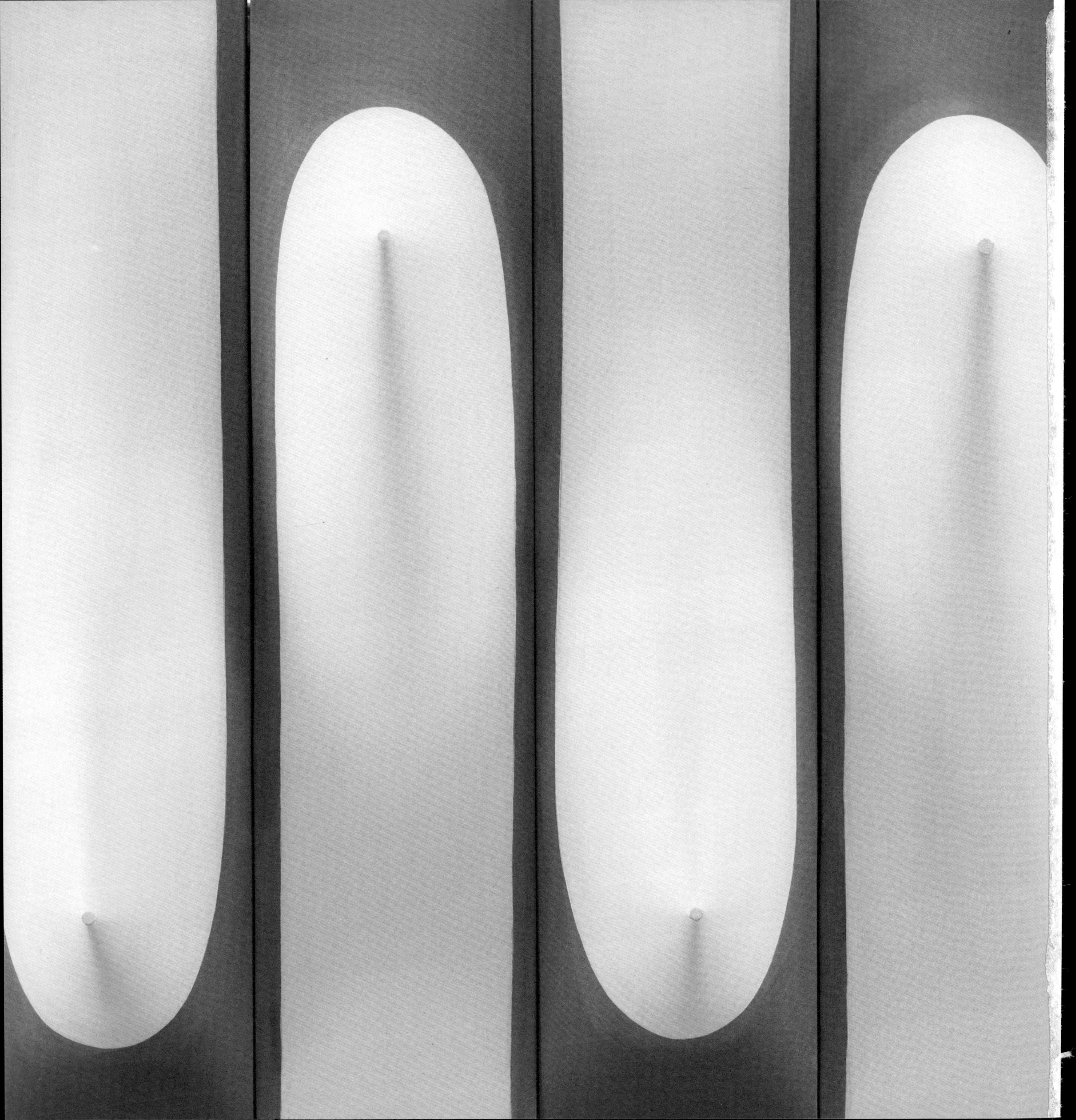

Zilia Sánchez

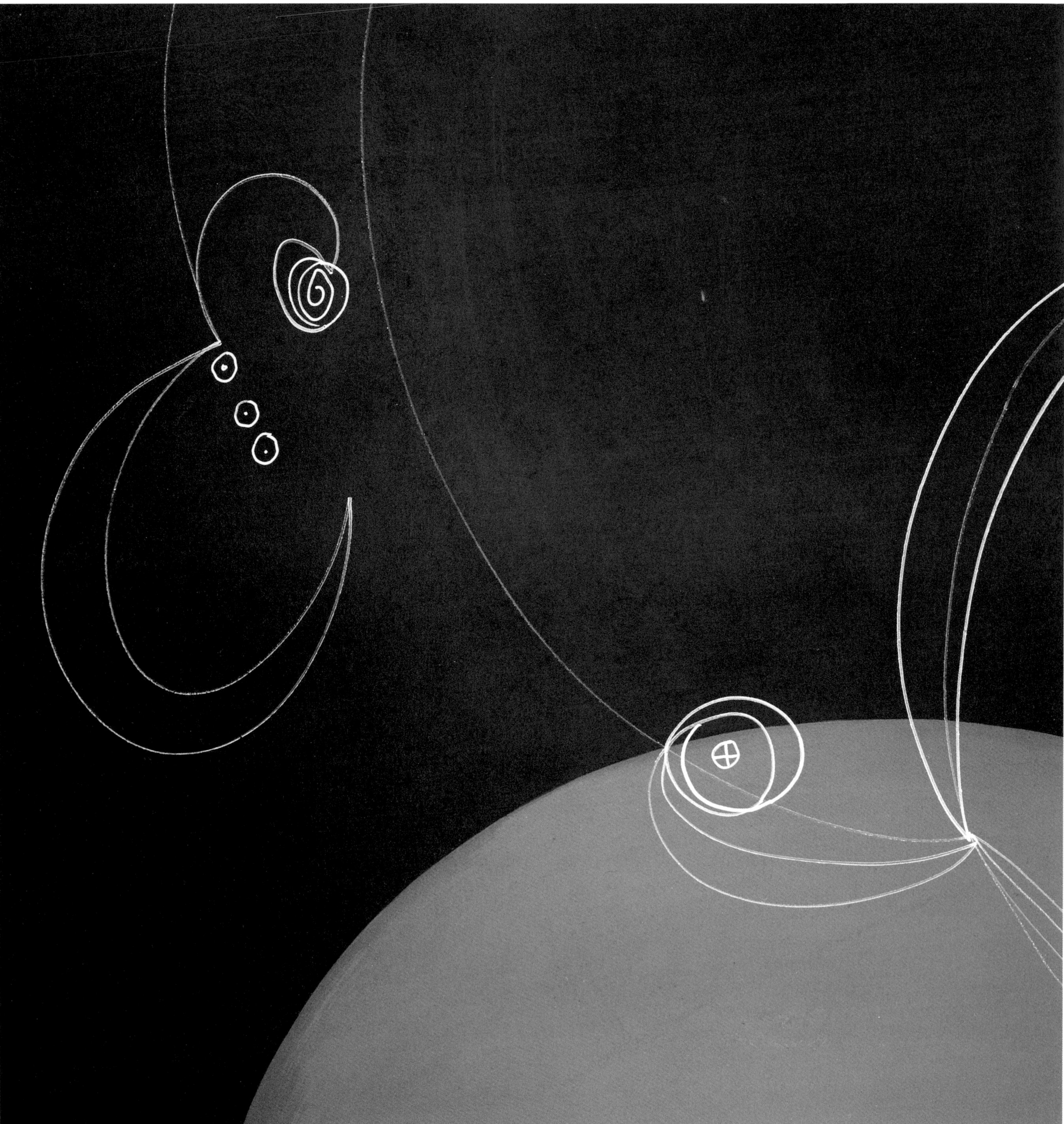

VESELA SRETENOVIĆ

Zilia Sánchez : Soy Isla

With contributions by
Carla Acevedo-Yates
Mercedes Cortázar
Ingrid W. Elliott
Abigail McEwen

Chronology by Alyson Cluck

Yale University Press, New Haven and London
in association with
The Phillips Collection, Washington, DC

Published on the occasion of the exhibition
Zilia Sánchez: Soy Isla

The Phillips Collection, Washington, DC
February 16–May 19, 2019

Museo de Arte de Ponce
June 15–October 21, 2019

El Museo del Barrio, New York
November 20, 2019–March 22, 2020

The exhibition is organized by The Phillips Collection.

With lead exhibition support and a Curatorial Fellowship from The Andy Warhol Foundation for the Visual Arts.

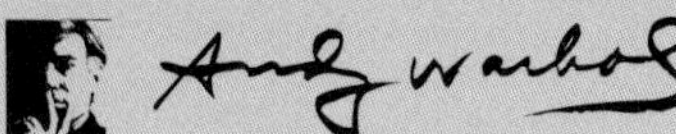

The Andy Warhol Foundation for the Visual Arts

Generous funding is provided by the Diane and Bruce Halle Foundation.

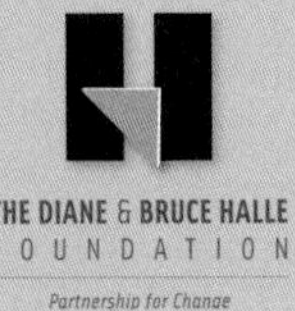

Additional exhibition support from the Marion F. Goldin Charitable Fund.

The artist documentary is made possible by Beatriz Bolton and the Dosal Family Foundation.

Further funding is provided by PHILLIPS.

In-kind support is provided by

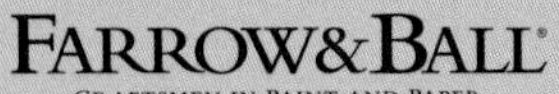

yalebooks.com/art

Designed by Margaret Bauer, Washington, DC
Set in FF Profile
Printed in Italy by Verona Libri

Library of Congress Control Number: 2018944525
ISBN 978-0-300-23390-2

A catalogue record for this book is available from the British Library.

The paper in this book meets the requirements of ANSI/NISO Z39.48-1992 (Permanence of Paper).

10 9 8 7 6 5 4 3 2 1

Jacket illustrations: (front) detail of cat. 53; (back) cat. 50. Details: (front endsheet) *Troyanas* (Trojan Women), 2016. Acrylic on stretched canvas, 23 ¼ × 22 ¼ × 4 ½ in. (59 × 56.5 × 11.4 cm). Collection of the artist, Courtesy Galerie Lelong & Co., New York; (p. ii) cat. 55; (p. vi) cat. 35; (p. xii) cat. 56; (pp. 16–17) cat. 56; (p. 18) Zilia Sánchez on the beach, 2018; (pp. 26–27) cat. 19; (p. 28) cat. 5; (pp. 42–43) cat. 42; (p. 44) *Afrocubano*, 1957 (see p. 173); (pp. 56–57) cat. 45; (p. 58) cat. 29; (pp. 68–69) cat. 37; (p. 70) cat. 46; (pp. 80–81) cat. 18; (pp. 148–49) cat. 4; (p. 150) Zilia Sánchez, 2018; (pp. 164–65) cat. 43; (p. 166) cat. 1; (p. 172) cat. 48; (p. 178) cat. 54; (p. 186) cat. 39; (p. 188) artist's hand in front of a painting, 2018; (back endsheet) cat. 56

Contents

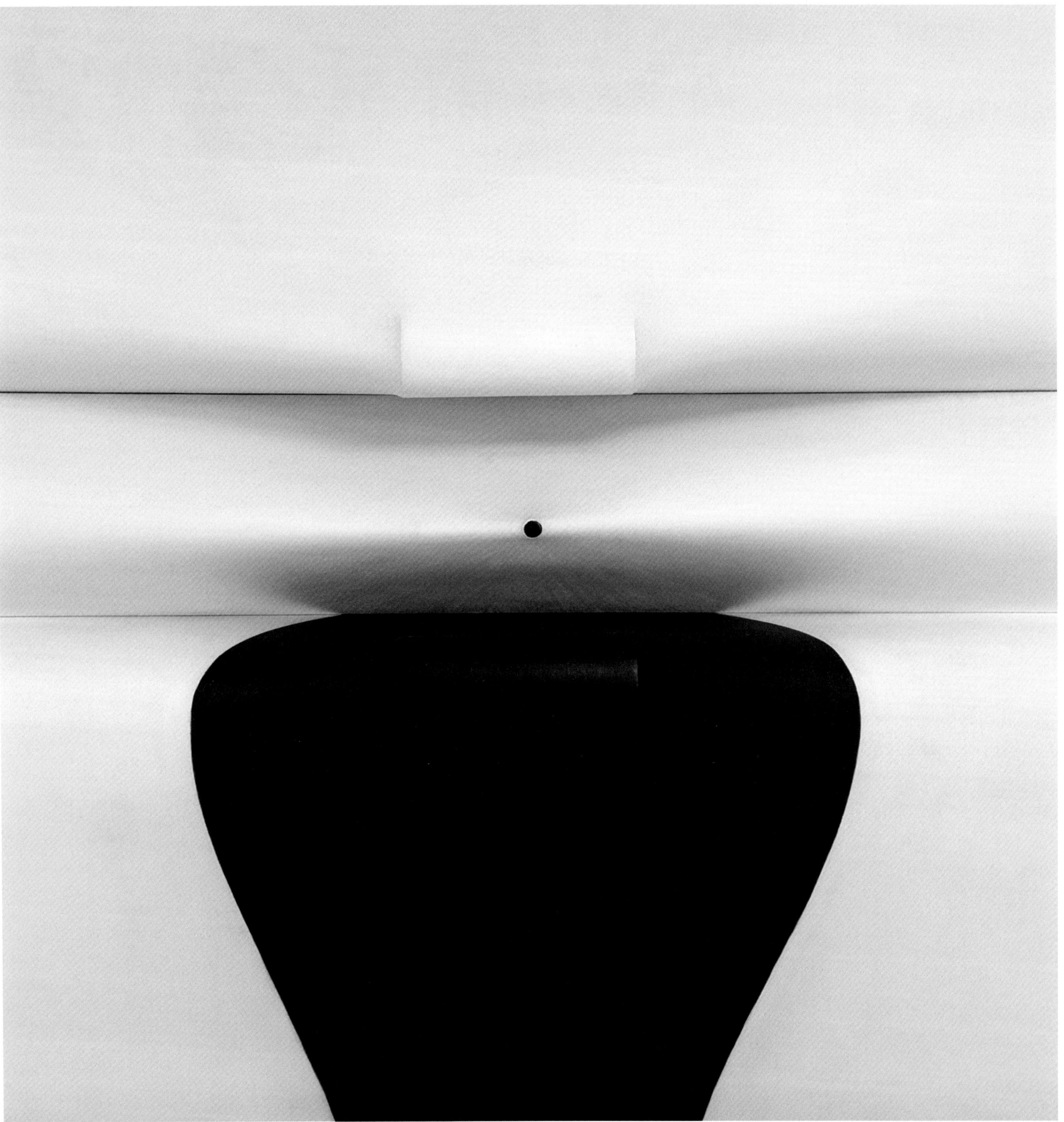

Foreword and Acknowledgments

Zilia Sánchez: Soy Isla (I Am an Island) is the first museum retrospective of a prolific, innovative, and yet largely unknown Cuban artist, Zilia Sánchez (b. 1926, Havana). It features about sixty-five works from the early 1950s to the present, including paintings, works on paper, shaped canvases, sculptural pieces, graphic illustrations, and ephemera. The exhibition is organized chronologically, tracing Sánchez's journey from her beginnings as an artist in Cuba to her travels to Europe in the 1950s and residence in New York in the 1960s to her move to Puerto Rico in the early 1970s, where she still lives and works.

For most of Sánchez's extraordinary seventy-year career, her art has been underrepresented in the United States. Her works only began to gain attention in the country in the past few years,

DOROTHY KOSINSKI

starting with solo exhibitions at Artists Space (2013) and Galerie Lelong (2014, 2015, 2016) and group shows at El Museo del Barrio and White Columns (2014). A number of art institutions, including the Colby College Museum of Art, the Museum of Modern Art, New York, the Pérez Art Museum Miami, the Princeton University Art Museum, the Rose Art Museum, Brandeis University, and the Solomon R. Guggenheim Museum, New York, have also recently begun adding her work to their collections. The Phillips acquired a 2008 work, the diptych *Maquinista* (Machinist; cat. 58), in 2016. The main objective of this exhibition, then, is to shed new light on Sánchez's artistic production and provide the recognition she deserves.

Throughout Sánchez's career, abstraction has prevailed, and her subjects have largely remained the same: the female body and its surrounding space. Due to its reductive geometric forms, Sánchez's work has often been aligned with the minimalist, post-minimalist, or neo-concrete movements. However, with its classical elegance, sensuality, and poetic narratives, her work resists traditional categorization and floats in-between; hence the exhibition title *Soy Isla* — "I am an island."

According to the exhibition's curator, Dr. Vesela Sretenović, "*Soy Isla* refers to an island — either Cuba, where Sánchez was born, grew up, and began her artistic career, or Puerto Rico, where she has long resided and worked, or both — surrounded by the vastness of the sea and the boundless horizon, yet never in complete isolation. It also recalls her own desire for solitary practice, forming an 'island' of her own within larger, mainstream art currents, concretism and neo-concretism in Cuba and Latin America, and lyrical and gestural abstraction in Europe and America, including minimalism in New York."

The title *Soy Isla* also refers to a series of Sánchez's works with the same name, some of which are featured in the exhibition, including a video from 2000 of a performance project called *encuentrismo — ofrenda o retorno de la serie Soy Isla: Compréndelo y retírate* (in loose translation, The Encounter: Offering or Return, from the series I am an Island: Understand and Retreat; cat. 57a–b). By showing her repeatedly pushing her painting *Soy Isla* into the ocean, and pulling it out again, the piece serves as a metaphor for Sánchez's life and art.

Still, an island exists within surrounding waters. The essays in this catalogue by outstanding scholars and curators contextualize Sánchez's work and lengthy career in a broader spectrum of global modernism. They include an introductory text and an interview with the artist by Dr. Sretenović, and essays by Dr. Ingrid Elliott, an independent scholar, who situates Sánchez in prerevolutionary Cuba and vis-à-vis Cuban vanguardist painters of landscape; Dr. Abigail McEwen, associate professor of Latin American art at the University of Maryland (UMD), who writes of Sánchez's life after leaving Cuba and her graphic works in exile; Carla Acevedo-Yates, associate curator at the Eli and Edythe Broad Art Museum, Michigan State University, who addresses the notion of homotextuality and the oblique queerness of Sánchez's work; and Mercedes Cortázar, Cuban poet and literary critic, who writes from a personal and artistic angle, highlighting Sánchez's work in 1960s New York. The illustrated chronology is by Alyson Cluck, a doctoral candidate in art history at UMD. We are grateful to these authors for their extensive research and invaluable scholarly and literary contributions.

The exhibition is also complemented by a short, newly commissioned video produced by VideoArt Productions, Inc. Shot in San Juan, this nonlinear, poetic documentary aims to capture Sánchez in places where she has lived and worked, including her studio, which is now being rebuilt after the devastation of Hurricane Maria. We express our deepest gratitude to Beatriz Bolton and the Dosal Family Foundation, whose generous support made this film possible. Our profound thanks go to the filmmaker Martin Huberman for his dedication and imagination in filming the artist and editing this video.

This marvelous exhibition would not have been possible without the assistance of the artist herself, with her inspirational energy, strong working ethic, and personal endurance. Our first and foremost applause thus goes to Zilia Sánchez and to her long-time partner Victoria Ruiz, who has been with her every step of the way in the past five decades.

The project has been a pioneering art historical and curatorial undertaking and a true labor of love for Dr. Sretenović, Phillips Senior Curator of Modern and Contemporary Art, who deserves special recognition for initiating this project and orchestrating all of its facets from beginning to end.

Dr. Sretenović's research was significantly facilitated by the artist's archives at Galerie Lelong in New York. Our profound appreciation goes to the gallery's vice president and partner, Mary Sabbatino, and assistant director for Latin America, Maria Heinz, who went out of their way to aid Dr. Sretenović's research travel and to introduce her to the artist's friends and collectors. We are also grateful to the other staff of Galerie Lelong, most importantly Bianca Cabrera and Danielle Wu.

Special praise for conducting scholarly detective work, for providing translations from Spanish to English, and for offering invaluable assistance during the project goes to Alyson Cluck, who is also a contributor to the catalogue and a doctoral candidate in art history at UMD, our academic partner. She has been Dr. Sretenović's left and right hand throughout the entire project. We are grateful to UMD's Department of Art History and Archaeology, which supported Cluck's graduate fellowships on all levels during the past two years. We are also grateful for additional assistance and personal insights into Cuban art and culture from another doctoral candidate at UMD, Cuban-born Patricia Ortega-Miranda.

Half of the works on view in the exhibition come from private collections. Our immense gratitude goes to the individual lenders, who include Beth Rudin DeWoody, Cleusa Garfinkel, Cecilia and Ernesto Poma, RosaMaría García Sarduy, and Laura Delaney Taft and John Taft. We are especially thankful to lenders in Puerto Rico, including the Andreu-Pietri Family, Marie Lynn Arrieta-Tartak, Ignacio J. López Beguiristain and Laura M. Guerra, the Berezdivin Collection, Luis R. de Corral, MD, Jose R. Landron, and Mima and César Reyes, who opened their homes to allow advanced study of Sánchez's works, despite the devastating obstacles caused by Hurricane Maria in 2017.

The Phillips is equally grateful to the institutions that have lent works to the exhibition, including the CINTAS Foundation Fellows Collection, the Colby College Museum of Art, the Compañía de Turismo de Puerto Rico, the Diane and Bruce Halle Foundation, the Instituto de Cultura Puertorriqueña, the Museo de Arte de Ponce, El Museo del Barrio, the Museum of Modern Art, New York, the Pérez Art Museum Miami, and the Princeton University Art Museum.

We greatly appreciate the guidance, insights into Sánchez's life and work, and encouragement from individuals who have helped champion this project, including Michy Marxuach, as well as former students of Sánchez in San Juan who are now accomplished artists, including Guillermo Calzadilla, Tony Cruz, Jorge González, Alana Iturralde, Carlos Rodríguez, and Chemi Rosado-Seijo, and her friends Rita Geada, Mercedes Cortázar, and RosaMaría García Sarduy.

For its generous support of the exhibition, we are indebted to The Andy Warhol Foundation for the Visual Arts, which provided a curatorial fellowship to Dr. Sretenović, enabling her to travel extensively and conduct critical research. A subsequent exhibition support grant from The Andy Warhol Foundation for the Visual Arts helped bring this project to fruition. In addition, we extend our gratitude to the Diane and Bruce Halle Foundation, the Marion F. Goldin Charitable Fund, PHILLIPS, and Farrow & Ball.

This beautiful catalogue was made possible by Yale University Press, where Amy Canonico, Mary Mayer, Kate Zanzucchi, and Raychel Rapazza coordinated many aspects of the publication. We extend our thanks to Margaret Bauer for her elegant design and to copyeditor Miranda Ottewell, proofreader Julia Smith, and indexer Cathy Dorsey. Our most sincere appreciations go to Raquel Pérez-Puig for her extraordinary photography, which made this catalogue visually rich and enticing, and to Esther Ferington, who edited the catalogue essays with the greatest patience, diligence, and perfectionism.

Many other people within and outside the Phillips contributed to this groundbreaking project, offering their expertise. The dedication and hard work of the Phillips staff needs a special acknowledgment. It goes to Haley Barton, Kelley Daley, Vivian Djen, Patti Favero, Bill Koberg, Alec MacKaye, Miriam Magdieli, Cherie Nichols, Sue Nichols, Klaus Ottmann, Victoria Potucek, Elizabeth Steele, Liza Strelka, Laura Tighe, Trish Waters, and Bridget Zangueneh, among many others.

In launching this exhibition and museum retrospective of an extraordinary artist, the Phillips remains true to its tradition of "firsts" in the field of modern art, which began when it opened to the public in 1921 as the first museum of modern art in the United States. We hope that this exhibition, like many of our "firsts," will not only share an amazing body of work by the artist but open a space for new research and scholarship in the years ahead.

Dorothy Kosinski, PhD
Vradenburg Director & CEO

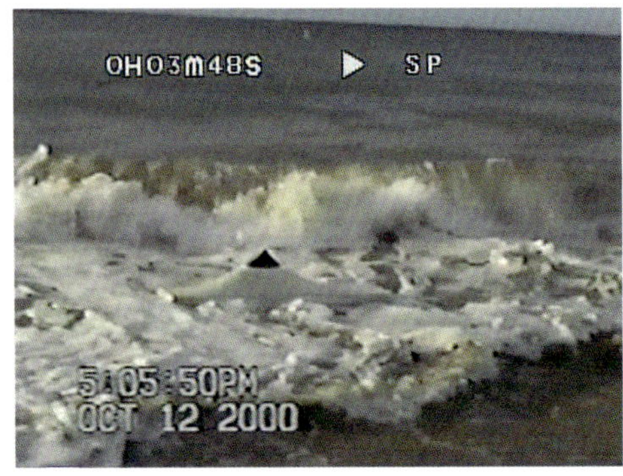
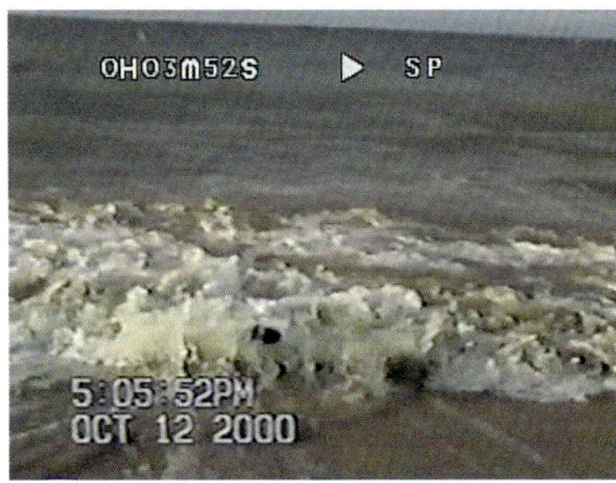
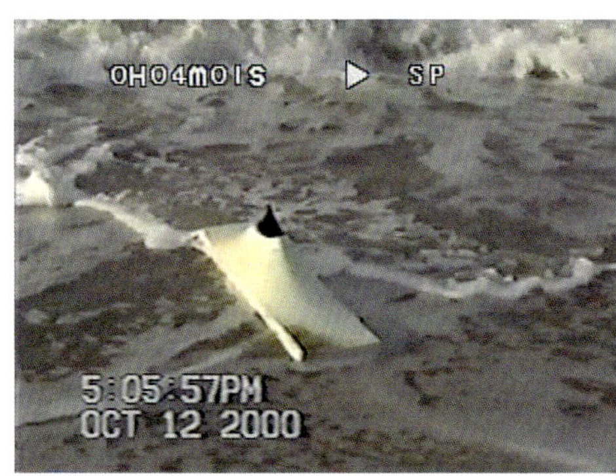
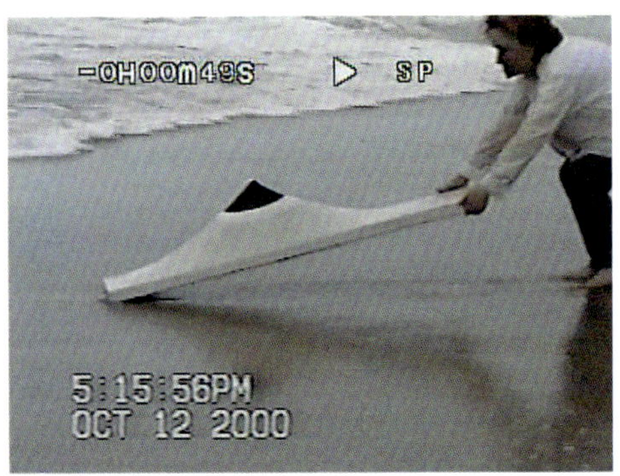
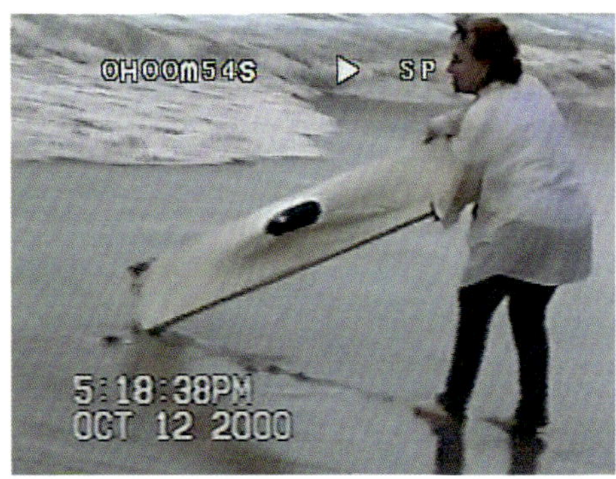
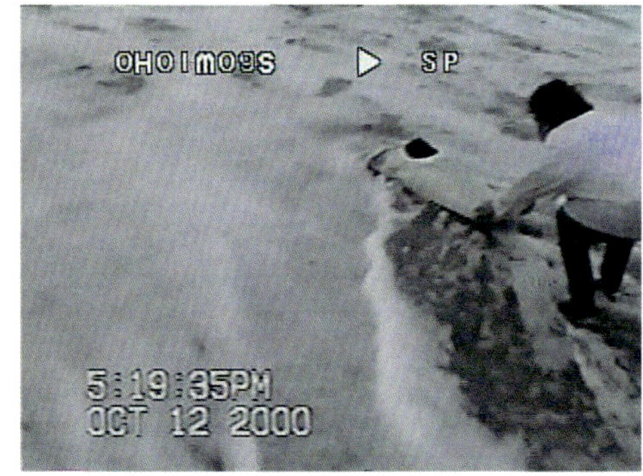
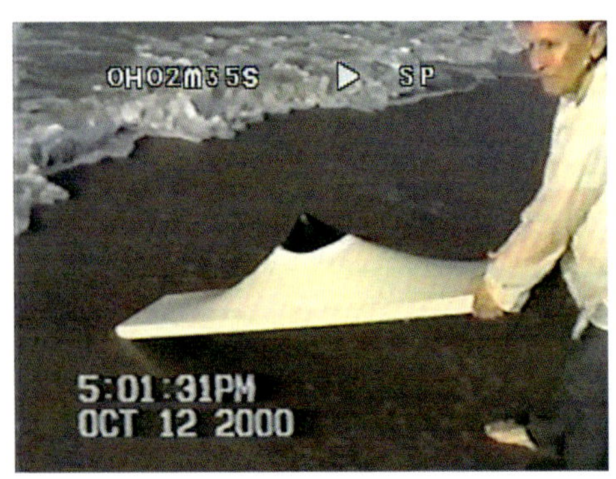
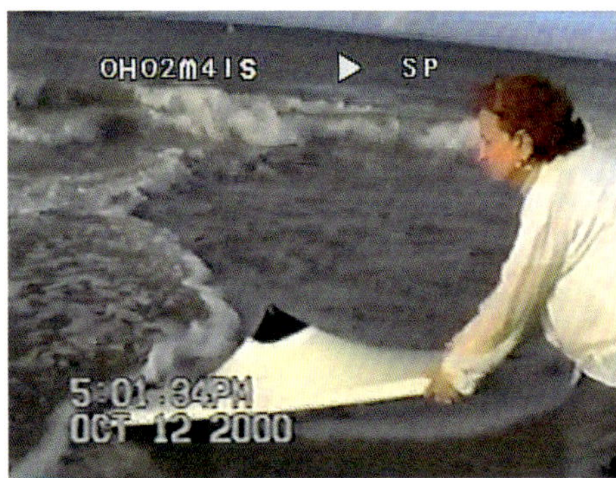
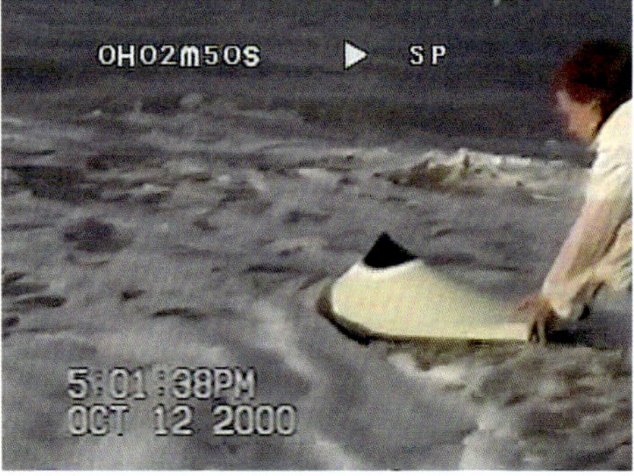

above Video stills from *encuentrismo —
ofrenda o retorno* (The Encounter —
Offering or Return), performance, 2000
(cat. 57a).

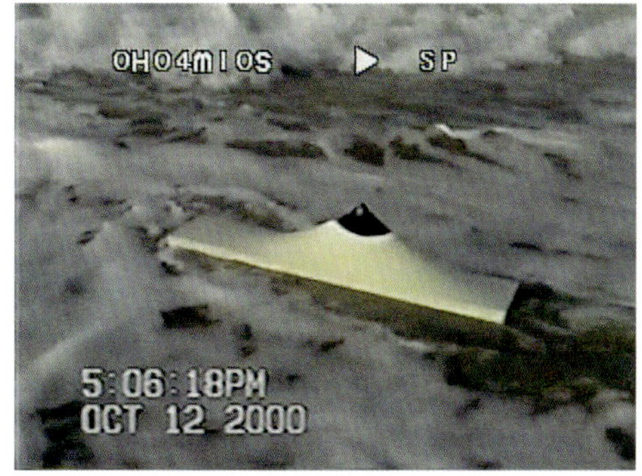
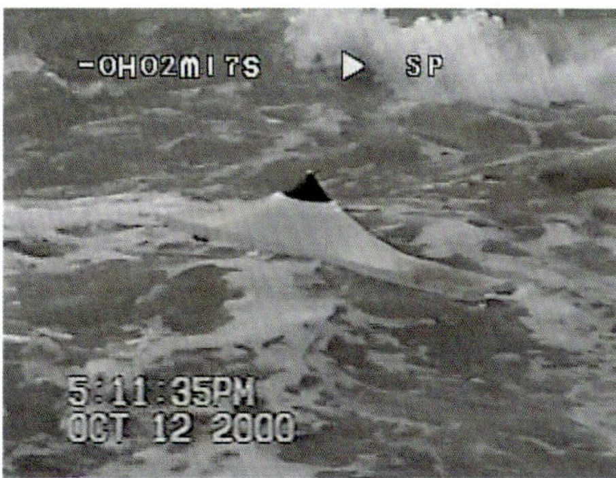
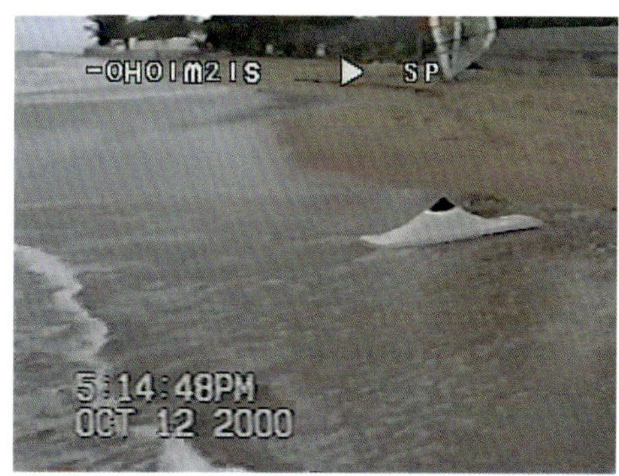
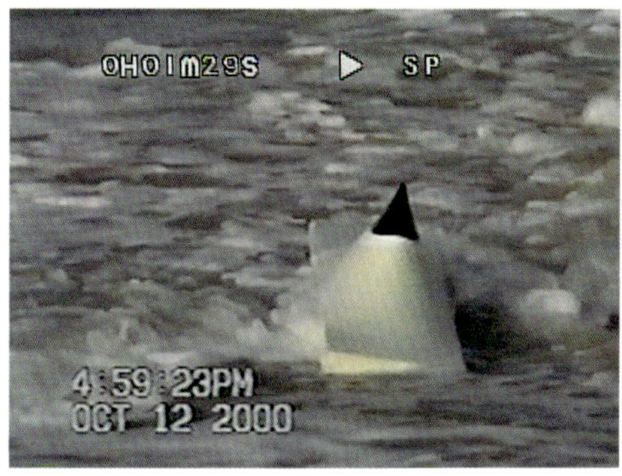
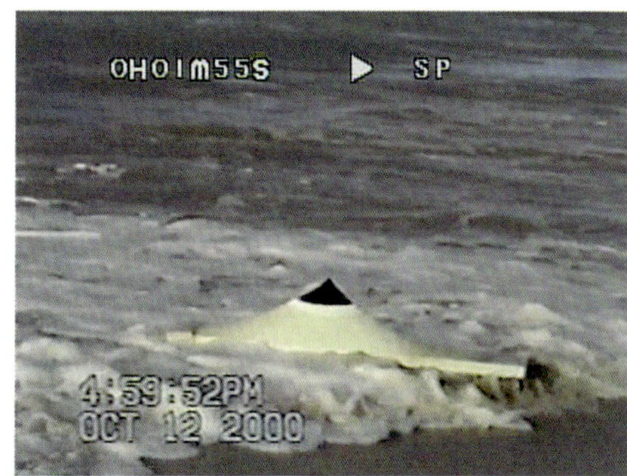
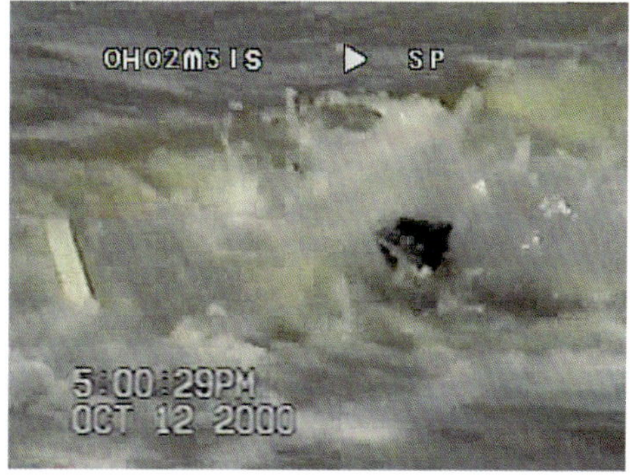
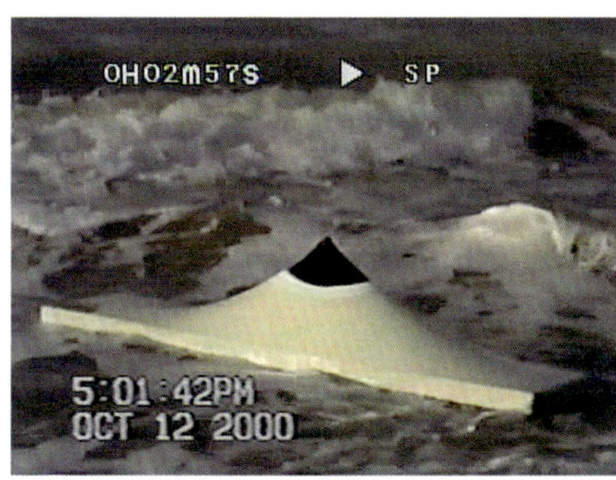
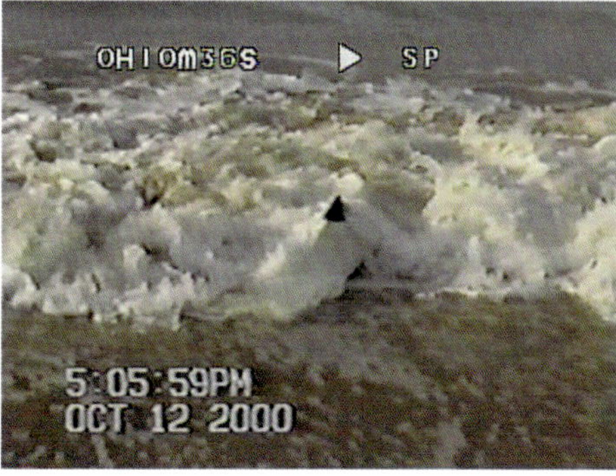
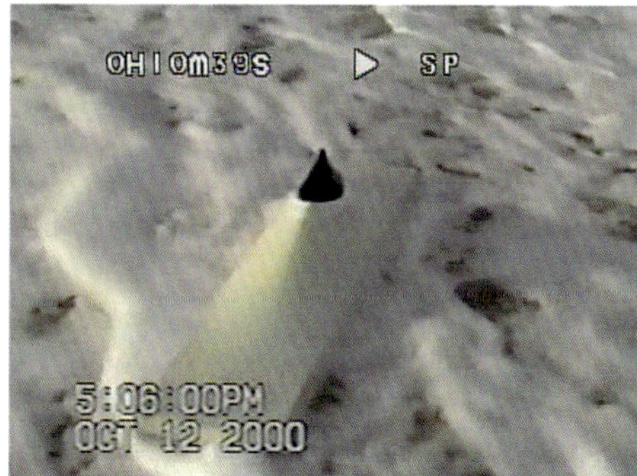

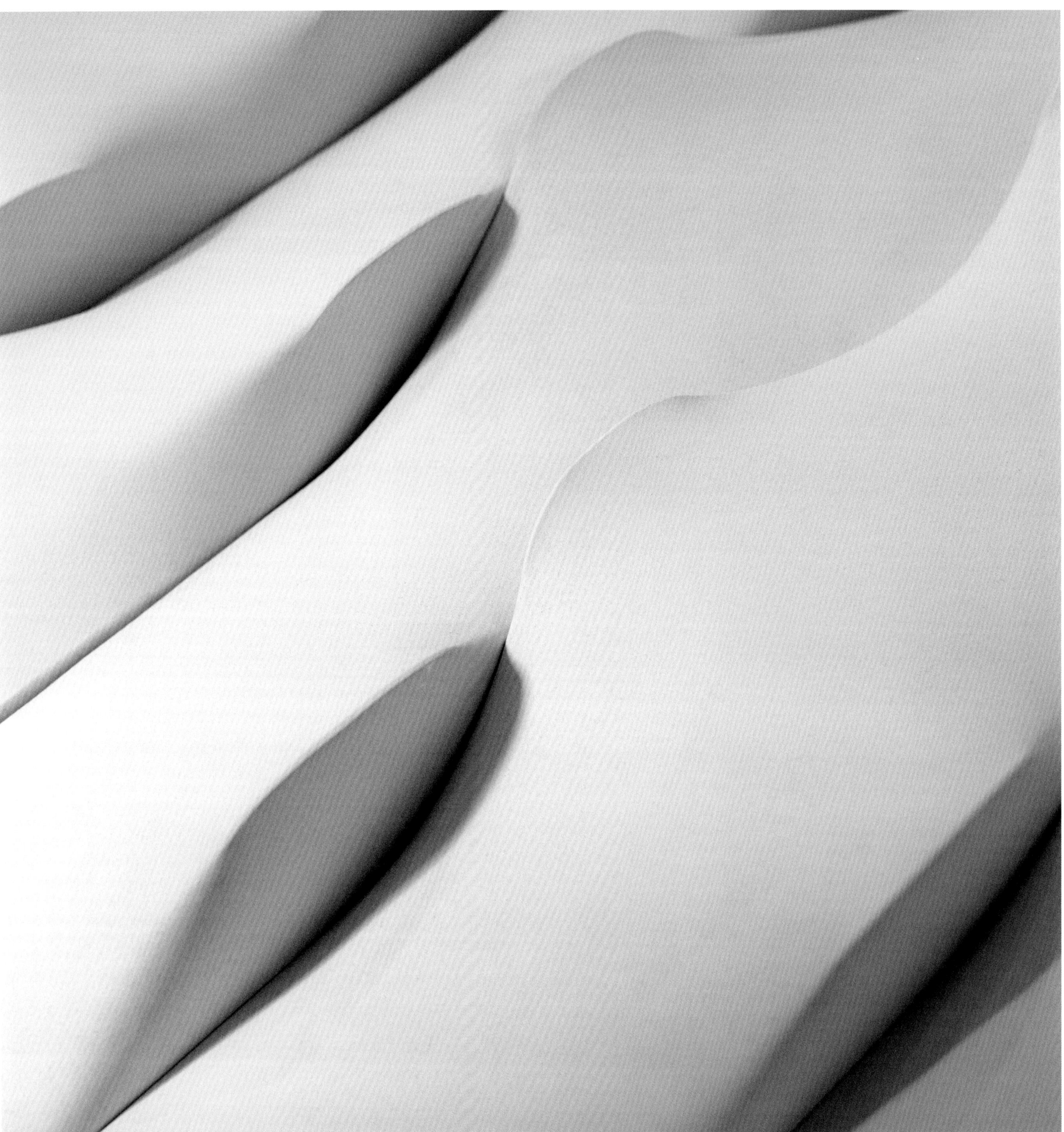

The power of art is like lightning — it strikes suddenly and out of nowhere. That is what I felt when I stumbled upon Zilia Sánchez's work during one of my visits to the New York galleries. I was hit by the work's serene presence, heroic scale, and sincerity. With curved, abstract forms suggestive of the body and a subdued palette of white, grays, blues, and flesh tones, Sánchez's paintings appeared at once subtle and monumental, plain and voluptuous, restrained and tactile. Impregnated with strong sculptural dimensions, they were swelling from the walls, pouring into the space. They were looking *at* me as much as I was looking at them,[1] and I felt an immediate visceral connection with the work.

I had never heard of the artist or her art, but a profound experience of being "in the presence of the sensuous," to borrow the

Embodied Spaces of Zilia Sánchez

VESELA SRETENOVIĆ

words of French philosopher Mikel Dufrenne (1910–1995),[2] stayed with me afterward. For Dufrenne, the "sensuous" refers to the experience of art as an open-ended possibility of perceptions and feelings. Like his French contemporary, Maurice Merleau-Ponty (1908–1961),[3] who privileges a sensory encounter with a work of art resulting in sensuous knowing, Dufrenne emphasizes the corporeal experience of art, in which the meaning operates implicitly via sensuousness and affectivity, rather than mere reflection. Along these lines, the American philosopher of the mind Susanne Langer (1895–1985)[4] argues that the power of art lies in its emotional or affective potential; it is "cognitive emotion"—combining the empirical, sensory, and conceptual knowledge—that leads to a full understanding of art. She considers the sensible as a nondiscursive language that operates through allusive thought or "emotive form,"[5] which begins in sensation and ends in reflection. In tune with this view, contemporary American philosopher Mark Johnson (b. 1949)[6] proposes the embodied meaning rooted in the physical encounter with the world and hence in sensorial, prereflective perception and motion. Art, or aesthetic experience, is for Johnson a culmination of the human attempt to find meaning through feelings, emotions, images, and metaphors, which in turn provide the basis for abstract thought — and thus, abstract art.

Correspondingly, but from two different sides of the globe, Brazilian theoretician Mário Pedrosa (1900–1981) and German American philosopher Herbert Marcuse (1898–1979) acknowledge that art has an affective power and, within it, a sociopolitical dimension. For Pedrosa, art has a revolutionary spirit, while for Marcuse, art offers sensual and emotional stimulations and, thus, knowledge. In that sense, art for both of them represents a call for liberation and transformation, individual and social. All of these interrelated philosophical propositions emphasize the embodied meaning and the coexistence of the sensorial and the mental. They fall somewhere between the phenomenological investigation of experience and the ontological quest for meaning, resonating with Sánchez's visual language, which stresses the emotional and the sensual. As she says, "I feel the form, rather than think it."[7] Drawing upon these theories, Sánchez's sensuality — particularly evident in her shaped canvases from the 1970s onward, best known as *topologías eróticas* (erotic topologies) — must be considered in a broader sense, surpassing its mere carnal or fleshy appearance to carry ontological and even political dimension. I will return to this in more depth, after charting, in brief, the artist's trajectory.

Sánchez was born in Havana in 1926 to a Spanish father and Cuban mother. She was exposed to art early on, first through her father, whose hobby was painting, and then through her neighbor, and later mentor, Víctor Manuel (1897–1969), a legendary Cuban landscape painter. After taking preparatory classes in drawing and modeling, she enrolled in the Academy of San Alejandro to study, at first, architecture — only for a semester — and then fine art. After graduating in 1948, she started to exhibit regularly, with a first solo show in 1953

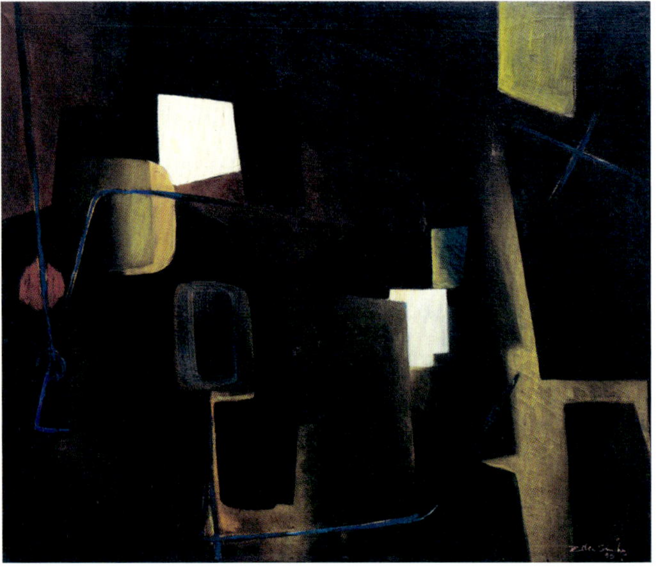

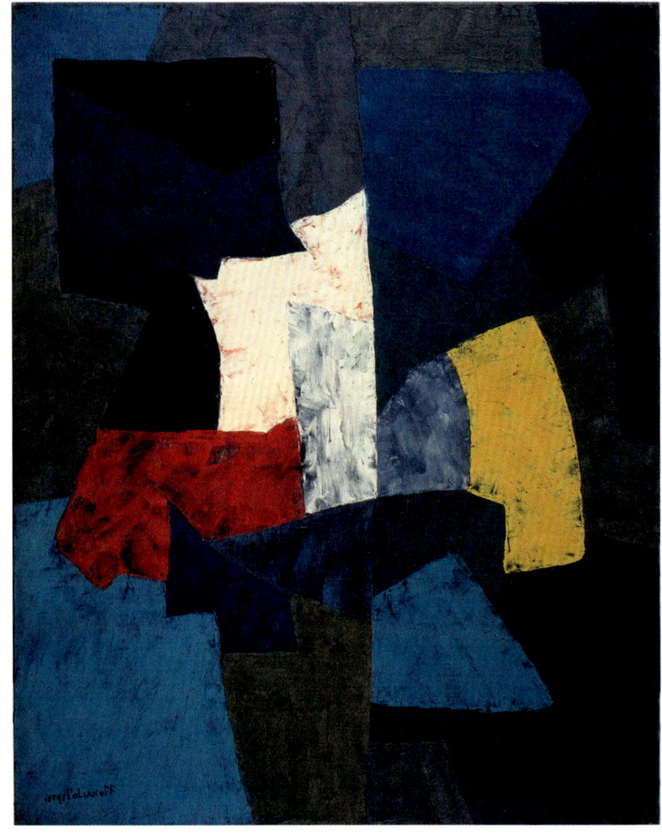

1 Zilia Sánchez, *Composition*, 1953. Mixed media on canvas, 28 ¾ × 33 in. (73 × 84 cm). Museo Nacional de Bellas Artes, Havana.

2 Serge Poliakoff, *Abstract Composition*, 1954. Oil on canvas, 45 ⅝ × 35 in. (115.9 × 88.9 cm). Tate Gallery, London, Purchased 1961.

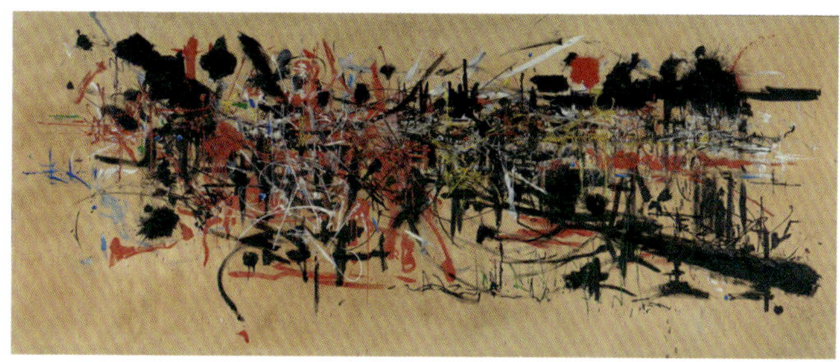

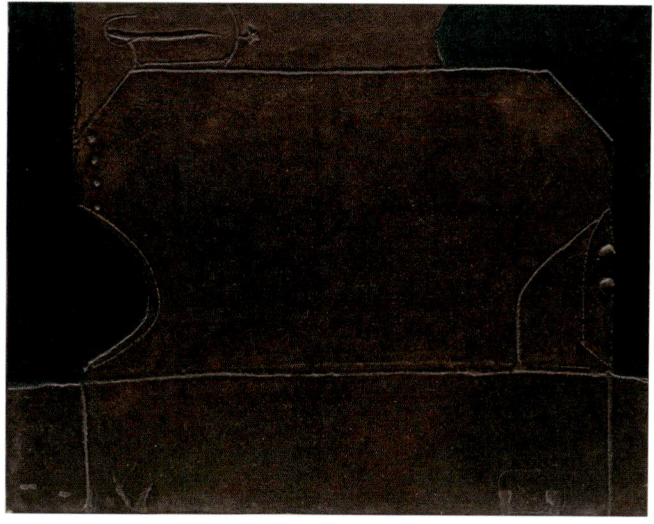

at the Lyceum in Havana, followed by frequent exhibitions with a group of young artists called Los Once (The Eleven), who shared her interest in gestural abstraction.[8] In addition, Sánchez was closely involved in anti-Batista intellectual and literary circles, working on graphic illustrations as well as doing scenography for theater production. While some of her very early works on paper portray adolescent girls or young women with big eyes and a hunted look full of anxiety, in the early 1950s she gradually shifted toward abstract compositions.

Throughout the mid- and late 1950s, Sánchez traveled intermittently to Spain and also visited Italy and France. She exhibited internationally in Madrid in 1957, Caracas in 1958, the São Paulo Bienal in 1959,[9] and Mexico City in 1960. At that time, her work was in tune with trends of European postwar abstraction, oscillating between lyrical and gestural expression. Her mid-1950s work — with soft palette and spontaneous brushwork (fig. 1), or intricate lines and scribble-like marks — reveals affinity with Tachisme[10] and the paintings of Serge Poliakoff (fig. 2), Georges Mathieu (fig. 3), Hans Hartung, and Wols. Her late 1950s and early 1960s work is entrenched in Art Informel (cat. 11),[11] which emphasizes the transformative qualities of found materials like earth, sand, rags, strings, and detritus and stands in opposition to the modernist canons of pure form. The heavy pigments, dark tones, and raw materiality of Antoni Tàpies (fig. 4), on the one hand, and the perforated surfaces of Lucio Fontana's monochromes (fig. 5),[12] on the other, were of particular importance to Sánchez, encouraging her to break away from the flatness of the pictorial plane and to develop her own idea of a curved or shaped canvas.

In 1960, the year after the Cuban Revolution, Sánchez left Havana for New York. In her words, it was a hard decision, but an inevitable one. At the core of it was her urge for liberation from established conventions — social, political, gender, and artistic. However, the experience of the New York period was a harsh one. Having to work many odd jobs in order to support herself left little time for art practice. The skyscrapers of Manhattan that blocked the horizon, the distance from the ocean, and the language barrier did not help. On

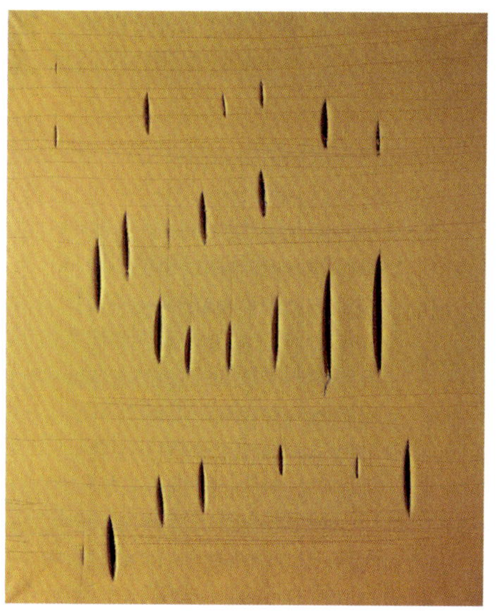

3   Georges Mathieu, *The Battle of Bouvines*, April 25, 1954. Oil on canvas, 23 ¾ × 98 ½ in. (60 × 250 cm). Musée National d'Art Moderne, Centre Georges Pompidou, Paris.

4   Antoni Tàpies, *Brown on Black*, 1959. Oil with sand on canvas, 51 ⅛ × 63 ¾ in. (129.9 × 161.9 cm). Solomon R. Guggenheim Museum, New York.

5   Lucio Fontana, *Spatial Concept*, 1959. Private collection.

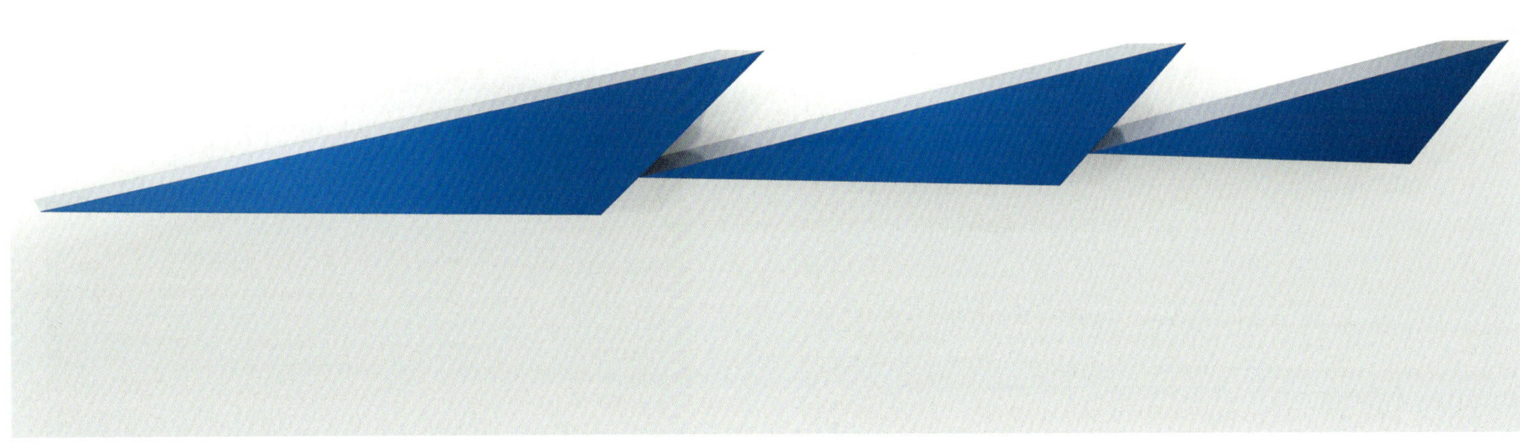

top of this, being a Cuban in exile was a tough position. Nonetheless, Sánchez managed the hardships of this time by traveling to Spain and France;[13] studying printmaking at the Pratt Graphic Art Center; participating in the literary circles of Cuban émigré friends and illustrating the journal *La nueva sangre* (The New Blood);[14] and showing her work at galleries with Latin American affiliations, including Galería Sudamericana, later called the Zegrí Gallery, the Sarduy Gallery, and the INTAR Gallery.

Although Sánchez spent time in New York during the heyday of minimalism, she found herself disconnected from some of her contemporaries — Donald Judd, John McCracken (fig. 6), Robert Morris, and even Louise Nevelson[15] — despite their shared aesthetic of reductive, geometric forms, modular units, and seriality. A closer parallel can be drawn between her work and that of artists who, although often associated with minimalists, focused on creating shaped canvases[16] — which challenged the rectangular shape of paintings and the constraints of two-dimensionality — including

Ellsworth Kelly, Frank Stella, Kenneth Noland, Charles Hinman,[17] and Carmen Herrera (fig. 7) in the United States and Enrico Castellani and, foremost, Agostino Bonalumi (fig. 8) in Italy. Although all of them, including Sánchez, pursued the same goal of shifting artwork from an object into the surrounding space or environment, their means of achieving it were slightly different. While many minimalist and shaped-canvas artists followed a path of strict geometry, Sánchez and Bonalumi, completely independently, were inspired by Fontana's sliced canvases. They turned to curved shapes, pushing them out from underneath and into space and creating their own poetic, humanist abstractions. For Sánchez, they were "topologies," and for Bonalumi, *estroflessioni* or *pitture-oggetti* (painting-objects).[18]

Sánchez diverged further from the minimalists regarding the notion of sequencing and its application. While for the minimalists seriality implied mechanical process and industrial fabrication, for Sánchez it retained a sense of touch and the human hand. Severo Sarduy — a poet, writer, and Sánchez's close friend — differentiated

6 John McCracken, *Arrow*, 1991. Polyester resin and fiberglass on wood, 20 ½ × 230 × 14 in. (52.1 × 584.2 × 35.6 cm). Albright-Knox Art Gallery, Buffalo, Purchased in Memory of Bernard D. Welt, Barbara D. Bernheim and Ida Z. Welt, 2004.

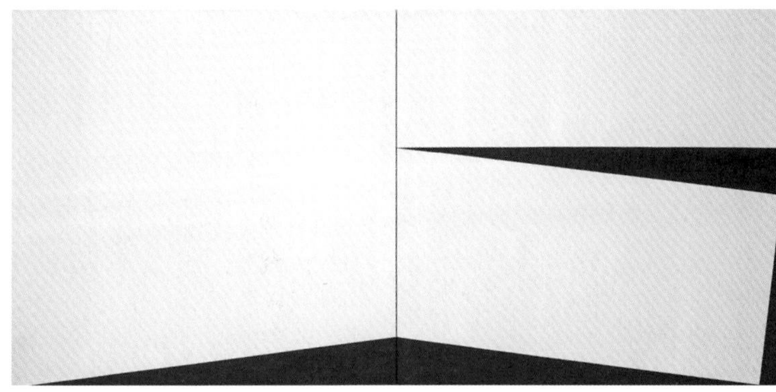

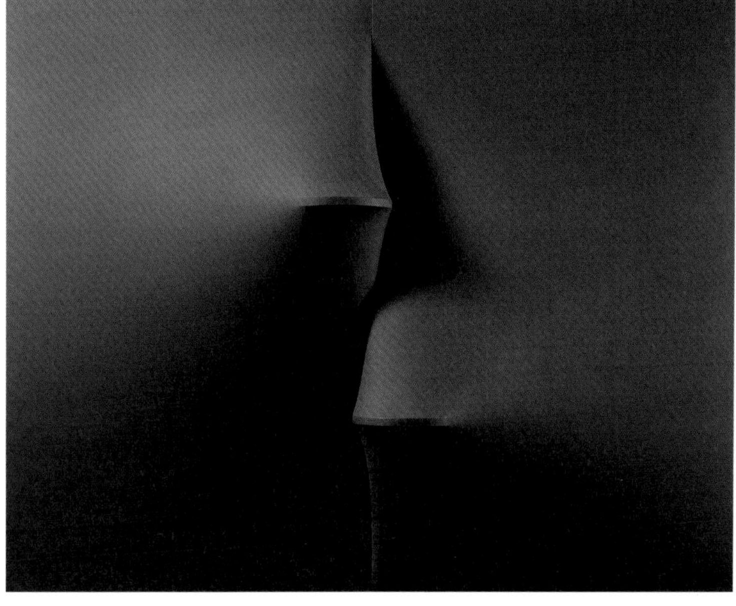

the artist from her contemporaries affiliated with minimalism in "Topologías eróticas" (Erotic Topologies), an essay for the catalogue of her 1970 solo exhibition at the Universidad de Puerto Rico in San Juan, *Estructuras en secuencia* (Structures in Sequence): "Zilia Sánchez's topologies participate little in this [minimalist] code. Although endowed with the same degree of formalization, of equal 'deconstructive' capacity, the allusions that these reliefs make, somatic or not, and the fact that they do not achieve their full definition but in the function of play, shift them toward a space of tactility, toward sensitive values, space configured by the bodies that inhabit it."[19]

In the same catalogue, Gordon Brown, the senior editor of the New York–based *Arts Magazine*, similarly situated Sánchez vis-à-vis her minimalist peers, describing her work as "fleshy sensuality of breasts and nipples."[20] In his view, "Zilia Sánchez is different from the minimal artists who have only their own puritanism to purify. … This makes all the more interesting her reduction of the pleasures of the flesh to the modern equivalent of Neo-Classicism."[21] In the same light, Mario Peña noted in his 1971 write-up in *El tiempo*, "[Minimalism] is considered a style devoid of warmth and feeling. But the painter Zilia Sánchez delivers to us in sequences of light and form a wealth of visual and sensitive poetry. … Zilia's art is transcendental, because by making sensory contact with her work, the viewer discovers many things, the most important perhaps being the feeling that is experienced in the presence of a work of art, or what one feels as that 'itching in the blood.' "[22]

Another degree of separation between Sánchez and the minimalists was on the subject of objecthood, in particular Donald Judd's "specific object," defined by him as "neither painting nor sculpture."[23] Although Sánchez's topologies could perfectly fit that category, what fundamentally differentiated them from the materiality and anti-illusionism of works by Judd and his peers was their associative meaning. Employing ancient mythology, as well as recurring lunar motifs and tattoo-like drawings, brought an elusive content and metaphorical significance to her work. In this respect,

7 Carmen Herrera, *Blanco y verde* (White and Green), 1960. Acrylic on canvas, 48 × 96 in. (121.9 × 243.8 cm). Smithsonian American Art Museum, Washington, DC, Museum purchase through the Luisita L. and Franz H. Denghausen Endowment.

8 Agostino Bonalumi, *Nero*, 1969. Shaped canvas and vinyl tempera, 47 ¾ × 57 in. (121 × 145 cm). Archivio Agostino Bonalumi, Milan.

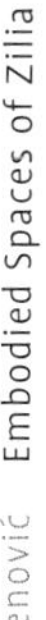

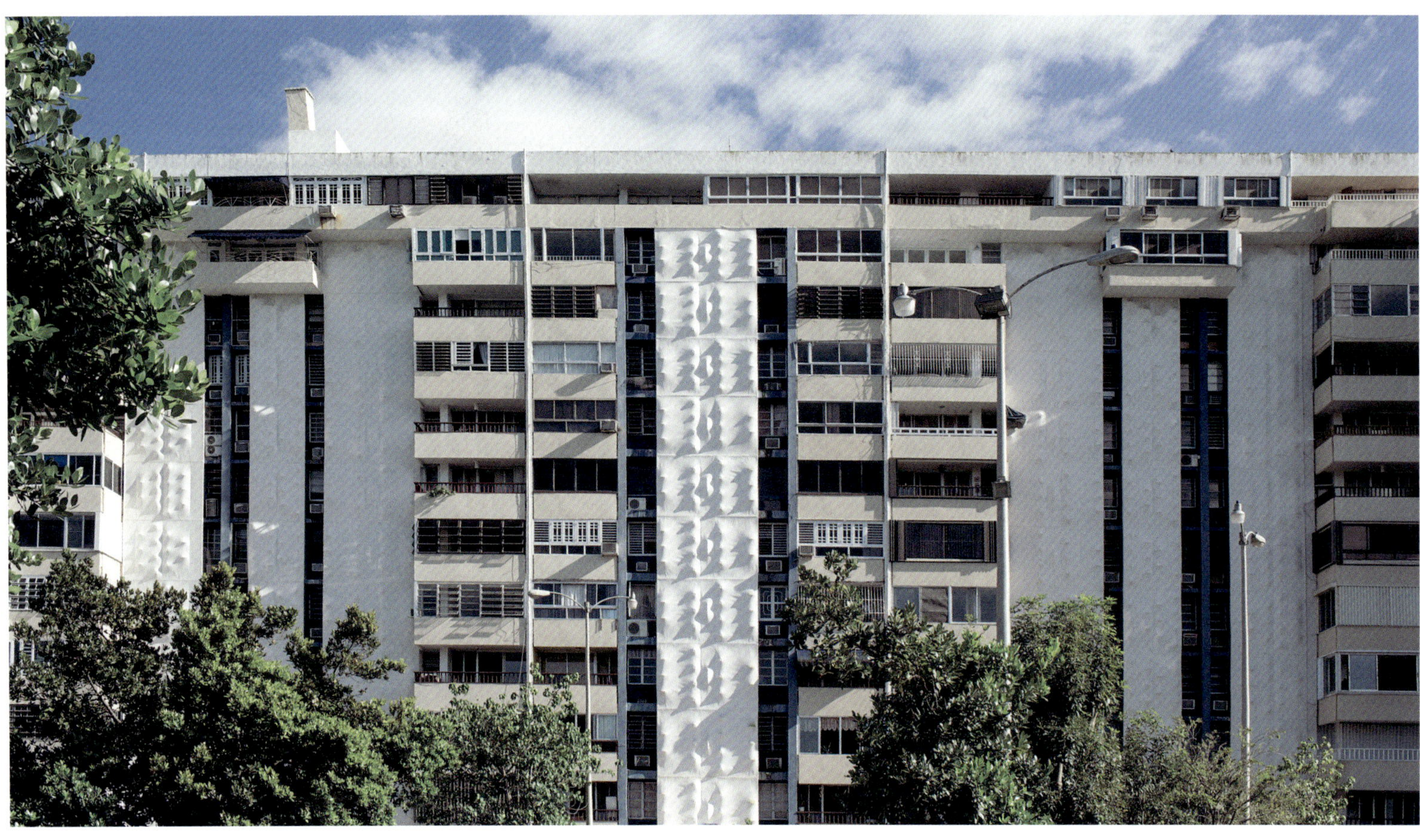

her topologies are correlated to the concept of "non-object," coined by Ferreira Gullar (1930–2016),[24] Brazilian poet and art critic. In fact, "non-object" is a counterpart to Judd's "specific object," for it operates between painting and sculpture, but is also in opposition to Judd's "specific object," for it unifies the sensorial and the mental, functioning as both the transparent body and zone of signification.

Floating somewhere between minimalists' cool geometry and her own corporeal forms, Sánchez called herself a *mulata minimalista*.[25] Recalling Louise Nevelson's serial work, she commented, "No title, no touching, no color, only construction modules. But I touch, too much. I like the names."[26] Given these irreconcilable differences, it comes as no surprise that she opted for seclusion from the mainstream, rather than connection to it. At the same time, New York City, the mecca of art, was not the most welcoming place for Latin American artists and especially women and gay artists. Hence, Sánchez turned inward and stayed true to herself—in essence, neutral. "Neutrality as harmony is a strong presence in my work," Sánchez has said,[27] and she has obviously pursued neutrality in her art and life.

9 Zilia Sánchez, *Mural in Cement*, 1971.
Laguna Gardens, San Juan.

Toward the end of 1971, Sánchez moved to San Juan. "I was searching for a warmer place, something more like my own country," she explains.[28] An island close to her original home, Puerto Rico offered her the blue sky and ocean that she needed, but also the language and culture from which she felt disconnected. Although she traveled to Puerto Rico relatively often and exhibited there,[29] it was a public commission for a cement mural on the building facade of a condominium complex in Laguna Gardens[30] that finally enabled her to settle in San Juan permanently. *Mural in Cement* (fig. 9) is a modular, relief-like structure in cement. With pointed lumps and painted in white, it is essentially architectural painting — similar to her shaped canvases or corporeal topologies, which convey abstractly the human body.

Immediately upon her arrival in San Juan, Sánchez found a small studio in Santurce, a neighborhood of San Juan that brought back memories of her grandmother's home in the small village of Cojímar, east of Havana, and therefore gave her a sense of comfort. She also became involved in a liberal magazine, *Zona. Carga y descarga* (Zone. Charge and Discharge [or Load and Unload]),[31] whose aim was to create an open, discursive space around the social, political, and cultural issues of the time, including anticolonialism, Puerto Rican independence, feminism, and homophobia. Although the journal had a short life (1972–75), and Sánchez participated only in the first few issues, her design was instrumental for the remaining ones. In many ways, involvement with *Zona* was a prolongation of her close engagement with the literary, intellectual, and political circles often aligned with the left. Sánchez was always critically engaged with social issues, yet she was never politically active. Her revolutionary spirit was her artistic practice, and she would inspire the same attitude in her students (many of whom, including Guillermo Calzadilla, Tony Cruz, Alana Iturralde, Jorge González, Carlos Rodríguez, and Chemi Rosado-Seijo, are now accomplished artists of installation and social practice) at the local art league, La Liga de Estudiantes de Arte, and the Escuela de Artes Plásticas y Diseño de Puerto Rico, where she taught for more than thirty years.

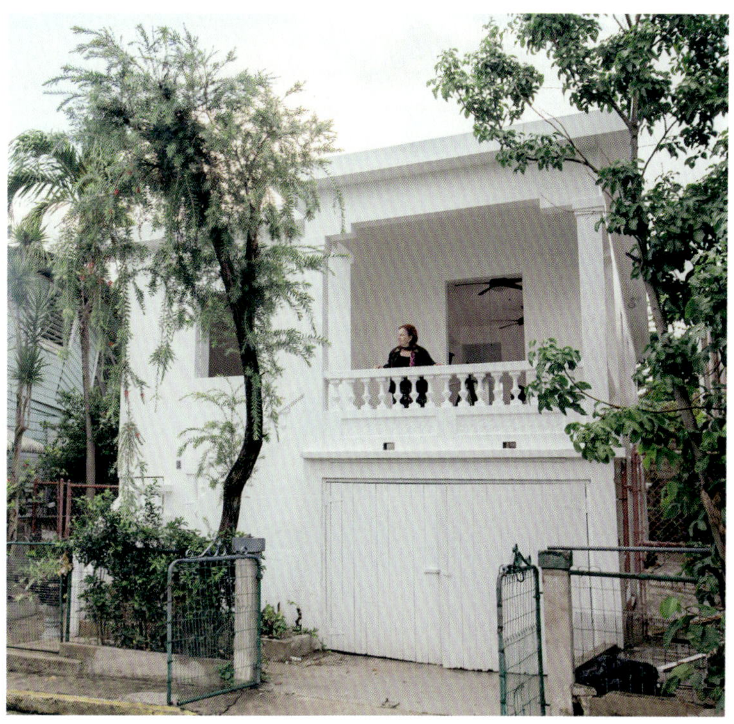

After almost fifty years in San Juan, Sánchez still works in the same studio (fig. 10). Within this period, she has perfected her signature style of erotic topologies: canvases stretched over wooden armature. It is uncertain exactly when Sánchez made her first shaped canvases. The idea was born, as the artist recollects, after her father passed away in 1955,[32] when she saw the washed sheet from the bed in which he died drying on the rooftop of her building, blowing in the wind and hitting a pipe or tube.[33] It was the constant movement of the sheet, lifted up in the air, that stayed with her, resulting later in a raised, relief-like painting — a painting that is infused with a third dimension, implying not only a spatial depth but a pulse of life, a living body, perhaps that of her deceased father. According to Sánchez, she tried showing some of her early reliefs with raised fabric when she was still in Cuba, but no one seemed to understand them, for they were neither paintings nor sculptures. "I went far away, too far for the time," she said later.[34] Over the years, the idea of relief as a "dimension in which the forms look more real"[35] kept percolating, and a number of works from the late 1950s and the early 1960s (fig. 11) reveal this. To this day, Sánchez is relentlessly pursuing her shaped

10 Sánchez on the balcony of her studio, Santurce, San Juan, February 2018.

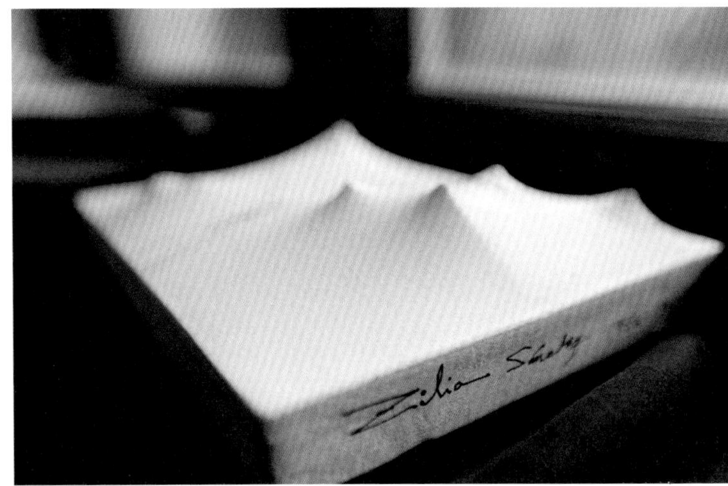

canvases, revisiting and reinvestigating old ideas with new vigor. The fact that the curved shapes and mute palette from decades ago remain constant, however, is by no means a sign of redundancy or idleness. Quite the opposite. Repetition in Sánchez's work is not just an aesthetic device; it is an intentional act, a sign of reworking and rethinking her own positions of "making my work to satisfy my feelings and spirit,"[36] and thus maintaining her desired sensuality.

———

Sánchez's erotic topologies[37] (fig. 12) are corporeal abstractions characterized by curvilinear geometry, sensual elegance, and formal and emotional ambiguities. In his 1975 review of a show by Sánchez in San Juan, Antonio J. Molina (b. 1928), Cuban exile writer and critic, describes her work as "sensory poetry." According to him, "these flesh-canvases seem to breathe in a sensual, silent expression of great harmony, yet full of vitality."[38] Critical writing that highlights Sánchez's sensuality and eroticism has been common since then. In a 2009 essay, Manuel Álvarez Lezama (b. 1950) considers Sánchez's topologies as "new metaphors about sensuality and eroticism,"[39] while more recent writing by Benigno Trigo underlines the explicit

sexual connotations of her work. Trigo approaches Sánchez's sexuality through the surface or skinlike quality of her work, where "the surface is stretched and extended to simulate folding, caressing, and touching feminine sexual body parts (highly abstract and stylized details that suggest nipples, labia, vulvas, clitoris)."[40] He continues, "The language of Sánchez's *Topologías eróticas* is *homotextuality*,"[41] a term coined by Rudi C. Bleys, denoting overt homoeroticism that is self-evident in a work of art, but not necessarily intended by an artist. Essentially, for Bleys and Trigo, homotextuality is a visualization of hidden content or *ambiente*, a queer space, or in Bleys's own words, "a diversity of (homo)sexual life or the simultaneous coexistence of various patterns of sexual behavior and identity."[42]

Nonetheless, Sánchez's erotic topologies, whether single panels or polyptychs (*módulos infinitos*; fig. 13), tattooed or plain, transcend pure formal concerns and erotic implications. There are other aspects of the artist's sensuality that have rarely, if at all, been mentioned: the embodied meaning (sensuousness) and the revolutionary potential (oblique politics). To address these overlooked aspects, I return to the philosophical concepts introduced earlier, which in their own ways assert the interconnection of bodily and cognitive experience, sensual and intellectual meaning, and claim the transformative and affective power of art.

The first critic to bring up a broader aspect of eroticism in Sánchez's work was Marta Traba (1930–1983), Argentinian art critic, writer, and feminist theorist. Although she too praised the sensuality of Sánchez's topologies, writing that Sánchez "produces ensembles whose ripples, depressions, and elevations are marked not only by an organic spirit but also by a sensual pleasure,"[43] she went further to touch explicitly on the erotic aspect or "epic eroticism" in Sánchez's work.[44] For Traba, eroticism is the most primal bonding between individuals, which goes beyond a mere sexual encounter and its pornographic representation into a deeper — sensual — connection among people. Moreover, eroticism is, in her view, a universal language of communication among people, restoring the purpose of art.

11 Side view of Zilia Sánchez, *Untitled*, 1956–99 (cat. 4).

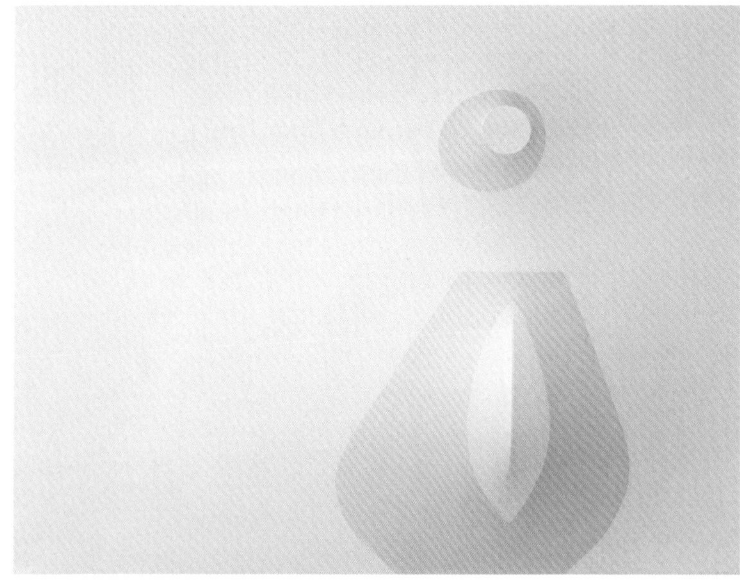

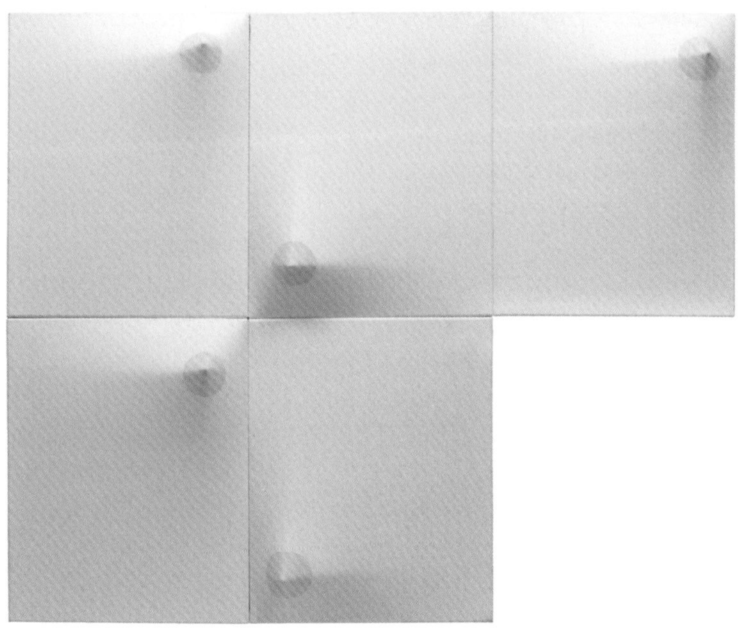

Traba recognizes and admires this potential of erotic pervasiveness, exemplified in Sánchez's purity of form and sensitive modulation of subdued colors.

Traba's writings are in tune with those of Herbert Marcuse, who claims that Eros carries liberating and constructive power against oppression.[45] In a 1978 essay, Marcuse states, "Today the fight for life, the fight for Eros is a political act."[46] Furthermore, he proposes a dialectic of Eros and Logos; for him eroticism, especially in art, is about not hedonistic pleasure but sensual knowing, which leads to the construction of a nonrepressive society, where the division of labor and leisure (Eros) is erased. This is similar to the view of Mário Pedrosa, who looks at art as a vital necessity that offers exercise in artistic freedom, which in turn aspires social freedom. Pedrosa advocates the politics of resistance, which claims that by resisting any demagogical thinking, art becomes political. Abstract art, in his opinion, has a revolutionary quality, for it awakens people's innate creativity without traditional narrative.[47]

Similarly, eroticism for Sánchez does not operate in terms of explicit sexual or biological function or any gender-oriented study. Instead, it infers a bonding principle or desire for human interconnection, an urge for fulfillment, and an impulse to live fully and uncompromisingly. Sánchez, too, believes that eroticism is a means for liberation, both politically and for women; a break from social conventions; and a path toward self-realization, artistic and otherwise. To that end Eleanor Hakim, a New York–based leftist writer, writes in a 1966 essay, "Sánchez's metaphoric visualizations fulfill her social function as an artist who searches for the root sources of reality and who re-establishes the possibilities of communication through regenerative creative experience."[48] As with many feminist artists of the time, for Sánchez, too, eroticism is a pledge of equality and gender liberation, a power to speak. Although never an outspoken activist or feminist, Sánchez has always been a free, nonconformist spirit, a rebel, a fury — *una furia*, as she would call herself. Therefore, by withstanding any ideological rhetoric, Sánchez's practice itself

12 Zilia Sánchez, *Nacimiento de Eros* (The Birth of Eros), 1971. Acrylic on stretched canvas, 90 11/16 × 114 15/16 × 16 in. (230.3 × 291.9 × 40.6 cm). Museo de Arte de Puerto Rico, San Juan.

13 Zilia Sánchez, *Troyanas* (Trojan Women), polyptych, 1990. Acrylic on stretched canvas, 36 × 42 × 4 1/2 in. (91.4 × 106.7 × 11.4 cm). Collection of American Friends of the Israel Museum, Jerusalem.

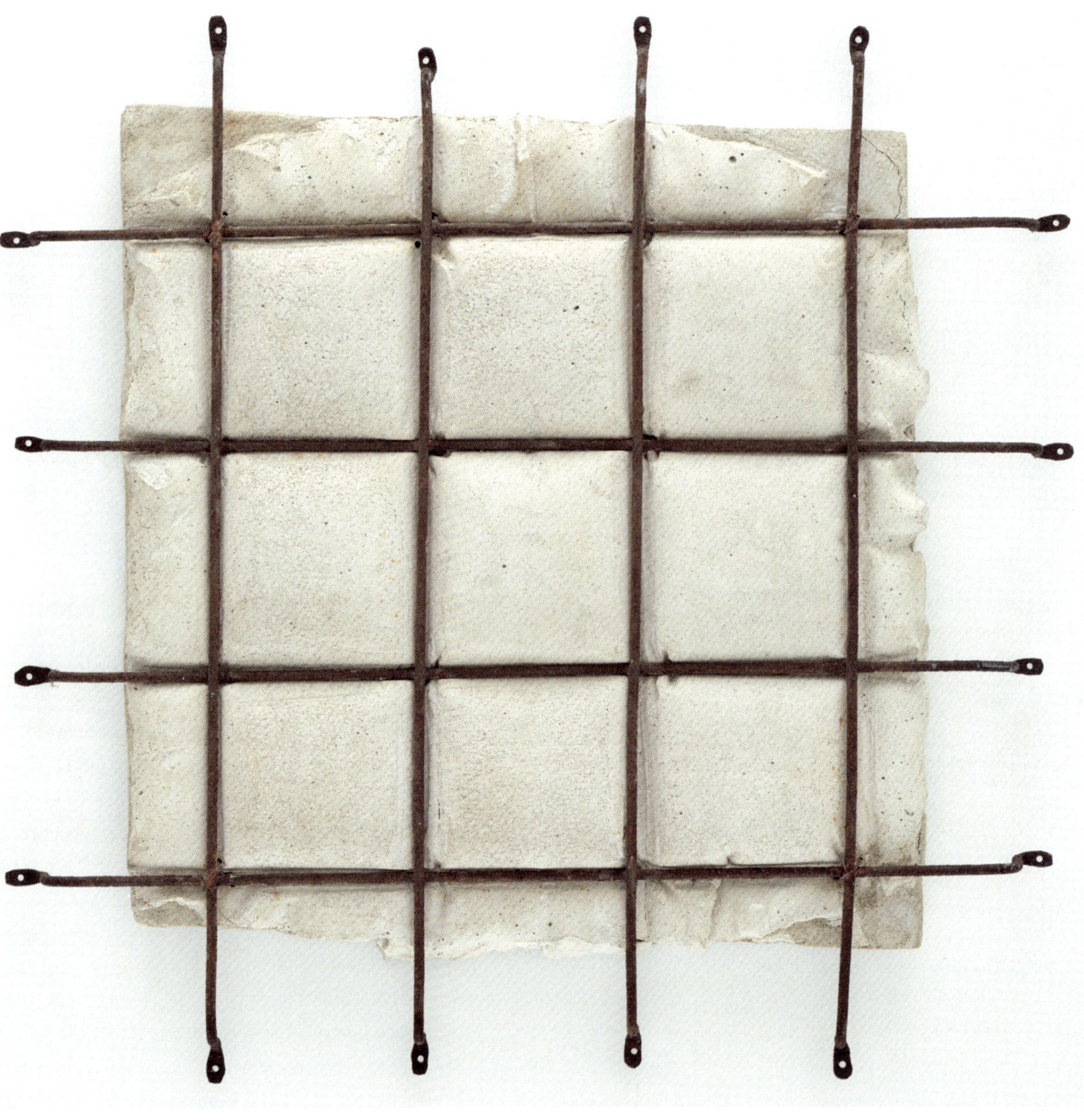

14 Zilia Sánchez, *Represión* (Repression), 1998. White cement with iron bars, 24 × 24 × 2 in. (61 × 61 × 5.1 cm), Collection of the artist, Courtesy Galerie Lelong & Co., New York.

becomes the art of resistance, art that is obliquely political (fig. 14). In this respect her topologies, although clearly anthropomorphic and seductive, are not simply studies of the eroticized female body that invoke lust or self-indulgence. Rather, they should be considered in a broader, ontological sense as embodied meanings.

Indeed, for Sánchez, seeing, feeling, and thinking are intermingled. By stating that "the heart and brain converse, and that is where my art comes from,"[49] Sánchez recalls Susanne Langer's cognitive emotion and Mikel Dufrenne's sensuous meaning. When she claims that "without search there is no art,"[50] she points directly to the ontological quest for meaning that is hidden, or in Maurice Merleau-Ponty's terms, silent, as it appears in his writing: "The sensible is that: to be evident in silence, to be understood implicitly."[51] By choosing the language of abstraction (in phenomenological terms, abstraction equals "bracketing," or reducing the reality to its essentials), Sánchez further camouflages her narrative and goes straight to the basics: "the egg, the world, the breast—three things."[52] In other words, or in symbolic terms, the egg as inception, the world as a permanent state of being, and the breast as nourishment are the pillars of life that merge the human and the natural world. Accordingly, the female body is, for Sánchez, an expression of nature, and the feminine principle is the governing norm of life. By the same token, the beauty of the human form is equal to the beauty of the landscape, and therefore breasts look like mountains.

This visual correlation of the human and the natural is in alignment with Merleau-Ponty's ontology of "flesh" (*chair*)[53] as an enveloping principle or "oneness," in which subject–object–world are inherently "reversible," and everything is intertwined with everything else. In this sense, Merleau-Ponty's "flesh" corresponds directly to Sánchez's treatment of canvas as skin, which envelops the protruding feminine forms inhabiting the space. The play of light and shadows only further emphasizes their palpable, sensual, and spatial quality. As Sánchez explains, they are "painting finding a third dimension,"[54] "sculptures dressed in fabric," or "paintings with air that breathe"[55]

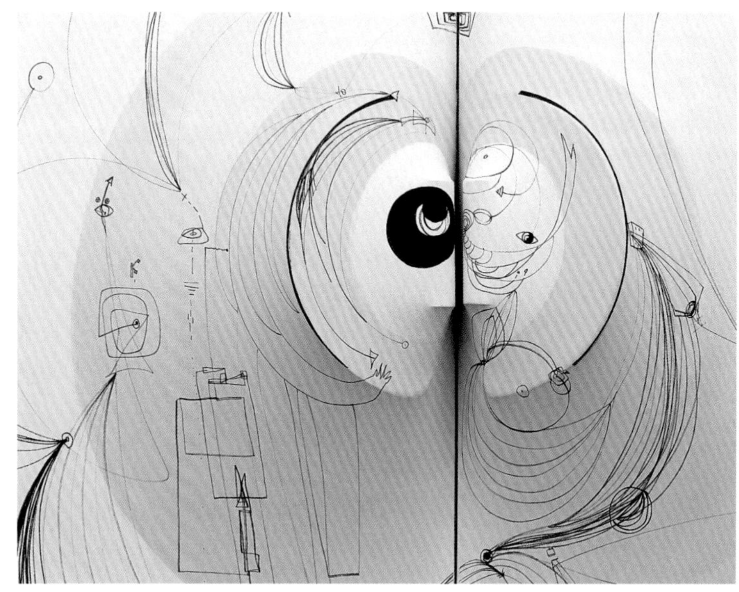

(cat. 41). Impregnated with air, they echo Merleau-Ponty's notion of "depth"—not only as a special dimension but as a place of intertwining or reversibility of perception and reflection, and the individual and the social. Consequently, such a perpetual reversibility leads to instability of signification and ultimately to ambiguous or latent meaning, which is the crux of both Merleau-Ponty's ontology and Sánchez's work. The open-endedness of her art is evident in the fact that many of Sánchez's works have dates that span decades or are rewritten; that she calls her topologies constructions or structures, interchangeably; that the orientation of her works is often uncertain (marked in multiple directions); and even that her signature shifts to different places.

Sánchez's intentional ambiguity is most evident in her *tatuajes*, or "tattooed" works (fig. 15), which bear gestural marks drawn in ink directly on the canvas, like tattoos on flesh. "Line is the first thing you do," says Sánchez. "Line is a release of expression."[56] In these tattooed works, including the *Soy Isla* paintings (such as

15 Detail of Zilia Sánchez, *Lunar con tatuaje* (Moon with Tattoo), c. 1968/96 (cat. 31).

cat. 33), the wiggly, sinuous, and calligraphic inscriptions present ambiguous trajectories and abstracted personal stories. Essentially, these paintings are maps or topographies of outer, physical space and inner, emotional space hovering among bodyscape, skyscape, and dreamscape. "I like to draw with my eyes closed" (fig. 16), Sánchez explains, which for her is a way to get in touch with feelings, to reach to the "movement that is of the body, but also of intellect,"[57] and achieve balance between two forces. By using names of the protagonists from Greek mythology for her titles, mostly female warriors and heroines — Amazonas, Troyanas, and Antígona (cat. 47) — Sánchez not only removes biographical elements from her narratives but also uses classical mythology to comment on contemporary conditions, especially the position of women in society. It is from this elusive content, lingering between the intimate and the epic, the individual and the collective, that the embodied, elliptical meaning of her work derives.

The elusive narratives also play out in Sánchez's *Lunar* works (including cat. 52), where her topology overlaps with cosmology and where the corporeal meets the celestial as part of a larger cosmic unit. The moon is the feminine symbol, universally representing time intervals. In Spanish, *lunar* has a double meaning, the moon or a mole/birthmark, which accentuates the synergy of the body and the universe in her work. By projecting light, the full moon is a symbol of subtlety and reflection, but also wholeness. This, too, parallels Sánchez's circular forms with silky surfaces in white, gray, and black tones, while echoing the Caribbean moonlight — *la noche lunar* — that provides her with comfort and tranquillity.

As with the mythological elements, Sánchez is drawn to lunar motifs because there is something hidden and subliminal about them. By employing direct symbols, whether mythological or astronomical, and choosing mystical and poetic silences, Sánchez's work is driven by — to use Mark Johnson's term —"meaning making," which is grounded in the body. For Johnson, embodied meaning[58] has a visceral origin and emerges from the human encounter with the

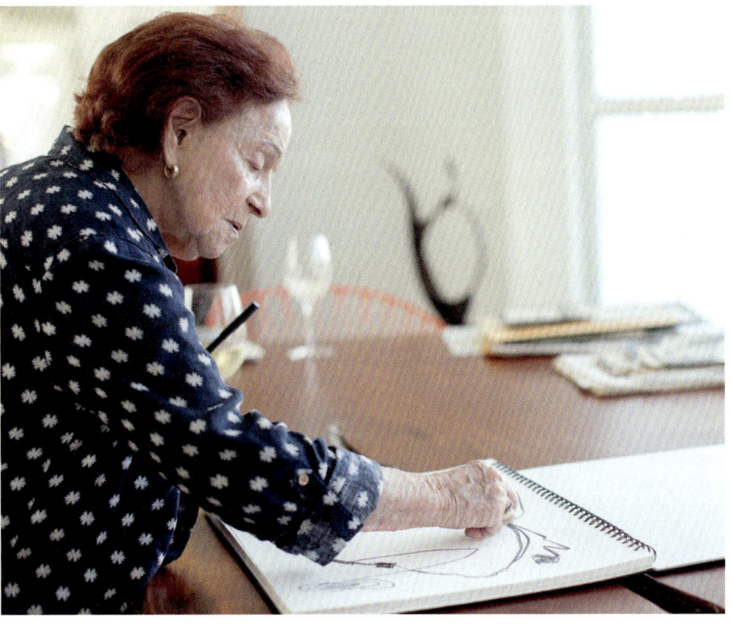

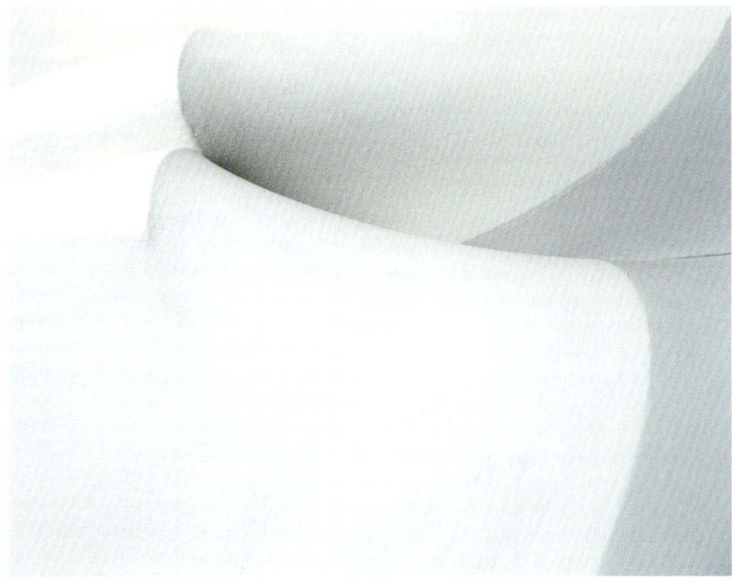

16 Sánchez drawing, San Juan, February 2018.

17 Detail of *El silencio de Eros* (The Silence of Eros), 1983 (cat. 46).

environment and from exchanges with others. Conversely, the notion of encounter holds a special place in Sánchez's work, with multiple implications: as a place of connection with others; as a place of divergence; and, above all, as a place of "investigation," from which harmony arises. Indeed, the concept of harmony has always had a strong presence in her work: "I am after a harmony between two forces. I compose the balance of the body," she has said.[59]

Clearly, over the years, Sánchez has pursued the same principles from the outset of her career: harmony, elegance, vigor, and sensuality. Her topologies are embodied spaces — physical, social, emotional, and metaphorical. They resonate with Sánchez's own view of them as "metaphors for humanity with reference to sensuality,"[60] as well as with those philosophies that stress the embodied, sensuous meaning and the affective and transformative power of art (fig. 17).

Vesela Sretenović, PhD, is senior curator of modern and contemporary art at The Phillips Collection.

NOTES

1. Sánchez talks about her work dominating the spectator. See Norma Niurka, "Zilia sublimiza el cuerpo femenino," *El Miami Herald*, January 24, 1982. Translated by Patricia Ortega-Miranda. This is also noticed by Dolores Prida when she asks, "Who watches whom?" when facing Zilia's work. Dolores Prida, "El erotismo espacial en la pintura de Zilia Sánchez," *La nueva sangre* 3, no. 9 (October 1970): 9–10.

2. From the title of Mikel Dufrenne's *In the Presence of the Sensuous: Essays in Aesthetics* (Atlantic Highlands, NJ: Humanities Press International, 1987).

3. Maurice Merleau-Ponty develops his ontology of vision as an "embodiment" and "reversibility" of sense perception and reflection, self and the world, and nature and culture from which all meaning derives. He calls this "sensuous meaning" or "sensuousness." Maurice Merleau-Ponty, *The Visible and the Invisible* (Evanston, IL: Northwestern University Press, 1968), 214.

4. Susanne Langer argues that art is a high form of expression, symbolizing direct or intuitive knowledge — e.g., feeling, motion, and emotion — that ordinary language is unable to convey. Langer attempts to trace the origin and development of the mind in her books *Feeling and Form* (New York: Scribner, 1953) and *Mind: An Essay on Human Feeling*, 3 vols. (Baltimore: Johns Hopkins Press, 1986).

5. Langer, *Feeling and Form*.

6. Mark Johnson is known for his contributions to embodied philosophy, cognitive science, and cognitive linguistics. In *The Meaning of the Body*, he argues for the embodied nature of human cognition and highlights the importance of body-based meaning making. Mark Johnson, *The Meaning of the Body: Aesthetics of Human Understanding* (Chicago: University of Chicago Press, 2007).

7. Zilia Sánchez, conversations with the author, September 2016–March 2018.

8. Los Once had a short life, from 1953 to 1955. Sánchez, who was never an official member, was the only woman associated with the group. The members included Francisco Antigua, René Ávila, Ignacio Bermúdez, Agustín Cárdenas, Hugo Consuegra, José Antonio Díaz Peláez, Viredo Espinosa, Fayad Jamís, Guido Llinás, Raúl Martínez, Tomás Oliva, and Antonio Vidal.

9. It is interesting to note that Sánchez chose to show *Composición en blanco*, when the whole Bienal was marked by a culmination of the Informel work.

10. Tachisme — derived from the word *tache*, "stain" — is a French style of abstract painting from the 1940s and 1950s that favors intuitive and lyrical expression.

11. The Art Informel movement of the 1950s — the name refers to an absence of form, structure, concept, or approach — represented a break with modernist tradition. It stressed the pursuit of spontaneity, looseness of form, the irrational, and the immaterial.

12. Sánchez has never met Tàpies or Fontana in person, but she has seen and admired their work throughout the years.

13. Sánchez was a CINTAS fellow in Madrid in 1966–67, taking courses in painting restoration at the Escuela de Restauración in the Casón del Buen Retiro, now part of the Museo Nacional del Prado.

———

14. *La nueva sangre*, a New York–based Spanish-language literary magazine founded in 1968, featured poems, drawings, theater reviews, literary criticism, exhibition listings, and cultural activities, aiming to share a vision of bilingual, bicultural, bisexual New York.

———

15. The only kinship that Sánchez has claimed to have among the minimalist artists is with Eva Hesse, because of their shared sensuality of forms and materials.

———

16. The shaped canvas, a hybrid of painting and sculpture, was one of the dominant forms of abstract painting in the United States in the 1960s and the 1970s. In 1964, the Solomon R. Guggenheim Museum organized the defining exhibition *The Shaped Canvas*, curated by Lawrence Alloway, and in 1965 a group show, *Shape and Structure* at Tibor de Nagy in New York, introduced three-dimensional shaped canvases by a number of artists. The 2014 exhibition *The Shaped Canvas Revisited* at the Luxembourg & Dayan Gallery in New York attempted to present this 1960s phenomenon in its full complexity, drawing a parallel between the United States and Europe.

———

17. Sánchez and Hinman are compared in Ernesto J. Ruiz de la Mata, "Purely Decorative? Why Not?," *San Juan Star Magazine*, November 4, 1979.

18. Agostino Bonalumi (1935–2013) was an Italian abstract artist known for his principal role in the postwar avant-garde. Bonalumi became fascinated with the plasticity of painting and issues of space and invented his *estroflessioni*, which he referred to as painting-objects. These were made from structures and frames, which, when placed at the backs of canvases, caused them to stretch, deform, and create unusual curvilinear shapes. He was friends with Enrico Castellani and was associated with the ZERO movement, which stood in opposition to the subjectivism of Tachisme and Art Informel and instead advocated light and motion.

———

19. Severo Sarduy, "Topologías eróticas," in *Estructuras en secuencia* (San Juan: Museo de la Universidad de Puerto Rico, 1970), n.p. Reprinted in *La provincia*, April 8, 1973, and in the 2000 exhibition catalogue *Zilia Sánchez: Heróicas eróticas* at the Museo de las Américas in San Juan. Translated by Alyson Cluck and Patricia Ortega-Miranda.

———

20. Gordon Brown, statement in ibid., n.p.

———

21. Ibid.

———

22. Mario Peña, "El minimalismo con poesía de Zilia," *El tiempo*, January 4, 1971. Translated by Alyson Cluck.

———

23. Donald Judd, "Specific Objects," in *Donald Judd: Complete Writings, 1959–1975* (Halifax: Press of the Nova Scotia College of Art and Design; New York: New York University Press, 2005), 181–89. Originally published in *Contemporary Sculpture: Arts Yearbook 8* (New York: Art Digest, 1965), 74–82.

24. Ferreira Gullar was instrumental in the formation of the neo-concrete movement, which held that artwork should interact with spectators and make them aware of their physical bodies and metaphysical existence. He embraced phenomenology in order to overcome the acute rationalism of geometric abstraction, especially concretism. In December 1959 Gullar published his essay "Theory of the Non-Object" in the national newspaper *Jornal do Brasil*. For translation and analysis of his text, see Michael Asbury, "Neoconcretism and Minimalism: On Ferreira Gullar's Theory of the Non-Object," in *Cosmopolitan Modernisms*, ed. Kobena Mercer (Cambridge, MA: MIT Press, 2005), 168–89.

———

25. Stefan Kalmár and Richard Birkett, "Zilia Sánchez Interview," San Juan, March 2013, Artists Space video, http://artistsspace.org/materials/zilia-sanchez-interview. Translated by Carla Acevedo-Yates.

———

26. Ibid.

———

27. Alberto Barral, "Zilia Sánchez," *Art Nexus*, no. 104 (March–May 2017): 49.

———

28. Sánchez, conversations with the author.

———

29. The artist's major solo exhibition *Estructuras en secuencia* was held at the Museo de la Universidad de Puerto Rico in 1970.

———

30. The Laguna Gardens complex was built by an exiled Cuban architect, Henry Gutiérrez (b. 1931).

31. *Zona* was an important left-oriented and pro-independence magazine. There are different spellings of the magazine, both commonly used. One is the primary source, *Zona. Carga y descarga*, and the other is *Zona de carga y descarga*. Similarly, translations of the magazine vary from "Charge and Discharge" to "Load(ing) and Unload(ing)." All are correct.

32. Sánchez's father's death was confirmed in a meeting with her brother, Ramiro Sánchez, in Havana in early March 2018.

33. The artist's own recollection of her first shaped canvases slightly varies. Therefore, she retells the story with different details; at times, the bedsheet is hitting against a tube or a pipe, and other times against a wooden space divider. In the most recent conversation, in February 2018, Sánchez talked about her initial experimentation using small tile-like wooden pieces and a tube, and wanting to make an entire wall out of them.

34. Ileana Delgado Castro, "Encuentro con Zilia Sánchez," *El nuevo día*, sec. Revista Domingo, March 20, 2005. Translated by Alyson Cluck.

35. Ibid.

36. Sánchez, conversations with the author.

37. Sánchez credits Severo Sarduy for naming her shaped canvases *topologías eróticas* as well as for her title references to ancient Greek mythological narratives.

38. Antonio J. Molina, "Zilia Sánchez y su obra," *El mundo*, May 5, 1975. Translated by Alyson Cluck.

39. Manuel Álvarez Lezama, "Zilia Sánchez: Poeta de la sensualidad," in *Zilia Sánchez: Construcciones en secuencia* (San Juan: Casa Sofía de Puerto Rico, 2009), n.p. Translated by Alyson Cluck.

40. Benigno Trigo, "Zona. Carga y descarga," in *Malady and Genius: Self-Sacrifice in Puerto Rican Literature* (Albany: State University of New York Press, 2016), 100.

41. Ibid., 102.

42. Rudi C. Bleys, *Images of Ambiente: Homotextuality and Latin American Art, 1810–Today* (London: Continuum, 2000), 8.

43. Marta Traba, "A la búsqueda del signo perdido," in *Dos décadas vulnerables en las artes plásticas latinoamericanas, 1950–1970* (Mexico City: Siglo Veintiuno, 1973), 174. Translated by Alyson Cluck.

44. Marta Traba, "El erotismo y la comunicación," *Zona. Carga y descarga* 1, no. 2 (November–December 1972): 11. Translated by Alyson Cluck.

45. Herbert Marcuse, *Eros and Civilization: A Philosophical Inquiry into Freud* (Boston: Beacon Press, 1955). Marcuse attempts to synthesize Marxist and psychoanalytic theory, alluding to Freud's *Civilization and Its Discontents* (1930).

46. Herbert Marcuse, *The Aesthetic Dimension: Toward a Critique of Marxist Aesthetics* (Boston: Beacon Press, 1978). Marcuse calls for radical subjectivity and looks for spaces of a critical consciousness that can fight oppressive forces of capitalism; art offers that possibility.

47. Gloria Ferreira, ed., *Mário Pedrosa: Primary Documents* (New York: Museum of Modern Art, 2015).

48. Eleanor Hakim, "Zilia Sánchez: Metaphoric Visualizations of Reality," in *Zilia Sánchez: Paintings* (New York: Zegrí Gallery, 1966), n.p.

49. Sánchez, conversations with the author.

50. Ibid.

51. Merleau-Ponty, *Visible and the Invisible*, 214.

52. Kalmár and Birkett, "Zilia Sánchez Interview."

53. Merleau-Ponty's ontology of "flesh" was fully developed in his unfinished manuscript, *The Visible and the Invisible*, published posthumously in 1961. The basic idea was to resolve the Cartesian dualism of body and mind, not through a dialectical synthesis but rather with the ontology of "Being," in which everything is intertwined or reversible. In this sense, "flesh" is the embodied character of existence.

54. Delgado Castro, "Encuentro con Zilia Sánchez."

55. Niurka, "Zilia sublimiza el cuerpo femenino."

56. Kalmár and Birkett, "Zilia Sánchez Interview."

57. Ibid.

58. Johnson, *Meaning of the Body*.

59. Barral, "Zilia Sánchez," 49.

60. Delgado Castro, "Encuentro con Zilia Sánchez."

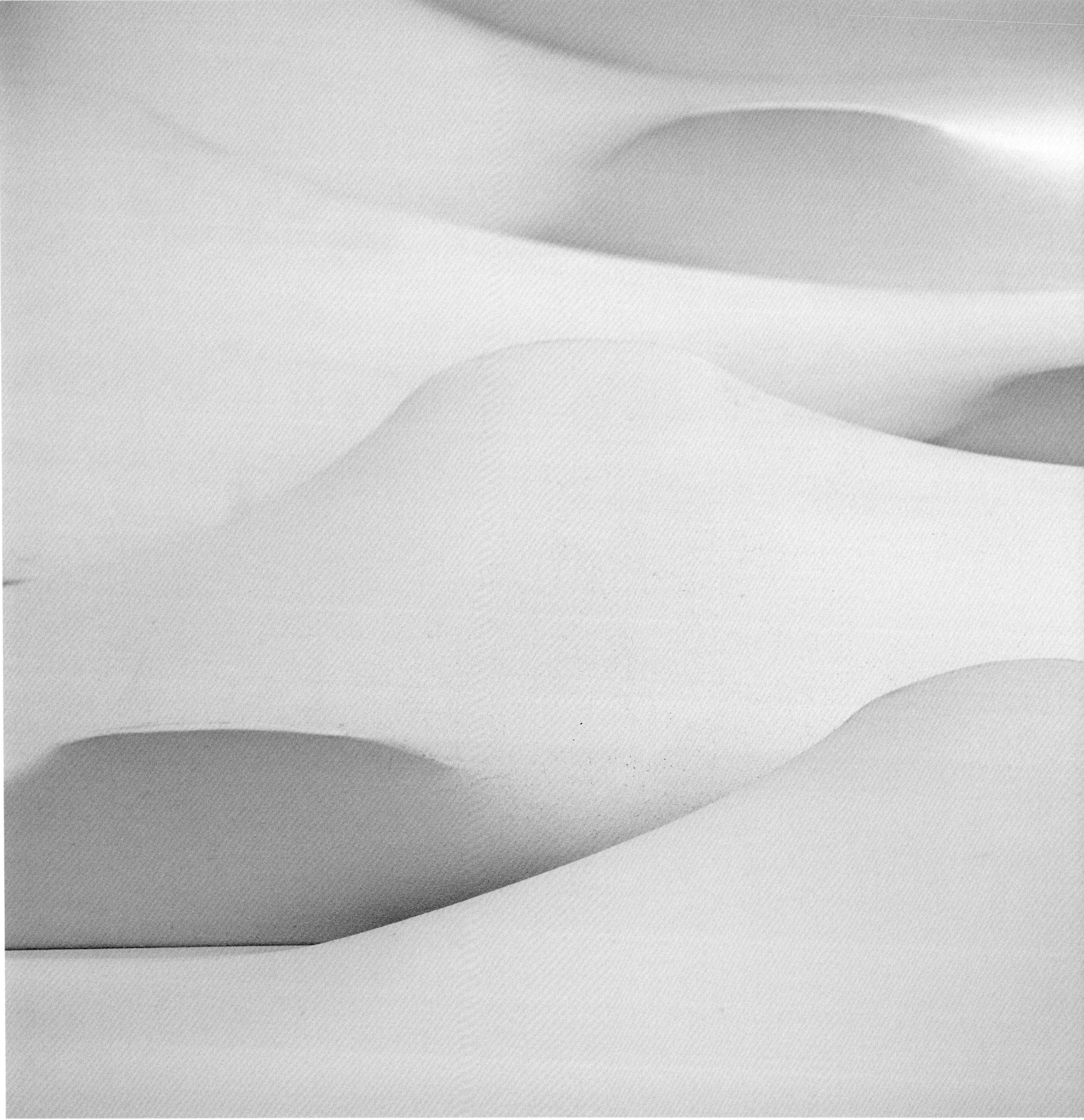

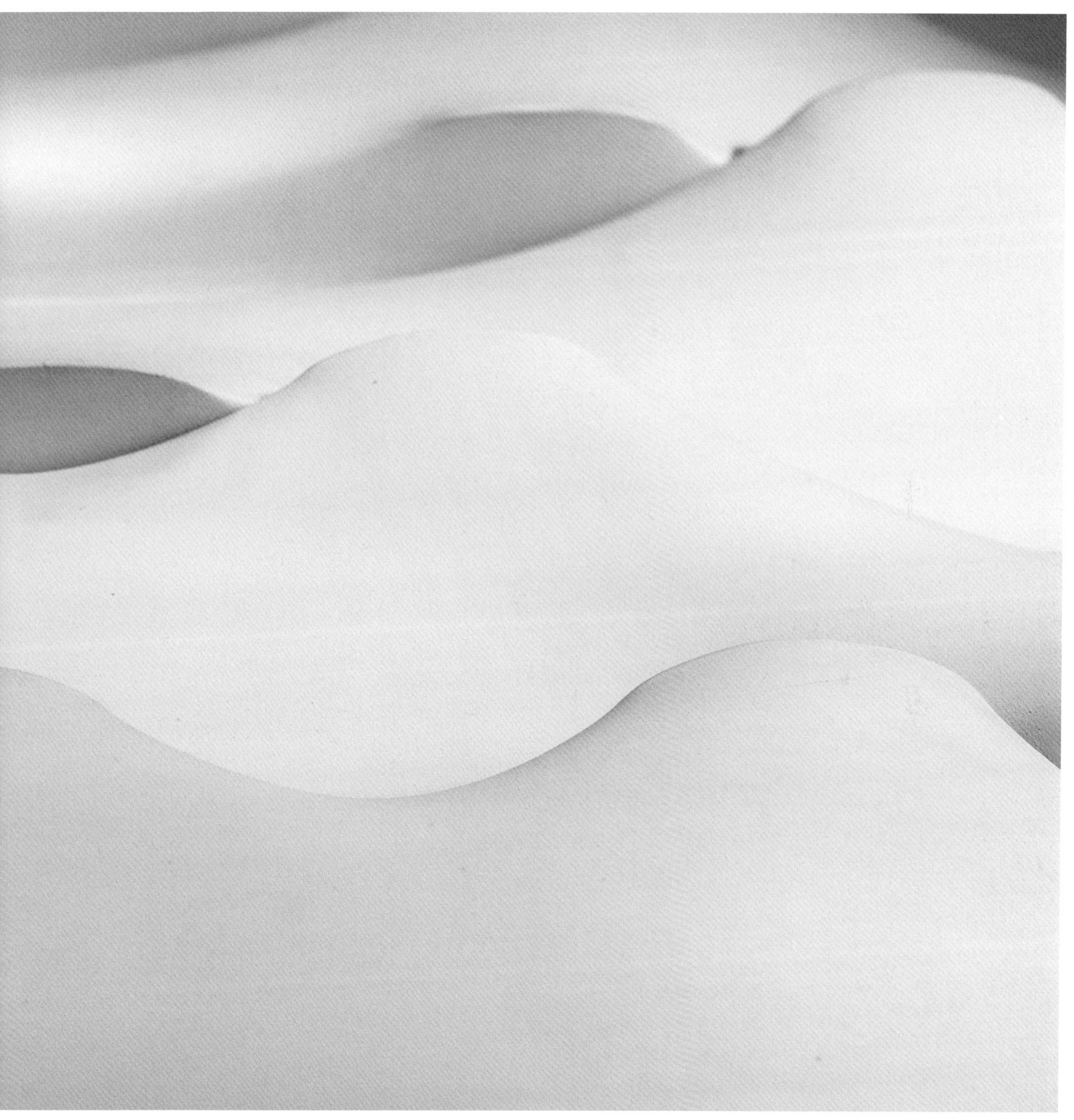

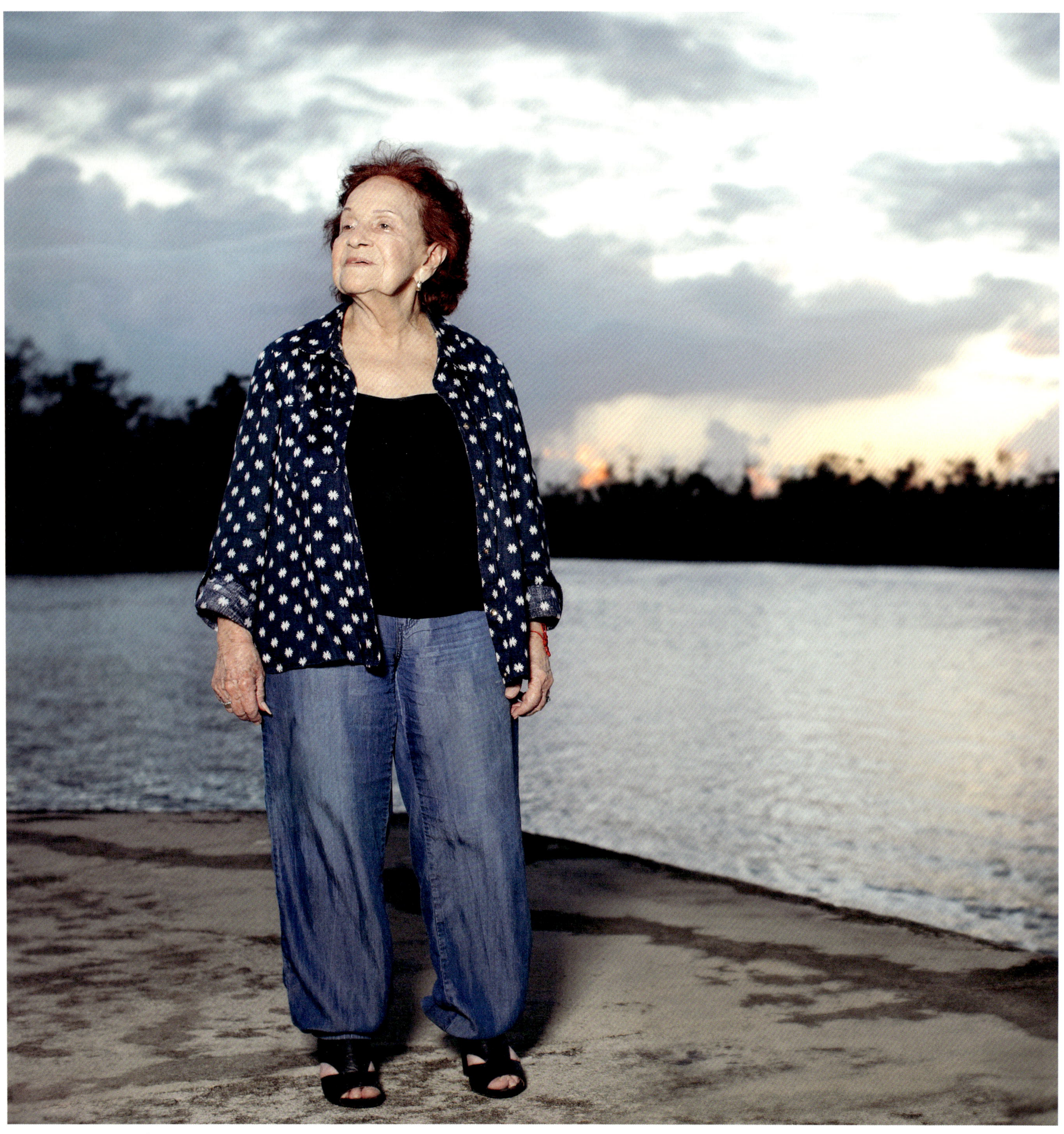

In Retrospect: Talking with Zilia Sánchez

VESELA SRETENOVIĆ Tell us more about your upbringing in Havana.
ZILIA SÁNCHEZ It was happy, although I remember that I cried a lot when I was little, and the only way for my mother to console me was to take me outside to see the moonlight. I was very close to my father. He loved painting and taught himself how to paint, especially landscapes. He worked in business administration, like my grandfather, but in his free time he would always paint. I would scream until I was seated next to him, so that I could paint too. As long as I was next to my father, working, I was calm and happy.

VS So you were drawn to art from early on at home. Did you and your family go out to see art exhibitions?
ZS Yes, when there was something new, we would go to see it, but

VESELA SRETENOVIĆ

I don't remember much more. What I do remember vividly is my father's death [in 1955]; it was so awful. The day he died felt like I had died. I remember I saw his bedsheet, the sheet that my mother washed because he was throwing up. The sheet was drying, and since it was windy, it was hitting against a wooden space divider, and this image of the blowing bedsheet against wood got stuck in my mind. I think that such moments of internalizing the outside world, especially when you are young, are of crucial importance, and you never forget them.

VS When did you decide to go to the academy?
ZS My schoolteacher from fourth to sixth grade told my mother that I should go and study drawing, so I went to the Academy of San Alejandro. First I studied architecture, but only for a semester; the studies required advanced math, so I ran away. I never liked exact numbers or precise things — I preferred to be free, and art offered that. After I graduated, I got a scholarship to go to Spain.

vs I assume that the training at the academy was very traditional.

zs It was horrible. Very academic, prescriptive, monotonous. I wanted to take off and leave. I was always searching for something new and different.

vs And who were the artists you were looking at around that time?

zs Víctor Manuel, foremost. He was a neighbor, living a floor below us, and my mom would often sit me down on our balcony so I could watch him paint. He was very important to me, but he was also a very important Cuban painter. He was bohemian, self-trained, very academic, but he had grace and charm, and he would often give me his drawings.

vs What was the most significant thing about him?

zs He was a marvelous person, a true artist without going to an art school. And that was inspirational for me, because art can be expressed through a technique or a spirit. Technique can be taught, but an inner spirit cannot.

vs It seems that, from the very beginning, you wanted to escape from the established conventions, and that the language of abstraction gave you a way to express an imaginary, inner world, rather than external reality.

zs Right, right. I was always searching for the invisible and the unknown. That is why I don't like it when people ask me how I make my work — it's irrelevant. It is the feeling that matters, and the technique comes second.

vs This makes me think of transitions in your work, from very poetic, dreamy, even surreal imagery in the vein of 1950s European lyrical abstraction to the 1960s shift toward more robust, textural work in the Informel style, followed by another change toward shaped canvas. Can you tell us more about those trajectories in your work?

zs I don't realize when a big change occurs. One is born every day. I read a lot, and when something affects me, I don't realize it at first, nor do I control it or myself. I just surrender. And only later do I say to myself: What did I do? What happened?

vs So your process is both introspective and retrospective.

zs It's very internal. One day it can be one way, the next day it could be another way. And the changes I make in the works happen the same way — they are not preconceived but intuitive.

vs Let's step now from the internal aspect of your work to your social surroundings and put your work in a broader historical context. After your earlier travel to Spain in the mid-1950s, you returned to Cuba in the late 1950s; was it different then than when you left?

zs Yes, it was different, and I didn't want to stay.

vs Why?

zs I felt that I didn't have a lot of freedom. I thought about staying and talked about that a lot with my family. But you know, one becomes selfish with one's work. When I want to paint, I want to be alone. This doesn't mean that I don't love my family. On the contrary, they gave me so much, to the point that I didn't want to paint, but to be with them instead. I realized then that I had to leave in order to be alone and find myself, and they understood. But after I left, I missed them badly and wanted to go back. One has nostalgia for freedom, but also for having everything, but you can't have everything. Life, at times, presents us with hard choices.

vs Was art politicized at that time?

zs Some artists were more political than others. I never liked politics. We were all against Batista's regime, but many of us didn't go to protest, and many wanted to leave, especially after 1959 — mostly the young intellectuals, including my close friend, poet Severo Sarduy, who settled in Paris.

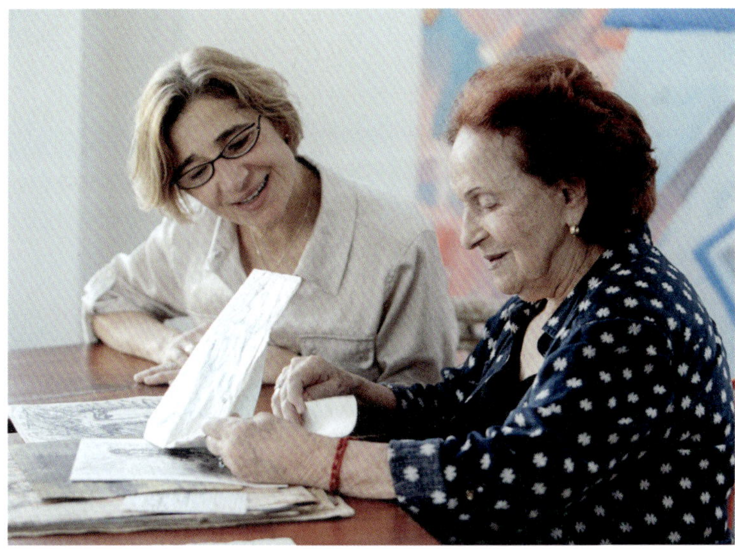

vs Did you have a sense at that time of what the next regime would bring?

zs Not really. Many thought that it would be wonderful, but it turned out to be the same—as the saying goes, the same donkey with different ears. Batista was a dictator, but he was loved by many. People seemed to prefer to be dominated than to have a democratic government for the people; they were scared of disorder. Like Batista, Fidel was a politician who wanted to dominate the community, the people—and soon after, everything fell apart.

vs And you left Cuba in 1960 to go to New York, right?

zs Yes, Severo was in New York at that time and invited me to visit him, so I did. We stayed first in the Lower East Side and eventually we settled on the Upper East Side, close to the East River—I always looked for water.

vs Eventually, you started to show your work, including at the Sarduy Gallery. Tell us more about those days.

zs It was RosaMaría García Sarduy, Severo's cousin, who opened the gallery, and I showed my work there. It was very close to where we lived on the Upper East Side. It was a community place for many Cuban artists and poets to meet and exchange ideas. But I worked a lot of jobs, from factory work to restoration, in order to pay the rent, so I didn't interact with people that much.

vs Did you go to the galleries and attend openings? New York in the mid-sixties was an art mecca, where both Pop and minimalism flourished, and artists like Donald Judd, Ellsworth Kelly, Lee Bontecou, Eva Hesse, Agnes Martin, and Carmen Herrera—whose aesthetic is similar to yours—were working and living. Did you know them?

zs I would go to the openings and see the shows occasionally, but I didn't hang out with others very often. I didn't know Kelly or Judd in person, but I knew of their work. I did meet Herrera, whose work I found very interesting. But overall, New York was tough for me. I didn't like the climate there, and I didn't connect with people either.

vs However, in the video interview from your first solo presentation in New York, at the Artists Space in 2013, you called yourself a *mulata minimalista*. What was your connection to minimalism? You hadn't met most of these artists, but where did you see their work?

zs Well, "mulatto" is a mix, so I wanted to call myself that because every Cuban has some black blood, and I liked this reference to race. By the same token, minimalism also has a "mulatto" or mixture component, of something small and something big. So, I called myself a "mulata minimalista" because I am a mix myself. I still call myself that.

vs Around that time, you also attended Pratt Graphic Art Center. Were you enrolled in the program or just taking classes?

zs I just signed up for printmaking classes. Serigraphy interested me the most because I was unfamiliar with its technique; I knew lithography but I wanted to learn more about colors and the use of cut paper.

above Sretenović and Sánchez in San Juan, February 2018.

vs I'm very curious to ask about the books on eroticism that you came across in New York, which confirmed your new direction emphasizing bodily forms. What were those books?

zs I read so many books on sexuality, eroticism, and communication. And then, one day, Severo came to visit and whispered: "Those are *tetas* [boobs] — you did breasts, Zilia!" That's why I started to use "Eros" in my titles.

vs But before that, you didn't think that way?

zs No, they were mountains to me.

vs While in New York, you were awarded the CINTAS Fellowship twice [1966 and 1968], which enabled you to travel to Spain again.

zs Yes, and I decided to spend my time in Madrid and study conservation at Prado. I always loved looking at old paintings, and I wanted to learn more about painting restoration. I also learned about porcelain, because it is a material used for curved forms, and a painting is flat. I never liked porcelain itself, but learning a technique gave me the needed skills to make molds and then to make up things in my own way.

vs While at Prado, what was the most influential art for you?

zs Goya! He laid his heart into his painting. He liberated the painting by putting it inside of him — he ate the paint.

vs What about your contemporaries?

zs I very much liked the Informel artists, Antoni Tàpies, Manolo Millares, and Rafael Canogar.

vs And did you meet Tàpies?

zs No, no. But I liked his work and the whole group — their creativity, their energy, originality, honesty. Making art is about being honest. And being honest is when you say what you feel and do not make things to please or to be liked.

vs All in all, being in Spain was good for you. Did you have a chance to travel?

zs Spain felt like home. My father was Spanish; my aunts, my father's sisters, lived in Spain (in Cuenca), and everyone spoke Spanish. I didn't travel that much; I preferred to be in the studio, although we went to Old Salamanca, where my grandfather was from. I also went to Paris to visit Severo and passed through Italy.

vs Then you returned to New York again and became involved in *La nueva sangre*, a Spanish literary magazine founded by Cuban and Puerto Rican poets living in New York, including Mercedes Cortázar and Dolores Prida, whose aim was to give visibility to Hispanic, bilingual, bicultural, bisexual, bi-everything in New York.

zs Yes, yes. I did drawings and illustrations for some of the issues.

vs I'm also interested in your 1968 series of ink drawings, *El significado del significante* [The Signified of the Signifier] (cats. 27–30), a title that directly echoed French structuralism and the semiotics of the late sixties. Were you aware of those theories, or perhaps familiar with *Tel quel*, a journal of literary criticism established in Paris in 1960 by a group of philosophers, writers, and poets [including Barthes, Derrida, Lacan, François Wahl (Sarduy's partner), and Sarduy]?

zs I don't think so, but given that Severo was in those circles, he could have introduced me to their ideas, because we would talk a lot. He was a little younger than me, but we had known each other from childhood. He was extremely supportive of me and wrote beautifully about my work. He was an exceptional person — he was also the one who said to me early on: "Stay abroad."

vs And how was it, watching the turbulent events in Cuba from New York?

zs Well, you know, it was sad. I wish that things didn't go the way they did, but I am not a dramatic person. I always turn the page and go on. Some people would call me to go to the streets and protest, and I would just say, "It's too *hot*!"

vs But then, in the early 1970s, you left New York for a hot place — Puerto Rico. How come?

zs Hmm. The physical heat can't hurt. The other heat — the heat of the mind — is what is dangerous. And going to the blue sky and the ocean of Puerto Rico was almost like going home. Besides, the language is the same, and the people are similar. We're built from the same mold. Cuba and Puerto Rico are two small islands that cannot fight big powers. I say this because I am not a rebel; I am a realist.

vs When you arrived in San Juan, you were commissioned to do a large cement mural on the facade of an apartment building in Laguna Gardens. How did that come about?

zs A Cuban architect/developer contacted me and offered the commission. I made different molds that had depth to them, which, when multiplied and organized in different combinations, resulted in a large relief on the facade.

vs Was this architectural undertaking an extension of painting for you?

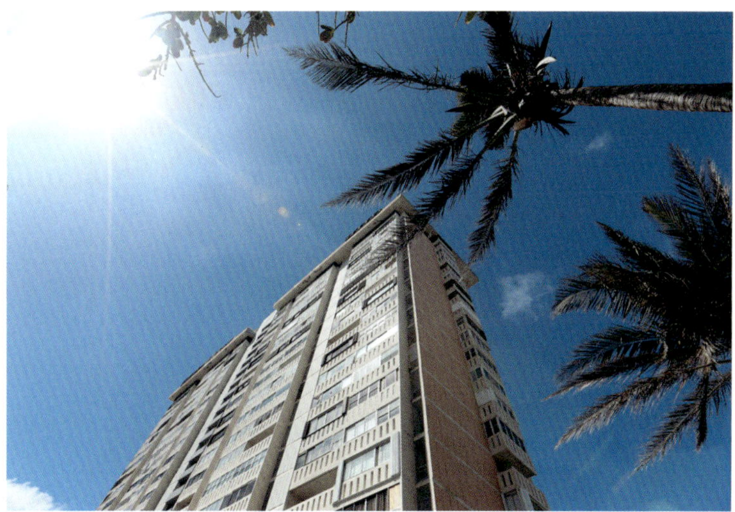

zs Yes, but frankly, it was also a job that enabled me to earn money to live on for a while and to make my work.

vs This is also the beginning, if I may say, of your mature style of *topologías*, in which paintings gain a strong sculptural dimension and a tactile quality, suggesting eroticized female forms and bearing mythological titles. Tell us more about this body of work.

zs I always start with a small sketch in my notebook and work from there. I make the form, i.e., wooden armature, first, and then I stretch the muslin over the armature until the fabric sets completely. I keep a variety of small wooden pieces and use them as needed for a new composition. Color comes last. I use acrylic because oil paint is susceptible to cracks and it dries very slowly. As to my frequent references to mythology — oh, mythology within the artists' minds opens an enormous window. Thank you, mythology!

vs In San Juan, you helped Rosario Ferré to start a very important but short-lived magazine: *Zona. Carga y descarga*. Could you tell us a little more about it?

zs *Zona* was Rosario's invention, and I worked on the graphic design. There were nine issues altogether, and I did graphic design for only three or four issues. After Rosario went to New York in the mid-1970s, the magazine was discontinued.

vs Looking at *Zona*'s design and contents, it makes me think of Stéphane Mallarmé and his concrete poetry, where the sounds and the typography were part of the poetry. It also once more brings to mind the *Tel quel* design and concept, which were geared toward experimental, nonlinear writing, the protection of human rights, and the politics of the far left, the values that *Zona* cherished as well.

zs Severo talked to me about Mallarmé, but I didn't read anything by him at that time. As I said, Severo was very cultured and a marvelous man on so many levels, and I learned a lot from him.

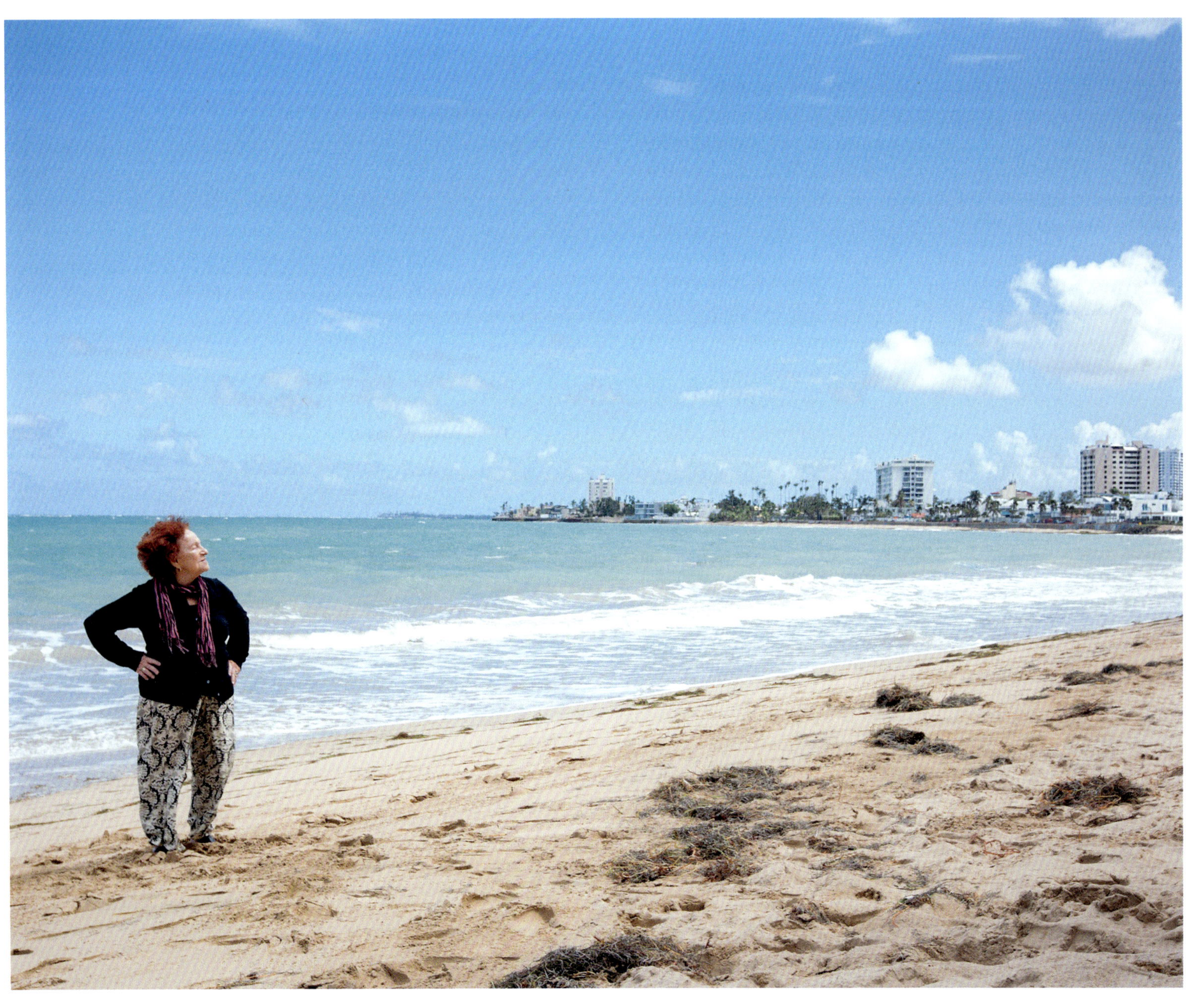

above Sánchez on the beach, San Juan,
February 2018.

vs You also started to teach in San Juan? You were a beloved teacher.

zs I liked teaching because I never took a traditional approach, based on observation. Instead, I would bring an apple to a class and say, "This is an apple, look at it now," and then I would take it away. Or I would give them a square and ask them to put anything they wanted inside the square — that way they could learn basic geometry. I preferred free form to copying because I like to work with feelings more than with eyes. I was a terrible teacher!

vs But how come your students loved you and still talk about you with admiration and great affection?

zs Because they had to finish the program, ha-ha! Many started not because they liked drawing but because they had to graduate — and also they liked my work. So I taught them how to do my work, and that was unusual at that time. And then, on Tuesdays and Thursdays, we had exams — and they could do whatever they wanted. If you want to be an artist, you have to have your own head, your own eyes, and your own pencils. Essentially, you cannot teach art.

vs In your long life, filled with numerous challenges, what would you say were the best and the worst, the happiest and the most difficult moments?

zs It is always nostalgia, both in the good and the bad. I left Cuba and my beloved ones, and that was difficult, but at the same time that is what I wanted and needed to do, so that was good. I often say, "I am an island. Understand it and walk away." The earth and the rocks are solid, but they don't float. I like to float and feel free.

vs And how do you maintain hope, faith, power?

zs I don't believe in bad. I have anguish, but I am not a dramatic person. If something goes wrong, I'll come back to it and try it again. The day is long, the night is long, and tomorrow is another day. I don't make a tragedy out of anything. I believe in the ocean because the ocean comes and goes and comes again. Tragedy does not exist.

vs But so many of your titles are from Greek mythology. And all of them are tragic stories, like *Amazons*, *Antigone*, *Trojan Women*, and *Joan of Arc* (cats. 44, 47, 51).

zs Yes, I believe that they are also heroic. They had to go through a lot of suffering, yet they overpowered the tragic and became heroines. Women have always been tragic and heroic. It is better to see them as love — Eros — or a life force, than Thanatos, or an impulse to die. Dying has no strength. It is just inevitable.

vs You are an extremely prolific artist. What do you consider to be your most productive period?

zs The most productive period is now!

Vesela Sretenović conducted a series of conversations with Zilia Sánchez from September 2016 to March 2018 in person and via phone calls and email facilitated through translation by Maria Heinz.

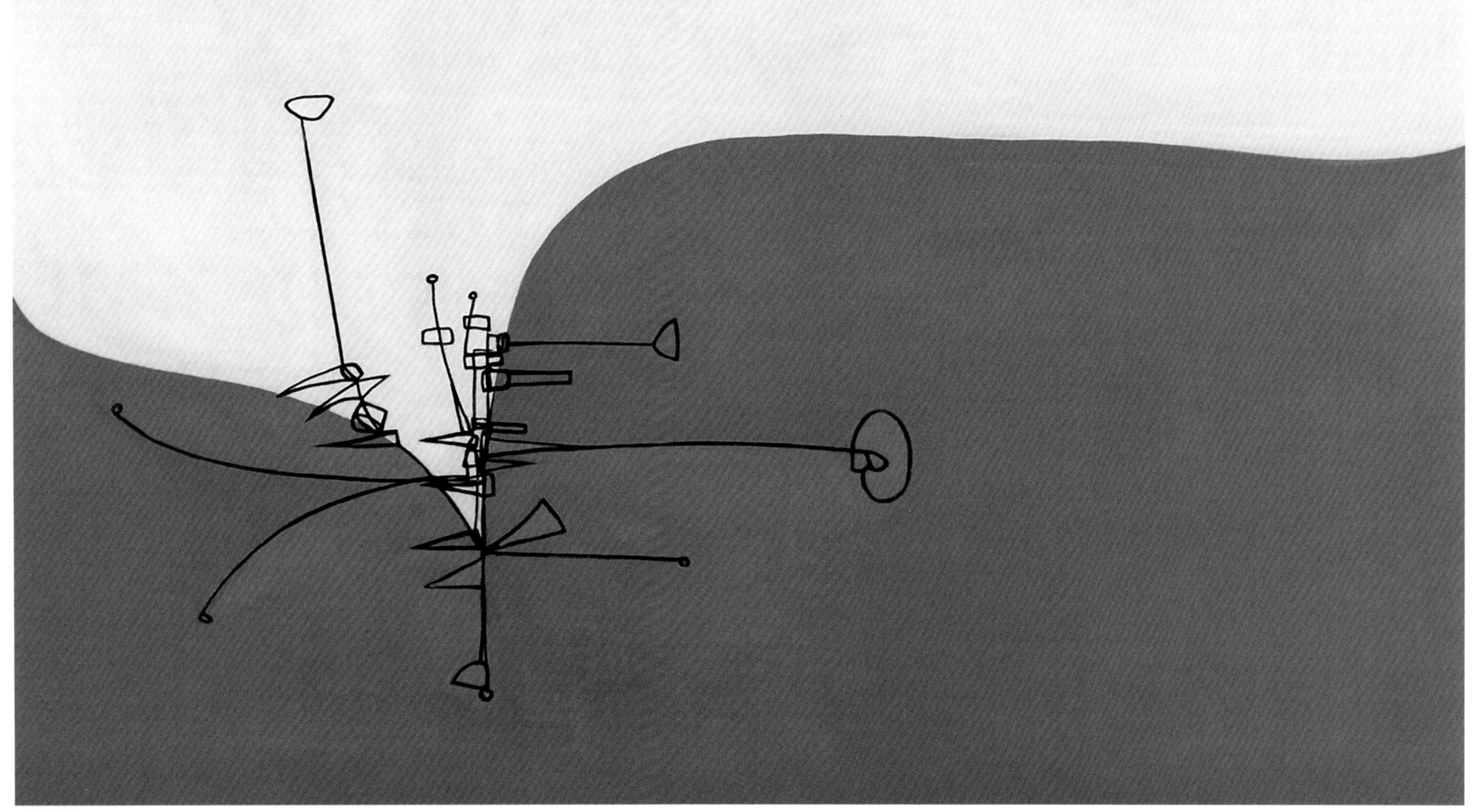

Zilia Sánchez: Sensuality and Desire in Cuban Landscape Painting

Zilia Sánchez created *Lo que es de isla y piel* (Belonging to Island and Skin; cat. 5) in Havana in 1958, when she was still pursuing colorful geometries and expressionist brushwork with superimposed line drawings. Yet in *Isla y piel*, Sánchez embarks on the cool white and gray that would distinguish her mature palette. She also minimizes the geometry to a few flatly painted broad shapes, which contrast with what she calls "tattoos": drawings applied in fine black marking pen on the canvas or "skin" of the painting. The tensions between the work's unpredictable curvature and linear drawing, and between the control of the flat paint and the spontaneity of drawn gesture, prefigure the aesthetic tensions of Sánchez's later, voluptuously shaped works. The title also foretells her obsession with these subjects. In the years to come, Sánchez would dramatically explore

INGRID W. ELLIOTT

the sensuality of desire in relation to geography and the body, specifically the female body. The title also suggests that these themes may "belong" to Cuban tradition or create a sense of "belonging" for the Cuban artist.

Isla y piel is from the *Afrocubanos* series. The series title may be an expression of Sánchez's admiration for Wifredo Lam (fig. 1), considered Cuba's greatest Afro-Cuban artist and a pioneer in bringing Cuba's African traditions into paint.[1] Lam studied and worked in Europe for years. After his return to Cuba in 1941, he explored the relationship between the female body and the Cuban landscape in a highly sensual fashion. In her mature work, Sánchez fuses bodies with the landscape just as Lam did before her, joining her work to a Cuban tradition that had associated landscape and desire with national art since the colonial era.

In 1941, the same year that Lam returned from Europe, Cuba's leading art critic, Guy Pérez Cisneros, argued that desire should be the linchpin of a new national landscape painting style, the Tropical

Baroque.[2] The name derived from both Cuba's tropical climate and environs and the history of conquest and plunder during Europe's Baroque era. Pérez Cisneros argued that Cubans needed to recapture the land, which was both the object of foreigners' colonial desires and the root of their exoticizing perceptions. To do so, he urged artists to create from their own desires, rather than from foreign ones; desire could be the starting place for self-determination. This was, in effect, an anticolonial stance. It was also an aesthetic strategy. Pérez Cisneros urged contemporary painters to leave the confines of the early Cuban vanguard — an artistic movement that emerged in 1927, which sought to create work that was both current with European modernism and true to national sensibilities. He wrote that painters should invigorate Cuban art by tapping into sexual desire, which he argued depended on the pursuit of the unknown.[3] But even this approach had nationalist implications connected with the land. Pérez Cisneros suggested that the fertility of the soil was analogous to human sensuality, as in the intuitive landscapes of vanguard painter Mariano Rodríguez (fig. 2).[4]

Lam's interrogation of geography and femininity reflected a tradition dating back to the 1920s, when vanguard artists like Víctor Manuel, Carlos Enríquez, and Amelia Peláez explored similar themes in the pursuit of a nationally relevant avant-garde. Sánchez's ties to this tradition suggest that the question of desire in her oeuvre is intrinsically tied to her relationship with the island that she left in 1960.

Despite the geometric and abstract orientation of her early work in Havana, Sánchez claimed a connection to nature and the body. In the late 1940s and early 1950s, when she first began to exhibit, her work tended toward a combination of geometric, painterly color and rectilinear drawing. In this way Sánchez was current with the latest trends in avant-garde painting, which oscillated between the concrete geometry of Sandú Darié and Mario Carreño (who emerged in 1950 and 1951, respectively) and the gestural abstraction of the Los Once artist group (1953–55).[5] That being

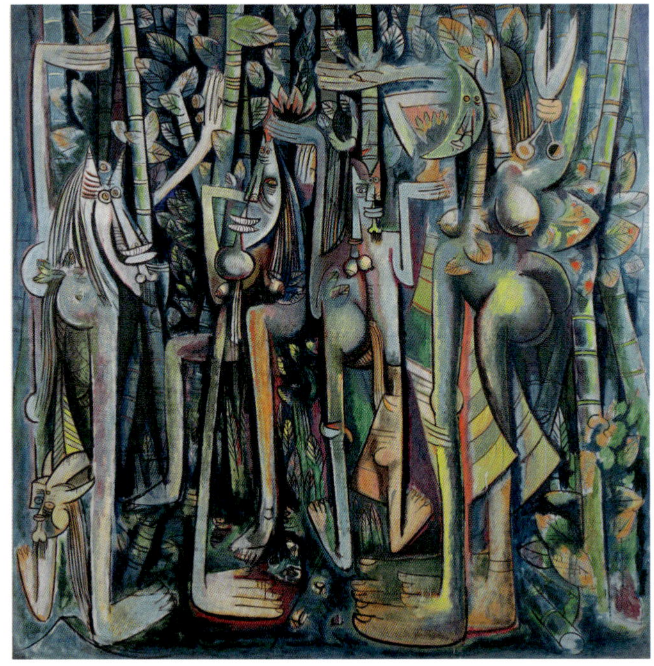

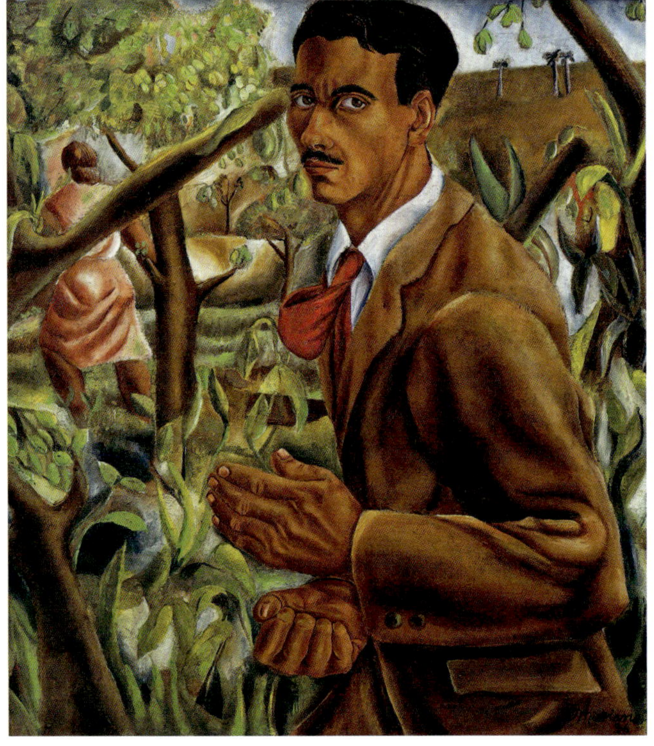

1 Wifredo Lam, *The Jungle*, 1943. Gouache on paper mounted on canvas, 94 ¼ × 90 ½ in. (239.4 × 229.9 cm). Museum of Modern Art, New York, Inter-American Fund.

2 Mariano Rodríguez, *Self-Portrait*, c. 1938. Oil on canvas, 25 ¾ × 22 ¼ in. (65.5 × 56.5 cm). Collection of Alejandro Rodríguez, Havana.

said, her brushwork in the 1950s may bear a closer resemblance to the Impressionist application of her mentor, the early vanguard painter Víctor Manuel. Sánchez's unwillingness to choose between these trends in contemporary art is demonstrated in her first solo exhibition, at Havana's Lyceum gallery in 1953 (figs. 3–4). The works reproduced in the exhibition pamphlet and by the press also merge painterly and geometric forms with rectilinear drawing, revealing an early impulse to conjoin that which had been deemed separate.

Rather than choosing a side in the debates about abstraction, Sánchez describes another target in the exhibition pamphlet.[6] Here she refers to the assumed opposition between naturalism and modern art. She challenges the reader by asking, "Has anyone ever seen a natural work of art?" Her retort is that "nature and art, because they are different things, can never be the same. With art we express our concept of that which is not nature."[7]

Yet she goes on to make a poetic connection between Cuba's landscape and the artist's brush: "The young island extends its body, and your hand constructs geometric ghosts with the dust of the *madrepora* (coral) vegetation that is entangled in your young brush." Youth, in other words, connects the island and the artist's brush. When Sánchez insists that traces of the "young" island's air, light, and sea are present in her "young brush" and her geometry, she resists a separation between nature and modern painting or abstraction. This fusion of nature and abstraction is continued in works Sánchez executed in the 1960s in New York and Madrid, which convey the rich brown color and texture of dirt and reveal an awareness of the Informel style, particularly the work of the Catalan artist Antoni Tàpies.

Those later international references and developments were preceded, however, by the influence of the Cuban vanguard. In the 1953 pamphlet, when Sánchez emphasizes the "youth" of the island and of her brush, she is using a vanguard buzzword. This suggests that she may see her work as aligned with the earlier artists' efforts to create a nationally relevant modern art. Indeed, early exposure to

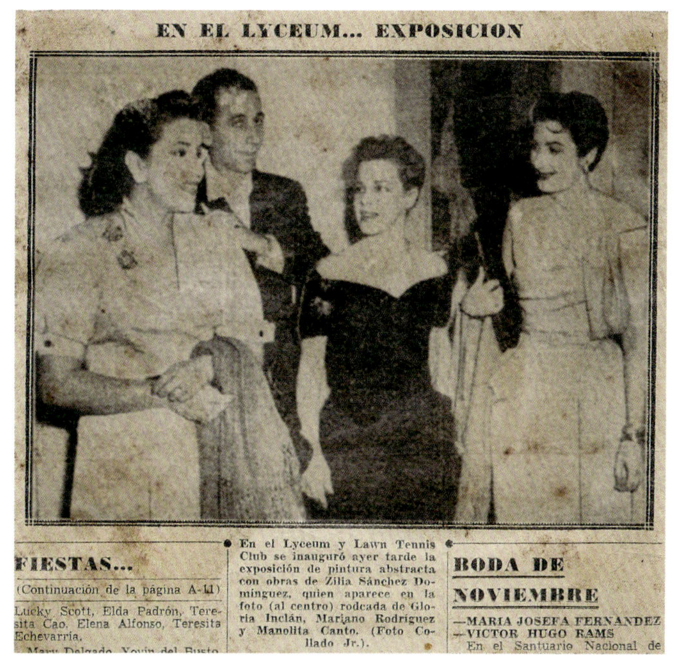

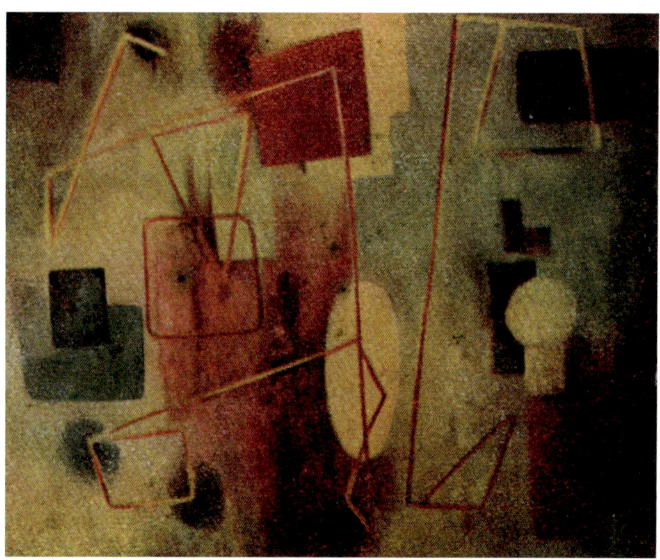

3 Press clipping, Sánchez in the Lyceum, 1953.

4 Zilia Sánchez, *Untitled*, c. 1953, from Lyceum exhibition pamphlet.

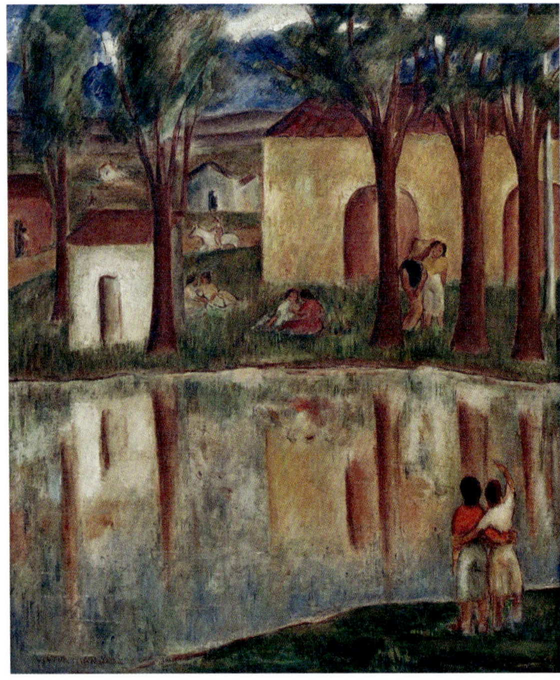

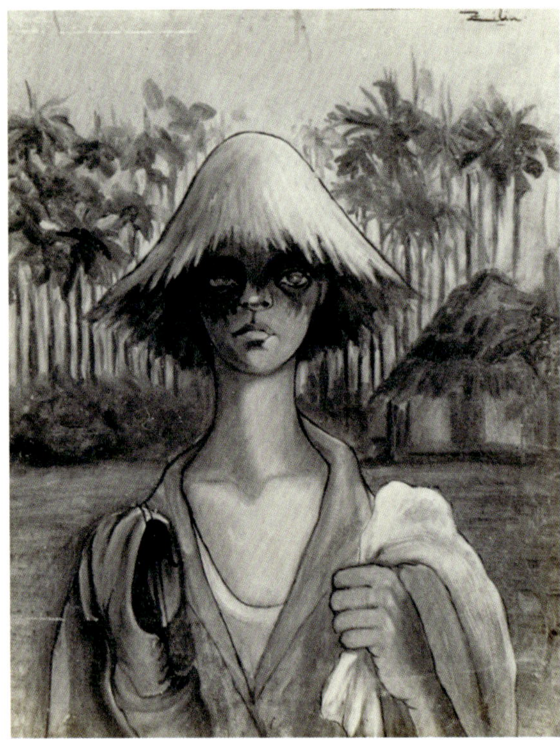

the mingling of nature and modernism in national painting may have come from Manuel (fig. 5), a pioneer of Cuban modernism who was a neighbor to Sánchez's family. In a 1984 interview with Giulio Blanc, Sánchez testified that Manuel was more important to her than her teachers at Havana's national art school, the Academy of San Alejandro, where she studied with landscape painter Domingo Ramos and the Impressionist-leaning Leopoldo Romañach.[8] She called Manuel her "true professor," despite the fact that he was outside the academy. The most important thing he taught her was to paint "from the inside out." This maxim was consistent with the interiority of the early vanguard, which put a great emphasis on honesty, sincerity, and an authentic expression of one's interior world.[9] Sánchez explores these sentiments as well and associates them with Manuel in the interview in this catalogue.[10] His importance to Sánchez is further demonstrated by two mementos in her personal archive: a 1964 *El mundo* clipping detailing Manuel's legacy, which would have been sent to her in New York, and a photo of a work by Sánchez in Manuel's style.[11]

Sánchez's painting after Víctor Manuel depicts a gaunt *guajiro*, or peasant, with a straw hat, wide eyes, and a blank expression (fig. 6). The hat echoes the shape of his presumed dwelling place, the hut in the background. It also physically locates the head and therefore the imagination of the peasant in the stand of palms and the natural landscape where he lives and labors. His elongated body echoes the tree trunks behind him, and his large hat emulates the bushy palm fronds. These associations may be an early connection for Sánchez between bodies and landscapes and an attempt at emotional expression on behalf of the land. Sánchez's image emphasizes the *guajiro*'s desolate poverty and is perhaps more realistic than Manuel's romanticized images of the 1920s. Manuel made his name in Cuban art with expressionist paintings of amorous peasants in rural or urban landscapes that associated their romance with idyllic natural settings. Such works were considered the first forays into modern Cuban art.

5 Víctor Manuel, *Paisaje con parejas* (Landscape with Couples), c. 1943. Oil on canvas, 26 ½ × 21 ⅝ in. (67.3 × 54.9 cm). Museo Nacional de Bellas Artes, Havana.

6 Zilia Sánchez, *Untitled*, n.d.

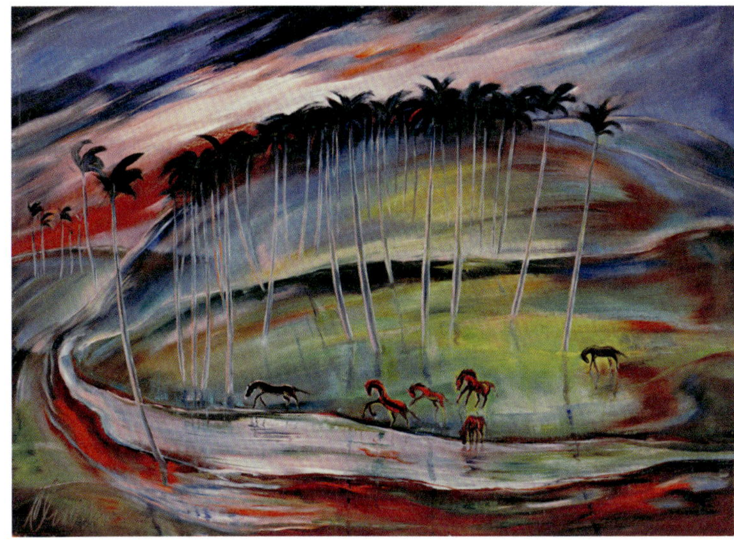

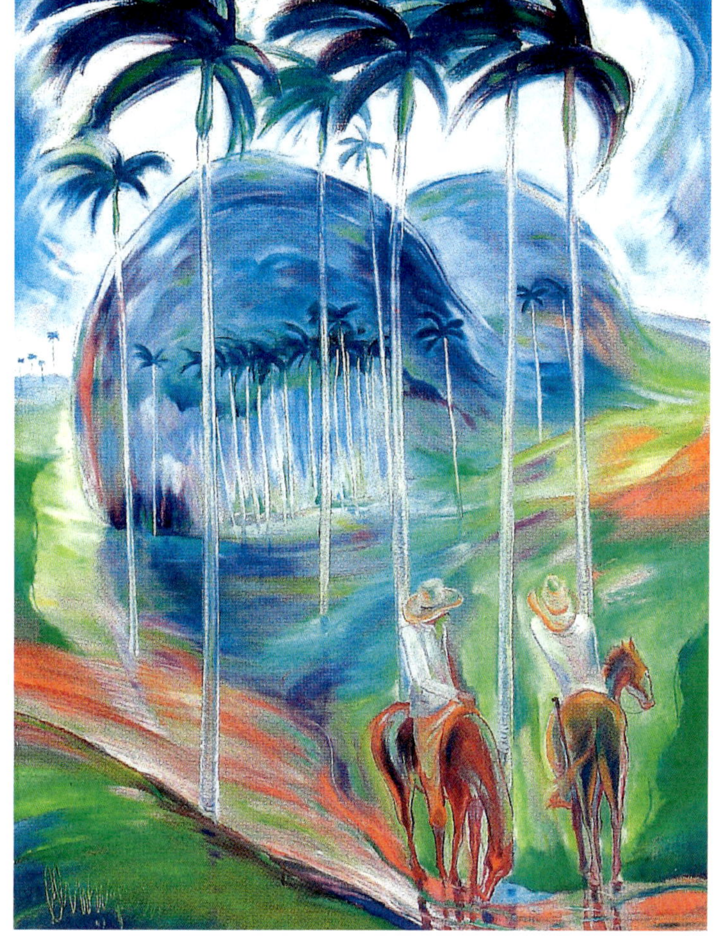

Sánchez also embraced Víctor Manuel's advice to "paint what one feels."[12] When asked in the 1984 interview what she feels when she paints, Sánchez answers: "Cuba." She goes on to say: "What interests me is the sensuality, the eroticism that is Cuba, its landscape, its people. An elegant sensuality; look at the *Tropical Gypsy* of Víctor, [or the works of] Carlos Enríquez, Lam."[13] Indeed, the prevailing theme of the art criticism on Sánchez's work has been her eroticism; this is the overriding emotion driving her oeuvre, a feeling that has been successfully conveyed. What is less apparent is the central importance of this emotional state to her connection to Cuba.

Without the biographical and archival data, we might not guess the importance of Manuel to Zilia Sánchez. The sensual landscapes of Enríquez need no such evidence, however, as the visual likenesses speak for themselves. Enríquez's mountains and hills frequently resemble breasts and vulvas, as in *Paisaje con caballos salvajes* (Landscape with Wild Horses; fig. 7) and *Tetas de Madruga* (Breasts of Madruga; fig. 8).

While these correspondences in his paintings are not subtle and would have been apparent to someone as visually sensitive as Sánchez, critics also called attention to them just as Sánchez embarked on her own erotic bodyscapes. In 1957, using language that could equally apply to Sánchez, vanguard painter Marcelo Pogolotti identified

7 Carlos Enríquez, *Puisaje con caballos salvajes* (Landscape with Wild Horses), 1941. Oil on composition board, 17 ½ × 23 ⅝ in. (44.5 × 60 cm). Museum of Modern Art, New York, Gift of Dr. C. M. Ramírez Corría.

8 Carlos Enríquez, *Tetas de Madruga* (Breasts of Madruga), 1943. Oil on canvas, 35 × 28 in. (88.9 × 71.1 cm). Collection of Sergio Delgado, Miami.

a correspondence between earth and flesh or topography and anatomy in his friend Enríquez's work.[14] Sánchez conflates the body with natural phenomena as early as 1956 in an untitled ink on canvas in which breast forms become stars of the night sky. *Lo que es de isla y piel* suggests that this topic was on Sánchez's mind, though it isn't until the early 1960s that the body becomes the focus of her exploration, and the 1970s before breasts emerge in mountain-like majesty.

If eroticism forges ties to Cuba for Sánchez by connecting her to a history of sensuality in Cuban art and national identity, the question remains: How does Sánchez intervene in this tradition? For Enríquez, the erotic was part of a national mythology of masculinity, which Sánchez seems to counter with works inspired by mythical female warriors. Enríquez's erotic landscapes were part of his *romancero guajiro* (peasant ballads) credo. This artistic philosophy was inspired by the heroes of the Cuban countryside in the wars for Cuban independence from 1868 to 1898. As with Víctor Manuel, Enríquez's *guajiros* are closely tied to the land, but Enríquez elevates their contributions to Cuban life by linking them to national heroes like Manuel García and José Martí. These figures were paragons of Cuban masculinity, something further emphasized by Enríquez's unabashed male eroticism — a gaze that often objectified Cuban *criollas* and *mulatas*, women of Spanish or African descent.

The virulent masculinity of the nineteenth-century freedom fighters and their relationship to the Cuban countryside and to male sexual prowess is apparent in one of Enríquez's most famous works: *El rapto de las mulatas* (The Abduction of the Mulatto Women; fig. 9). This is an image of sexual conquest in the art historical tradition of the abduction of the Sabine women, a Roman mythological incident painted by Nicolas Poussin (1634 and 1637) and Peter Paul Rubens (1635), among others. One of the *mulatas* in Enríquez's work clearly resists her assailant with outstretched arms. Her companion, however, has a sly expression that may be interpreted with more ambivalence and is suggestive of the stereotype of the *mulata* as a

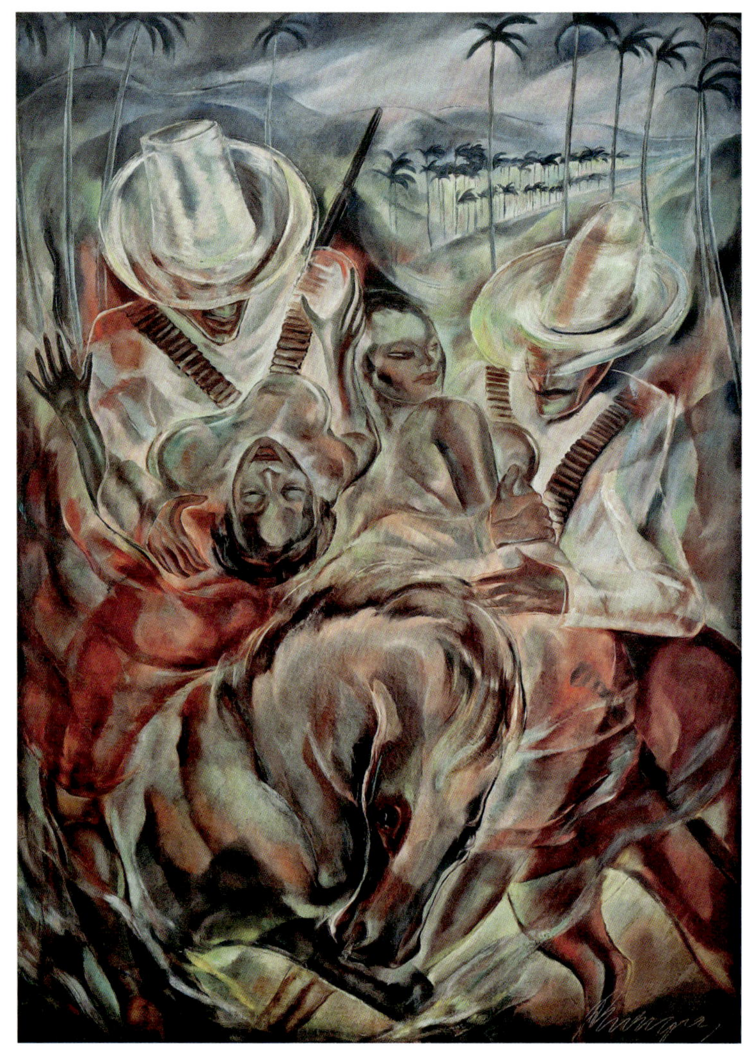

9 Carlos Enríquez, *El rapto de las mulatas* (The Abduction of the Mulatto Women), 1938. Oil on canvas, 24 ¾ × 17 ¾ in. (65 × 45 cm). Museo Nacional de Bellas Artes, Havana.

sexually salacious being. There is no question that this work is painted according to male fantasies regarding the excitement of sexual conquest, so that the women's bodies are sexually available to both the *mambises* or freedom fighters and the presumably male viewer.

Sánchez also turns to classical mythology for inspiration, but she does so on female terms. Sánchez has treated individual female heroes like Antigone and Joan of Arc (cat. 51). But the women warriors of the *Amazonas* (Amazons) and *Troyanas* (Trojan Women; cats. 25, 44, 47, 56) series were subjects that she returned to repeatedly from 1960 to the present. The early Amazonian works focus on erotic anatomy: vagina and buttocks, perhaps, in an untitled piece from 1960–71, and buttocks and breasts in *Topología erótica* (Erotic Topology) from 1968 (cat. 26). This suggests that Sánchez's strident female eroticism is part of a warrior stance, perhaps as a counter to the male virility of works like Enríquez's *El rapto de las mulatas* or more generally to a society — be it Cuba, Spain, or the United States — where women are too frequently objectified by the male gaze, both in art and in life.

In works from 1978 and 1993, Sánchez makes more direct reference to Amazonian mythology, seemingly referring to the story of Amazon warriors cutting off a breast to allow space for greater precision in archery. In these paintings, the breast itself becomes a shield; a symbol of male objectification of the female body becomes the locus of its defense. The breast similarly serves as shield, and a sign of courage and sacrifice, in the *Troyanas* series. It can hardly be coincidental that rape or other male abuses of power are part of all three of these narratives. Sánchez's works provide a defiant response.[15]

While Sánchez departs from Enríquez's Cuban male mythologies by embracing mythical female figures from the European tradition, she also turns toward his fascination with Cubans of African descent. Such themes appealed broadly to the vanguard generation just before Sánchez, including Enríquez, one of the early adopters of

Afro-Cubanismo as a pathway to national painting, preceded only by Eduardo Abela. Enríquez was obsessed with what he understood to be the highly sexualized figure of the *mulata*. Sánchez, in contrast, divorces the Afro-Cuban theme from her eroticism. Instead, she isolates her racial references in titles and perhaps the black drawings evocative of Lam's Afro-Cuban motifs.[16] See, for example, her 1957 and 1958 works from the *Afrocubanos* series (cats. 5 and 6), and her 2006 *Serigrafía* (Serigraph), from the series *Dibujos Afrocubanos*.

Nevertheless, Sánchez personalized her relationship to Afro-Cuban culture when she declared "Soy mulata" (I am a mulatta).[17] The racial identity of the bodies that inspired her, however, is not really apparent. Her palette ranges from stark black and white to sky blue to various grays, with beige and pink that can be read as flesh tones. The most obvious anatomical features are frequently white or pinkish, implying European heritage. Yet there are also a host of navy and gray breasts in various works, and a black-breasted Amazon shield. Race has an important yet ambiguous place in Sánchez's oeuvre.

"Soy mulata" is certainly a reference to Sánchez's penchant for mixing cultures and genres together in her work, as she indicates in the interview in this catalogue.[18] She consistently merges the artistic traditions available to her: Cuba's Afro-Cuban, sensual, and landscape traditions; European expressionism, Cubism, and Constructivism; and painting, sculpture, and drawing.[19] Yet, given the sexual myths and stereotypes of the Cuban *mulata* and Sánchez's celebration of female sexuality, we would be remiss in not considering Sánchez's relationship to such conventions.

Sánchez's celebration of female sexuality both invokes and resists the stereotype of the Cuban *mulata* as an exclusively sexual being (fig. 10).[20] Despite Sánchez's obsession with sensuality, she puts this theme aside in her Afro-Cuban works. When she does celebrate female desire, she heralds female agency rather than objectifying the female body. By Sánchez's isolating the erotic features of a woman's body and treating them as shapes worthy of artistic

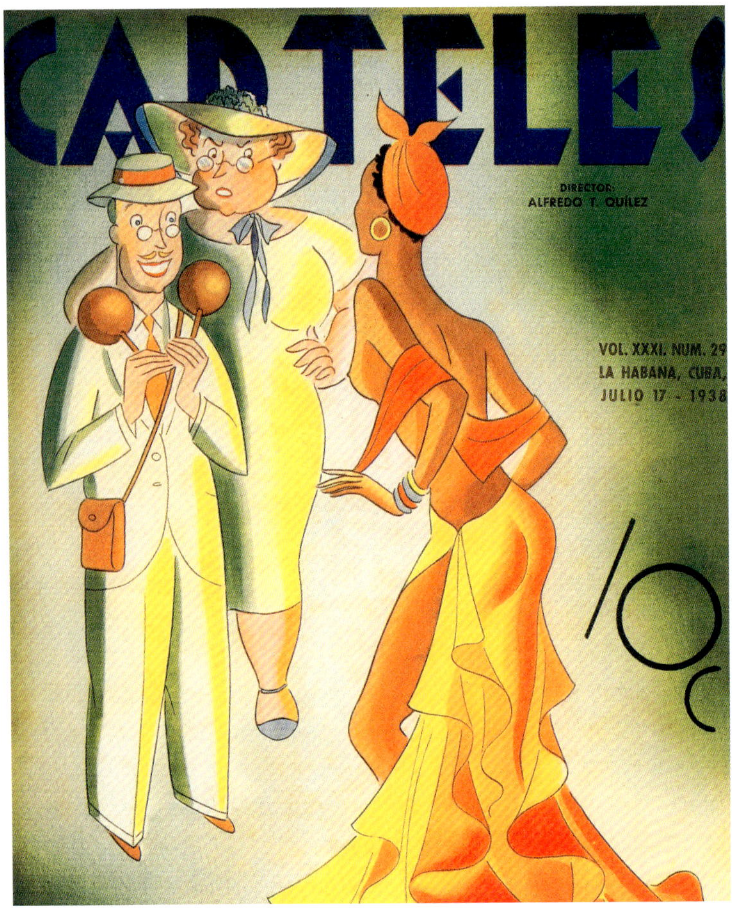

10 Andrés García Benítez, illustration for
the cover of *Carteles*, July 1938.

attention, the inspiration for her efforts, and the topographies of a
semiabstract art, those features become one with the national
landscape, recalling the genre closely tied to national identity by
the vanguard painters of the 1920s like Manuel. They become
part of a national art tradition, venerated art objects, rather than
aspects of a female body to be possessed in some male sexual fan-
tasy. Where Enríquez or Lam look at the landscape and intuit female
sexuality, Sánchez looks at the female body and sees the landscape. In doing so, she emphasizes the beauty of the human form
in a way that is more sensual than sexual. This is buttressed by
her "classicizing" approach, in which cool colors and painted precision convey control, as opposed to the erotic frenzy of Enríquez's
works. In this sense, Sánchez's statement "Soy mulata" can be
understood as claiming ownership of her sexual agency in the face
of historical and art-historical objectification of the female body,
African or otherwise.

The artistic drive inherent in this stance recalls the "creative
eroticism" that Cuban anthropologist Fernando Ortiz identified in
Lam's work in a 1950 essay, which is now considered the first serious
assessment of his art.[21] His description of how this creative eroticism
functioned in Lam's *The Jungle* can be equally applied to Sánchez's
oeuvre, raising the possibility that Sánchez was inspired by more
than Lam's drawing. Ortiz suggests this creative eroticism derived
from what he considered a carnal femininity that was not African,
but rather grounded in the "mixed-race sensuality of Cuba." Noting
that symbols of femininity abound in *The Jungle* (breasts and buttocks punctuate the forest), he claims that this nudity is a sign of a
"primitive humanity," as well as the "vital force" of love. These body
parts, as well as animal parts (beaks, wings, claws, tails, hooves, and
horns), and plant parts (fruits, stems, and leaves), stand in for the
whole and contribute to an "unreality" expressive of a psychological
world.[22] Ortiz celebrates Lam's elevation of dream, ecstasy, or hypno-
sis over intellectual concerns.[23] This praise for unreality and subconscious states over the rational mind suggests an admiration for

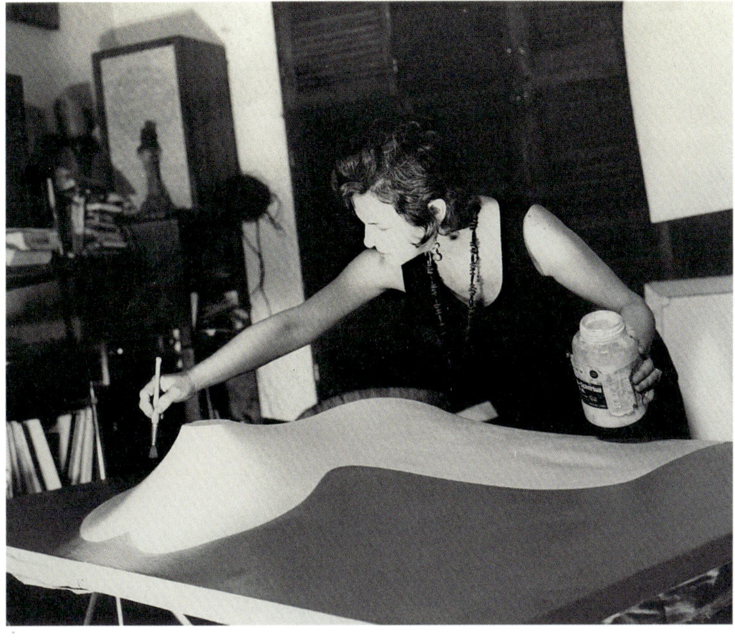

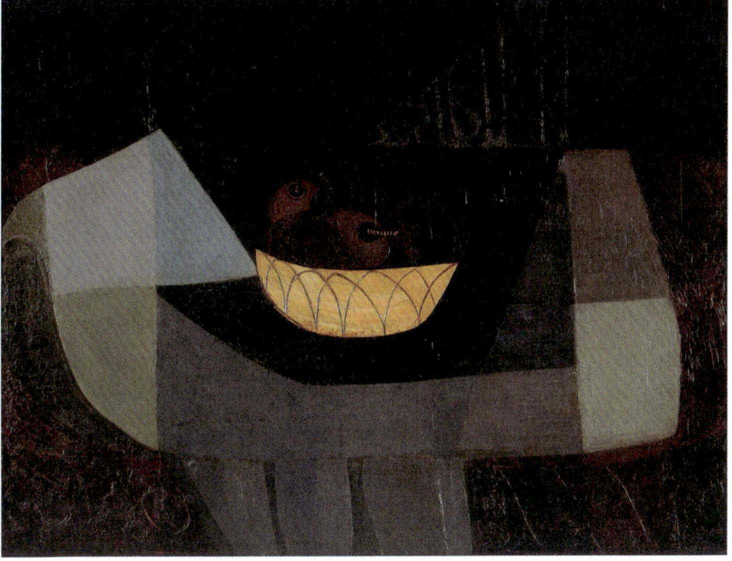

the principles of Surrealism, a movement with which Lam had ties in France and on the Caribbean island of Martinique.

Sánchez's eroticism shares this attention to psychological drives, but what may be more compelling is her analogous attention to the details of the human body. Sánchez enlarges the elements that Lam had isolated before her, and re-creates them in three dimensions, frequently on a larger than life scale. When she works these forms on the horizontal (fig. 11), the enlarged human shapes become islands and skin. Pale body parts also become islands in contrast to the dark sea around them. But whether the shapes are horizontal and maplike, or vertical and humanoid, we understand that they relate to a living body, a form in its entirety. Her intense focus on the details of that body, and their re-creation in three dimensions, conveys a desire to know that detail intimately, a desire to touch that is inherent in the creation of the work and invited by a close view. This gaze conveys desire in a loving fashion, a celebration of the beauty and sensual curves of the female body. That those curves often express their desire by reaching for the other half of the bifurcated canvas suggests that this is an activated subject, rather than an objectified body.

For Sánchez, the land was what she lost when she chose not to return to Cuba. Her engagement with notions of landscape and desire can be understood as a connection to that lost land and the art it inspired when she was growing up — Enríquez's landscapes and his writing in the 1930s and 1940s, as well as Lam's groundbreaking works in the 1940s and the first significant appreciation of that work in the 1950s, just as Sánchez emerged as an artist herself. Landscape and desire were similarly at the center of the still lifes she admired by the leading female artist of the Cuban vanguard generation, Amelia Peláez (fig. 12).[24]

From the mid-1930s to the 1940s, Peláez created semi-abstract works that critics and intellectuals regarded as establishing the first truly Cuban art style. She linked erotic aspects of the female body to the fruits of the Cuban landscape, painting still lifes with vagina-like fish and papayas, breast-like mamey fruits, and

11 Sánchez in her studio, n.d.

12 Amelia Peláez, *Naturaleza muerta con mameyes* (Still Life with Mameys), c. 1935. Oil on canvas, 25 ½ × 32 in. (64.8 × 81.3 cm). Museo Nacional de Bellas Artes, Havana.

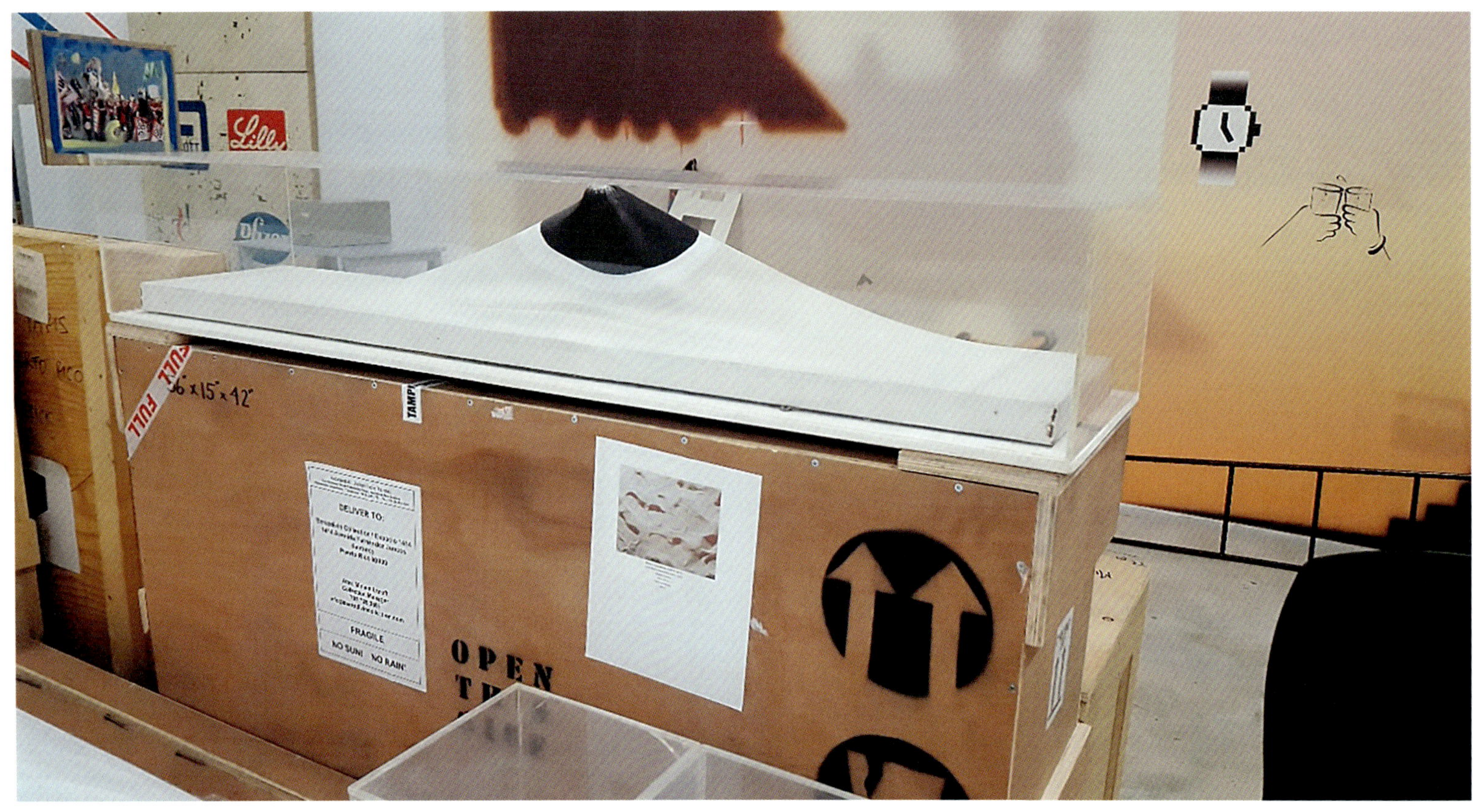

uterus-shaped guanabanas.[25] What's more, Peláez's works prefigure
the tension between the geometric austerity and sensual aspects
of Sánchez's mature work.[26]

As Sánchez puts it in the 1984 interview,

For me, Cuban painting has much to do with the purity of forms, structure.
This you see in the figures of Víctor, in the black line of Amelia, in Lam. . . .
It is the purity of forms seen in the white light of midday. . . . What interests
me is the sensual, the erotic elegance, but with simplicity and structure.
Color does not interest me as much; my colors are white, black, gray,
pink. In the tropics, in the strongest sun of the day, everything is relief,

and what doesn't exist are the more varied colors of the morning (the hour
that Domingo Ramos likes) and the fall of the afternoon (as in many of
Amelia's paintings).[27]

Sánchez relates her aesthetic choices — her predilection for
sculptural topography and minimalist color — to Cuba's climate and
art history. Structure in Cuban art may have first emerged in Peláez's
preference for the Cubist and Constructivist lessons of Paris, which
are apparent in her multiperspectival approach to the tablecloth and
the geometric planning of her compositions. Then, in the 1950s,
a group of artists known as Los Diez (1957–61) pursued painting that

13 Storage view of *Soy Isla*, painting from
encuentrismo — ofrenda o retorno
(The Encounter — Offering or Return),
performance, 2000 (cat. 57b).

was focused exclusively on geometric forms, under the leadership of another remarkable female painter, curator, and gallerist, Loló Soldevilla.[28] Sánchez exhibited with both of these artists as she began to participate in the Havana art scene in the 1950s.[29] She created ceramics — in effect, paintings in three dimensions — with Peláez, and likely attended the decisive, groundbreaking European geometric abstraction show organized by Soldevilla at the National Museum upon Soldevilla's return from Paris in 1956.[30] This must be some of what Sánchez had in mind when she remarked on the enthusiasm and productivity of Cuban art as she came of age in the 1950s. She brought this energy and dedication, along with Cuban themes and aesthetics, into exile.[31] Perhaps propelled by postrevolution biases against abstraction that were already apparent in 1959, Sánchez moved abroad in 1960: first to New York, then to Madrid, and then back to New York, finally settling in Puerto Rico in the early 1970s.

Despite her life abroad, Sánchez has never abandoned her emotional attachment to Cuba and has been drawn to landscape for that reason. As the interview in this catalogue suggests, Sánchez was first exposed to artistic practice by her father, who was an amateur landscape painter. She spent her childhood at his side, watching while he painted.[32] Moreover, grief for her father's death was wrapped up in the revelation that led to her first shaped canvases.[33] As she watched the bedsheets of his final days drying on a clothesline, the wind brushed them against a pipe or a wooden object on the rooftop.[34] This prompted the first thought of building the armature that could bring three-dimensional shape to her canvases. It is possible that his inert body beneath the sheets was also at the back of her mind. Grief, longing, and love for her father and for Cuba are clearly bound to landscape for Sánchez.

Exile is, after all, yet another form of loss. Titles such as *Lo que es de isla y piel* and *Soy Isla* (fig. 13) personally identify Sánchez with the land — an island. The island is never named, so it could be Cuba or Puerto Rico, or both. Bifurcated canvases, particularly those with forms that reach past the divide, likewise suggest an island

divided and a yearning for a connection or communication to create a whole across some separation, speaking to the physical and emotional divisions of exile.

Sánchez has never relinquished her Cuban citizenship, despite nearly fifty years in Puerto Rico; in a sense, this represents a yearning for Cuba's landscape that she shares with artists who remained in Cuba. As we have seen, Cuban artists of the past also expressed a strong desire for the land and suggested it wasn't fully theirs. Enríquez's erotic landscapes bristled at the influence of US landowners, Lam's jungle can be understood as staking a claim not permitted to slaves, and Pérez Cisneros's Tropical Baroque was an effort to replace the neocolonial desire for the land with Cuban desire. In each case, desire is at the heart of self-determination. There may be a parallel between Cubans' desire for self-determination with respect to the land or the nation, and Sánchez's activation of a female subject who takes charge of her sexuality and her body in a radical act of personal autonomy.

We can also understand Sánchez's sensual revision of Cuba's artistic history of landscape and desire as an expression of her longing for the landscape she left behind and her desire to be in dialogue with Cuban art. This is all the more poignant given the particular desire that may be the reason for her departure from Cuba. While the Castro government's position on homosexuality was not blatant until the raids of 1961, these policies were consistent with long-standing homophobia in Cuba.[35] In this respect, a return to Havana may not have been particularly appealing for a young woman with a homoerotic gaze. Desire, then, may be emblematic of the reason for Sánchez's exile, as well as her attachment to Cuba and its artistic traditions.

Ingrid W. Elliott, PhD, is an independent scholar and curator.

NOTES

1. Another possible influence might have been Lydia Cabrera's 1954 publication of *El Monte*, a work that explores Afro-Cuban religious practices and whose title refers to Cuba's woodlands, also depicted in Lam's *The Jungle*. Regarding Sánchez's admiration for Lam, see Eva Fuchs, "Zilia Sánchez at Galerie Lelong, New York," *Ocula Insight*, June 10, 2016, https://ocula.com/magazine/insights/zilia-sanchez-at-galerie-lelong-new-york.

———

2. Guy Pérez Cisneros, "Víctor Manuel y la pintura cubana contemporánea," in *Las estrategias de un crítico: Antología de la crítica de arte de Guy Pérez Cisneros*, ed. Luz Merino Acosta (Havana: Letras Cubanas, 2000), 117–40. Previously published in *Universidad de la Habana*, no. 34 (January–February 1941): 218–30.

———

3. Ibid.

———

4. Pérez Cisneros, "Sexo, símbolo y paisaje," in Merino Acosta, *Las estrategias de un crítico*, 99–104.

———

5. For more on these trends in Cuban art in the 1950s, see Abigail McEwen, *Revolutionary Horizons: Art and Polemics in 1950s Cuba* (New Haven, CT: Yale University Press, 2016); for Sánchez's exhibition history with Los Once, see chapter 3. While Sánchez exhibited intermittently with Los Once from 1953 to 1955, she also exhibited with geometric painters at the Lyceum and Nuestro Tiempo in 1954 and at the Galería Cubana in 1956. In 1954 Sánchez exhibited in the Lyceum's *Homenaje a José Martí*, a comprehensive vanguard show also known as the Anti-Bienal, as well as Nuestro Tiempo's inaugural exhibition, which included the gestural *onceños* and Mario Carreño and Sandú Darié's geometries. In 1956 Sánchez exhibited in *El tema religioso en la pintura cubana* at the Galería Cubana with geometric painter Loló Soldevilla.

———

6. *Exposición de pintura, Zilia*, November 9–16, 1953, Lyceum, Havana. A review of the exhibition quotes the pamphlet text and attributes it to Zilia Sánchez: Adela Jaume, "Z. Sánchez y su obra de pintura abstracta en la Sociedad Lyceum," clipping from unknown newspaper, in Zilia Sánchez archive, Galerie Lelong, GA0832.

———

7. Ibid., GA0164.

———

8. Giulio V. Blanc, "Conversation with Zilia Sánchez," *Mariel* 2, no. 7 (Fall 1984): 37.

———

9. Ingrid W. Elliott, "National Values: The Havana Vanguard in La revista de avance and the Lyceum Women's Gallery," in *A Companion to Modern and Contemporary Latin American and Latino Art*, eds. Alejandro Anreus, Robin Greeley, and Megan Sullivan (Hoboken, NJ: Wiley-Blackwell Press, forthcoming).

———

10. Vesela Sretenović, "In Retrospect: Talking with Zilia Sánchez," in this catalogue.

———

11. Nydia Sarabia, "Víctor Manuel, todo un pintor" (photos by Korda), *El mundo*, May 10, 1964, in Sánchez archive, GA0886A-H; painting of *guajiro* in style of Víctor Manuel, ibid., GA0120.

———

12. Blanc, "Conversation with Zilia Sánchez."

———

13. Ibid.

———

14. Juan A. Martínez, *Carlos Enríquez: The Painter of Cuban Ballads* (Miami: Cernuda Arte, 2010), 66.

———

15. The original 415 BC story by Euripides focuses on the suffering, including rape, of the Trojan women at the hands of the Greek conquerors. In modern times it's taken to be a critique of colonization, and we could view Sánchez's *Joan of Arc*—who fought with her fellow French soldiers to expel English invaders—and even her *Antígona*—a figure who contests state authority—as female protests against male abuse of power. Both Joan of Arc and Antigone lose their lives due to official censure of their heroism.

———

16. Similar drawings in Lam's oeuvre may have been inspired by the Anaforuana lines, which are intended to invite spiritual possession in Afro-Cuban Santería practices.

———

17. Sánchez refers to herself variously as "soy mulata" or "mulata minimalista"; see, for example, her March 2013 interview for her Artists Space monographic show, https://vimeo.com/66332817.

———

18. Sretenović, "In Retrospect."

———

19. For more on Sánchez's relationship to various schools of European art, see Ingrid W. Elliott, "Between the Real and the Invisible," in *Diálogos constructivistas en la vanguardia cubana: Amelia Peláez, Loló Soldevilla, y Zilia Sánchez* (New York: Galerie Lelong, 2016).

———

20. Vera M. Kutzinski, *Sugar's Secrets: Race and the Erotics of Cuban Nationalism* (Charlottesville, VA: University Press of Virginia, 1993).

———

21. Fernando Ortiz, *Wifredo Lam y su obra vista a través de significados críticos* (Havana: Ministerio de Educación, 1950), republished and translated as "Wifredo Lam and His Work as Seen by Famous Critics," in *The EY Exhibition: Wifredo Lam*, ed. Catherine David (London: Tate, 2016), 180–85.

22. Ibid., 183.

23. Ibid., 184.

24. Fuchs, "Zilia Sánchez at Galerie Lelong."

25. Ingrid W. Elliott, "Crafting Cuban Modernism," in *Amelia Peláez: The Craft of Modernity*, by Rene Morales and Ingrid Elliott (Miami: Pérez Art Museum Miami, 2013).

26. Elliott, "Between the Real and the Invisible."

27. Blanc, "Conversation with Zilia Sánchez."

28. Elliott, "Between the Real and the Invisible."

29. On Sánchez's shared exhibition history with Peláez and Soldevilla, see ibid., 12.

30. Regarding Sánchez's ceramics work with Peláez, see Blanc, "Conversation with Zilia Sánchez." For more on Soldevilla's 1956 exhibition *Pintura de hoy: Vanguardia de la escuela de París*, see McEwen, *Revolutionary Horizons*. Sánchez went to all of the major exhibitions at the National Museum with her family; see Sretenović, "In Retrospect."

31. Blanc, "Conversation with Zilia Sánchez."

32. Sretenović, "In Retrospect."

33. Fuchs, "Zilia Sánchez at Galerie Lelong."

34. Sánchez's recounting of this story has changed over time. In earlier published accounts she referred to the sheet flapping against a pipe; more recently, in conversations with the exhibition curator, she has mentioned a wooden room divider. See Ileana Delgado Castro, "Encuentro con Zilia Sánchez," *El nuevo día*, sec. Revista Domingo, March 20, 2005; and Sretenović, "In Retrospect."

35. Ian Lumsden, *Machos, Maricones, and Gays: Cuba and Homosexuality* (Philadelphia: Temple University Press, 1996), 58–59.

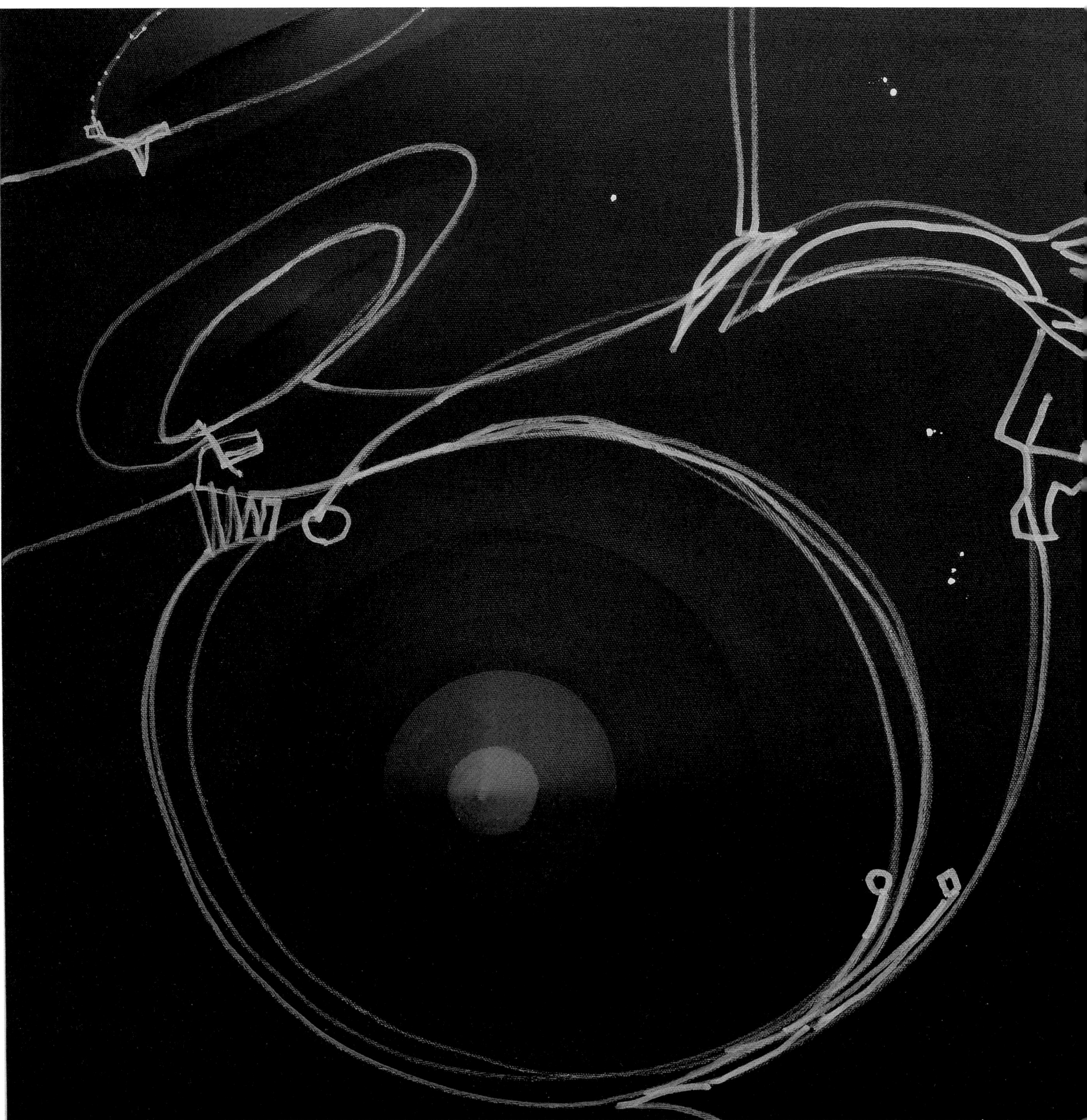

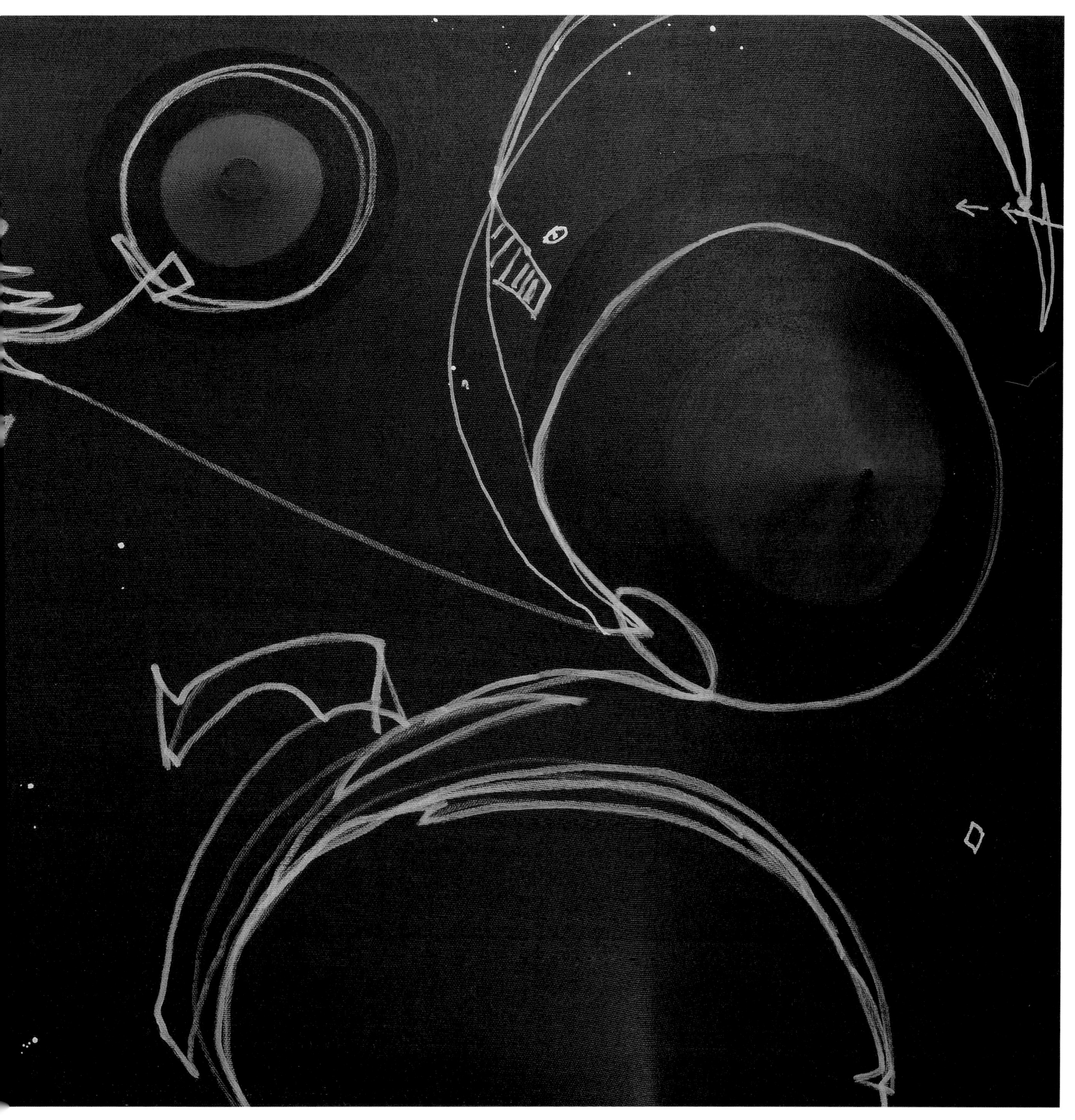

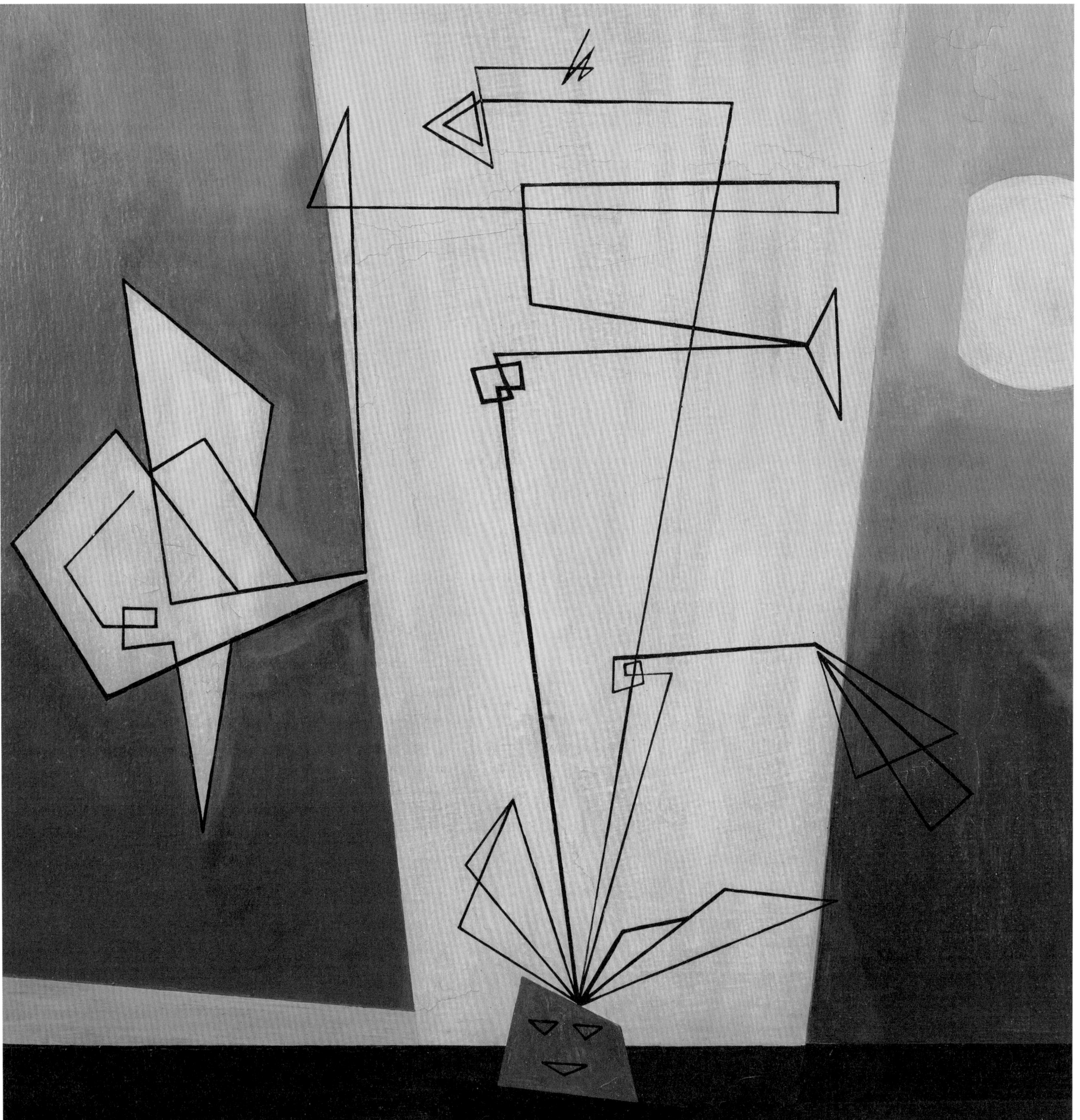

"What is true of all exile is not that home and love of home are lost," Edward Said once reflected, "but that loss is inherent in the very existence of both."[1] The anxieties of exile, whether in anticipation or in abeyance, internalized or diasporic, cast a shadow over the generation of Cuban artists who came of age in the 1950s and 1960s as they negotiated changed and often vexed relationships with their native country. Born in Havana but long resident abroad, in New York through the 1960s and since 1971 in Puerto Rico, Zilia Sánchez numbers among the untold artists alienated from the canon of Cuban art, who have but recently been brought back into the fold. The essence of *lo cubano* in her work is thus and unsurprisingly elliptical, conveyed through structures of feeling and memory—she recalls, for example, "the purity of forms seen in the white light of

The (Printed) Medium of Exile

ABIGAIL MCEWEN

midday"—rather than content. Although Sánchez considers herself an émigré, as she left before the imposition of exit visas in 1961, she has acknowledged that Cuba is what she feels when she paints "from the inside out"—"the sensuality, the eroticism that is Cuba, its landscape, its people."[2] The emphasis on feeling, or affect, in her accounting of Cuba reverberates across the erotic economy of her mature work, the estrangements of exile manifest in the corporeal topography of her "tattooed" canvases. Yet the shaped paintings, serial structures, and neutral palette that define Sánchez's mature practice did not emerge ex nihilo at the end of the 1960s. The political and cultural formations of the intervening years inexorably changed Sánchez's relationship to Cuba, the contingencies of which can be seen in the trajectory of her work as it moved in and out of abstraction, through portraiture, and across a range of media.

The scope and significance of Sánchez's practice during these early years abroad, as she faced a looming horizon of exile, remain largely uncharted. Although contemporary with the rise of minimalism and, later, of postminimalism in New York, her work progressed on the margins of the art world, in less apparent dialogue with the downtown scene than with the left-leaning literary and cultural circles connected to the emergent émigré community. Her many illustrations for ephemeral publications rendered the existential poetics of this circle, which included her friends Mercedes Cortázar and Isel Rivero, with graphic agitation, gleaned in part from her study of printmaking at the Pratt Graphic Art Center, an extension of the Pratt Institute that opened in 1956. Although it may be tempting to dismiss her graphic and occasional scenographic work as merely commercial or incidental to her contemporary painting, her collaborations anticipate the topographic and conceptual insinuations of her mature painting, cultivated clearly within the period context of Cuban New York. Indeed, the development of Sánchez's work across printed media makes visible a worlding process that unfolded in the early years of exile, in which her changing responsiveness to revolutionary Cuba and engagement with the Left saw an existential progression in her work, one reflective of an evolving understanding of herself in the world. The nature of her embodiment in time and history is inscribed in the prints and drawings that she published under the auspices of Cuban New York, the generational culture of which defined the formative years of her career.

In addressing her work on paper principally through the positionality of exile, this essay troubles essentialized notions of self or Cuban identity, instead emphasizing the mediated nature of Sánchez's work and its formal and conceptual praxis. Her work on paper is heavily concentrated in this period, and the intimacy of the medium, no less than its amenability to print, afforded a means of coping — privately and communally — with the gradual permanence of her place outside of Cuba. In a more personal way than her contemporary painting, Sánchez's printed work illuminates the context of her lived transatlantic experience of the 1960s and early 1970s, the social and artistic circles in which she moved, and, over time, her cognition of exile itself.

Sánchez arrived in New York as a young artist with a promising pedigree and early international exposure, her work conversant with lyrical postwar expressionism from Havana to Madrid. Her earliest paintings betray her exposure to the gestural abstraction of the Havana-based group Los Once (The Eleven), with whom she occasionally exhibited during the 1950s. Their incipient architectonics and painterliness relate in particular to contemporary work by Hugo Consuegra and Agustín Fernández, both of whom later settled in New York.[3] In the wake of Sánchez's travel to Madrid in 1957, her abstraction acquired the textured, convulsive materiality reminiscent of such Informel artists as Alberto Burri and Antoni Tàpies. The decade also saw the rise of concrete art, championed by Mario Carreño, Sandú Darié, and the group Los Diez (The Ten); their promulgation of geometric abstraction, in exhibitions at home and abroad, headlined the Havana scene over the late 1950s.[4] Sánchez represented Cuba in the São Paulo (1959) and Mexico City (1960) biennials before leaving for New York in 1960. Although the catalogue of Sánchez's work from the 1950s and 1960s is incompletely known, by the time of her arrival in New York she had a working knowledge of the formal and material possibilities of abstraction and its contemporary, transatlantic context. She soon came into contact with two cultural spheres: contemporary printmaking, which she studied at the Pratt Graphic Art Center beginning in 1962, and the Cuban community, just beginning to define itself in exile.

The opening of the Pratt Graphic Art Center in 1956 heralded the "print boom" of the 1960s and 1970s in the United States, which saw growing interest in the technical innovations offered by prints and multiples.[5] Notably, the center designed the Spring 1962 issue of its journal, *Artist's Proof*, around the "underdeveloped" topic of "The Contemporary American Book Illustrated with Original Prints."[6] Among the many artists who printed at the center in the early 1960s were the Abstract Expressionists Barnett Newman and Lee Krasner and the Venezuelan sculptor Gertrud "Gego" Goldschmidt. The conceptual artists Liliana Porter and Luis Camnitzer met at the

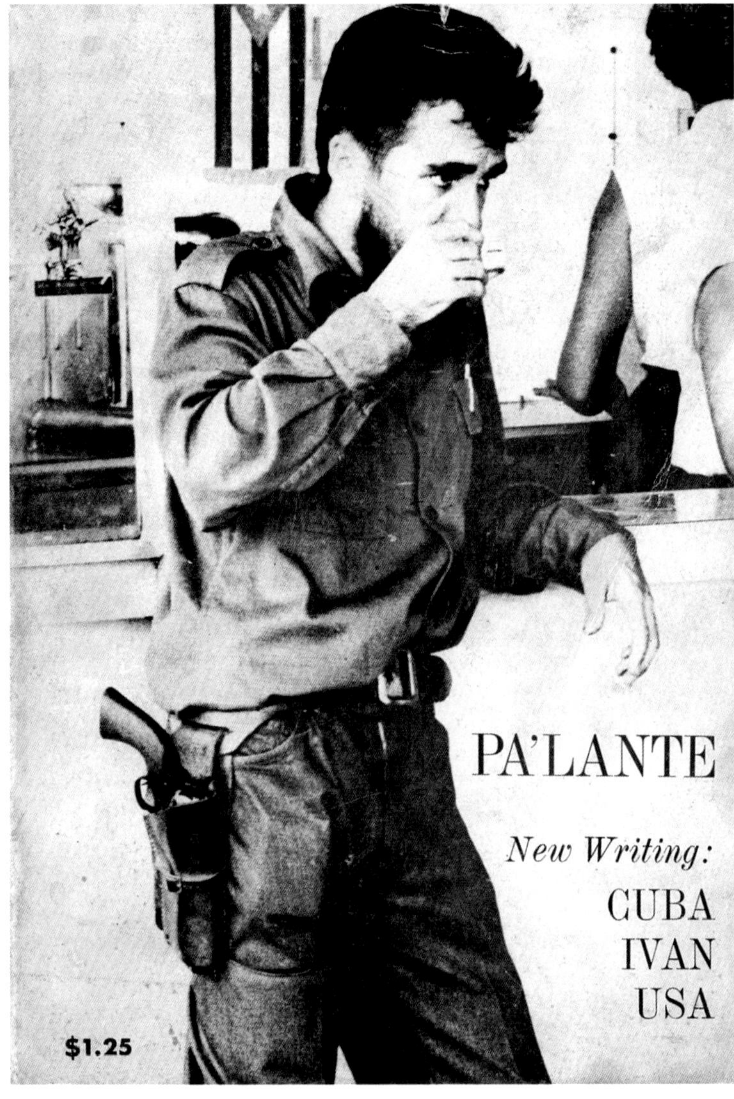

1 Leroy McLucas, cover of *Pa'Lante: Poetry, Polity, Prose of a New World*, May 19, 1962.

center in 1964; the next year, they founded the New York Graphic Workshop with José Guillermo Castillo. The center's foundational role in the elevation of printmaking as an art form doubtless drew Sánchez's notice upon her arrival in New York. While her graphic work takes clear cues from her painting, it also served as the principal medium through which she participated in the early ideation of Cuban New York.

Sánchez illustrated a number of publications during these years, mixing commercial work with contributions to new, and sometimes ephemeral, projects that ranged across the New York intellectual Left and the generation of young Cuban writers who arrived in the city in the early 1960s. Approximately 250,000 Cubans left the island between 1959 and 1962, the period bracketed by the Cuban Revolution and the Cuban Missile Crisis. This first exodus encompassed many of the island's elites and professional class, who initially imagined a temporary rather than permanent exile.[7]

Sánchez described herself as a "young *Cubana revolucionaria*" in the first and only issue of *Pa'Lante*, a journal published in 1962 by the leftist League of Militant Poets (fig. 1). "This new world is the world of our future whose image may be found in the fraternal socialist countries," the league declared, admonishing "the pseudo-ethic of anticommunism that has replaced our Jeffersonian tradition of moral revolution" and concluding with an appeal: "America, we are Yankee poets who believe that socialism will make you more beautiful, hundreds of times richer, and sane."[8] It published early translations of writers of the Cuban Revolution — among them Rolando Escardó, Nicolás Guillén, and Guillermo Cabrera Infante — alongside the Beat circle and an excerpt from Sergei Eisenstein's suggestively anti-Stalinist screenplay *Ivan the Terrible*. Poets Allen Ginsberg and Michael McClure directly addressed Cuba, the former obliquely in relation to Beat aesthetics and the latter more clearly in support of Fidel. "Letters from Cuba," contributed by the photographer Leroy McLucas, reflected mounting disillusionment with socialism on the island, a skepticism soon shared by the league, which led to *Pa'Lante*'s abrupt demise.

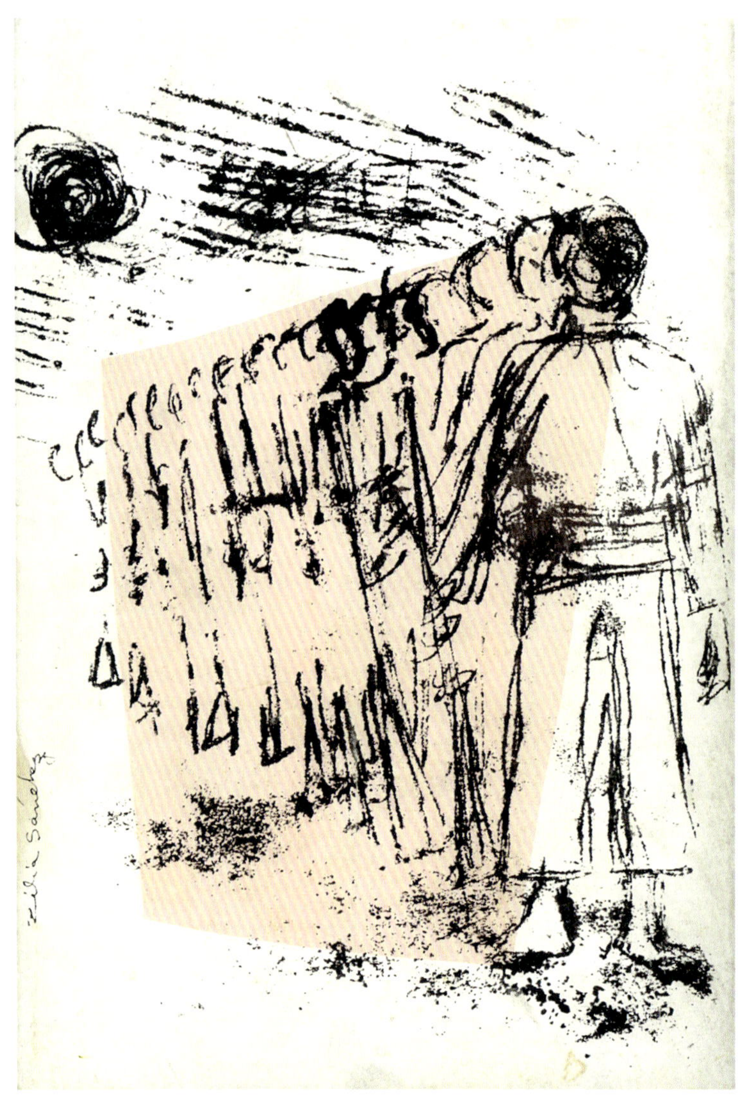

2 Zilia Sánchez, back cover of *Pa'Lante:
Poetry, Polity, Prose of a New World*,
May 19, 1962.

Sánchez, the sole female contributor — and the only Cuban contributor based in New York — provided three illustrations to *Pa'Lante*, including the striking back cover (fig. 2). Her inclusion is curious. The issue's only other illustrations are photographs by McLucas (cover) and Robert Frank (inside cover); the vaunted photographers of the Cuban Revolution — Raúl Corrales, Alberto Korda, Mario García Joya ("Mayito") — would have seemed more obvious choices. The back cover depicts a line of faceless Cuban *milicianos*, shotguns resting in hand. Their foreshortened bodies, indicated by a strong black line, are framed by a pink polygon, an unexpectedly feminine and geometric overlay. The drawing lacks the rebellious machismo of McLucas's bearded soldier, pistol at his side, on the front cover; Sánchez's figures are instead abstracted and anonymous, their forms increasingly schematic as they recede into the distance. The interior illustrations are similarly ambivalent: the first is a rendering of two soldiers and an oversize dove against a heavily textured ground, and the second is a portrait, formed economically by broad, visible brushstrokes. Among the most explicitly political images that Sánchez made, both in terms of their subjects and the context of publication, the illustrations convey a visceral unease and disquietude. Figural and graphic, they stand well apart from the rest of her work. The extent to which she shared the Left's disenchantment with the Cuban regime is difficult to precisely state for many reasons, not least the political upheaval of 1961–62. Her subsequent collaborations would be almost exclusively connected to the emergent Cuban exile community.

In 1962, the same year that *Pa'Lante* appeared, Cortázar published the first and only issue of *Protesta* (fig. 3), considered the first literary magazine of Cuban writers in exile. Cortázar, who had recently arrived in New York, belonged to Cuba's postrevolutionary group El Puente (The Bridge), composed of young writers interested in Beat literature and what Rafael Rojas has described as "an aesthetics of difference centered on individual solitude."[9] A compact volume of five folded sheets, *Protesta* published work by fellow *puentistas* Rivero and René Ariza alongside Beat poets Jack Micheline and William Bush.

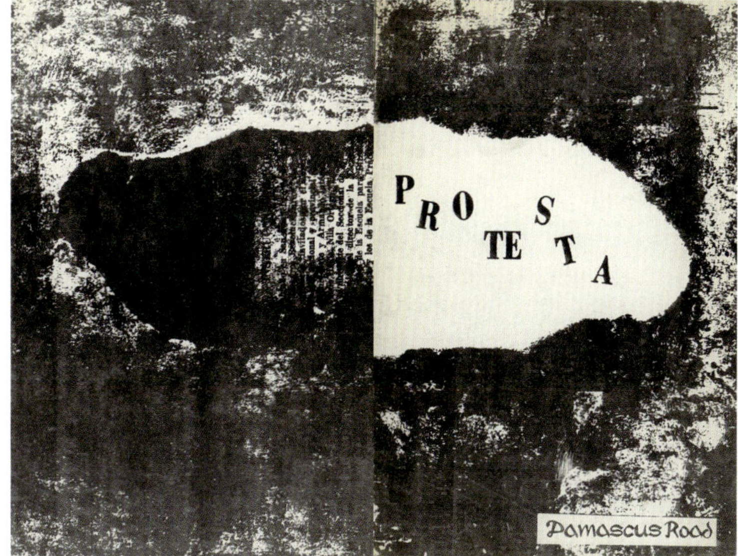

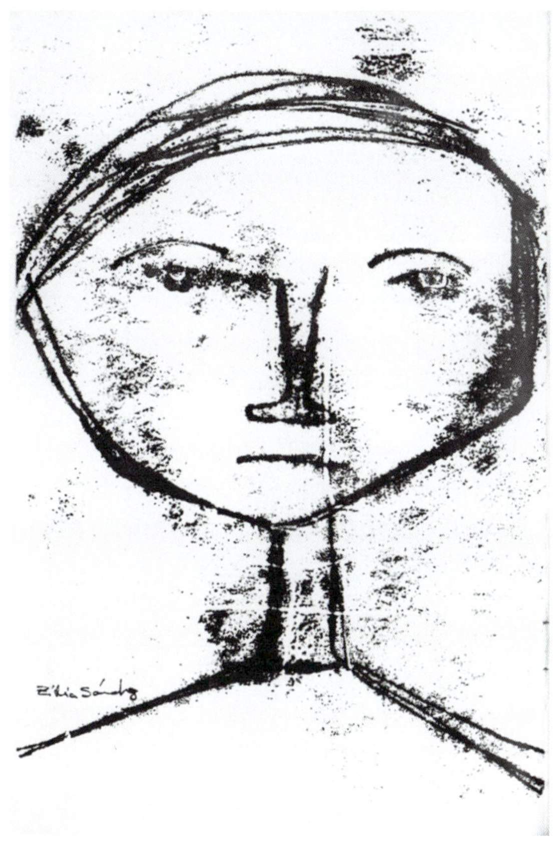

Sánchez contributed a drawing (fig. 4) — a spare, searching portrait — and the front and back cover. The issue contains neither editorial statement nor mention of Cuba per se but is pregnant with allusion, from the *gusanos* ("worms," Castro's term for the early exiles) mentioned in Rivero's poem to the title of Cortázar's poem, "Epitasis," and its intimation of an unfolding, classical drama. Sánchez's cover is notable for its typographic interest, which anticipates her later work on the journals *La nueva sangre* (The New Blood) and, in Puerto Rico, *Zona de carga y descarga* (Loading and Unloading Zone). The journal's title is printed on half of an island-like, plausibly phallic shape that extends to the back cover, upon which is overlaid what appears to be a passage from a newspaper article, its letters blurred. The background is dark and tortured, a stark chiaroscuro of black and white. Sánchez's closeness to the group around Cortázar brought her well within the orbit of the exile community, which continued to nurture her work.

Sánchez explored the textural, material properties of the page in a number of subsequent collaborations, adapting the raw expressionism of Informel painting to the existential poetry of her friends. She illustrated a number of books printed by Las Américas Publishing Company, which specialized in Hispanic culture and literature. Notable among them are Ramón Sender's *The Affable Hangman* (1963), for which she designed the cover, and Rivero's dialogic poem *Tundra* (1963). A poem in nine parts, *Tundra* traces the exquisite cruelties of the world and of man, and Sánchez's four black-and-white illustrations (fig. 5) distill the pain of a postapocalyptic world through a blur of flecked, atmospheric marks, abstractions of a void. The two illustrations that accompany Cortázar's *2 poèmes* (1965) are similarly cosmic and convulsive, their scarred surfaces instantiating the internalized turmoil —"and, maddened, to rack my brain against the world"— of the verse.[10] One of the two poems was first published in revolutionary Cuba, but its existential self-reckoning surely assumed new dimensions in its reprinting in exile, and Sánchez plumbed the plaintive, telluric pathos of the poems in her

3 Zilia Sánchez, front and back cover of *Protesta* 1, no. 1 (1962).

4 Zilia Sánchez, untitled drawing, *Protesta* 1, no. 1 (1962), n.p.

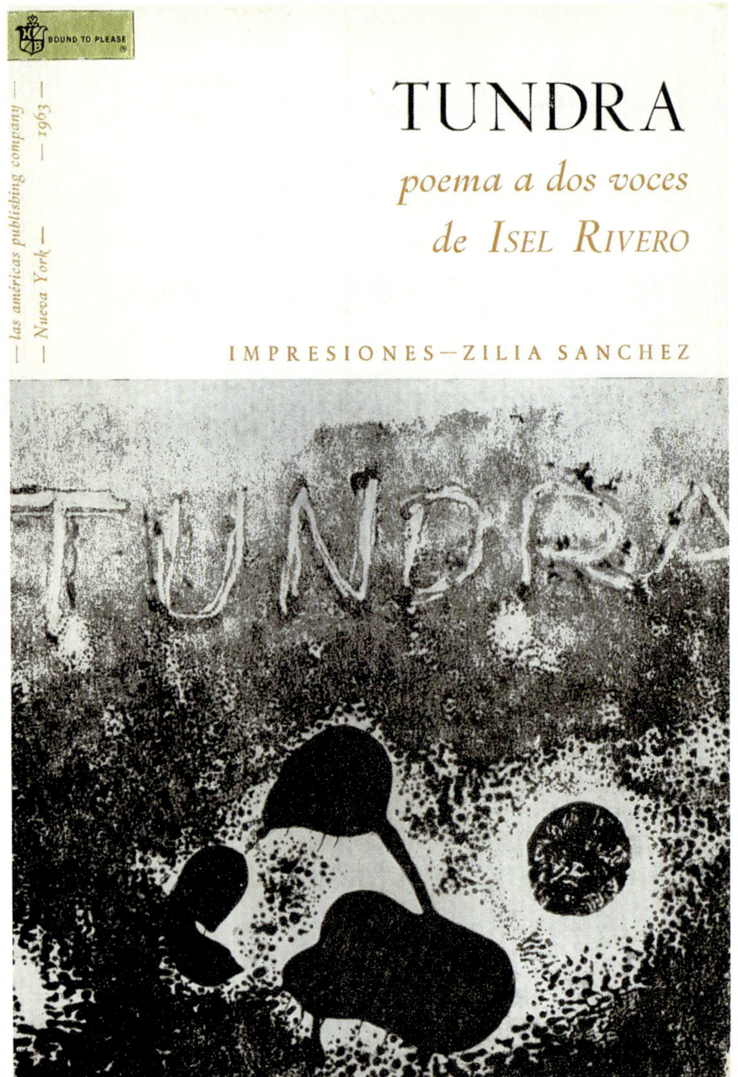

illustrations, in each case interpreting the text through a dense, dramatic stippling of pigment that spews the angst of her generation.

In 1966–67, Sánchez spent a year in Madrid supported by a CINTAS Fellowship. By the time she returned to New York, she had outwardly abandoned the existentialist expression of her previous New York work, and her work became newly minimalist in feeling. Minimalism was already well established in New York before she left for Madrid, developing apace in work and in theory by Robert Morris and Donald Judd, among others, and already periodized in Kynaston McShine's seminal exhibition *Primary Structures* at the Jewish Museum (1966), on view at the same time as Sánchez's solo show at the Zegrí Gallery. Sánchez likely just missed the stirrings of post-minimalism in *Eccentric Abstraction*, curated by Lucy Lippard at New York's Fischbach Gallery. The transformation of Sánchez's work in Spain appeared sudden, as architect and historian Fernando Chueca Goitia wrote in the catalogue for her show at Galería El Bosco in Madrid: "Her painting, yesterday informalist, also housed a secret chrysalis. It has not combined the informal and the formal, but has condemned its previous trajectory to make way for the new one. …One state annuls the other, although there exists a strange genetic relationship."[11] The fourteen paintings that she showed convey an occasionally agitated asceticism, distilled in a tensile line varyingly described as "poetic," "mathematical," "automatic," "discursive," and "Oriental" in many rave reviews. Its further recharacterization by Sánchez as a "tattoo" suggests an inscription on a body — and a nod to Severo Sarduy, exiled and in Paris since late 1959 and among Sánchez's closest friends.

The synergies between Sarduy and Sánchez's work are complex, but suffice it to note that through Sarduy and his association with the *Tel quel* group, Sánchez was introduced to structuralism and its critique of existentialist philosophy. Sarduy's book of essays *Escrito sobre un cuerpo* (Written on a Body), published in 1969, explored a Barthesian erotics of the text ("literature is an art of tattooing"). It further praised the graphic literalness and tautologies of "primary

5 Zilia Sánchez, cover of Isel Rivero,
Tundra: Poema a dos voces (New York:
Las Américas, 1963).

structures" by Robert Morris, Sol LeWitt, and Larry Bell, seen as exemplars of "urban painting. … pure groupings of signals, conventions, codes."[12] Sarduy served as Sánchez's most cogent and serious interlocutor during these years, and the somatic semiotics of her evolving shaped canvases derived substantially from his writings. The eroticism of the body in pieces suffuses the splendid ink-on-paper series *El significado del significante* (The Signified of the Signifier; cats. 27–30), which nominally refers to Saussurean psychologies of language. The drawings commingle the modular and the (faintly) masochistic in ways that recall the contemporary practice of fellow Cuban exile Agustín Fernández (fig. 6), who moved from Paris to Puerto Rico in 1968, as first observed by the Argentine critic Marta Traba.[13] Like

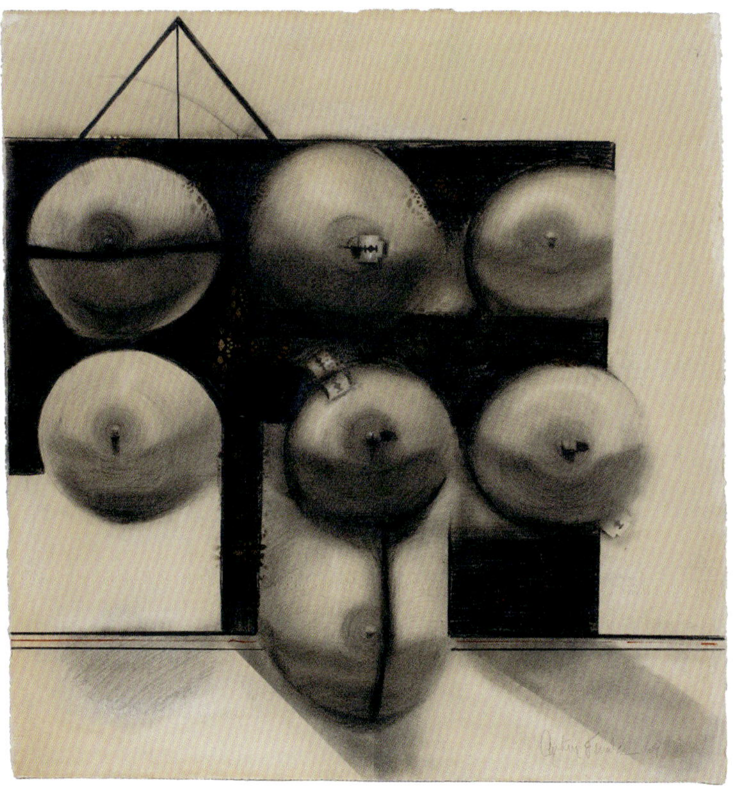

6 Agustín Fernández, *Untitled*, 1964. Pencil on paper, 24 × 22 ¼ in. (61 × 56.5 cm). Private collection, New York.

Fernández, Sánchez's apprehension of minimalism came at least as much from Europe — and from Sarduyan analysis — as from her observation of the New York scene, in which she struggled to find a place upon her return.

"In 1967, in New York," Sánchez later recalled, "four reliefs were rejected. … I felt very bad about this rejection, especially because I was convinced that they were good."[14] Sánchez has acknowledged Sarduy's epistolary support during this period, but she also found sustenance in the Cuban community in exile, no longer in the thrall of Beat poetry and increasingly invested in defining its own cultural (and political) space. The increasing Sovietization of the island, from the formalization of the Communist Party in 1965 to its integration with the socialist economic bloc (Comecon) in 1972, alienated many of the Cuban Left in New York, who faced the prospect of indefinite exile.

Into this space entered the new literary magazine *La nueva sangre* (1968–72). Cofounded by Cortázar and Cuban-born playwright and journalist Dolores Prida, among others, it carried the mantle of "Hispanic, bilingual, bicultural, bisexual, bicrazy, bieverything" New York.[15] The magazine regularly supported Sánchez's work within its charge, as articulated by the Puerto Rican writer Víctor Fernández-Fragoso, to provide a nucleus for young Hispanic culture by printing listings of activities and events in addition to reviews, poetry, and criticism.[16] It was explicitly not a publication "in exile," in distinction to the many émigré periodicals that began to appear, largely in South Florida, such as *Patria* and *Bohemia Libre*. A venue as well for Puerto Rican intellectuals, *La nueva sangre* existed rather in the interstices of "Nueva Yorksangre," as the magazine defined its conceptual place.[17] Among the New York–based Cuban artists who contributed drawings were Waldo Díaz-Balart and José Ángel Rosabal Fajardo, both of whom worked within modes of geometric abstraction. Sánchez's scenographic work for Cuban productions of Jean Anouilh's adaptation of *Antigone* (1969) and Virgilio Piñera's *Dos viejos pánicos* (1969) were reviewed in the magazine; records of her sets (and, indeed, the full extent of her scenography) have unfortunately not survived.[18] That she worked on a production of *Antigone* is notable not only for the play's classical leitmotifs of citizenship and homelessness — a theme resonant to Cuban and Puerto Rican audiences — but also for its anticipation of her shaped painting of the same name from 1970.[19]

The transformation of Sánchez's work from the existential agita of the first half of the decade to cool, minimalist erotics played out in the pages of *La nueva sangre*. The drawings that she contributed encompass portraiture, familiarly graphic but now self-consciously bifurcated (fig. 7), as seen in the magazine's sixth issue, dated March–April 1969, and even caricature, in the Fall 1969 issue. She shared "art and design" credits with Rafael Rodríguez in the latter issue, one notable for its typographical inventiveness. More pro-vocative is the cover of the tenth issue, dated February 1971, which featured a silkscreen from her time in Madrid. Spare and sensual, the lines — tattoos — traverse an elliptical field, fathomless and faintly feminized against a dark ground. A month later the same image, now printed in red, graced the cover of Prida's poem "Women of the Hour," published on the occasion of International Women's Day by Ediciones Nuevasangre, an extension of the magazine. Prida's bilingual poem, presented as "cosmic feminist poetry," sounded a call for liber-ation and present-day peace in an apostrophic paean to women's empowerment and eternity.

A Cuban-born playwright and journalist, Prida had arrived in New York in 1961. Her essay "Spatial Eroticism in the Painting of Zilia Sánchez," published in the ninth issue of *La nueva sangre* (October 1970), was the first to directly address the cosmic feminism, as it were, of Sánchez's work. Like Chueca, Prida identified an evolutionary link between the self-searching introversion of the earlier, textured abstractions and the sparely minimalist work that followed. Referring to the earlier work, she quotes Rivero's text from the 1966 Zegrí Gallery exhibition catalogue: "Man, our civilization, must recoil to its center, to its origins, in order to recuperate the lost self." She argues

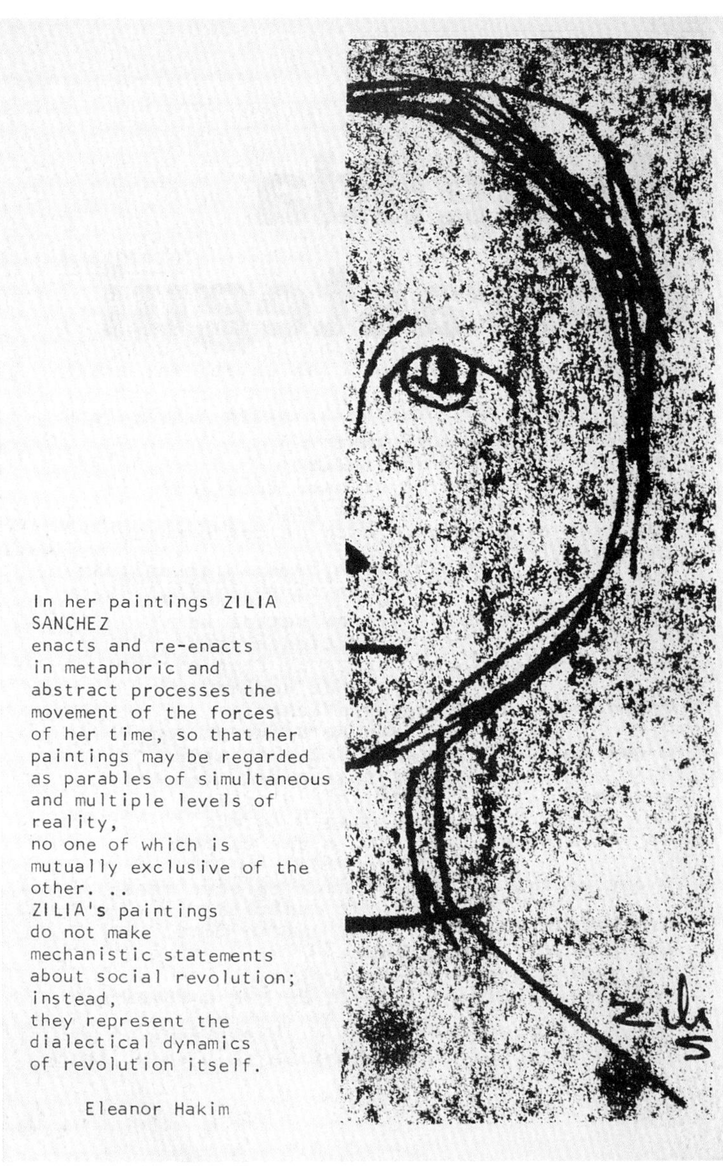

7 Zilia Sánchez, untitled drawing, *La nueva sangre* 1, no. 6 (March–April 1969): 12.

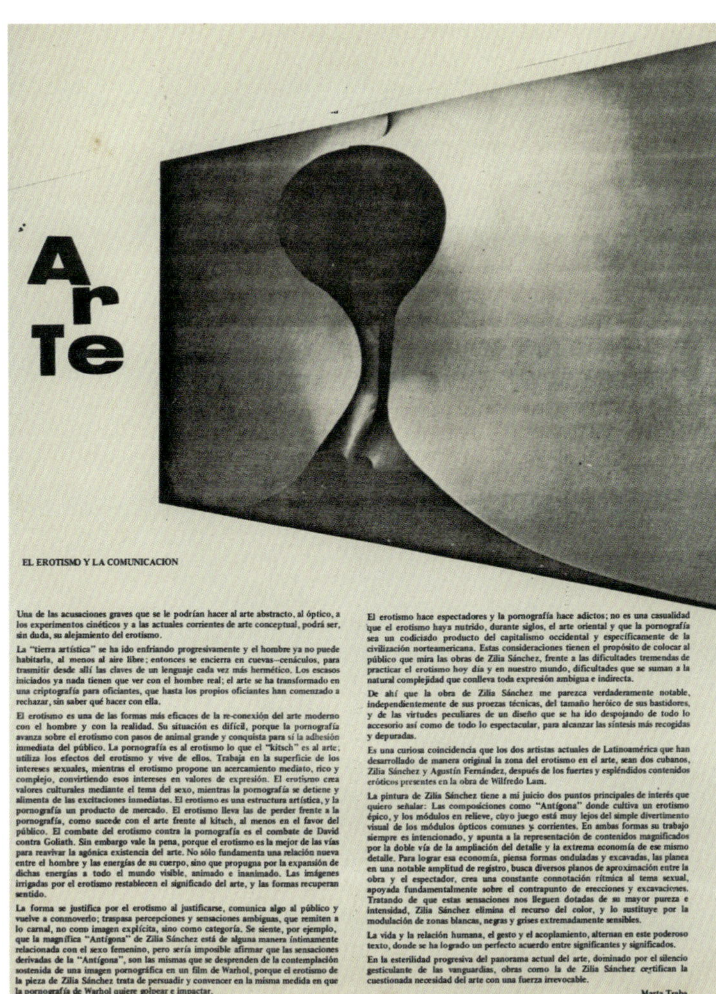

EL EROTISMO Y LA COMUNICACION

Una de las acusaciones graves que se le podrían hacer al arte abstracto, al óptico, a los experimentos cinéticos y a las actuales corrientes de arte conceptual, podrá ser, sin duda, su alejamiento del erotismo.

La "tierra artística" se ha ido enfriando progresivamente y el hombre ya no puede habitarla, al menos al aire libre; entonces se encierra en cuevas–cenáculos, para trasmitir desde allí las claves de un lenguaje cada vez más hermético. Los escasos iniciados ya nada tienen que ver con el hombre real; el arte se ha transformado en una criptografía para oficiantes, que hasta los propios oficiantes han comenzado a rechazar, sin saber qué hacer con ella.

El erotismo es una de las formas más eficaces de la re-conexión del arte moderno con el hombre y con la realidad. Su situación es difícil, porque la pornografía avanza sobre el erotismo con pasos de animal grande y conquista para sí la adhesión inmediata del público. La pornografía es al erotismo lo que el "kitsch" es al arte; utiliza los efectos del erotismo y vive de ellos. Trabaja en la superficie de los intereses sexuales, mientras el erotismo propone un acercamiento mediato, rico y complejo, convirtiendo esos intereses en valores de expresión. El erotismo crea valores culturales mediante el tema del sexo, mientras la pornografía se detiene y alimenta de las excitaciones inmediatas. El erotismo es una estructura artística, y la pornografía un producto de mercado. El erotismo lleva las de perder frente a la pornografía, como sucede con el arte frente al kitsch, al menos en el favor del público. El combate del erotismo contra la pornografía es el combate de David contra Goliath. Sin embargo vale la pena, porque el erotismo es la mejor de las vías para reavivar la agónica existencia del arte. No sólo fundamenta una relación nueva entre el hombre y las energías de su cuerpo, sino que propugna por la expansión de dichas energías a todo el mundo visible, animado e inanimado. Las imágenes irrigadas por el erotismo restablecen el significado del arte, y las formas recuperan sentido.

La forma se justifica por el erotismo al justificarse, comunica algo al público y vuelve a conmoverlo; traspasa percepciones y sensaciones ambiguas, que remiten a lo carnal, no como imagen explícita, sino como categoría. Se siente, por ejemplo, que la magnífica "Antígona" de Zilia Sánchez está de alguna manera íntimamente relacionada con el sexo femenino, pero sería imposible afirmar que las sensaciones derivadas de la "Antígona", son las mismas que se desprenden de la contemplación sostenida de una imagen pornográfica en un film de Warhol, porque el erotismo de la pieza de Zilia Sánchez trata de persuadir y convencer en la misma medida en que la pornografía de Warhol quiere golpear e impactar.

El erotismo hace espectadores y la pornografía hace adictos; no es una casualidad que el erotismo haya nutrido, durante siglos, el arte oriental y que la pornografía sea un codiciado producto del capitalismo occidental y específicamente de la civilización norteamericana. Estas consideraciones tienen el propósito de colocar al público que mira las obras de Zilia Sánchez, frente a las dificultades tremendas de practicar el erotismo hoy día y en nuestro mundo, dificultades que se suman a la natural complejidad que conlleva toda expresión ambigua e indirecta.

De ahí que la obra de Zilia Sánchez me parezca verdaderamente notable, independientemente de sus proezas técnicas, del tamaño heróico de sus bastidores, y de las virtudes peculiares de un diseño que se ha ido despojando de todo lo accesorio así como de todo lo espectacular, para alcanzar las síntesis más recogidas y depuradas.

Es una curiosa coincidencia que los dos artistas actuales de Latinoamérica que han desarrollado de manera original la zona del erotismo en el arte, sean dos cubanos, Zilia Sánchez y Agustín Fernández, después de los fuertes y espléndidos contenidos eróticos presentes en la obra de Wilfredo Lam.

La pintura de Zilia Sánchez tiene a mi juicio dos puntos principales de interés que quiero señalar: Las composiciones como "Antígona" donde cultiva un erotismo épico, y los módulos en relieve, cuyo juego está muy lejos del simple divertimento visual de los módulos ópticos comunes y corrientes. En ambas formas su trabajo siempre es intencionado, y apunta a la representación de contenidos magnificados por la doble vía de la ampliación del detalle y la extrema economía de ese mismo detalle. Para lograr esa economía, piensa formas onduladas y excavadas, las planea en una notable amplitud de registro, busca diversos planos de aproximación entre la obra y el espectador, crea una constante connotación rítmica al tema sexual, apoyada fundamentalmente sobre el contrapunto de erecciones y excavaciones. Tratando de que estas sensaciones nos lleguen dotadas de su mayor pureza e intensidad, Zilia Sánchez elimina el recurso del color, y lo sustituye por la modulación de zonas blancas, negras y grises extremadamente sensibles.

La vida y la relación humana, el gesto y el acoplamiento, alternan en este poderoso texto, donde se ha logrado un perfecto acuerdo entre significantes y significados.

En la esterilidad progresiva del panorama actual del arte, dominado por el silencio gesticulante de las vanguardias, obras como la de Zilia Sánchez certifican la cuestionada necesidad del arte con una fuerza irrevocable.

Marta Traba

that Sánchez's subject has "already arrived at its center … and now reveals it ready to project itself — naked — outwards, toward the universe, toward other men and other worlds."[20] This externalization of the self, made explicit in the tattoos and the shaped sex hypostatized in her canvases, is inscribed finally in the familiarly feminist and lunar terms that have long since defined Sánchez's practice. A consummate example of this inside-out projection is the black-and-white *Untitled* (cat. 16), in which the canvas stretches — skinlike — over a body insinuated by crescent-shaped contours both reflexively sculptural and viscerally inscripted, in the pliant geometry of a lunar tattoo. This painting and Sánchez's last collaborations with Prida

came at the end of her residence in Nueva Yorksangre, and they convey the maturation of her work and its new extraversion.

They also anticipate her work the following year, in Puerto Rico, on the magazine *Zona de carga y descarga* (1972–75, nine issues).[21] Cofounded by the writers Rosario Ferré and Olga Nolla, *Zona* marked a radical, postmodern position within Puerto Rican culture, advocating social and political revolution (in other words, feminism and independence). Sánchez had recently settled in San Juan, though she had exhibited regularly on the island since her solo show at the Universidad de Puerto Rico in 1965.[22] "It was Zilia who taught us how to make the journal," Ferré recalled, and Sánchez contributed expertise both technical and conceptual, producing a journal with the material sensibility of an artist's book.[23]

The magazine published Sarduy, among others of the Latin American "Boom generation," across oversize pages whose topologies of image and text — rotated and "tattooed," collaged and mimetic — were rooted in Sánchez's contemporary practice. For example, in the layout of the essay "El erotismo y la comunicación" by Traba, who spent eight months in San Juan in 1970–71, Sánchez oriented one of her reliefs at an angle, insisting upon its spatial projection outward as a play on a "pop-up" book, contrasting the flatness of the oversize page against the relief of the work itself and its printed angularity (fig. 8).

Zona bridged Sánchez's work from New York to San Juan. It also marked the conclusion of her decade-long focus on the print medium, as she turned her attention increasingly to shaped and modular canvases. The earlier anxieties of exile, so palpably graphic and personal in the previous decade, feel less acute in her work from Puerto Rico. Their sublimation into the erotic and semiotic economy of postminimalism suggests an evolved critical, no less than geographical, perspective.

8 Zilia Sánchez's work in Marta Traba, "El erotismo y la comunicación," *Zona. Carga y descarga* 1, no. 2 (November–December 1972): 11.

Long overlooked, the prints and drawings that Sánchez made during the formative years of the 1960s and early 1970s document an evolving self- and world-consciousness as she apprehended the conditions of exile, a new home, and eventually the corporeal presence of minimalist art. Throughout this time, her work was nurtured by the esprit de corps that bound the Cuban émigré community, from its early associations with the New York Left to its subsequent solidarity with the Puerto Rican intelligentsia. Training in printmaking in New York gave her a technical understanding of materials, creating a sensibility that became a throughline in her work. Her illustrations supported and interpreted the writings of her contemporaries who had also come from Cuba, particularly the poets Rivero, Cortázar, and Prida. The ephemeral publications on which they collaborated — *Pa'Lante*, *Protesta*, *La nueva sangre* — provided a singular creative forum and archive for the work of Cuba's earliest exiles. Collectively, her contributions marked her changing responsiveness to her place in the world, seen first in unblinking portraits and dense, mineral-like abstractions, and later in minimalist inscription. Although Sánchez has long remained reticent about her early work and de facto exile, she recently allowed that "those who emigrate are always seeking to know and learn more."[24] The plastic and existential knowledge gained during this period have long and productively informed her work, still and distinctively grounded in its graphic sensibility and sensuous surface.

Abigail McEwen, PhD, is associate professor of Latin American art and director of undergraduate studies, University of Maryland.

NOTES

1. Edward Said, "The Mind of Winter: Reflections on Life in Exile," *Harper's* 269 (September 1984): 55.

2. Zilia Sánchez, quoted in Giulio V. Blanc, "Conversación con Zilia Sánchez," *Mariel* 2, no. 7 (Fall 1984): 37. All translations from Spanish by the author.

3. Los Once exhibited between 1953 and 1955, repeatedly staging their practice of gestural abstraction in opposition to the Fulgencio Batista dictatorship. Among the group's best-known members are Guido Llinás (1923–2005), Raúl Martínez (1927–1995), Hugo Consuegra (1929–2003), and Agustín Cárdenas (1927–2001). Sánchez showed in two of Los Once's exhibitions — in 1953 (Nuestro Tiempo) and in 1955 (Galería Habana) — and with many of the group's members in other venues during the decade.

4. *Concrete Cuba: Cuban Geometric Abstraction from the 1950s* (New York: David Zwirner Books, 2016).

5. For more on the "print boom," see Deborah Wye, "Artists and Prints in Context," in *Artists and Prints: Masterworks from the Museum of Modern Art* (New York: Museum of Modern Art, 2004), 22–27.

6. Fritz Eichenberg, "Editorial: The Contemporary Print and the Book," *Artist's Proof* 2, no. 1 (Spring 1962): 1.

7. Jorge Duany, "Cuban Communities in the United States: Migration Waves, Settlement Patterns and Socioeconomic Diversity," *Pouvoirs dans la Caraïbe* 11 (1999): 71.

8. "A Statement by the League of Militant Poets," *Pa'Lante: Poetry, Polity, Prose of a New World*, no. 1 (May 19, 1962): 5. *Pa'Lante* was edited by Howard Schulman, Elizabeth Sutherland Martínez, and José Yglesias. The title derived from a line from a conga song popular at the time in Havana. For more on *Pa'Lante*, see Rafael Rojas, "The League of Militant Poets," chap. 7 in *Fighting over Fidel: The New York Intellectuals and the Cuban Revolution* (Princeton, NJ: Princeton University Press, 2016), 195–219.

9. Rojas, *Fighting over Fidel*, 155.

10. Mercedes Cortázar, "El largo canto," in *2 poèmes* (New York: Osmar Press, 1965), 28.

11. Fernando Chueca Goitia, *Zilia Sánchez* (Madrid: Galería El Bosco, 1967).

12. Severo Sarduy, *Written on a Body*, trans. Carol Maier (New York: Lumen Books, 1992), 41, 80–81.

13. Marta Traba, "A la búsqueda del signo perdido," in *Dos décadas vulnerables en las artes plásticas latinoamericanas, 1950–1970* (Mexico City: Siglo Veintiuno, 1973), 173–74.

14. Zilia Sánchez, quoted in Ileana Delgado Castro, "Encuentro con Zilia Sánchez," *El nuevo día*, sec. Revista Domingo, March 20, 2005.

15. Dolores Prida, "Comentario: La nueva sangre," *La nueva sangre* 3, no. 9 (October 1970): 2. The magazine was cofounded by Prida, Rolando Campins, Edwin Rodríguez, Víctor R. Fernández-Fragoso, and Mercedes Cortázar. Beginning with the ninth issue (October 1970), published after a year-long hiatus, only Prida remained on the

masthead. I am indebted to Alyson Cluck, who produced the chronology for this catalogue, for her extensive research on *La nueva sangre.*

———

16. Víctor R. Fernández-Fragoso, "*La nueva sangre* y el ambiente literario de Nueva York," *La nueva sangre* 1, no. 2 (June–July 1968). For more on émigré publications, see María Cristina García, "Defining an Identity in the United States," chap. 3 in *Havana USA: Cuban Exiles and Cuban Americans in South Florida, 1959–1994* (Berkeley: University of California Press, 1996), 83–119.

———

17. The magazine's first issue opens with an editorial, "*La nueva sangre* se define," in which seven writers define its objectives; it is dated "Nueva Yorksangre, a 12 de abril de 1968."

———

18. Sánchez had previously worked as a scenographer in Havana, for the guerrilla group Las Máscaras, in the 1950s. Her theater credits include *Mambí* (March 31, 1960) and *El milagro de Anaquillé* (July 1960) at Havana's Teatro Nacional.

———

19. Marta Traba, "El erotismo y la comunicación," *Zona. Carga y descarga* 1, no. 2 (November–December 1972): 11.

———

20. Isel Rivero, "Historical Situation and Retrospective," quoted in Dolores Prida, "El erotismo espacial en la pintura de Zilia Sánchez," *La nueva sangre* 3, no. 9 (October 1970): 9.

———

21. For more on *Zona*, see Benigno Trigo, "*Zona. Carga y descarga*: Minor Literature in a Penal Colony," *MLN* 124, no. 2 (March 2009): 481–508.

22. *Zilia Sánchez* (San Juan: Museo de la Universidad de Puerto Rico, 1965).

———

23. Rosario Ferré, quoted in Trigo, "*Zona. Carga y descarga*," 487.

———

24. Sánchez, quoted in "Zilia Sánchez Interview," *Design Porteur*, May 3, 2013, http://design-porteur.com/2013/05/03/zilia-sanchez-interview/.

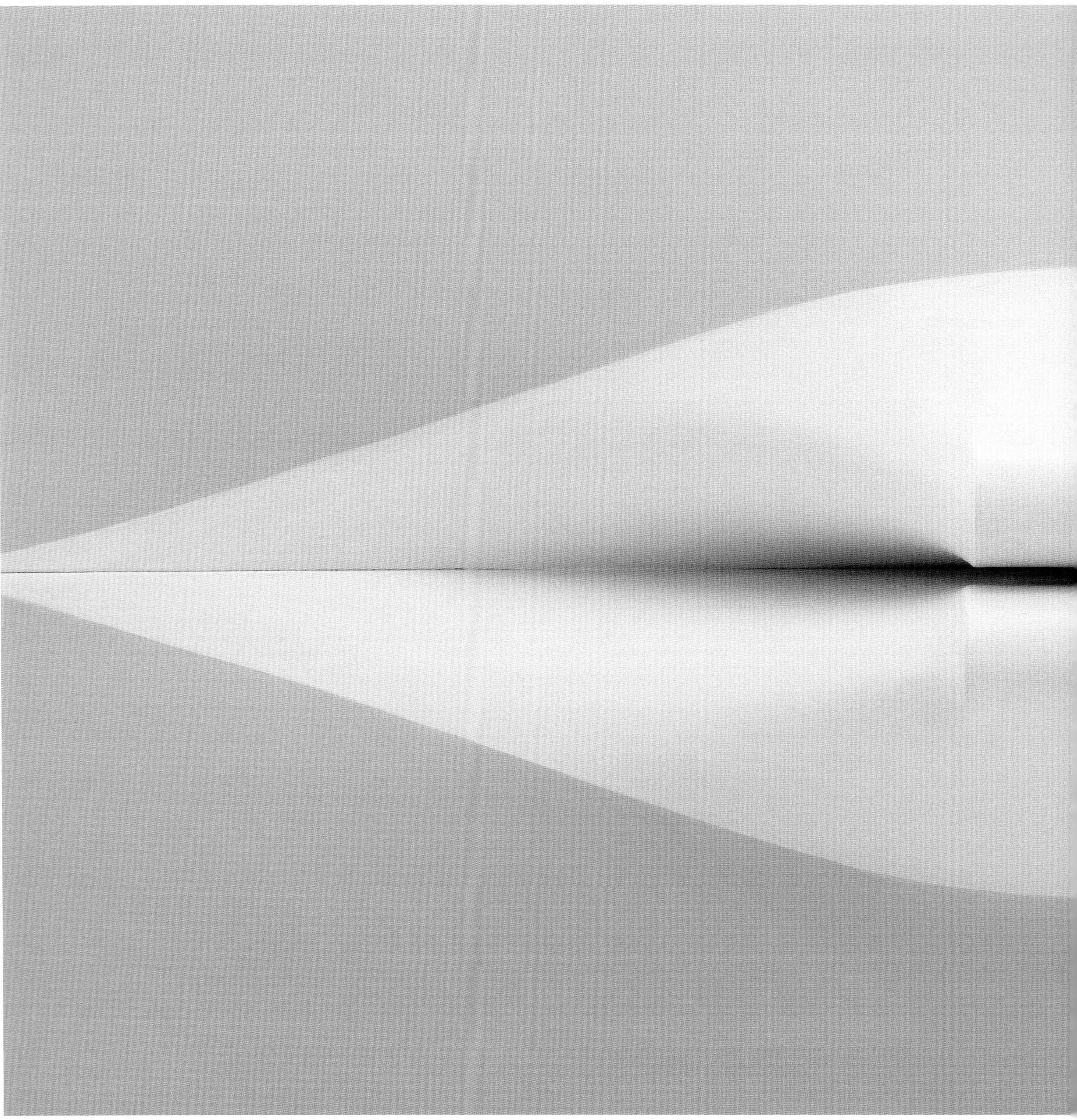

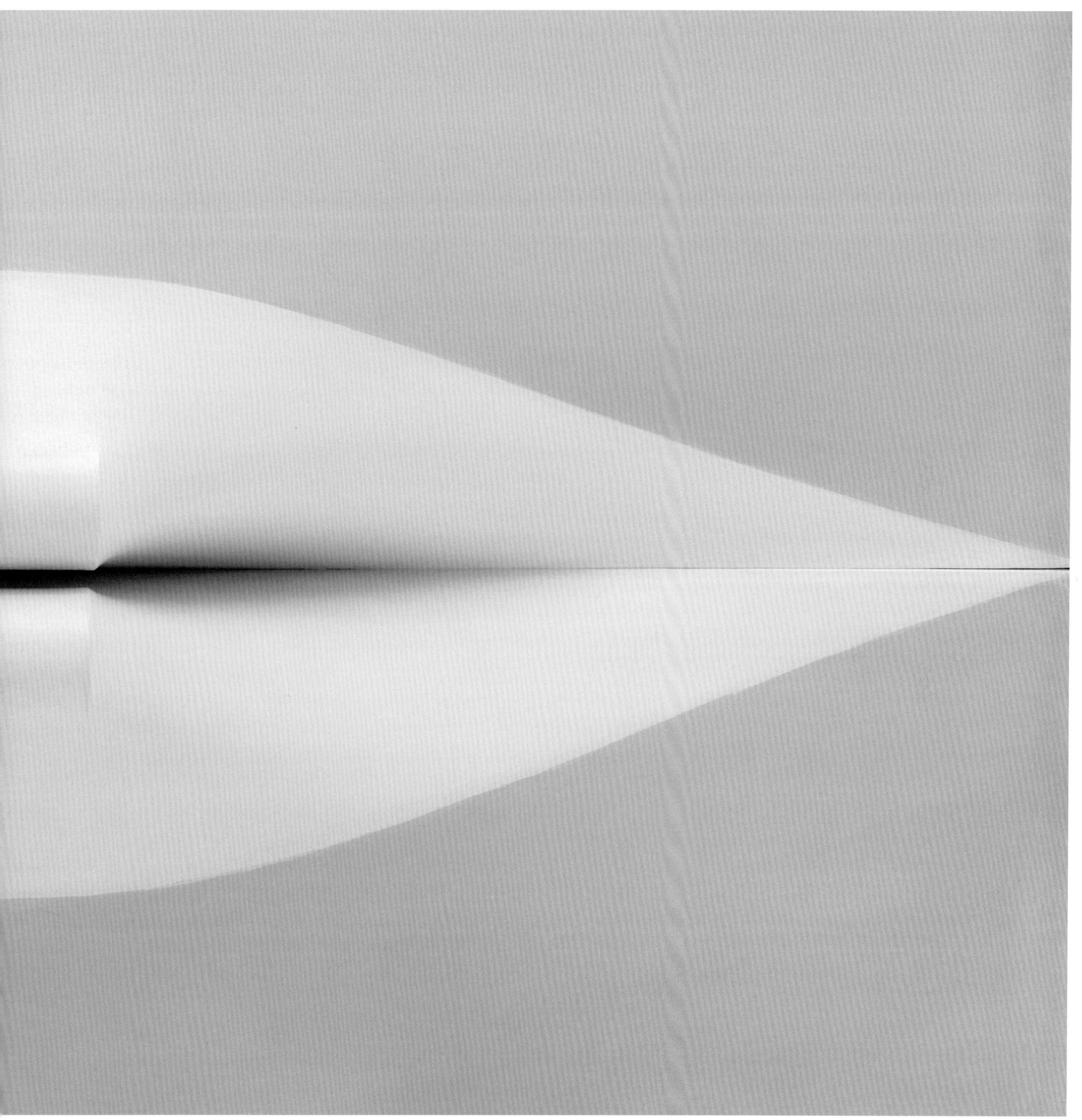

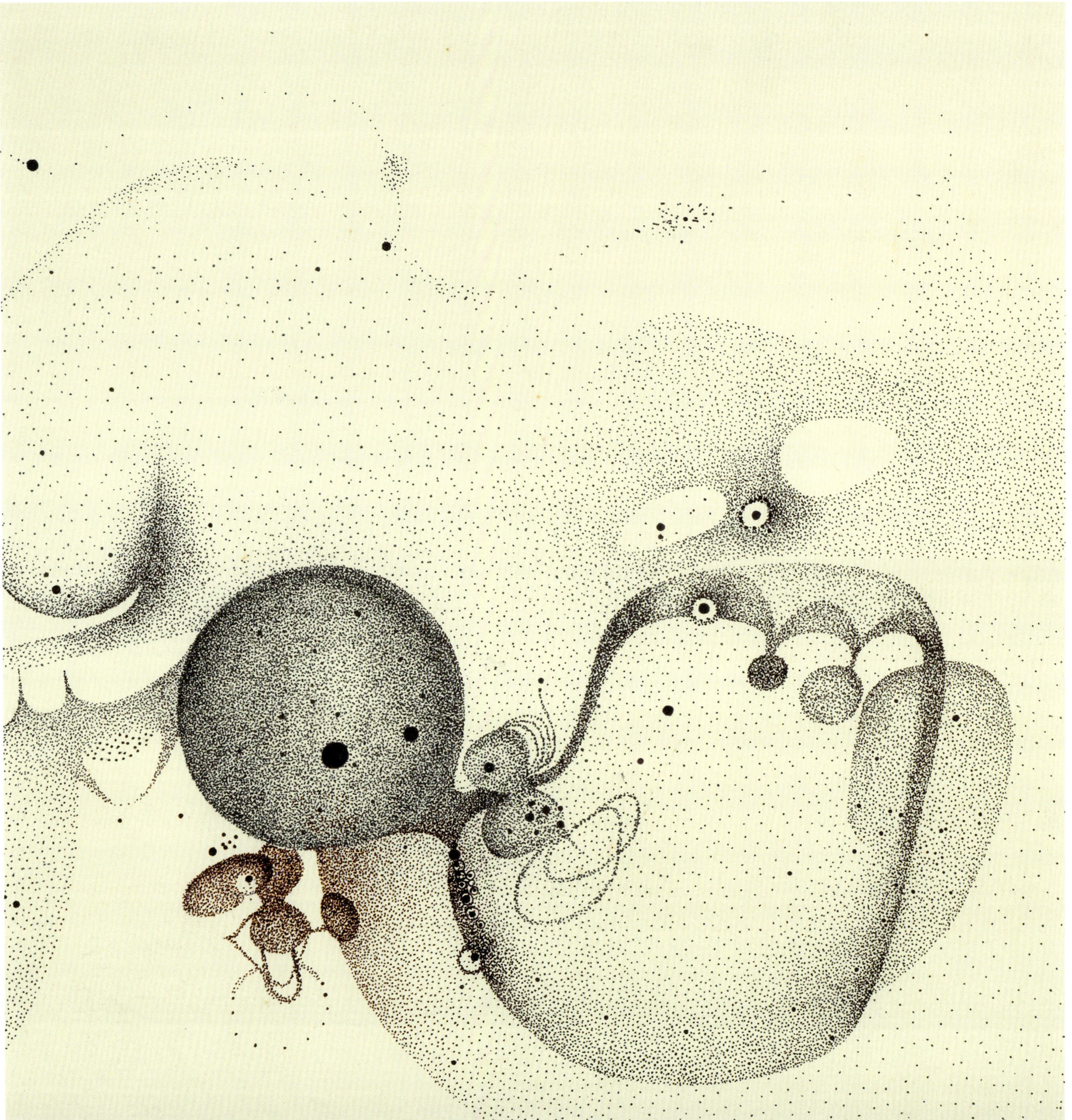

Decoding Homotextuality in the Work of Zilia Sánchez

CARLA ACEVEDO-YATES

Cobra, the main character of Severo Sarduy's 1972 experimental novel of the same name, is one of the most obsessive transgender characters in Latin American literature (fig. 1).[1] A lifelong friend and confidant of Zilia Sánchez, Sarduy gave Sánchez many books, including a first edition of *Cobra*. His inscription, dated November 17, 1972, in Paris, is on the half-title page. Above the title, "Cobra," to which he added quote marks, Sarduy wrote, "To Zilia, to Zilia again," and below it, "With love always, SEVERO" (fig. 2).

In the book, after years of performing as a drag queen at the Teatro Lírico de Muñecas, Cobra goes on a wild mission to find Dr. Ktazob,[2] a sadistic doctor who she hopes will perform on her the "morphological change." The novel describes Cobra's relentless obsession with bodily transformation, approaching the body as a blank page to be written, erased, and rewritten. At the end, Cobra's search and unbridled desire for a stable identity escape her, anticipating fundamental ideas on fluid identity and gender performativity in queer theory.

Sarduy's novel offers a compelling, and rather unorthodox, point of comparison with Sánchez's art. Much like the main character of the novel, Sánchez's work also undergoes morphological transformations, navigating the liminal space between painting and sculpture and challenging traditional assumptions regarding gender, sexuality, and binary categories more broadly. Taking as a starting point the groundbreaking literary and theoretical work of Sarduy, I will provide a partial semiotic analysis of Sánchez's complex art through the lens of homotextuality.

A homotextual work is one that, although it may not be intentionally created as homosexual, reveals a complex, codified hermeneutics in which desire and sexual and gender difference are inscribed. Coined by Rudi C. Bleys in his seminal book *Images of*

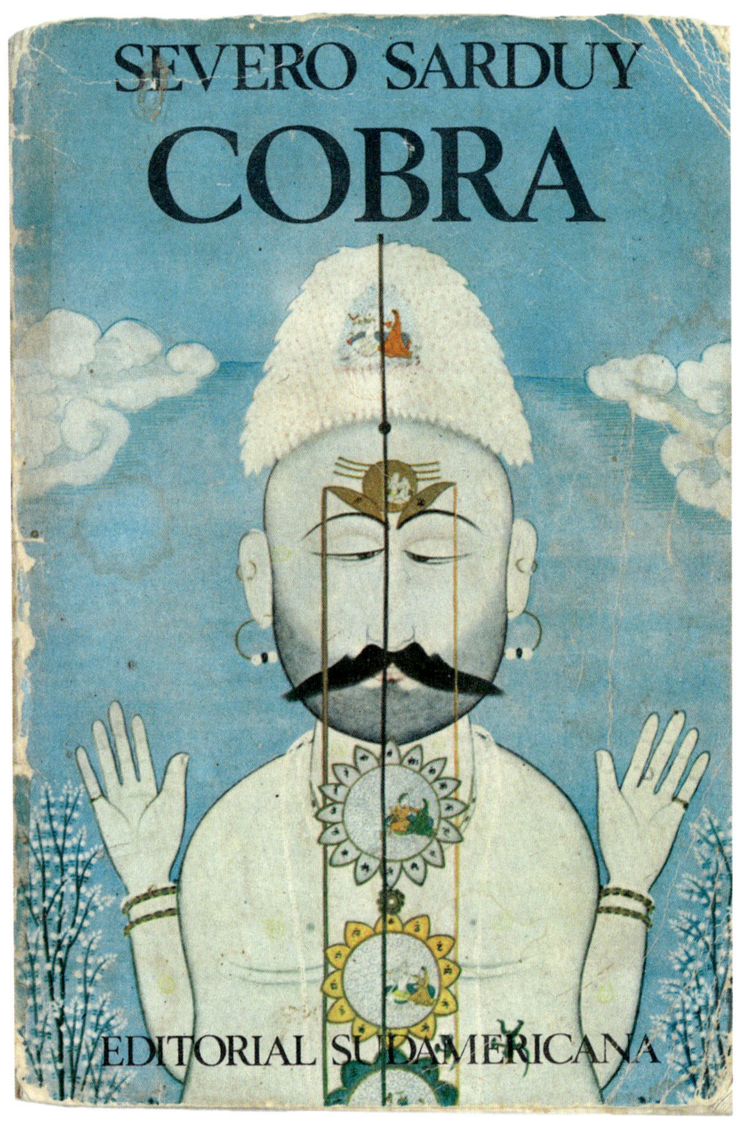

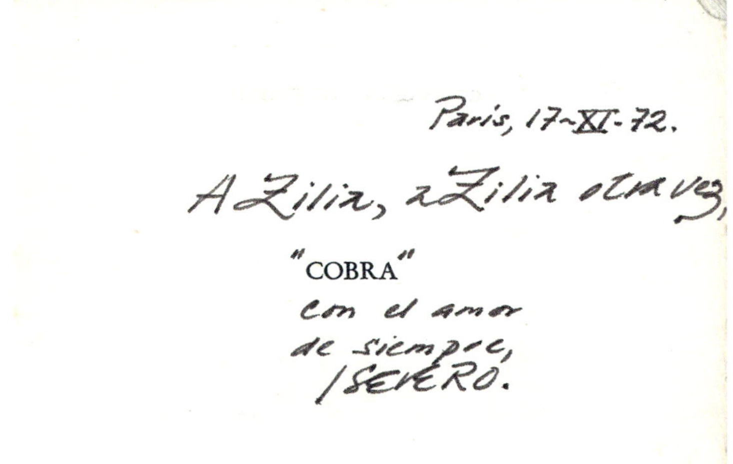

Ambiente: Homotextuality and Latin American Art, 1810–Today, published in 2000, *homotextuality* is defined as "a heuristic catch-all term, which is diachronic instead of being tied to all-too-reifying notions of 'homosexual' or 'gay' identity. … It embraces an image's potential reception as a site of homotextual meaning, even when not intended [to do] so by the artist him/herself."[3] In his book, Bleys argues that "a codified, if only implicitly 'lesbian,' aesthetic seems to be present"[4] in Sánchez's work. Expanding upon Bleys's analysis and drawing on Sarduy's writings, I argue that Sánchez's work, highly coded and homotextual, performs a formal, technical, and semiotic "drag" that navigates between forms, referents, and mediums, radicalizing the act of painting.

Sarduy: Artist, Writer, and Friend

Born in 1937 in Havana, Sarduy moved to Paris in 1960, the year after Fidel Castro came to power, with a government-sponsored scholarship to study painting. It is not clear if Sarduy fled Havana because of the revolution. In an article by Sarduy titled "Exiled from Himself," published a year before his death due to AIDS in 1993, he affirms that

1 Cover of Severo Sarduy, *Cobra* (Buenos Aires: Editorial Sudamericana, 1972).

2 Sarduy's dedication to Sánchez in *Cobra*.

"I only consider myself a *quedado* [one who stayed], or if you will —
I come from an island — an *aislado* [isolated one]. I stayed like that
from one day to the other. Maybe I'll return tomorrow."[5] The revolution and the new regime were not sympathetic to political differences
or to differences in sexual orientation or gender identity. But even
before Castro came to power, Sarduy struggled to fit into Cuba's very
conservative society and was considered "weird"[6] by some of his
family members (fig. 3).

Sarduy's literary career started in earnest when he arrived
in Paris, where he almost immediately met François Wahl[7] and was
introduced to a group of French intellectuals involved with the
magazine *Tel quel*. Sarduy was particularly drawn to Roland Barthes's
ideas, regularly attending his seminars at the École Pratique des
Hautes Études and then at the Collège de France. Sarduy's literary
and theoretical work owes much to Barthes's semiology, which
shaped his ideas on the baroque and its reconceptualization into the
neo-baroque. In 1972, at the same time that *Cobra* was published,
Sarduy also produced the essay *El barroco y el neobarroco*, which out-
lines a semiology for a Latin American neo-baroque. In this essay
he argues that the concept of the baroque — inherited from Europe,
but essentially transformed in the Americas — is crucial to understanding Latin American arts and letters.

The term *neo-baroque* distances itself from the ornate,
overwrought, and kitsch aesthetics that come to mind when we think
of seventeenth- to eighteenth-century Baroque art. Instead, Sarduy
employs a semiotic approach with an erotic queering of the term —
one that is based on careful semiotic analysis and looks to ety-
mological references. The meaning of the word *barroco* in Portuguese
is "irregular pearl," and Sarduy's concept of the baroque, similarly,
implies a deviation from the norm, a queering of Roland Barthes's
semiology. Sarduy identifies a series of precise semiotic operations
that define a "process of masking or artificialization" composed
of codified signifiers. These include substitution, proliferation, and
condensation.

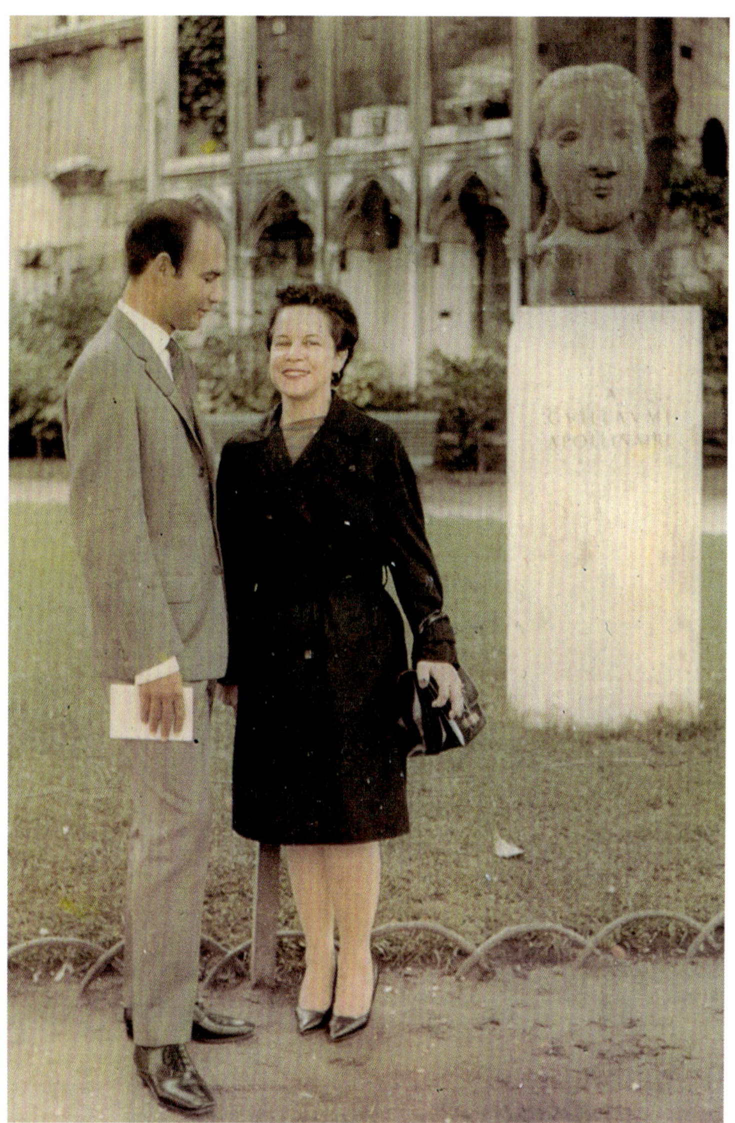

3   Sarduy and Sánchez in Paris, c. 1960.

Substitution, Proliferation, and Condensation

The first operation of artifice described by Sarduy is that of *substitution*, in which the visual signifier (form) that corresponds to the signified (concept) is replaced by another signifier, which only makes sense within the larger structure of the object of study. In Sánchez's work, this substitution occurs on the level of the signified, which shifts and changes according to the viewer's subjective positioning, thereby destabilizing fixed meaning and challenging binary positions and the heteronormative gaze.[8]

Take Sánchez's series of drawings from the late 1960s, *El significado del significante* (The Signified of the Signifier), in which an initial form (a signifier, exemplified by the dot) is constantly substituted with different concepts (the signifieds; cats. 27–30 and fig. 4). Sánchez has referred to the forms in these drawings as simultaneously embodying different ideas: "This is an egg, it's the world, and it's a breast. Three things."[9] In these works, there is a visual and semiotic exploration of the dot, which is the beginning of the line and of drawing as an artistic medium. By an operation of semiotic substitution, the dot becomes full of interpretive possibilities. In one of these drawings, an accumulation of dots comprises an egg-shaped form or lump that becomes a breast, approaching two round shapes that resemble buttocks or two breasts slightly touching each other. A line made of dots moves through one of these shapes and extends upward to what appears to be a nipple or a radiating sun.

In another drawing from the same suite, Sánchez plays with the dot as density, expanding and contracting its formal possibilities in a constellation of possible, abstract significations. Here, the dot as the primordial gesture of drawing, the mark on paper that is the signifier, becomes the site of multiple conceptual substitutions. It is only within the context of Sánchez's larger body of work, the sculptural canvases that she was working on at the same time as these drawings, that these works together acquire increasing erotic signifiers.

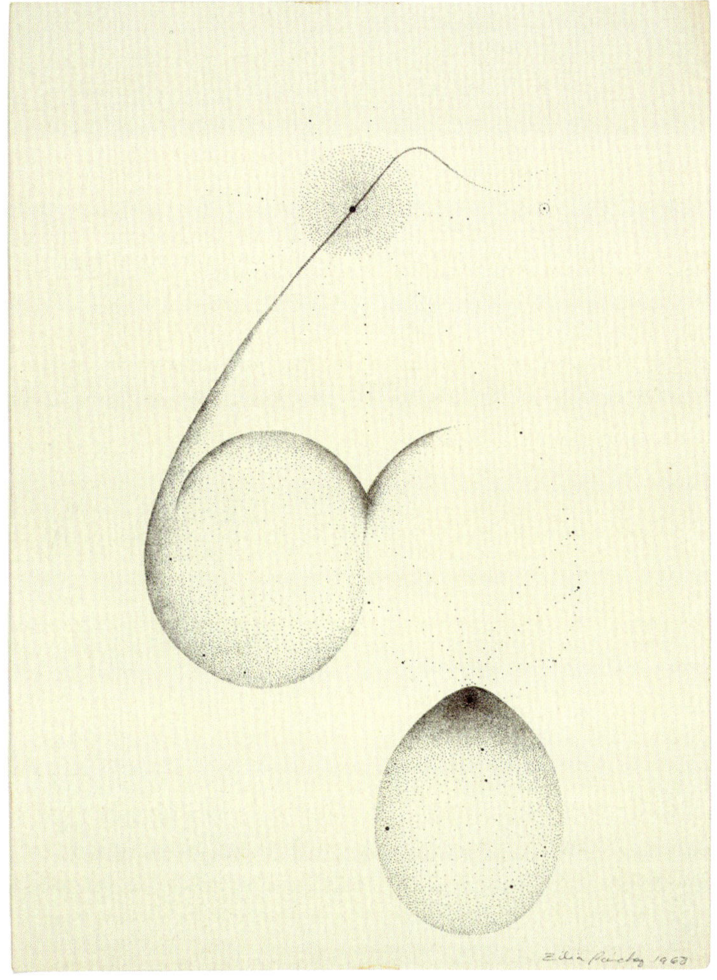

The second operation of artifice is *proliferation*, which "consists of obliterating the given signifier of a signified, but not by replacing it with another…but [instead] by a chain of signifiers that progresses metonymically."[10] This mechanism is perhaps most evident in Sánchez's modular works, where the signifier (the form of a breast, for example) is erased through a process of serial repetition and what Sarduy calls "visual isomorphy."

In *Amazonas* (fig. 5), for instance, the form of a breast or a nipple is accumulated in odd intervals as a chain of signifiers in a rhythmic "optical staccato."[11] Together with the implied meaning of the work's title, this creates a metonymic operation, in which one

4 Zilia Sánchez, *El significado del significante* (The Signified of the Signifier), c. 1968. India ink on paper, 19 ¾ × 14 in. (50.2 × 35.6 cm). Walker Art Center, Minneapolis, Gift of the artist and Galerie Lelong & Co., New York, in honor of Olga Viso, 2014.

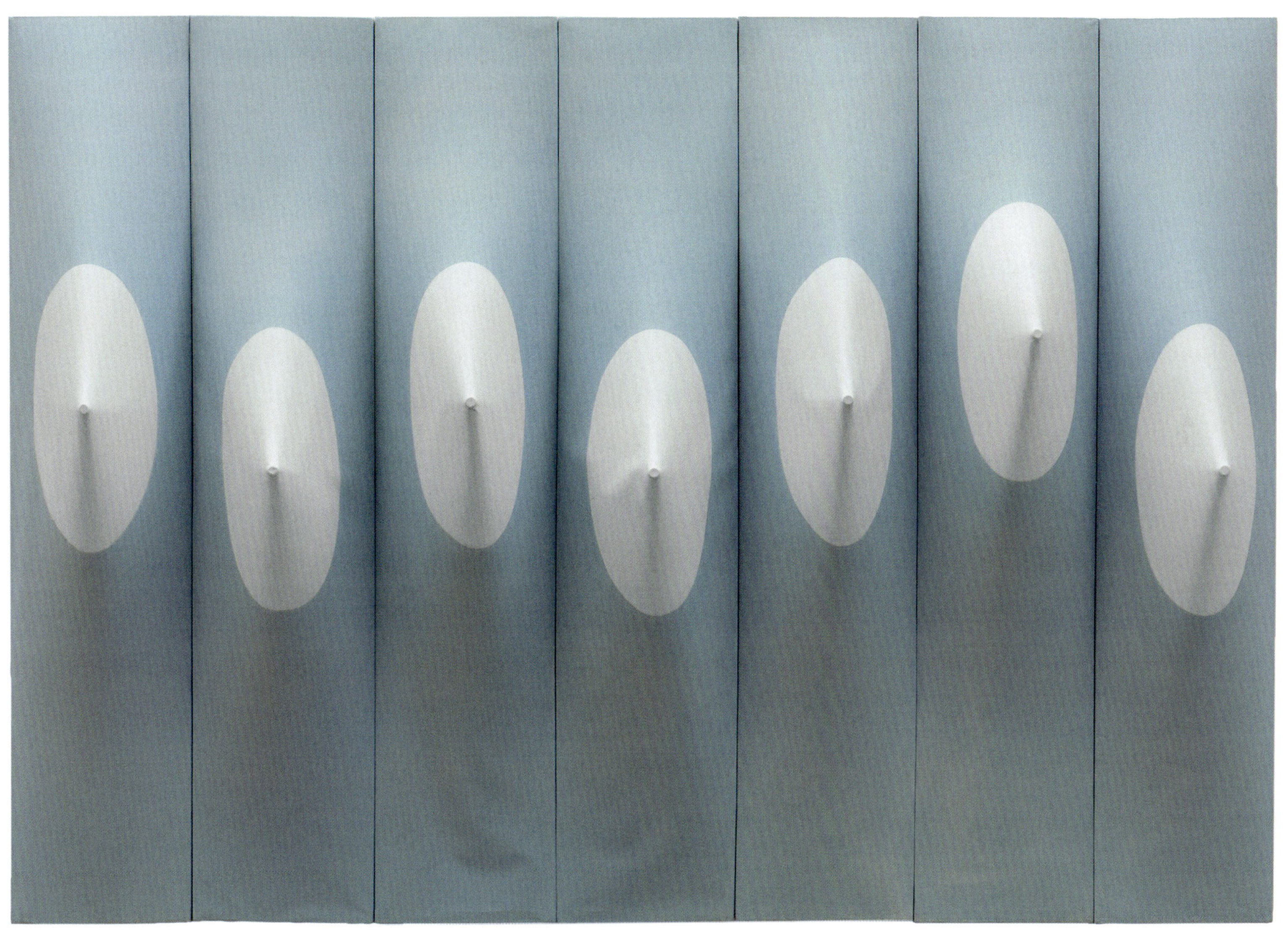

5 Zilia Sánchez, *Amazonas* (Amazons), 1972.
Acrylic on stretched canvas, 53 ¾ ×
74 ¼ × 11 ¼ in. (136.5 × 188.6 × 28.6 cm).
Private collection, Canada. Courtesy
Galerie Lelong & Co, New York.

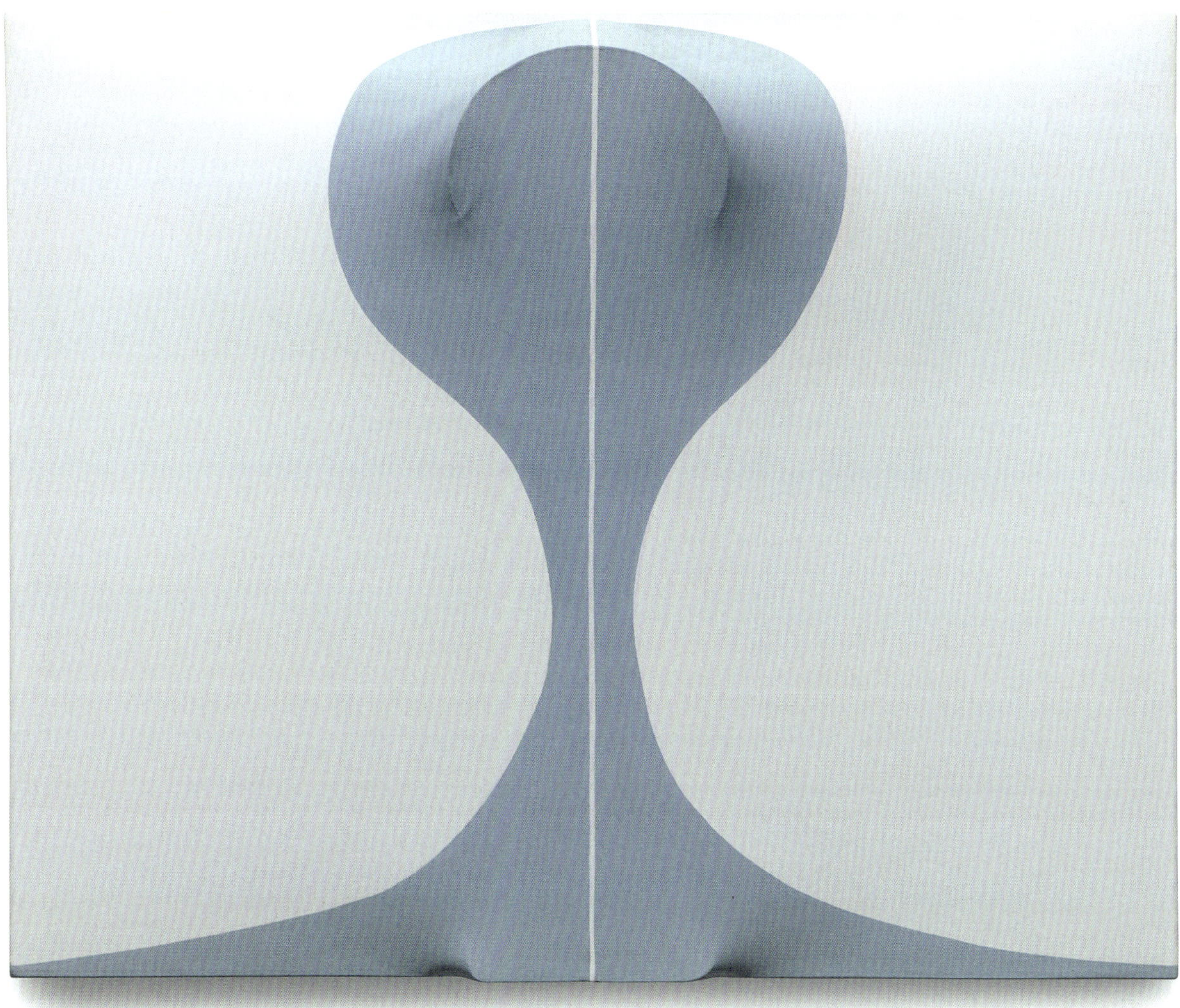

part (the breast) represents the thing that is meant. The title makes reference to the ancient myth of the Amazons, a matriarchal society of warrior women who, according to some classical writers, removed their right breasts in order to better use bows and arrows. The displaced breast appears again and again in Sánchez's work, isolated, as a pronounced peak or elevation — a form with multiple significations.

After all, the breast is the metonymic representation of the mother, but also of pleasure and of the world.[12]

The third operation, *condensation*, is, according to Sarduy, "the unification of two signifieds that come together in the exterior space of the screen, the frame or inside memory." In *Lunar blanco* (White Moon; cat. 20), for example, the given signified or concept of

6 Zilia Sánchez, *Antígona* (Antigone), 1970. Acrylic on stretched canvas, 30 × 36 × 10 in. (76.2 × 91.4 × 25.4 cm). Museum of Modern Art, New York, Acquired through the generosity of Agnes Gund, María Luisa Ferré Rangel, Bertita and Guillermo L. Martínez, Luisa Rangel de Ferré, an anonymous donor, and the Latin American and Caribbean Fund.

the moon, which in reality is not completely round but egg-shaped, is condensed into the semblance of a nipple in its form (signified). Sánchez's use of visual metaphors that condense two or more signi-fieds — egg, world, and breast, or moon and nipple — are good examples of the process of semiotic artificialization that Sarduy describes.

Sarduy adds that "the baroque presents itself, then, as a network of connections, of successive filigrees, whose graphic expression is not lineal, bidimensional, flat, but voluminous, spatial, and dynamic."[13] This seems to describe very well Sánchez's volup-tuous serial and three-dimensional paintings, where the conventional flat picture plane is radicalized by way of successive protrusions, elevations, and eruptions.

Erotic Topologies

In both her drawings and her sculptural paintings, Sánchez deliberately uses a coded vocabulary of erotic signifiers that operate through a process of semiotic artificialization, a reduced visual vocabulary, and the magnification of her subject matter. The latter is made through the isolation of parts of the female body and its sexual organs. Here, *lunares* (a term that, when translated from English, means "mole" or "beauty mark," but in Spanish also invokes the moon, as *luna* means "moon") becomes both celestial body and body mark.

In *Antígona* (fig. 6), curved contours delineated by color are both buttock and breast. In other works, one might catch the contour of a buttock, the semicircular shape of the vulva, or the roundness of the clitoris. These female bodily forms, further abstracted, magni-fied, and disembodied from the whole, become "erotic topologies."

In handwritten notes found at her studio in Santurce, Puerto Rico, Sánchez writes that "topos is place, but also a science that studies mathematical reasoning without consideration to any concrete meaning."[14] She adds, "the personal element and the emotion [are] the basis of every work."[15] Sánchez's "erotic topologies" are, then, personal and intimate expressions of her emotions and personal life, erotic spaces where meaning is abstracted.

Deviating from Minimalism

A homotextual and neo-baroque reading of Sánchez's work also implies a de facto deviation from art historical canons. Although Sán-chez's work has been often compared to Western art movements, especially minimalism, it broadly deviates from minimalist precepts. Writing about Sánchez's work for her exhibition *Estructuras en secuencia* (Structures in Sequence) at the Museo de la Universidad de Puerto Rico in 1970, Sarduy mentions the works of minimalists as a point of comparison, but quickly rejects any relationship between Sánchez and their work. He writes that "Zilia Sánchez's topologies barely participate in this code."[16] The elements that he mentions, which separate her work from that of John McCracken, Robert Morris, Sol LeWitt, and Donald Judd despite their formal affinities, are eroticism and tactility.

Eroticism is, in fact, a determining element in Sarduy's articulation of the neo-baroque. He describes it as "game, loss, waste, and pleasure, that is, eroticism as an activity that is always purely ludic, that is nothing more than a parody of the function of repro-duction, a transgression of the useful, of the 'natural' dialogue of bodies."[17] This playful erotic proliferation, which, according to Sarduy, is a parody of the function of reproduction, can be seen in Sán-chez's modular serial works such as the *Amazonas* and her polyptych *Troyanas* (Trojan Women; 1999), where the elevated forms of the breast and nipple are repeated and divorced from their reproductive function. In other works, such as *Juana de Arco* (Joan of Arc; cat. 51), these elevations caress each other, almost touching. In this diptych, perhaps one of Sánchez's most suggestive works, curves delineated by color reference the form of the vulva. The titles of these works, together with their visual signifiers, bring together female heroicism and eroticism, in what could be defined as an erotic painterly femi-nism that focuses on tactility and the proliferation of a magnified, unapologetic female sexuality.

The tactile, ludic eroticism, one that eschews sexual repro-duction to focus instead on the pleasures and rhythms of the female body, is found in the visual content of Sánchez's work, implicit in its forms, shapes, and contours, and in the intimate process of its making. Sánchez often describes her finished works as "bodies" and the fabric she stretches as "skin." She first builds a structure made of reclaimed wood or plastic, which she often finds on the streets of Santurce. These "constructions," as she calls them — sculptures in their own right — are the basis from which she makes and shapes the elevations and protrusions characteristic of her work. For the fabric, Sánchez has chosen a local type of linen known as *blanquín*, which is primarily used for upholstery. After dipping the *blanquín* in a glue-like mixture, Sánchez extends it over her constructions, stretching it over several days until it achieves the desired effect.

Sánchez frequently talks to her works and listens to what they have to say during this process of making. Sometimes they "behave well," she says, while at other times they do not. Curiously, the humid climate of the Caribbean plays a major role in their misconduct. The misbehaving works, which wrinkle and crease under Puerto Rico's humid weather conditions, might take longer to finish or might undergo what Sánchez has described as *la furia* or "the fury"—"tattooing" or writing on the surface of the work with black marker. Sánchez performs "the fury," in part, with her eyes closed, instinctively creating movements in her mind that she then proceeds to translate through her hand. She paints with her entire body, in a performative gesture that alludes to the privileged place the body occupies in her work — not only as a source but also as the site where painting occurs in its most intimate way.

Defying Definitions and Limits

Sánchez has recently referred to her paintings as bisexual,[18] further foregrounding the work's technical drag and liminal positionality: the constant oscillation that the work performs between painting and sculpture and between meaning and medium and its parallel upending of a heteronormative sexuality. However, her work has often suffered the imposition of a presumptive heterosexuality that,

together with schematic comparisons to Western art historical canons, runs the risk of reducing and collapsing the works' most radical operations.

As Bleys has noted, in what he defines as "art history's closet," art historians have often focused solely on the formal attributes of a work of art to the detriment of other readings, which include class, gender, and sexuality. He also adds that so-called erotic art "frequently remains fixed on female nudity, orgasmic pleasure and the consolidation of a straight male gaze,"[19] which avoids discussion of the social construction of gender.

For example, Argentinian art historian Marta Traba notes that Sánchez "looks for different planes of approximation between the work and the spectator [and] creates a constant rhythmic connotation to sexual subject matter, supported fundamentally on the counterpoint between erections and excavations."[20] In a similar way, Cuban American writer Dolores Prida describes Sánchez's work as "poetry spilled in female curves — man-woman."[21] It is helpful to remember that Spanish is a gendered language and that the binary classifications structure ways of thinking and approaching the world. Thus, these texts, although critical in their reception, in many ways reinforce binary categorizations and heteronormative readings of the work.

Whether it is deliberate or not, the obfuscation of Sánchez's work in addressing lesbian desire is made possible by the formal language of abstraction and the appropriation of minimalism's seriality. Here, a gendered and art historical myth[22] is created that is heteronormative and minimalist and, at its base, ideological: capitalist, depoliticized, and depersonalized.

The Queer Body in Exile

Curiously enough, Sarduy never addressed Sánchez's work himself in a homotextual way, opting instead to focus on an ambiguous reading, even though his literary and theoretical work was clearly queer. What is interesting is that Sánchez's artistic strategies seem to include both subscription and subversion of art historical trends in a deliberate artificialization of signifieds. For both Sarduy and Sánchez, this codification may have something to do with the Cuban Revolution and the queer body in exile. Forced to flee from its place of origin, from its *topos*, the body is no longer moored to one place or space. Displaced, it forever exists in between.

Perhaps some answers can also be found in the project *encuentrismo — ofrenda o retorno* (The Encounter — Offering or Return), from the series *Soy Isla: Compréndelo y retírate* (I Am an Island: Understand and Retreat; cat. 57a–b), consisting of the performance, video, and remaining painting. In arguably Sánchez's only performance documented on video, she proceeds to throw one of her paintings into the Atlantic Ocean on the north shore of Puerto Rico. Rhythmically, the tide keeps bringing back the painting, which she continues to push into the ocean. It is, metaphorically, the body that refuses to stay in one place, remaining in the constant back-and-forth of the tide. It is also a metaphor for Sánchez's work, which refuses to be one thing or the other.

Like Sarduy, who was exiled from himself, an *aislado*, Sánchez also identifies with an island. "Soy isla," she asserts, in a forceful statement of self-determination against foreign impositions of identity. After all, her work also exists like an island: resistant and independent of art historical categorizations, fluid and performative, and defiant to a heteronormative gaze.

Carla Acevedo-Yates is associate curator at the Eli and Edythe Broad Art Museum at Michigan State University. This article was supported by the Creative Capital | Andy Warhol Foundation Arts Writers Grant Program.

NOTES

1. Important precedents for Severo Sarduy's work are José Lezama Lima's *Paradiso* (1966) and José Donoso's *El lugar sin límites* (1966). Sarduy repeatedly mentions Lezama Lima and Donoso's influence on his work in his essay *El barroco y el neobarroco* (1972).

2. *Ktazob* in Arabic means "penis slasher." For a Lacanian psychoanalytic analysis of *Cobra*, see Ruben Gallo, "Sarduy avec Lacan: The Portrayal of French Psychoanalysis in *Cobra* and *La simulación*," *Revista Hispana Moderna* 60, no. 1 (2007).

3. Rudi C. Bleys, *Images of Ambiente: Homotextuality and Latin American Art, 1810–Today* (New York: Continuum, 2000), 11.

4. Ibid., 81.

5. Severo Sarduy, "Tribuna | Exilado de si mismo," *El país*, April 3, 1992, http://elpais.com/diario/1992/04/04/opinion/702338411_850215.html. Translated by the author.

6. Zilia Sánchez, interview with the author, June 9, 2016, San Juan.

7. François Wahl was Sarduy's longtime partner and the editor of many of Jacques Lacan's texts, notably his *Écrits*.

8. In queer theory, the heteronormative gaze not only sexualizes women but also presumes a heterosexual male viewer. In turn, heteronormativity presumes heterosexuality as the normal and "natural" sexual orientation. For more on the subject of imposed heterosexuality as it relates to women and lesbian experience specifically, see Adrienne Rich, "Compulsory Heterosexuality and Lesbian Existence," in *Feminism and Sexuality*, ed. Stevi Jackson and Sue Scott (New York: Columbia University Press, 1996).

9. Zilia Sánchez, interview by Stefan Kalmár and Richard Birkett, March 2013, on YouTube video posted November 7, 2013, https://www.youtube.com/watch?v=9LRddY6f9Kc.

10. Severo Sarduy, *El barroco y el neobarroco* (Buenos Aires: El Cuenco de Plata, 2011), 11. Translated by author.

11. Stephen Spector, "Zilia Sánchez at Sarduy," *Arts Magazine* 44 (Summer 1970): n.p.

12. Piera Aulagnier, *The Violence of Interpretation: From Pictogram to Statement*, trans. Alan Sheridan (Philadelphia: Brunner/Routledge, 2001), 56.

13. Sarduy, *El barroco*, 20.

14. Zilia Sánchez, handwritten notes, Santurce, PR. Translated by the author.

15. Ibid.

16. Severo Sarduy, "Las *topologías eróticas* de Zilia Sánchez," *Estructuras en secuencia* (San Juan: Museo de la Universidad de Puerto Rico, 1970).

17. Sarduy, *El barroco*, 33.

18. Zilia Sánchez, interview by the author, February 12, 2016, San Juan.

19. Bleys, *Images of Ambiente*, 4.

20. Marta Traba, "El erotismo y la comunicación," *Zona. Carga y descarga* 1, no. 2 (November–December 1972): 11.

21. Dolores Prida, "El erotismo espacial en la pintura de Zilia Sánchez," *La nueva sangre* 3, no. 9 (October 1970): 9–10.

22. For Roland Barthes, myth is a process of signification that is ideological at its basis. For more on this, see Barthes, *Mythologies*, trans. Richard Howard (New York: Hill and Wang, 2012).

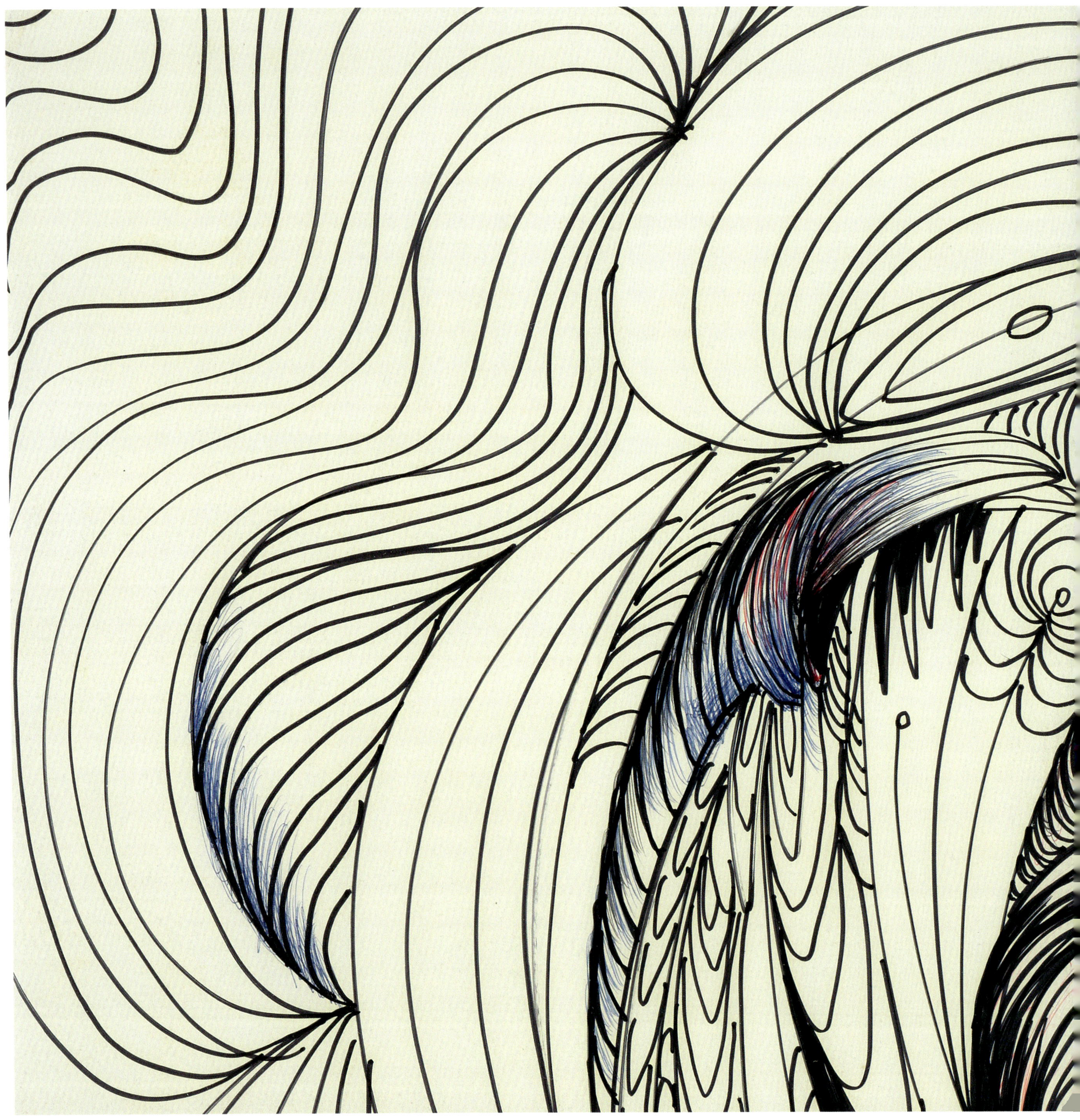

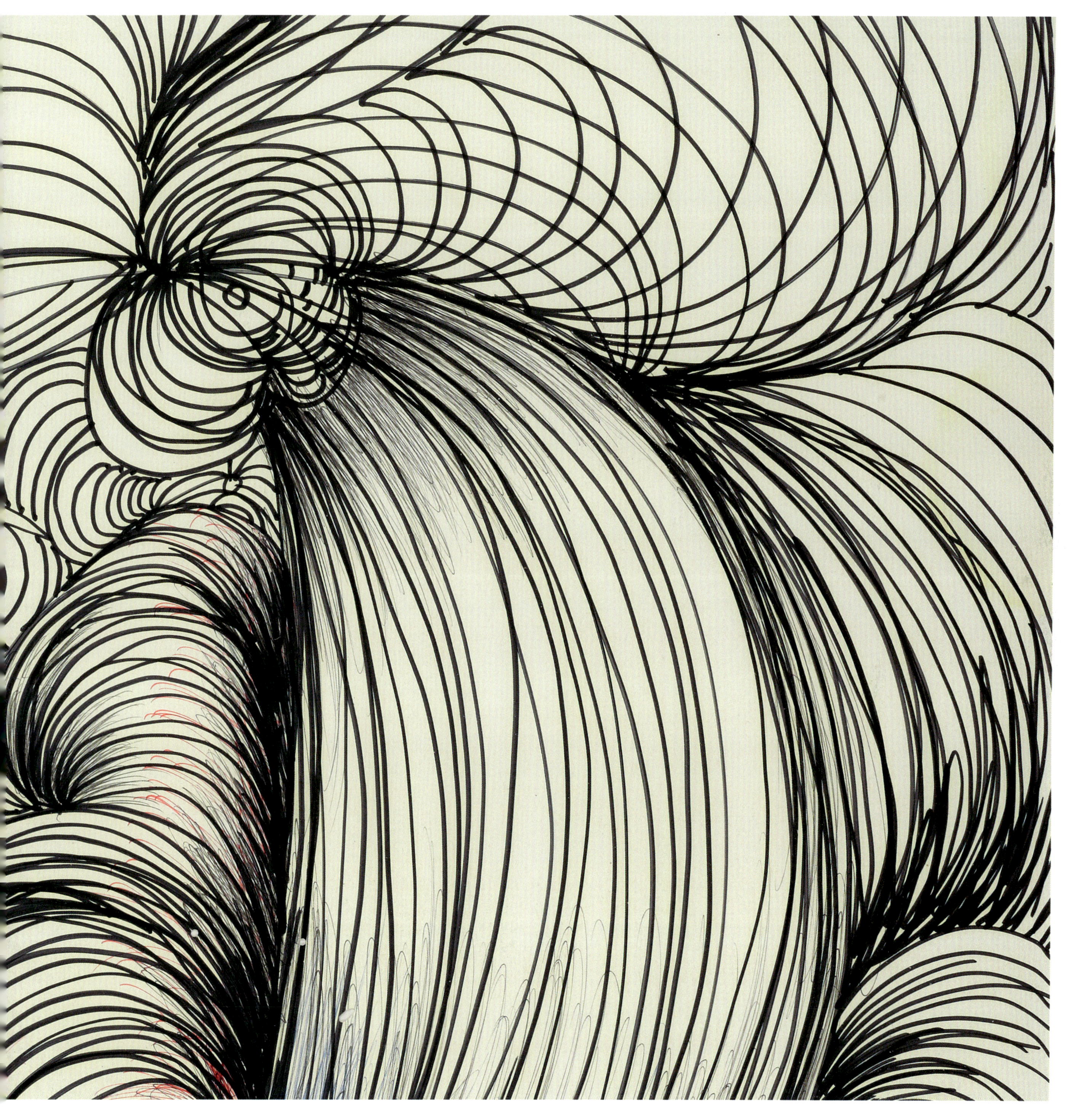

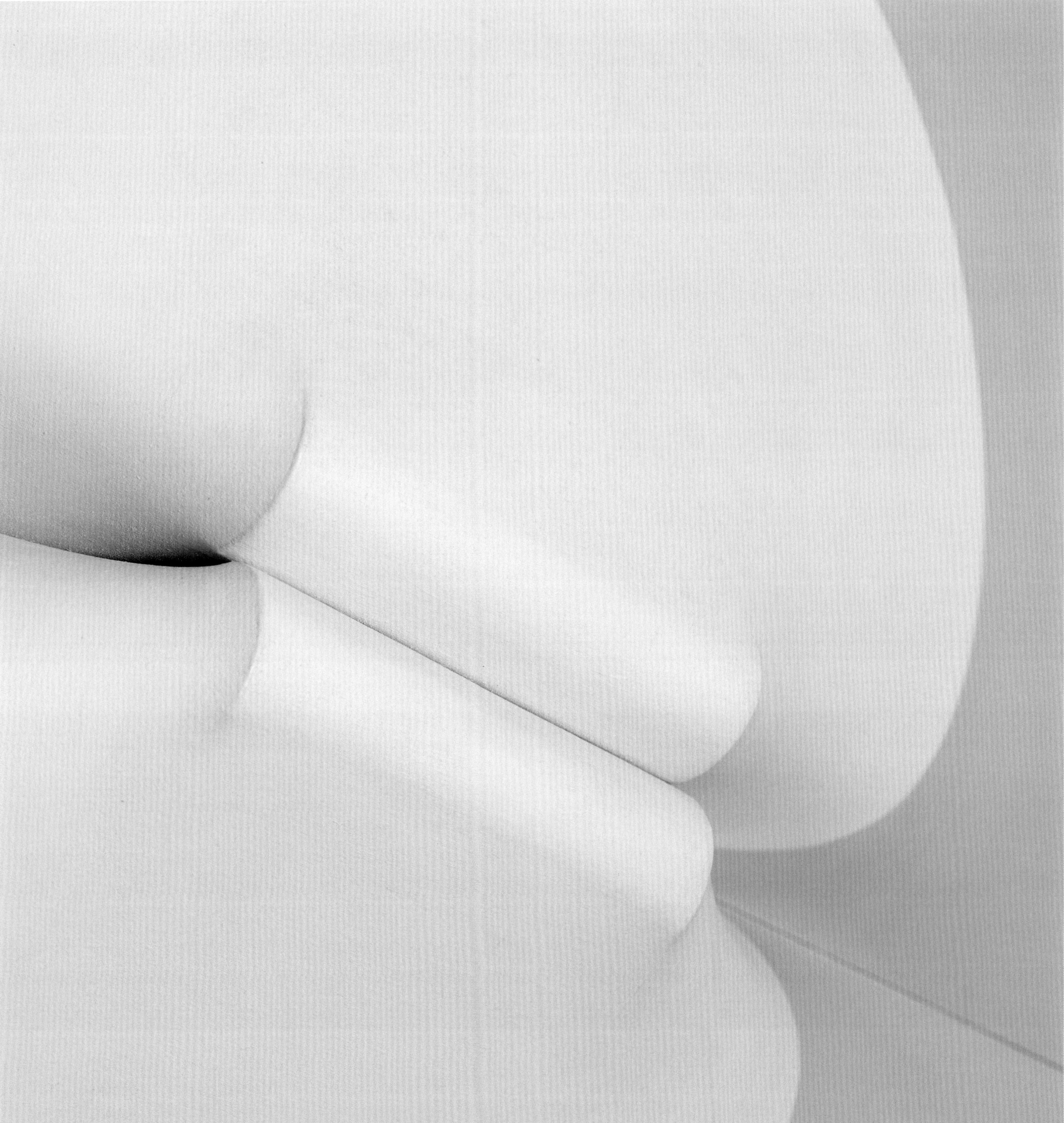

Personal Encounter: Zilia Sánchez in 1960s New York

MERCEDES CORTÁZAR

To look upon any great painting or sculpture requires active seeing, a penetrating stare that plunges us into the work's visual world and engages our total awareness in its essence. For some, this ability to perceive in a holistic way may be innate; others develop it. I owe my enjoyment of art to conversations with artists I have known over the years.[1] Of all these exceptional artists, Zilia Sánchez was the most important to me, because she is not only a great painter but also a great teacher. Above all, she understood poetry deeply and could communicate with me in the language of my own art.

My first encounter with Zilia took place in early 1959 at a small exhibition of Cuba's greatest living painters at the Lyceum in Havana. The show had been organized by the Woman's Club of Havana to present one of these artists with a monetary prize. Zilia was already a well-known artist with numerous solo and group exhibitions. Before this show, my attention had been engaged elsewhere, and I had never heard of her or any other Cuban painter.

No doubt I made a spectacle of myself as I plodded around the galleries looking like an early twentieth-century anarchist in a short black skirt, red shirt, glasses, and French bun. I scrutinized all these enigmatic paintings once, but then returned to the entrance and fixated on a spectacular painted frieze installed facing the door. This freestanding long, narrow, waist-level piece set on small wooden crosses resembled no other painting in the show. On the canvas's white ground, blue geometric shapes randomly underlay an irregular hatchwork of fine black lines — a long abstract "machine of dreams." To get the full effect, I had to back off to the sides.

The piece was by Zilia, whom I finally met through the Cuban poet Isel Rivero when I immigrated to New York in 1961. At the time, Isel was living with Zilia and RosaMaría García Sarduy. When José Mario Rodríguez, the publisher of Ediciones El Puente, heard I was leaving Cuba permanently, he asked me to take Isel copies of her epic poem *La marcha de los hurones* (The Parade of the Lemmings), which had just come out.

The basement apartment on West Forty-Sixth Street where Zilia lived had become a combination meeting place and youth hostel for the New York Cuban artistic community, including myself, RosaMaría, Isel, and many others. The first thing I said when I met Zilia was how extraordinary her painting at the Lyceum was. Famously suspicious of flatterers, she challenged me to describe the painting in detail, which, fortunately, I was able to do. Then she asked to read my poems. I showed her some writing in a notebook. A month or so later, the third book published by Ediciones El Puente, my *El largo canto*, arrived by mail directly from Cuba, addressed to me in care of Zilia.

Zilia said things to me about poetry that I had never read or heard. Her observations were original and deep and helped me to better understand my poems. We spoke just as much about her paintings. I would articulate the feelings and thoughts they produced in me, and she let me imagine that my comments helped to clarify her thinking.

This "clarification" might actually have inspired her assertiveness, because when I met Zilia, she was changing her approach, shifting to the Informel style. I was at first puzzled and disturbed by this more tactile painting, using textured matter affixed to the canvas (cat. 14), and wondered why she would abandon her unique dream machines. But her explanations let me see this shift as natural for a living artist. For example, Pablo Picasso, her favorite artist, had radically changed styles over the years. In no way did Zilia imitate Picasso, but like him, she viewed evolutions in style—"periods"—as natural to a fully committed creative personality.

Her inspiration had come from her earlier trips to Spain, where the anti-Franco group Dau al Set was active in Barcelona.[2] She was particularly drawn to the work of Antoni Tàpies, whose use of matter was an explosive protest against the continued repression in Spain that prevailed as a tragic result of the Spanish Civil War. Zilia's emotional connection with Dau al Set was entirely understandable, given that from a young age she had lived under regimes in Cuba that—except for a golden period during the Cuban Republic[3]—were in many ways as oppressive as Franco's. Also, the increasingly hot Cold War may have fed those paintings that I would later describe in a review of her show in Puerto Rico as "proclaiming a world of strange violences, savage rebellions" in which "the texture of the work acquires an absolute value and manages to imbue objects with sensory qualities they had not previously possessed."[4] These "violences" and "savage rebellions" were made even more powerful by their erotic undertones.

Zilia's process of composition, at the time, involved sticking a variety of textured materials on a large canvas using resins and glues. The palette comprised a somber array of black, brown, and sometimes blue. Her studio was a small room at the front of the apartment, where unsold canvases reclined against the wall. Working mostly at night under artificial light (incandescent bulbs, not deathly fluorescent lights), she sat on the floor and moved around the canvas. She "painted" with the gestures of a church organist operating keys and stops, grabbing the materials she had sorted out and put in strategically placed brown paper bags. She scooted and crawled, reaching here and there to deposit the stuff that she had carefully collected for inclusion in the piece.

Her aesthetic manipulation of matter gave her a break from her daytime job as a restorer of Old Master paintings, antique furniture, and even vintage lamps. Preserving valuable decorative items imbued her own assemblages with a precise and durable craftsmanship that lifted her work from the ironic jokiness of ephemeral aleatoric collage into the realm of masterpieces. These new works were a long way from the painting that had captivated me at the entrance to the Havana Lyceum show.

At one point, rather than have me staring at her as she worked, Zilia sat me down at a table with pencil, colored pencils, and paper. Her purpose was not to make me ashamed of my poor artistic skills but to give me a sense of delight in the creation of something visual. Then she would point to something she found interesting on my page. A natural teacher, she always found in my drawings something to praise.

To avoid wasting more of Zilia's precious studio time in this futile art-education practicum, I launched a campaign to visit museums. Here we were, near rich repositories of art all over New York. The trouble was that at that time Zilia loathed museums and avoided them, having determined that they contained more "bad" art than "good." "The moment you see a bad painting and decide it is bad, the inner destructive work has already been done," Zilia told me. I offered to lead her by the hand with her eyes closed only to good paintings and tell her when to open her eyes, and she acceded to this Dantesque travesty. I mainly wanted to look at Cézanne, Van Gogh, and the Impressionists. On my signal of a hand squeeze, she would open her eyes. If the work was "good," she would scrutinize it at length, looking up and down and around at all its details, saying nothing. If I chose badly, she put on a face and rolled her eyes. At the time, I thought this avoidance of "dreck" was the eccentricity of a genius, but now, when I am so open to art, I too suffer the inner disintegration caused by bad art.

A painter formed in the European tradition of art, Zilia found the New York art world pathetic and narrow-minded. Working against the mainstream — Abstract Expressionism — she continued to develop and refine a personal style that expressed her own ideas, feelings, and artistic vision. She showed photos of her work and catalogues from her previous exhibitions in Havana, Paris, Madrid, São Paulo, and Caracas to smug art gatekeepers, only to receive condescending critiques. Eventually her partner found the solution: open a showroom of her own. In 1969 a solo presentation of Zilia's work inaugurated a new space at 207 East Eighty-Fifth Street.

New York, supposedly the most open city in the United States, presented unspoken difficulties that had nothing to do with art, which Zilia and the rest of us confronted on a daily basis. Our foremost difficulty was the ghetto aspect of New York. It was a cliché that every wave of immigrants to New York had suffered rejection. Cubans in New York became part of the Spanish speakers — the block called "Latins," who, although once disdainful of each other, were now the target of New York's inextinguishable xenophobia. One of my painter friends, Waldo Díaz-Balart, Fidel Castro's ex-brother-in-law and a member of Andy Warhol's Factory, endured ten years of this xenophobia until, in 1970, he left New York for Madrid in disgust.

Our second major difficulty was the politics of the Cuban Revolution. Most of the comparatively few Cubans who chose to live in New York in the early 1960s were attracted by the city's intellectual and artistic reputation, by its theaters, music, universities, libraries, museums. Many New York intellectuals and artists sympathized with the Castro revolution and thought we were "lackeys of imperialism" and CIA moles, which we who had immigrated to New York were emphatically not.

Then there was the factor of styles of sexuality among artists. Cuba had always been hell for anyone who was queer. Even José Martí, Cuba's most famous poet and revolutionary, had been outspokenly homophobic, and Castro's revolution made homophobic persecution and aversion therapy part of the country's "utopian transformation." Fidel's dictum "Everything within the Revolution, nothing outside it"[5] was unmasked over time as a terrifying sham that hid electroshock treatment, UMAP forced-labor camps, and other appalling forms of punishment, but that had already been known to the LGBTQ Cuban emigrés who had flocked to New York in the 1960s and 1970s.[6] The world of art and literature in the New York of the 1960s was not yet the mecca for LGBTQ people it would become, but sexual preferences could be somewhat open if one was more or less discreet.

Setting aside all those obstacles, not just the New York of the 1960s but the art world everywhere had historically been supercilious about female artists and dismissive of the quality of their work. New York's art world in the 1960s functioned by game theory: money spent on art directly reflected a zero-sum battle of the sexes. Stories abounded of the excuses gallery owners gave for rejecting art by women, the most famous being the case of Cuban-born painter Carmen Herrera.[7] In one version of her rejection story, a female gallery owner liked Herrera's entire stock of paintings but refused to hang them for fear that her male artists would leave.

This blatant exclusion might have turned Zilia into a political or doctrinaire feminist. In fact, she was born with a feminist attitude toward art and life. She was proud of being female (she had the gestures and flirtatiousness of a brunette Marilyn Monroe), and had no psychological complexes about her sexuality. She wanted her paintings to express *life*, with movement that would explode toward the viewer and reveal the human condition as life's basic oneiric, erotic essence. The feminine body was for Zilia a metaphor for the source of us all. She conceived this not as a crude realistic image of the "obscene" (= "not-seen"), such as Gustave Courbet's *L'origine du monde* (The Origin of the World; 1866), but as a symbolic, almost metaphysical message. For Zilia, sex was not only a source of carnal pleasure but also the basic definition of what is really vital and strong, as well as beautiful and spiritual, in women.

Living in New York under the influence of Zilia, I felt that we needed a voice, and in 1962 I founded a magazine with a group of Cuban poets. Zilia's cover gave the magazine its name, *Protesta* (fig. 1) — and Zilia's drawing of a despondent person of ambiguous gender, placed on the last page, expressed the sadness we all felt in exile. This — the first poetry magazine of the postrevolutionary Cuban exile community — was financed by Jack Micheline, a poet who introduced himself to me at Le Figaro Café, a coffee house in Greenwich Village where I sometimes would write and compose poems.[8] The magazine was in Spanish, with English translations; Micheline's two long "Americana" poems, about sports and war, filled the centerfold. Taken as a whole, the magazine symbolized our unity — our poems

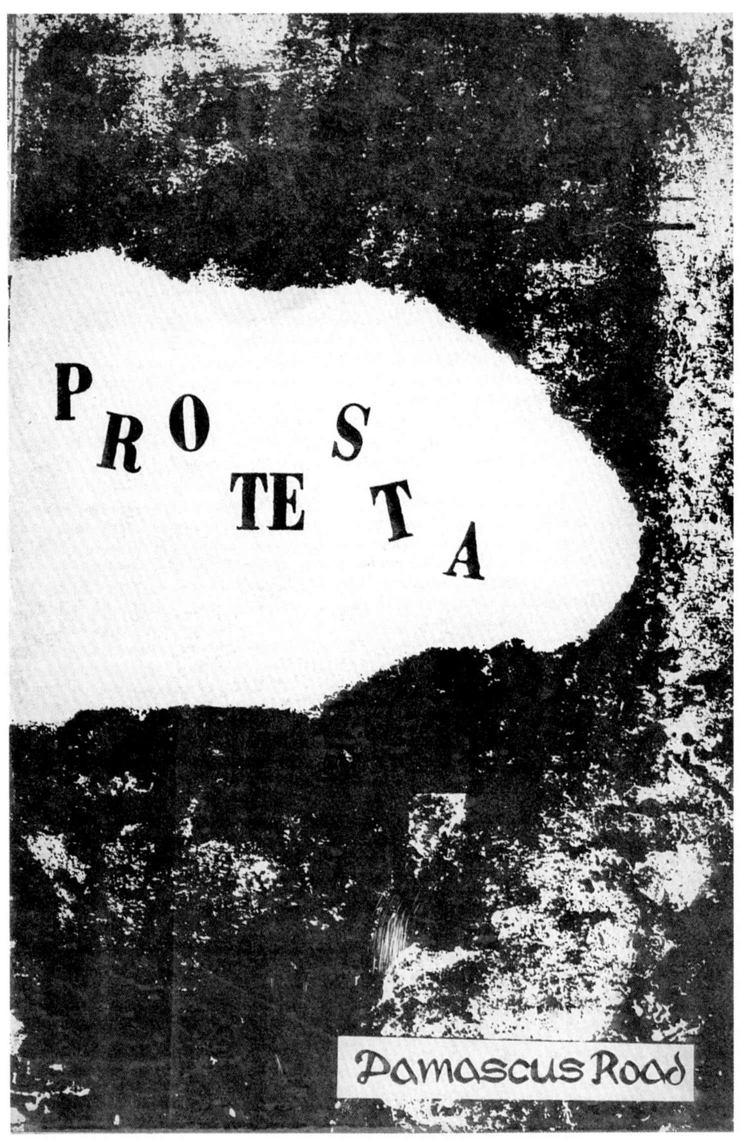

1 Zilia Sánchez, front cover of *Protesta* 1, no. 1 (1962).

and translations were our protest against the silence imposed on us in Cuba and in the United States.

My next project with Zilia came some years later, when she created the cover and designed the interior of my new book, *2 poèmes de Mercedes Cortázar* (fig. 2), published in Spanish with the French translation on facing pages. My job and my life fell apart in this period, and I traveled to Puerto Rico for Christmas. After a few days on the island I wanted to live there every day, speaking Spanish and gazing at the glorious blues and greens of the sea. I decided to stay.

For two and a half years I scraped a living in Puerto Rico as a journalist, writing for two newspapers. I met many interesting people, telephoning Zilia frequently to describe the wonders of life in San Juan. The painter Francisco Rodón, whom Zilia suggested I look up, introduced me to the cousins Rosario Ferré Ramírez de Arellano and Olga Nolla Ramírez de Arellano, well-connected heiresses. Both women were talking about leaving their husbands to take up "the literary life," and Rodón, a good friend, suggested they invite me to lunch to find out what they were getting into. I was appalled by their plan and told them, down to the grimmest detail, that writing was hell. Their financial position might or might not be helpful, I said, but it was crucial for them to get advanced degrees so they could at least become professors if writing didn't work out. Instead of being disheartened by my dour advice about the literary life, Rosario and Olga eventually took the first steps toward becoming muses of Puerto Rico's cultural revolution. Within a decade, they had become recognized as pioneers of radical Puerto Rican literature, feminism, and culture (fig. 3).

I returned to New York in 1967 and settled into a new job. My plan, I told Zilia, was to start another literary magazine with some Cuban and Puerto Rican poet friends. Called *La nueva sangre* (The New Blood), it would be paid for by subscriptions and out of our own pockets.

Meanwhile, Zilia had again changed her style and renewed her search for erotically charged forms and shapes. She told us to

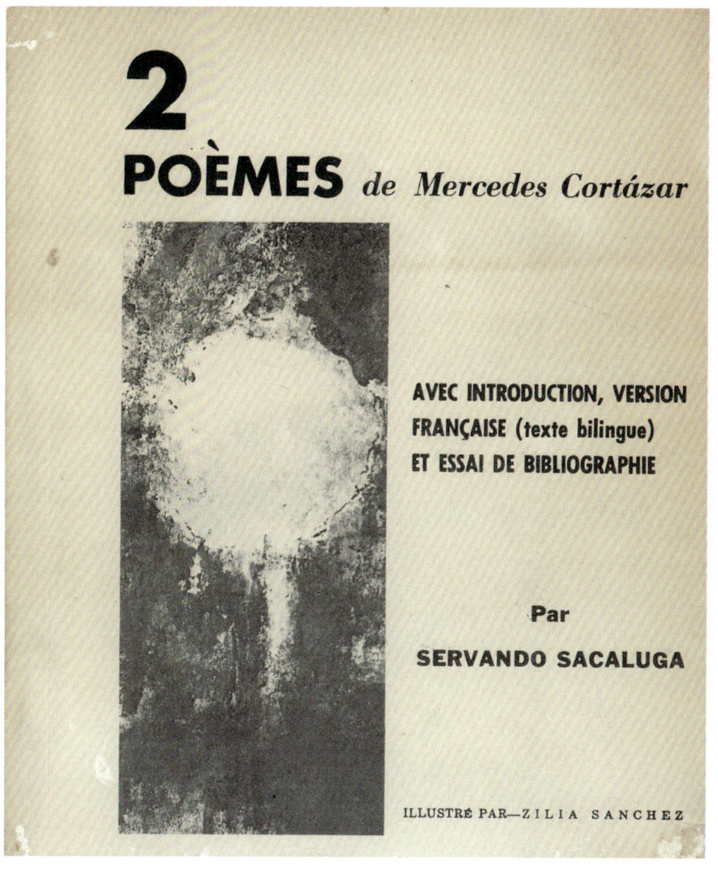

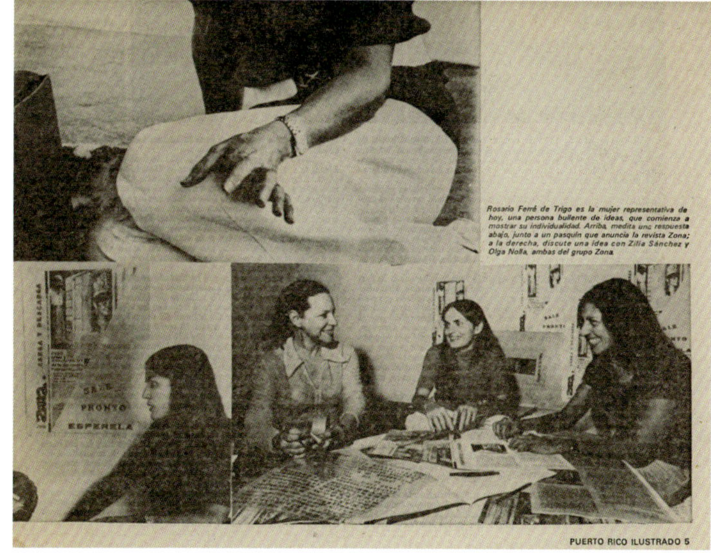

2 Cover, *2 poèmes de Mercedes Cortázar* (New York: Osmar Press, 1965).

3 Sánchez, Ferré, and Nolla, in *Puerto Rico ilustrado*, 1972.

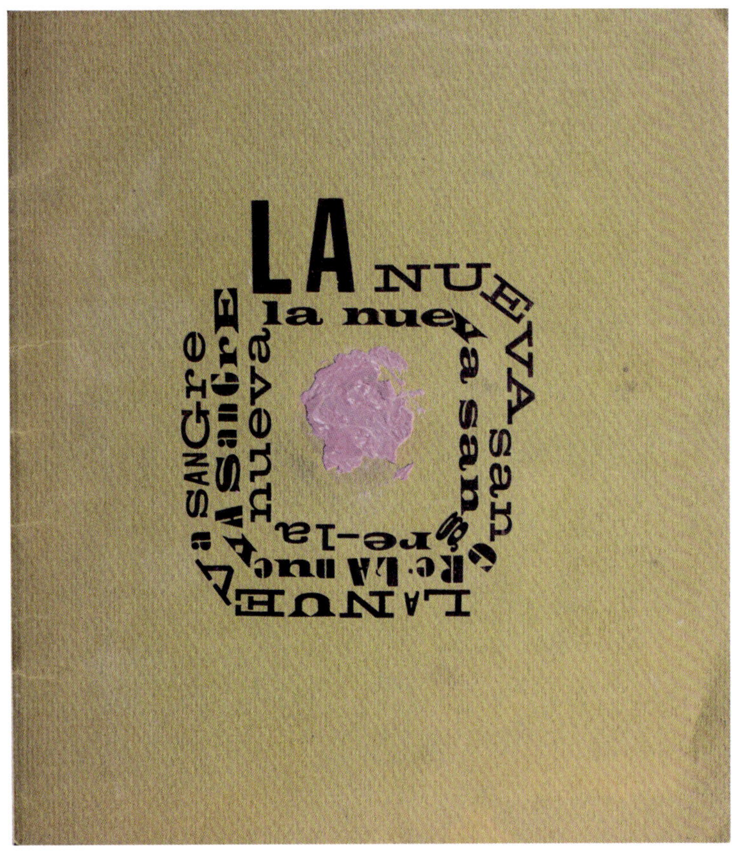

publish several issues and eventually agreed to design and illustrate the new magazine. I particularly remember one issue of *La nueva sangre*—volume 2, number 8, Fall 1969 (fig. 4). Zilia had designed a cover made of dark-brown construction paper with the magazine's name repeated in a pattern of diminishing squares and smaller type that framed a large blob of violet sealing wax at its center. At the last minute, I found myself melting and dripping sealing wax on each and every cover, exactly according to Zilia's specifications. She had finally found a use for my artistic skills.

My job as editor kept me busy corresponding with writers in the United States, Latin America, Spain, and France, soliciting contributions, and writing theater reviews—often scathing ones. I was the only one of us with theater training, having studied acting at Havana's Teatro Estudio and playwriting at Teatro Nacional de Cuba, and I desperately wanted Cuban theatrical work in New York to be astoundingly good. One play I looked forward to reviewing was Virgilio Piñera's now iconic *Dos viejos pánicos* (1968), in which an elderly couple freak out abusively at each other, in a black comic manner that has caused many critics to compare the play to Edward Albee's *Who's Afraid of Virginia Woolf?* (1962). Zilia's set design, I said enigmatically in my review, was "adequate to the task": it created an intense sensation of claustrophobia for this existential play that confronted the dishonesty of its two protagonists with the intrusiveness of the social system surrounding them. I was a great admirer of Piñera, but the acting and stage direction of this New York production of his most famous play left much to be desired.[9]

The work we published in *La nueva sangre* came from the United States, Latin America, Europe, Cuba, and Puerto Rico. The editorial board was made up of artists, poets, and writers, all Cuban and Puerto Rican friends who lived in New York. Unfortunately, they all eventually turned out to have all sorts of agendas other than publishing art and literature. Both Zilia and I drifted away from *La nueva sangre* out of a desire to develop in an original, authentic way, not to be a mouthpiece for an ideology or a circumstantial ethnicity.[10]

4 Zilia Sánchez, cover, *La nueva sangre 2,* no. 8 (Fall 1969).

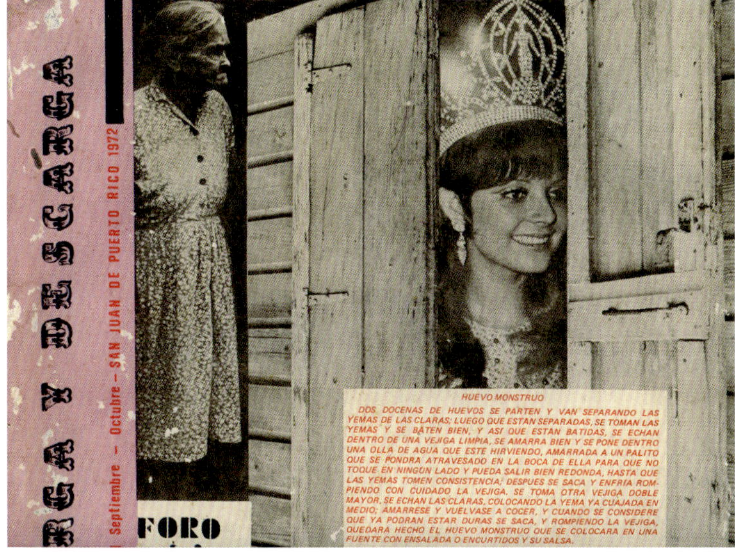

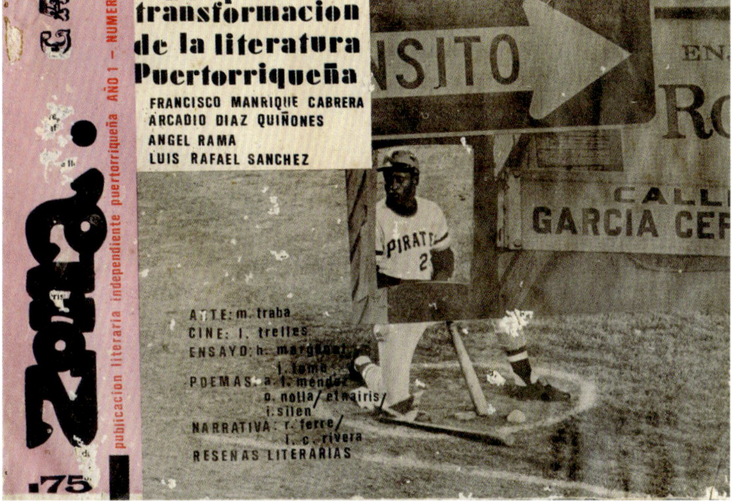

5 Zilia Sánchez, cover, *Zona. Carga y descarga* 1, no. 1 (September–October 1972).

designed by Zilia, shaping the magazine's look for its remaining run (fig. 5). Filled with lively work by students and professional writers who were feminist, antihomophobic, and pro–Puerto Rican independence, the magazine stood for a new, vital Puerto Rico, with Zilia Sánchez as its newest and most enthusiastic citizen.

From the moment Zilia moved to Puerto Rico, her paintings jumped from the canvas into the freedom of space. Although she had created sculptures with success, sculpture for her seemed too static and burdened by gravity by comparison with the lightness of being she could bring to her canvases. Although she was never self-conscious about audiences watching her paint (or restore paintings, most famously when, one day in New York, Greta Garbo stood watching her as she worked in the restorer's show window on East Fifty-Second Street), Zilia was never inclined to take the path of performance artists who transform painting into something staged in a museum. In the new, free trajectory that emerged from living in Puerto Rico, she pushed the basic two dimensions of the canvas toward viewers and their subconscious minds. She has continued to develop and perfect this style into masterpieces that, just as her work affected me so long ago at the Lyceum show in Havana, now arrest — no, *rivet* — viewers' attention when they are displayed on the walls of museums. In people's homes, they inspire years of contemplation and constant inner transformation.

Zilia today is not searching; like her role model, Picasso, she is continuing to discover. Her discoveries produce an inclusive expression of art and of being human, and her paintings of the past sixty-plus years are the map of this extraordinary voyage of discovery. Her palette acts like an ancient Greek chorus whose verses cheer on the heroic aspirations of the shapes protruding from the canvas. The enormous dimensions of some of her paintings seem to remind us that a murmur coming from our core is as important as jewels spewing from the depths of the Earth in a volcanic eruption.

In her *Topologías eróticas* (Erotic Topologies; fig. 6), as she calls them, Zilia eschews the garish superficiality of the spectrum

Terminally fed up with New York's literal and figurative cold, Zilia moved to Puerto Rico sometime between 1971 and 1972. By then the cousins Rosario Ferré and Olga Nolla had advanced their ambitious plans of making Puerto Rico a force in Latin American literature.[11] In 1972 they started *Zona. Carga y descarga* (Zone. Charge and Discharge [or Load and Unload]),[12] supported by well-respected writers such as Mario Vargas Llosa and Severo Sarduy. Zilia helped the cousins envision and design the magazine, which published nine issues over the three years of existence. The first four issues were

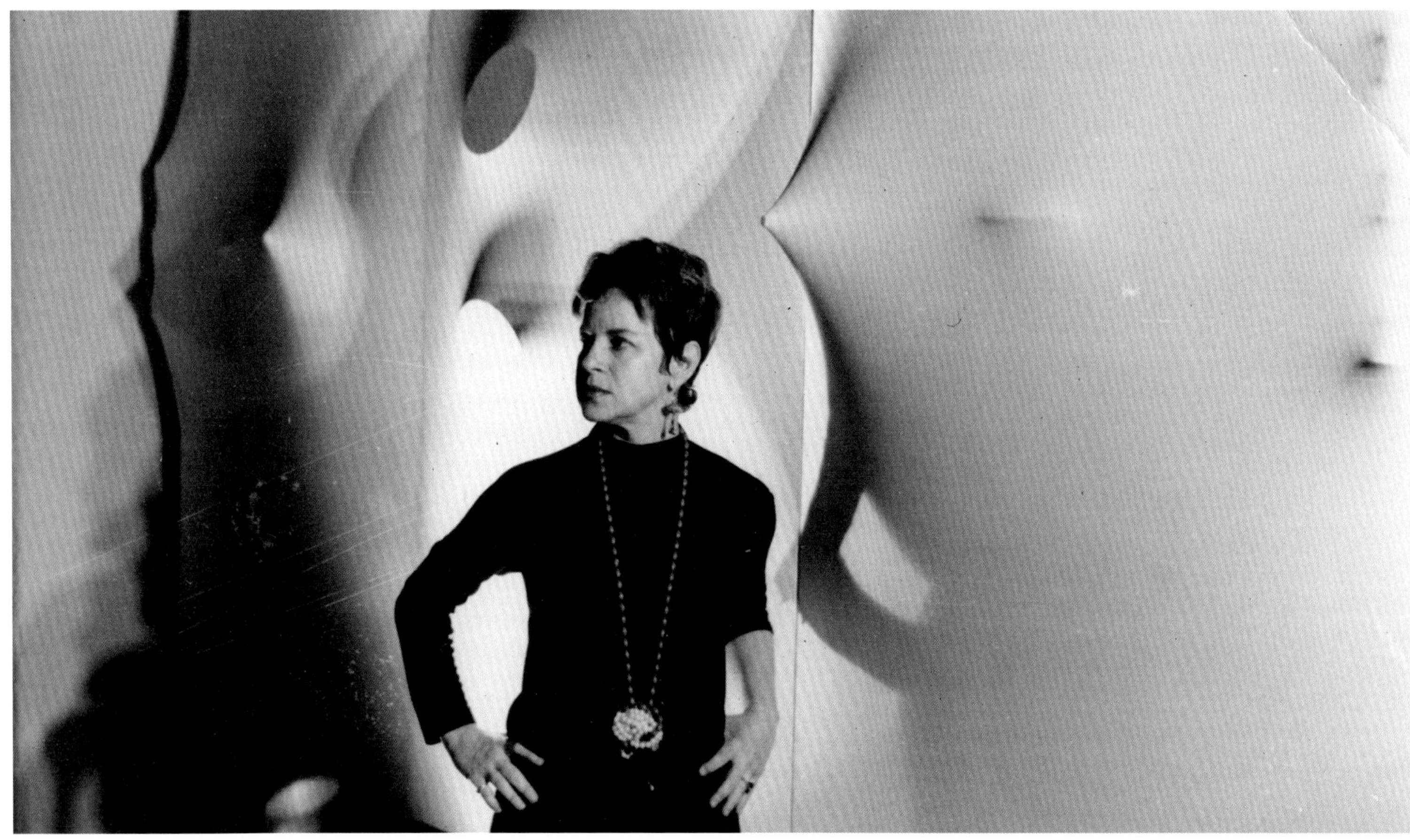

from reds to violets and favors the absence of color in black, the combination of all colors in white, earthy browns, natural clay tones of ocher (even soft and muted colors), dark or pale grays, delicate peaches, greens and pink skin tones, and, of course, tender blues — the colors of sea and sky — all of which whisper profound truths of the inner self. Most of the breast forms in her paintings have small "nipples"; at times they suggest truncation ("cut nipples"), not the product of sexual sadism but an artist's presentation of aggression elided. The forms of vulva and clitoris are suggestive everywhere, erotic, not pornographic. Semblances of body and organs in Zilia's paintings become daring metaphors of essential paths, signposts for women as artists and fulfilled beings, but also welcoming humankind as a whole.

Mercedes Cortázar is a Cuban poet, short story writer, novelist, and critic, presently working on the translation into English of her latest poetry book published in Spanish, Orbes.

6 Sánchez in front of one of her *Topología erótica* paintings, c. 1970.

NOTES

1. When I was in my late teens, after the Lyceum exhibit at which I saw Zilia's paintings for the first time, the famous painter Víctor Manuel taught me how to build and size a canvas, as well as mix colors. Later I befriended a number of painters in Havana: Cundo Bermúdez, José Mijares, Fayad Jamís, and Jorge Camacho. In New York, I connected with the Cuban artists Waldo Díaz-Balart, Inverna Lockpez, and José Ángel Rosabal Fajardo, and, in the late 1960s, with the Colombian Fernando Botero. In Puerto Rico during the 1960s and 1970s, the portrait artist Francisco Rodón personally expanded my understanding of art, while much later in Miami, Ramón Alejandro brought a new dimension to my understanding of figurative painting.

—

2. Dau al Set (Seven-Sided Dice) was a movement of Catalan artists, philosophers, and poets. The group's manifesto pledged them to strive beyond the limitations of conventions. The movement, which lasted from 1948 to 1953, was inspired by Dada, Surrealism, and the work of Joan Miró. Tàpies became its most famous exponent.

—

3. This period began with the adoption of the Cuban constitution in 1940 and lasted until Fulgencio Batista's coup d'état in March 1952.

—

4. My review of Zilia's show in *El mundo* is referenced at length by Alberto Alonso in "Alucinante exactitud del mundo de hoy en obras de Z. Sánchez," La Era Actual, *El diario–La prensa* (San Juan), May 20, 1966, 34. The original of my article is not preserved.

5. Fidel Castro, "Speech to Intellectuals," June 30, 1961. This speech may be consulted at Castro Speech Database, Latin American Network Information Center (lanic.utexas.edu), preferably with the Spanish text in hand (cuba.cu/gobierno /discursos/1961/esp/f300661e.html).

—

6. In 1980, the Cuban government advertised the Mariel boatlift as ridding the island of its remaining homosexuals and other criminals. One of the *marielitos* was my friend René Ariza, who stayed in Miami briefly before moving to San Francisco—long enough to tell me that an innocuous postcard I'd sent him and his poem I published in *Protesta* were part of the evidence that sent him to the UMAP. Most *marielitos* did not go to New York—it had become too expensive for those who did not aspire to lucrative professions—but among these new exiles who did was the influential poet and novelist Reinaldo García Ramos (b. 1944), who became a translator at the United Nations.

—

7. Herrera's retrospective, long overdue, was recently presented at the Whitney Museum in New York.

—

8. Micheline told me he wanted us (the Cubans in New York) to have a chance. Only later did I discover that he was a well-known poet, a friend of Jack Kerouac, and famous for helping people who were down and out.

—

9. Piñera was especially important to my early career (and to that of many other young writers). For one thing, he had persuaded Guillermo Cabrera Infante to publish my first short story, "Viaje a Camagüey," in *Lunes*, the highly influential cultural magazine of the newspaper *Revolución* (both were later replaced by the Cuban government organ *Granma*).

10. For me, the end of *La nueva sangre* came in 1971, when I realized that Cuban writers in New York were in limbo where everything they did was swallowed by silence. We were "outside History." The phrase "outside history" is G. F. W. Hegel's; see Hegel, *Introduction to the Philosophy of History*, trans. S. J. Quentin Lauer, marxists.org. I capitalized the word *History* to reflect its special meaning and foregrounding in the thinking of Fidel Castro, emphatically clear in the closing section of his "Speech to Intellectuals."

—

11. Rosario Ferré and Olga Nolla had not only divorced their husbands and simplified their names but also become *independentistas*, breaking politically with their families, which had long been associated with the cause of Puerto Rican statehood.

—

12. As Rosario's son Benigno Trigo, chair of the Spanish and Portuguese Department at Vanderbilt University, states unequivocally, the title of the magazine is *Zona. Carga y descarga*, with no *de* linking the title and subtitle. Trigo, "*Zona. Carga y descarga*: Minor Literature in a Penal Colony," *MLN* 124, no. 2 (March 2009): 481–508. The story behind the title is another Zilia anecdote. Zilia told me that Rosario insisted that the title be *Zona* (as in "cool" or "in the zone"), while Olga wanted the title to be *Carga y descarga* (as in "charge your batteries" or "get angry" versus "vent your spleen" or "tell it like it is"). Zilia, ever the Solomonic guru, suggested combining both in the magazine's title: hence *Zona. Carga y descarga*.

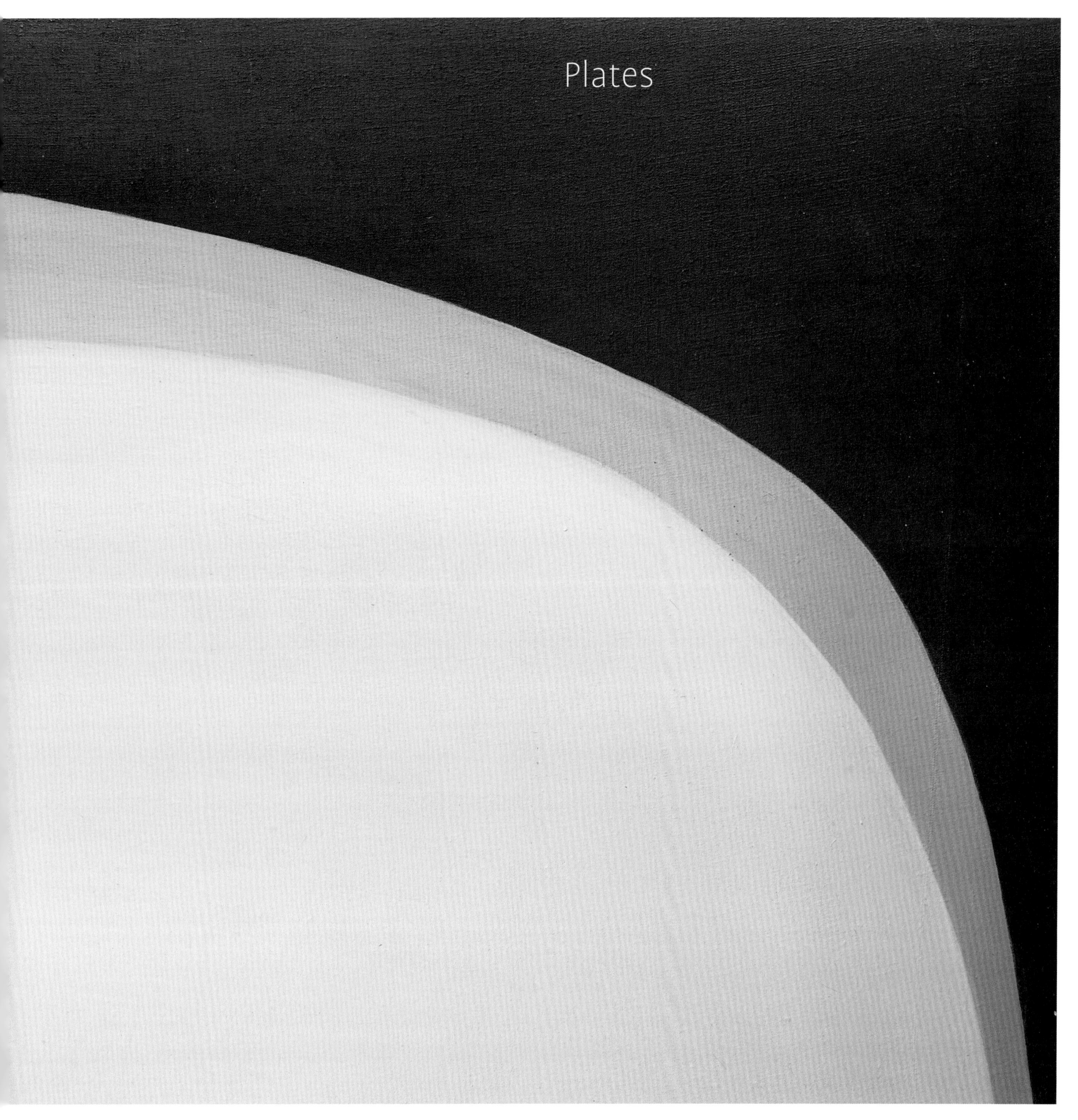
Plates

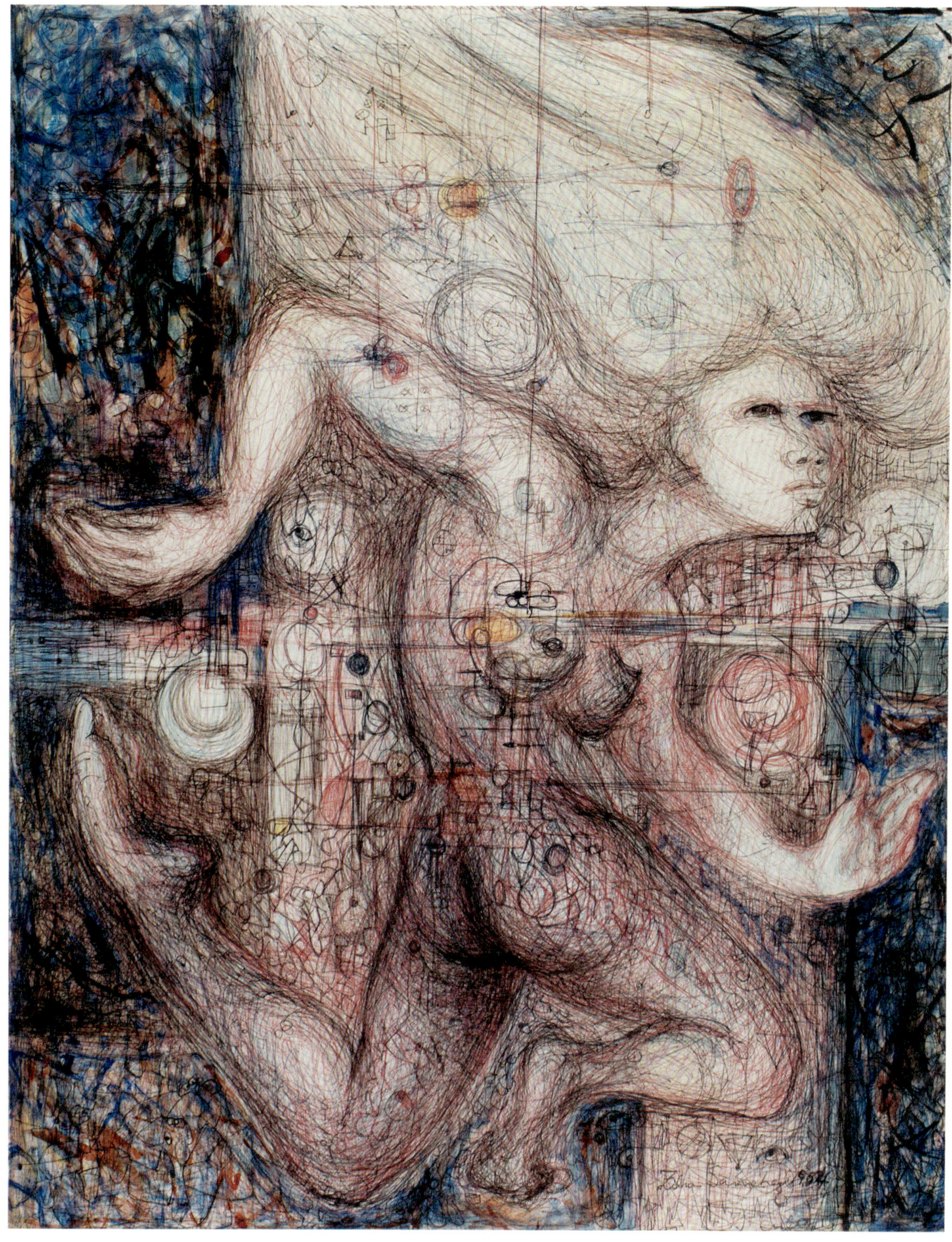

cat. 1 *Self Portrait*, 1954. Pen and ink on paper, 26 × 20 ⅛ in. (66.2 × 51.1 cm). Collection of the artist, San Juan.

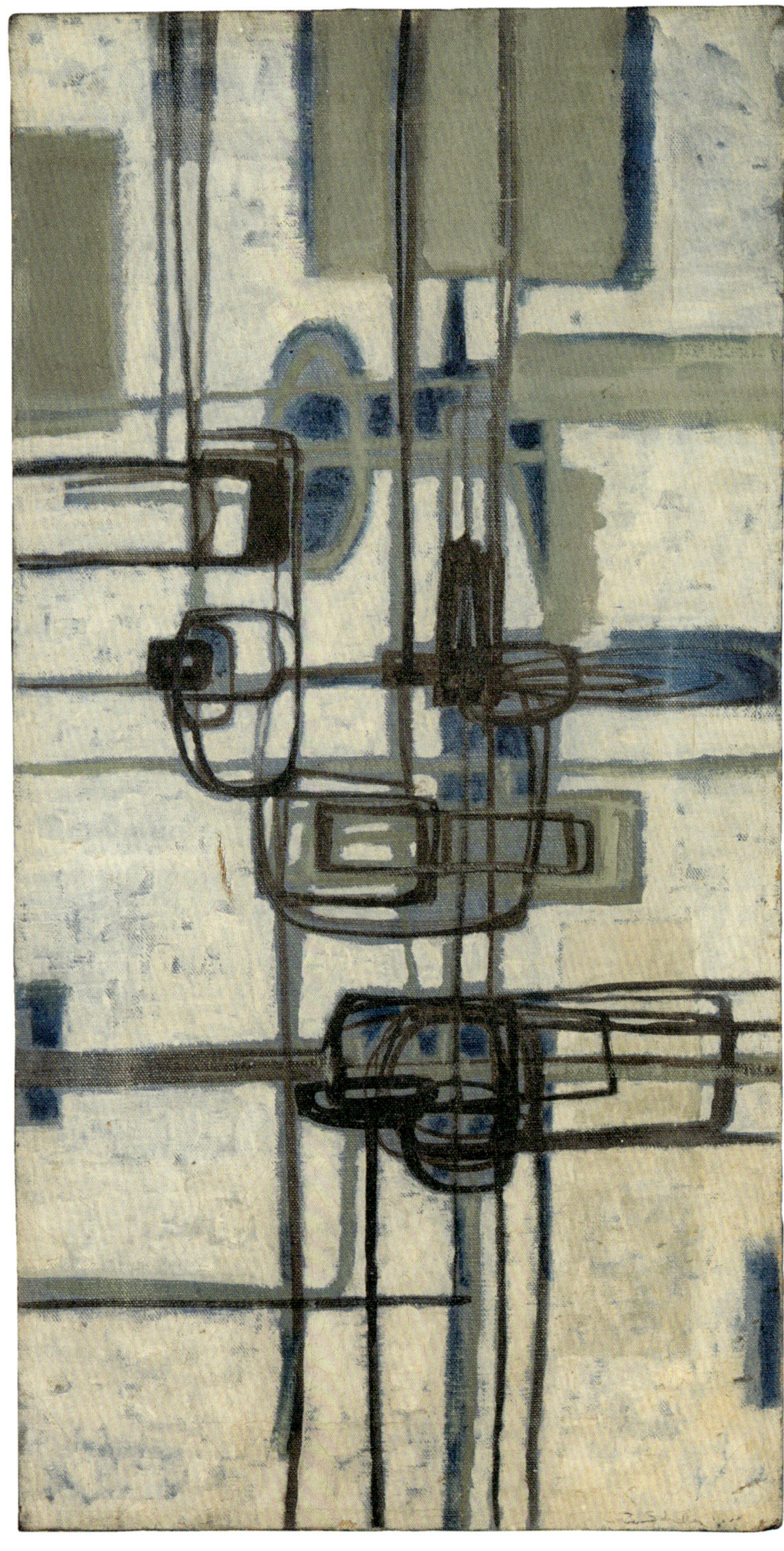

cat. 2   *Untitled*, c. mid-1950s. Acrylic on canvas, 22 ¼ × 11 ¼ in. (56.5 × 28.6 cm). Collection of RosaMaría García Sarduy, Miami.

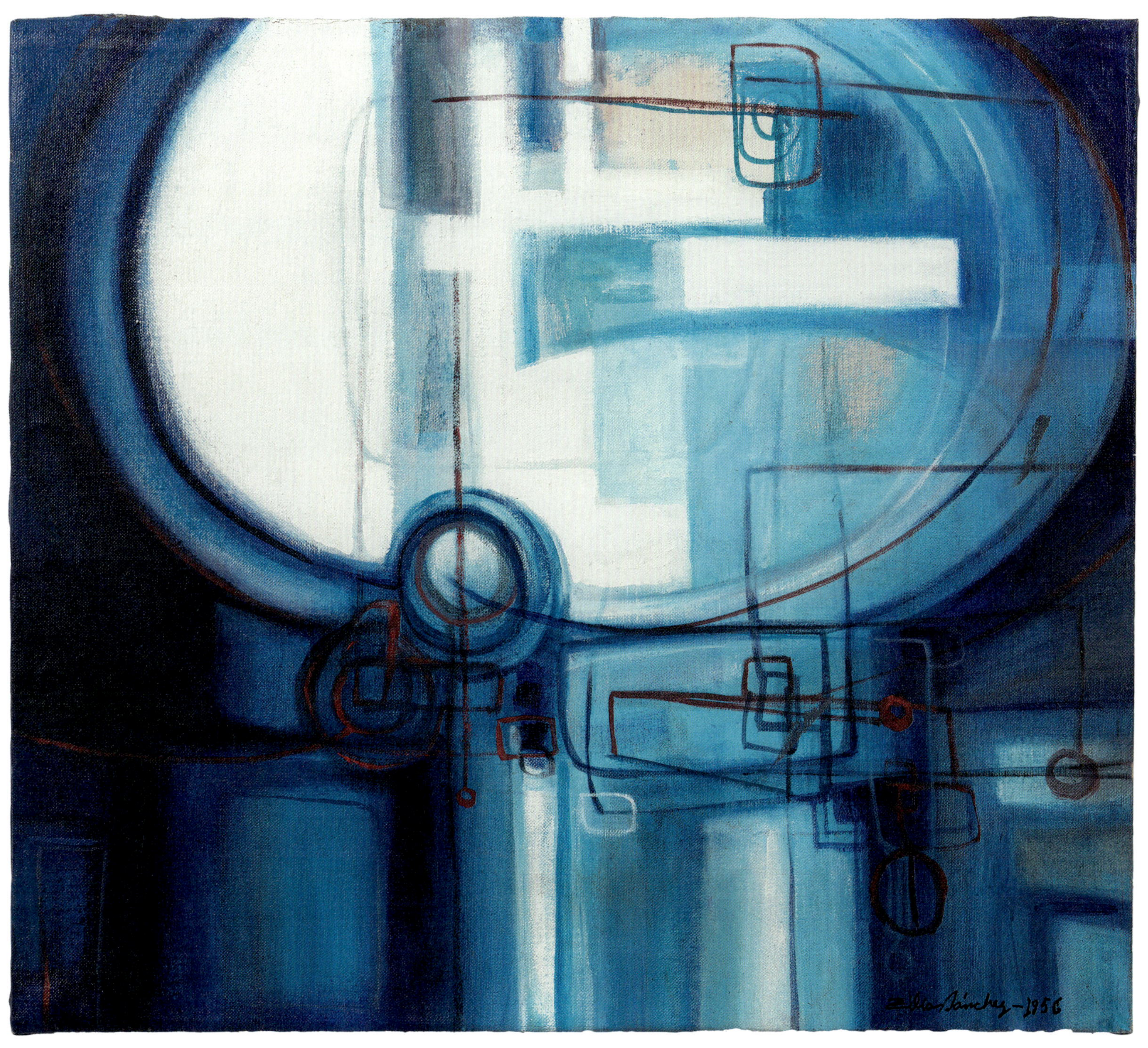

cat. 3   *Azul azul* (Blue Blue), 1956. Acrylic on canvas, 21 × 23 in. (53.3 × 58.4 cm). Collection of the artist, Courtesy Galerie Lelong & Co., New York.

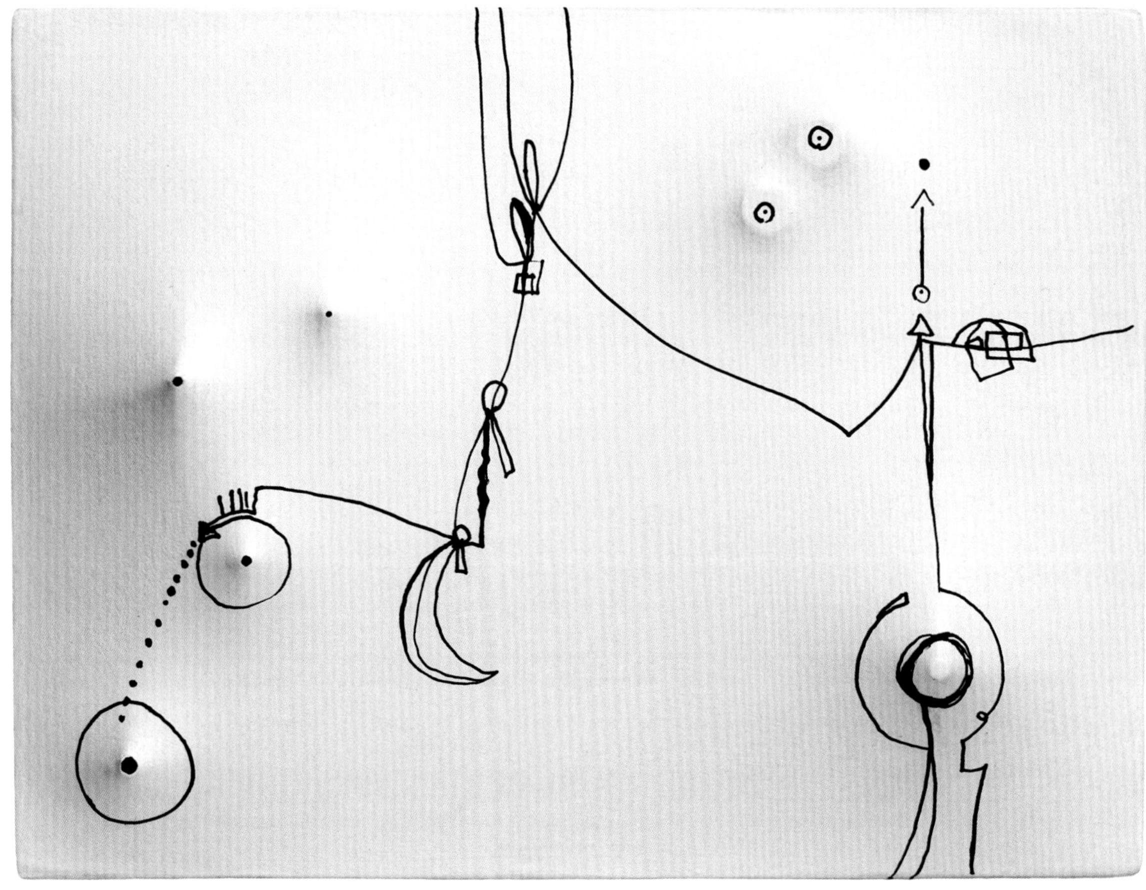

cat. 4   *Untitled*, 1956–99. Ink on stretched canvas, 7 × 9 ¼ × 2 ¾ in. (17.8 × 23.5 × 7 cm).
Collection of Ignacio J. López Beguiristain and Laura M. Guerra, San Juan.

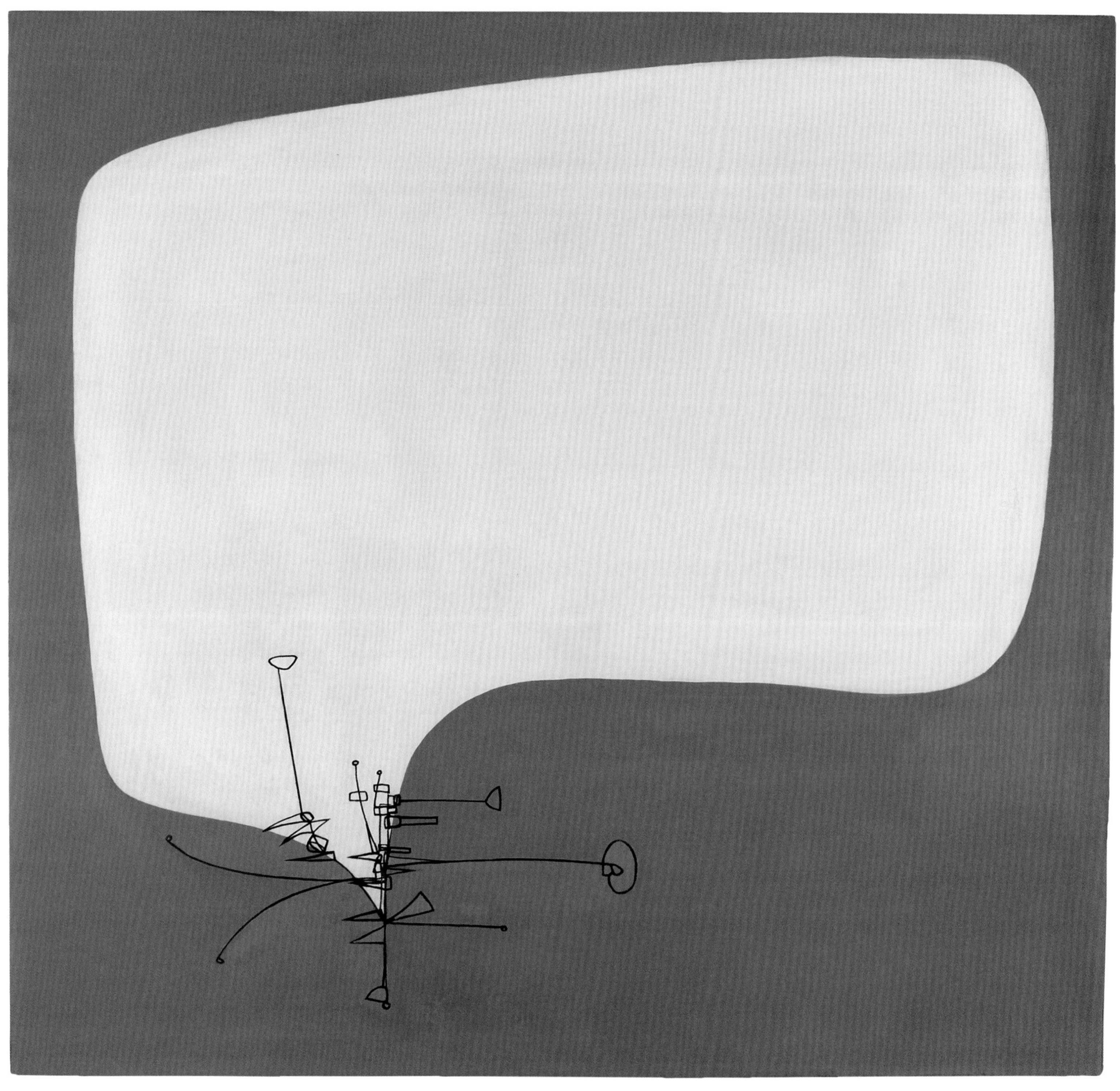

cat. 5 *Lo que es de isla y piel* (Belonging to Island and Skin), from the series *Afrocubanos*, 1958. Acrylic and ink on canvas,
39 ½ × 40 ½ in. (100.3 × 102.9 cm). Collection of Mima and César Reyes, San Juan.

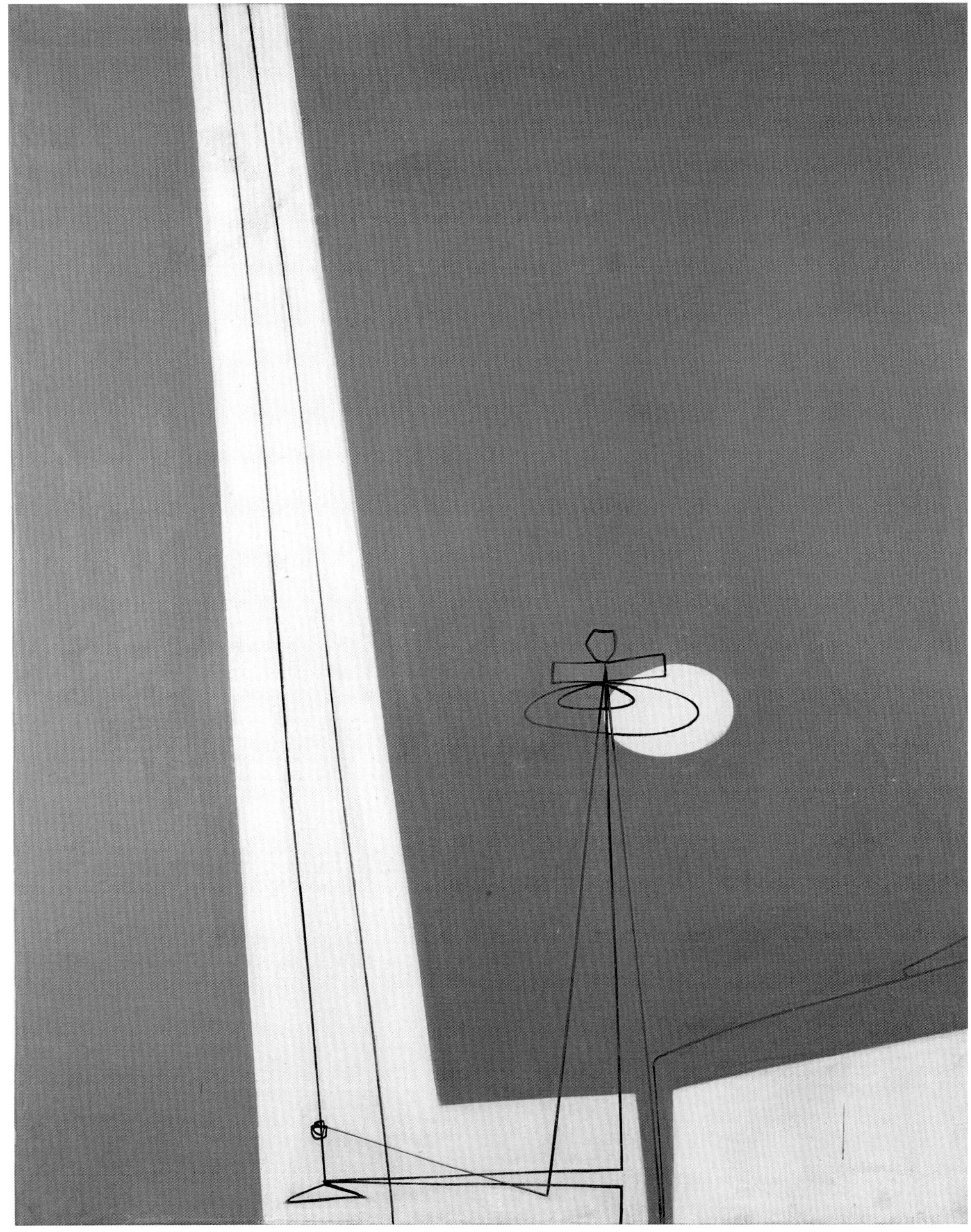

cat. 6 *Untitled*, from the series *Afrocubanos*, 1957. Acrylic and ink on canvas laid on board, 36 × 28 in. (91.4 × 71.1 cm).
Collection of the artist, Courtesy Galerie Lelong & Co., New York.

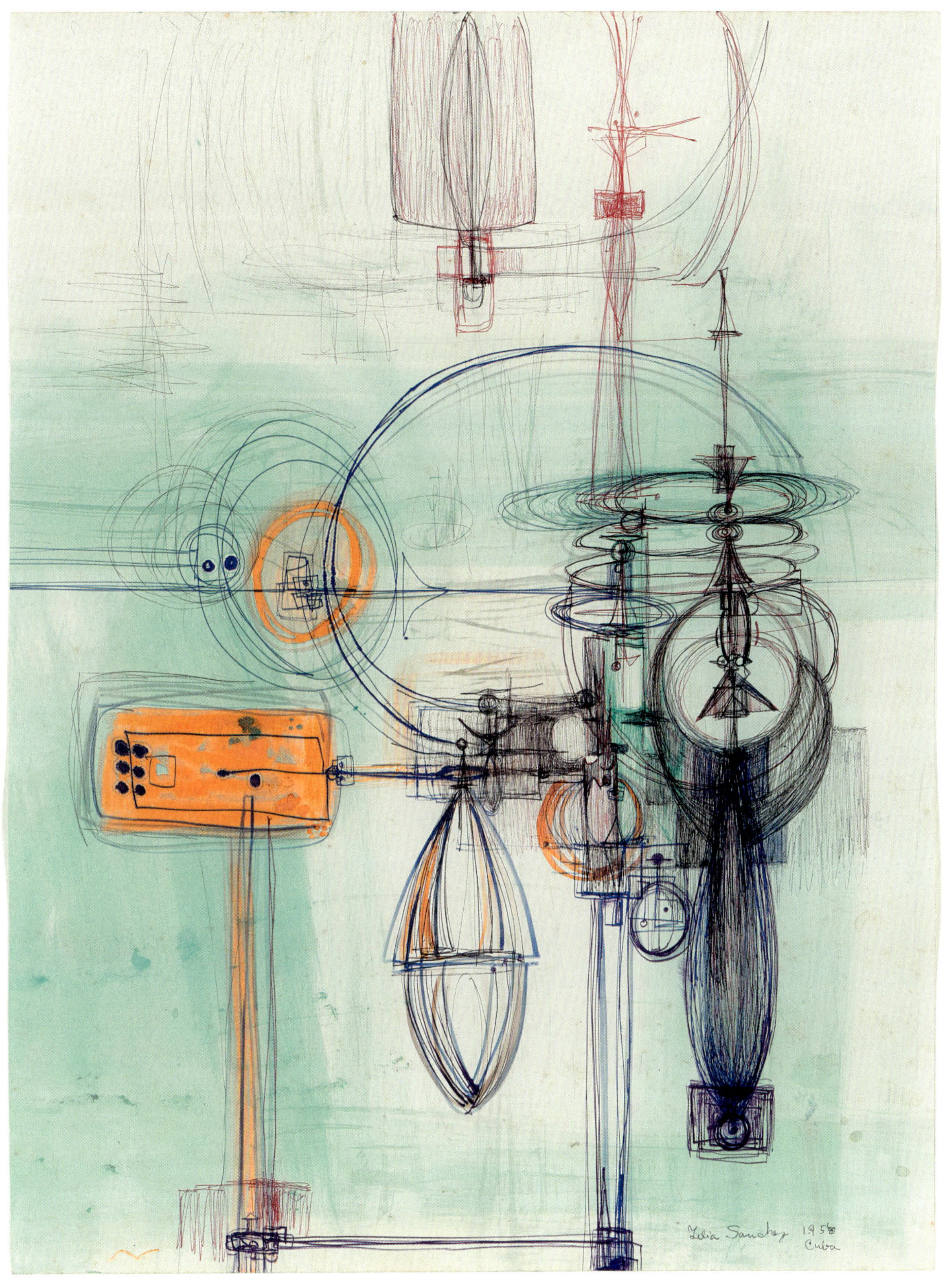

cat. 7 *Untitled*, 1958. Ink and watercolor on coated paper, 20 × 14 ⅝ in. (50.8 × 37.1 cm). Collection of the artist, Courtesy Galerie Lelong & Co., New York.

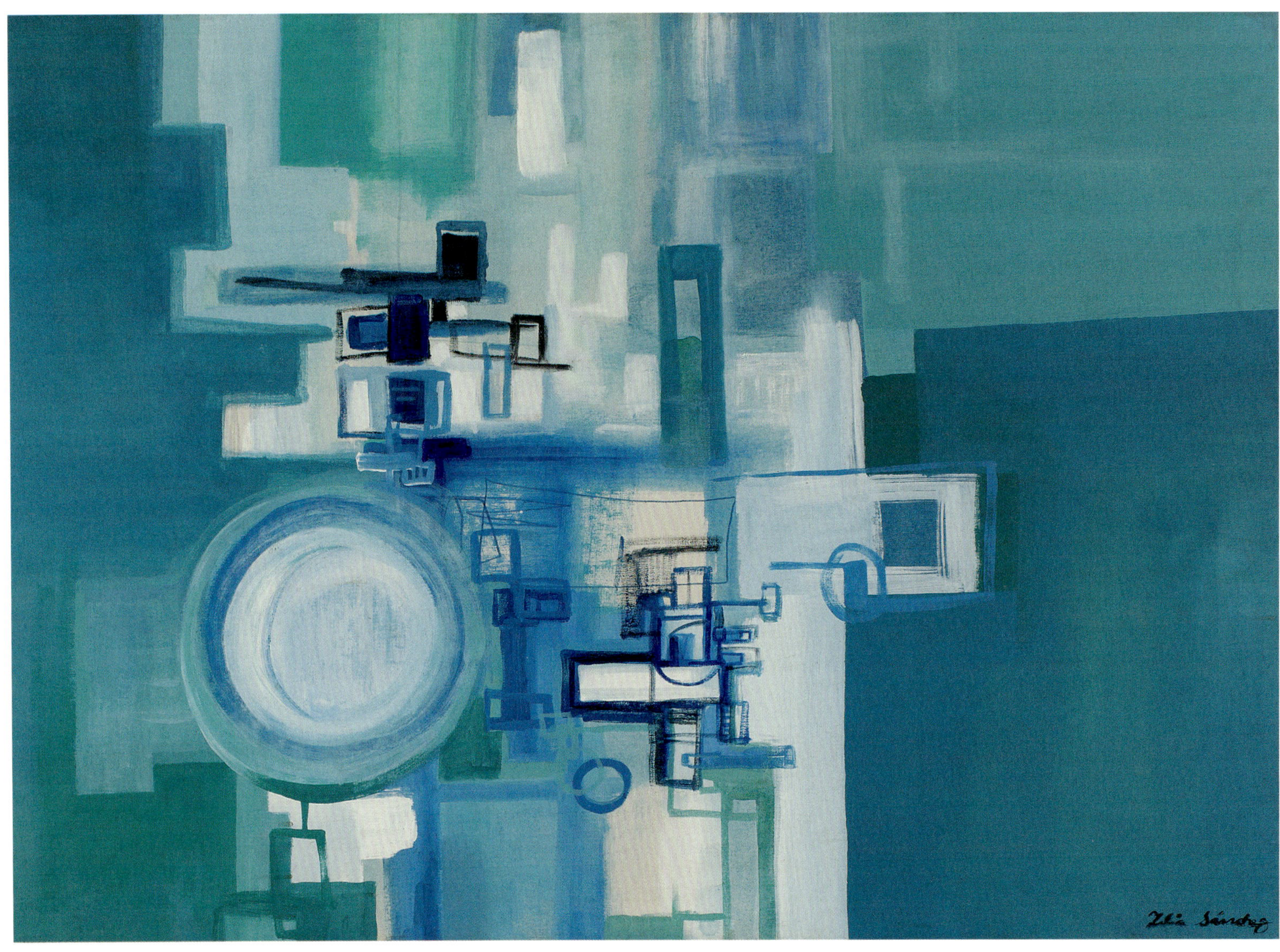

cat. 8 *Untitled*, 1958. Acrylic and ink on canvas, 34 × 49 ⅞ in. (86.4 × 126.7 cm). Collection of Mima and César Reyes, San Juan.

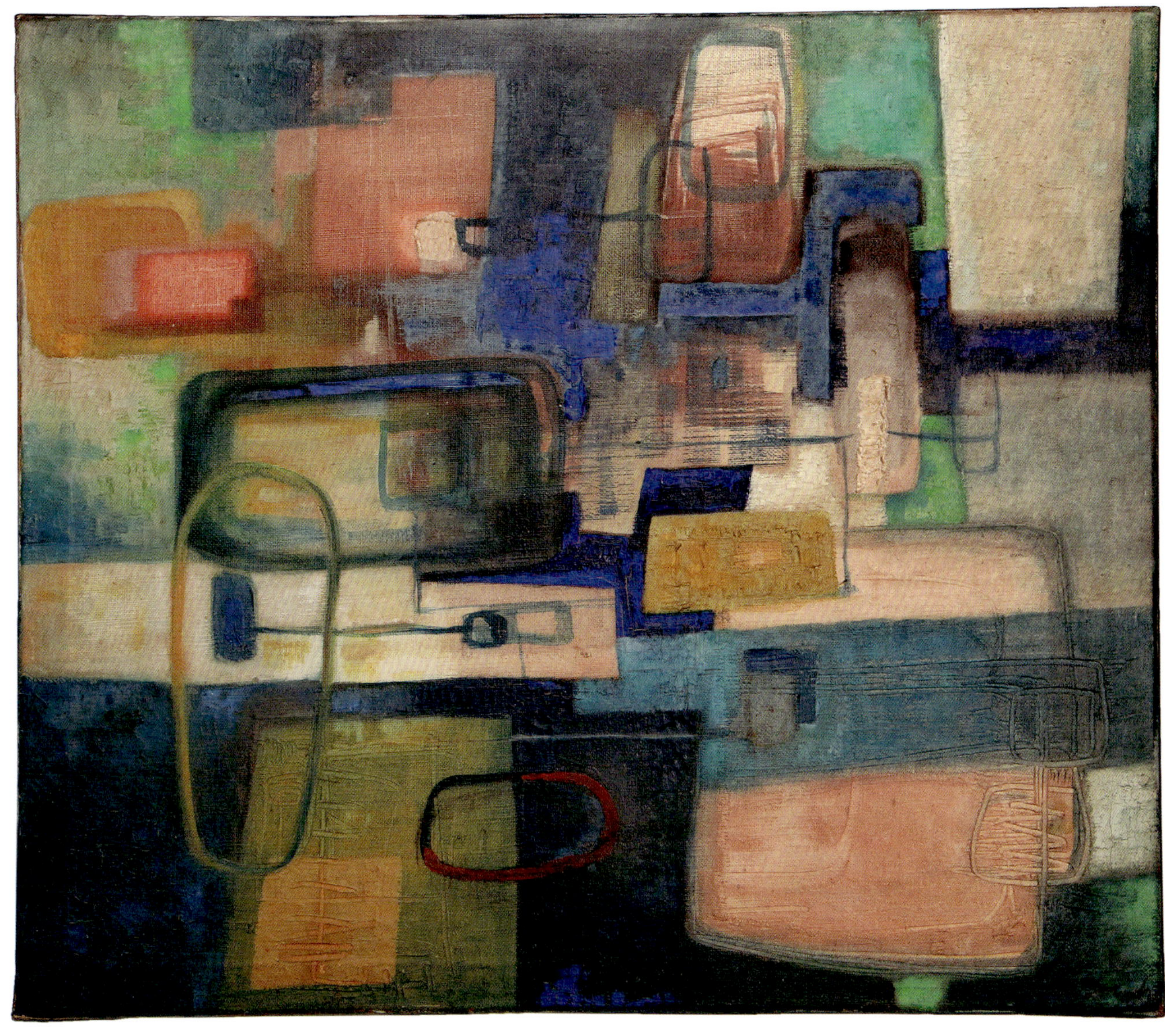

cat. 9 *Untitled*, mid-1950s–1962. Acrylic on canvas, 16 × 18 in. (40.6 × 45.7 cm). Collection of Cecilia and Ernesto Poma, Miami.

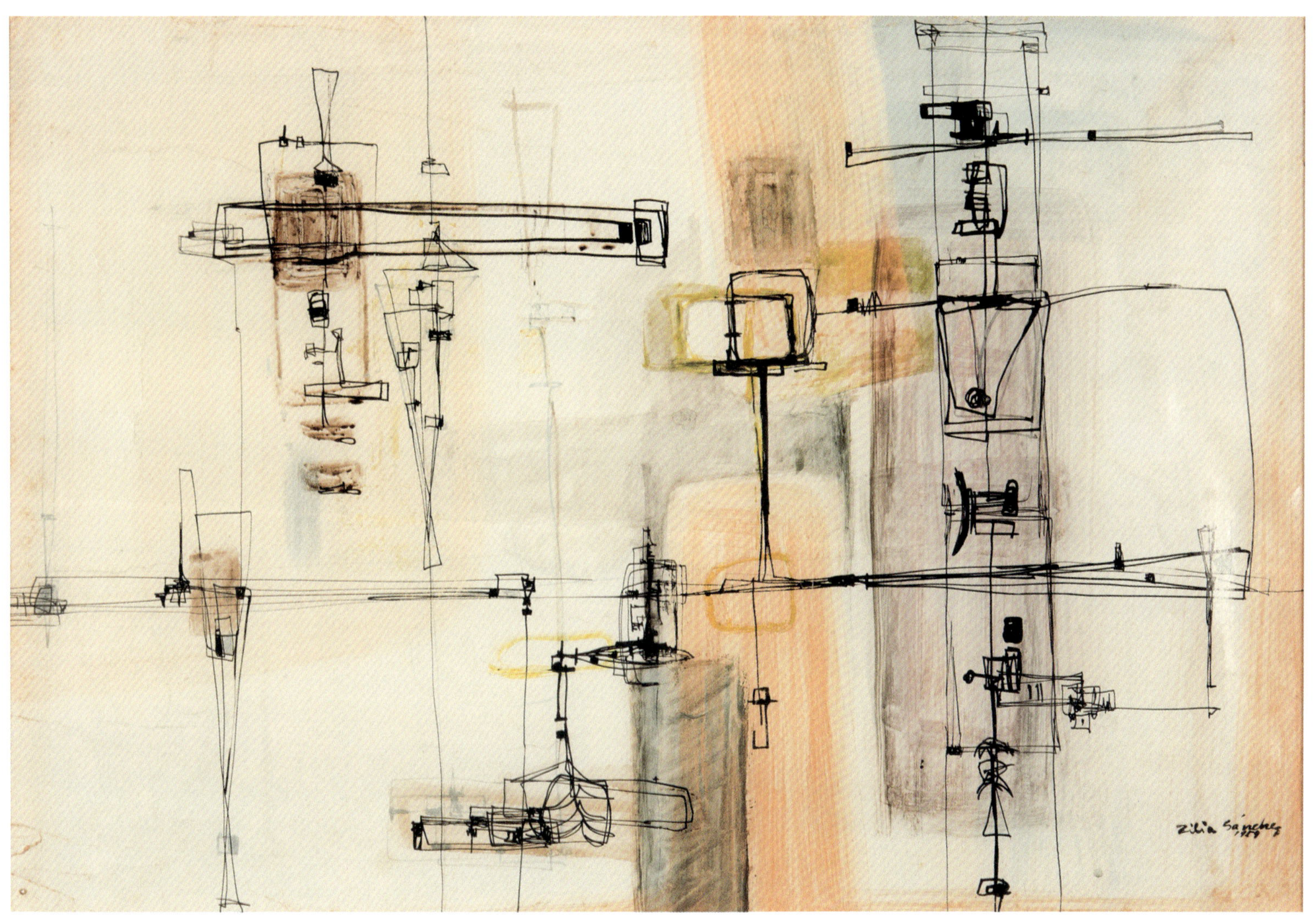

cat. 10   *Untitled*, 1959. Ink and gouache on paper, 14 × 20 in. (35.6 × 50.8 cm). Collection of RosaMaría García Sarduy, Miami.

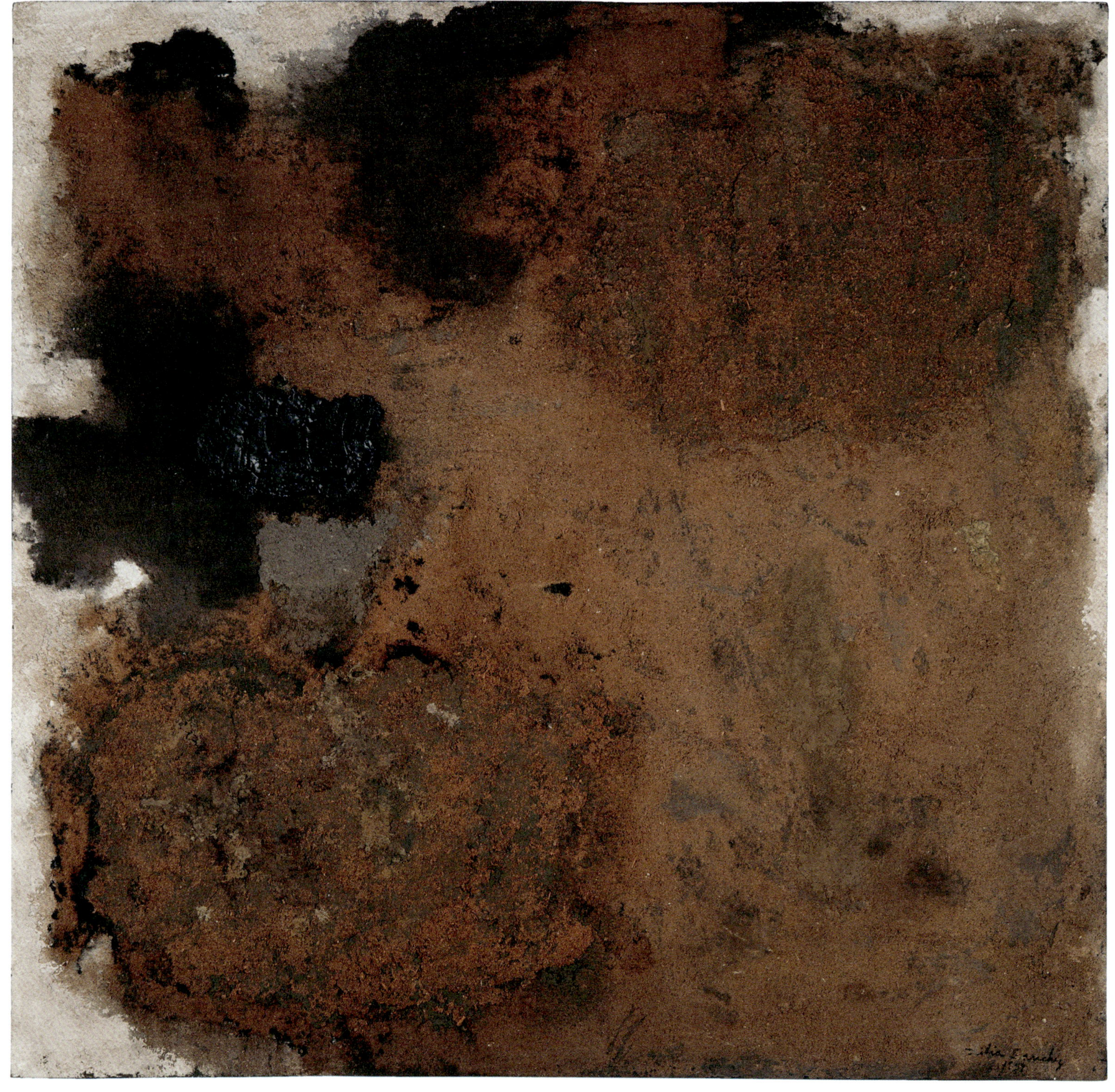

cat. 11   *Tierra* (The Earth), 1959. Mixed media on canvas, 48 ½ × 48 ¼ in. (123.2 × 122.6 cm). CINTAS Foundation Fellows Collection, Miami.

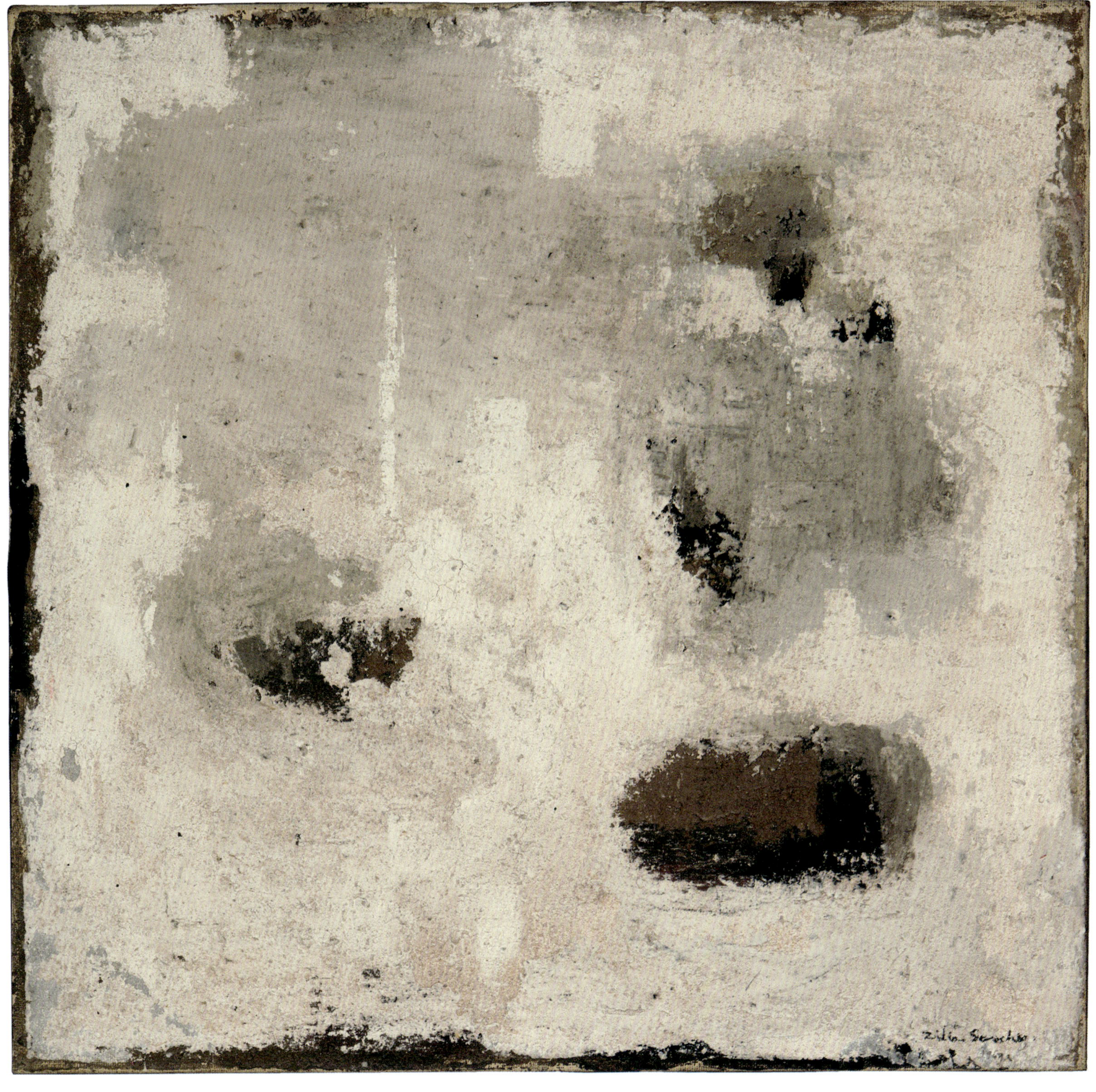

cat. 12 *Untitled (Agua)*, 1961. Mixed media on canvas, 38 ¼ × 37 ⅞ in. (97.2 × 96.2 cm). Collection of RosaMaría García Sarduy, Miami.

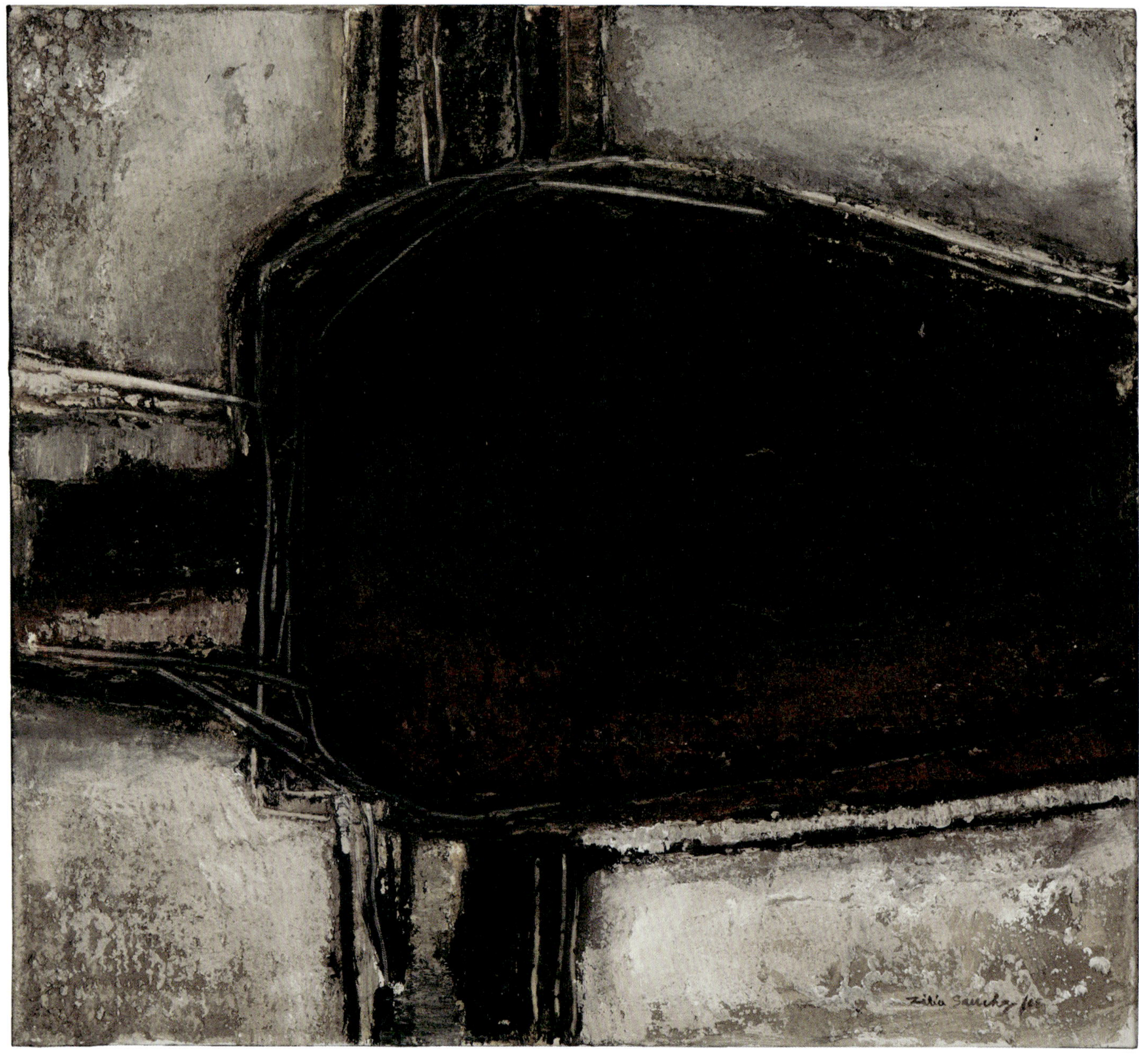

cat. 13 *Untitled*, 1965. Mixed media on canvas, 33 ½ × 36 in. (85.1 × 91.4 cm). Collection of RosaMaría García Sarduy, Miami.

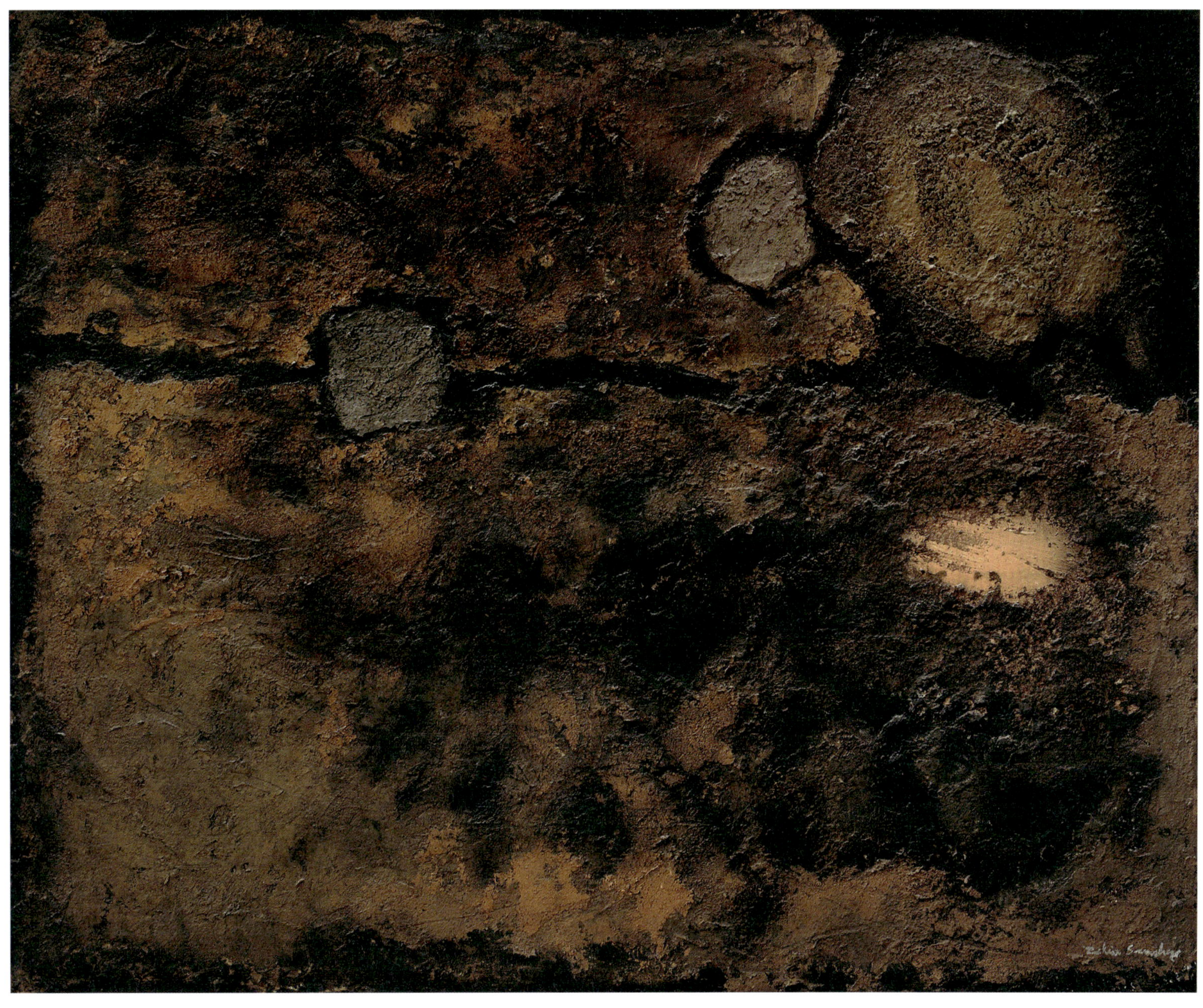

cat. 14   *Untitled*, c. 1960s. Mixed media on canvas, 38 × 42 in. (96.5 × 106.7 cm). Private collection, Miami.

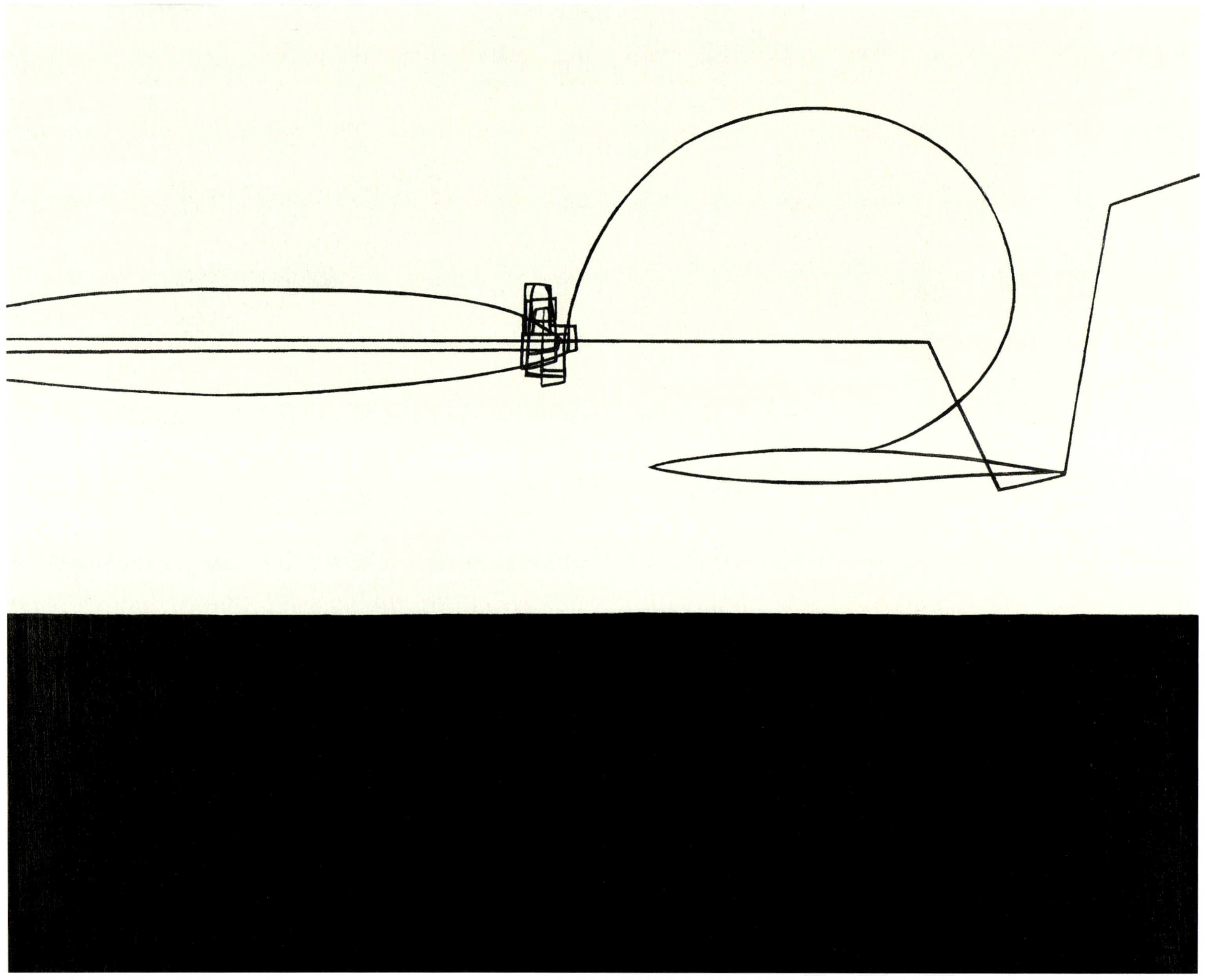

cat. 15 *Concepto Z*, 1964. Acrylic on canvas, 23 ⅛ × 28 ⅛ in. (58.7 × 71.4 cm). Instituto de Cultura Puertorriqueña, San Juan.

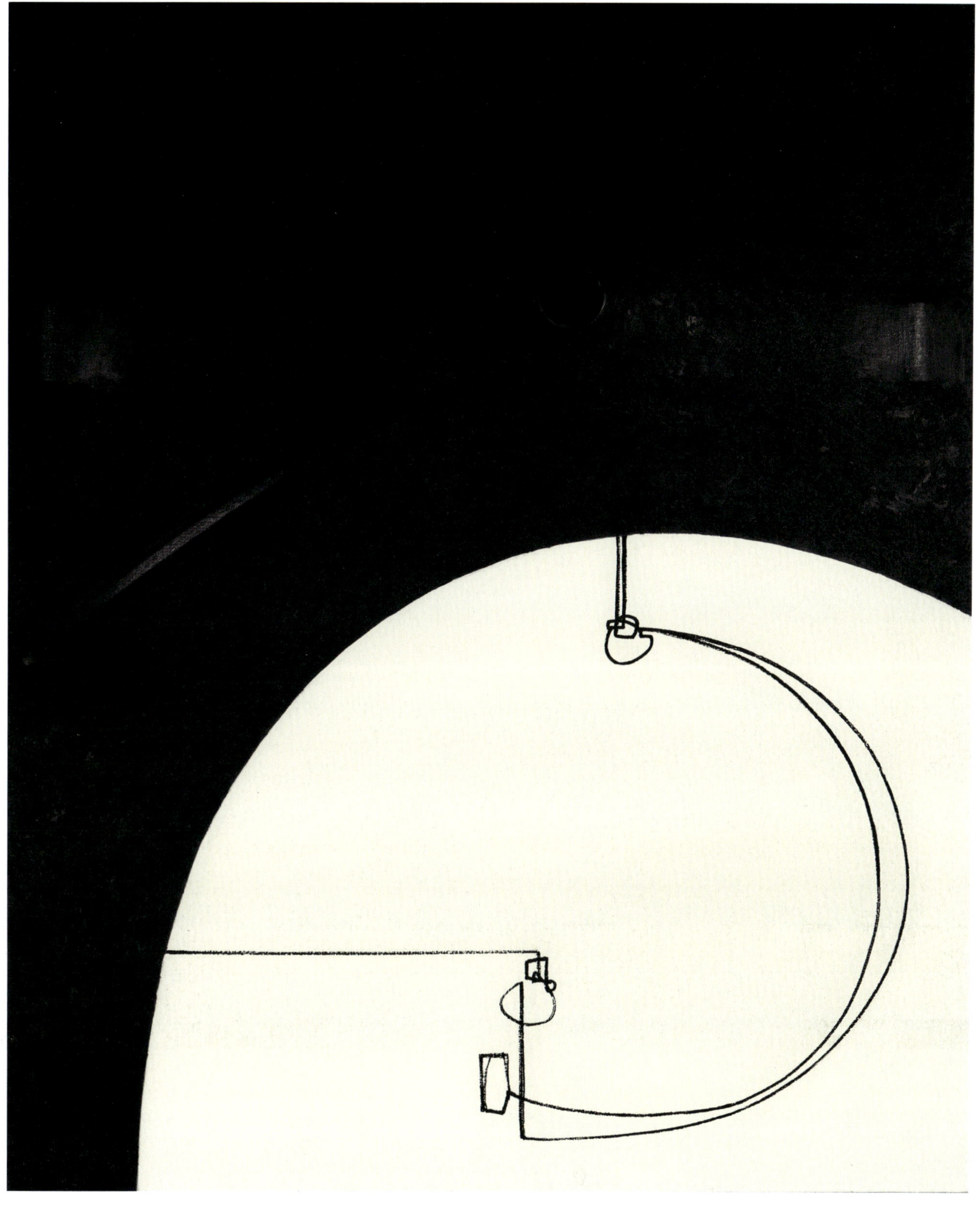

cat. 16 *Untitled*, c. 1960s. Mixed media on stretched canvas, 31 × 23 × approx. 2 in. (78.7 × 58.4 × approx. 5 cm).
CINTAS Foundation Fellows Collection, Miami.

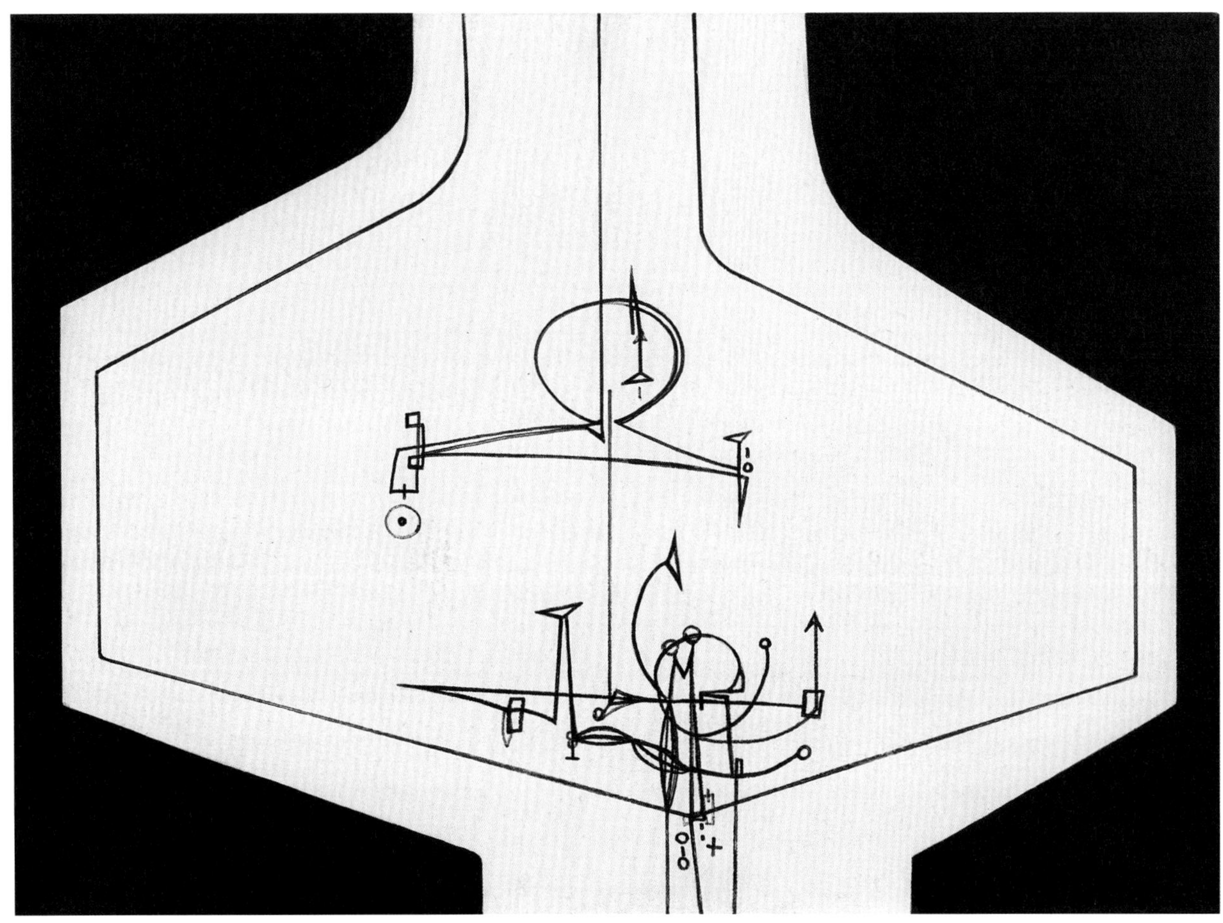

cat. 17 *Topología* (Topology), 1965/93. Acrylic and ink on canvas, 15 × 20 in. (38.1 × 50.8 cm).
Collection of the artist, Courtesy Galerie Lelong & Co., New York.

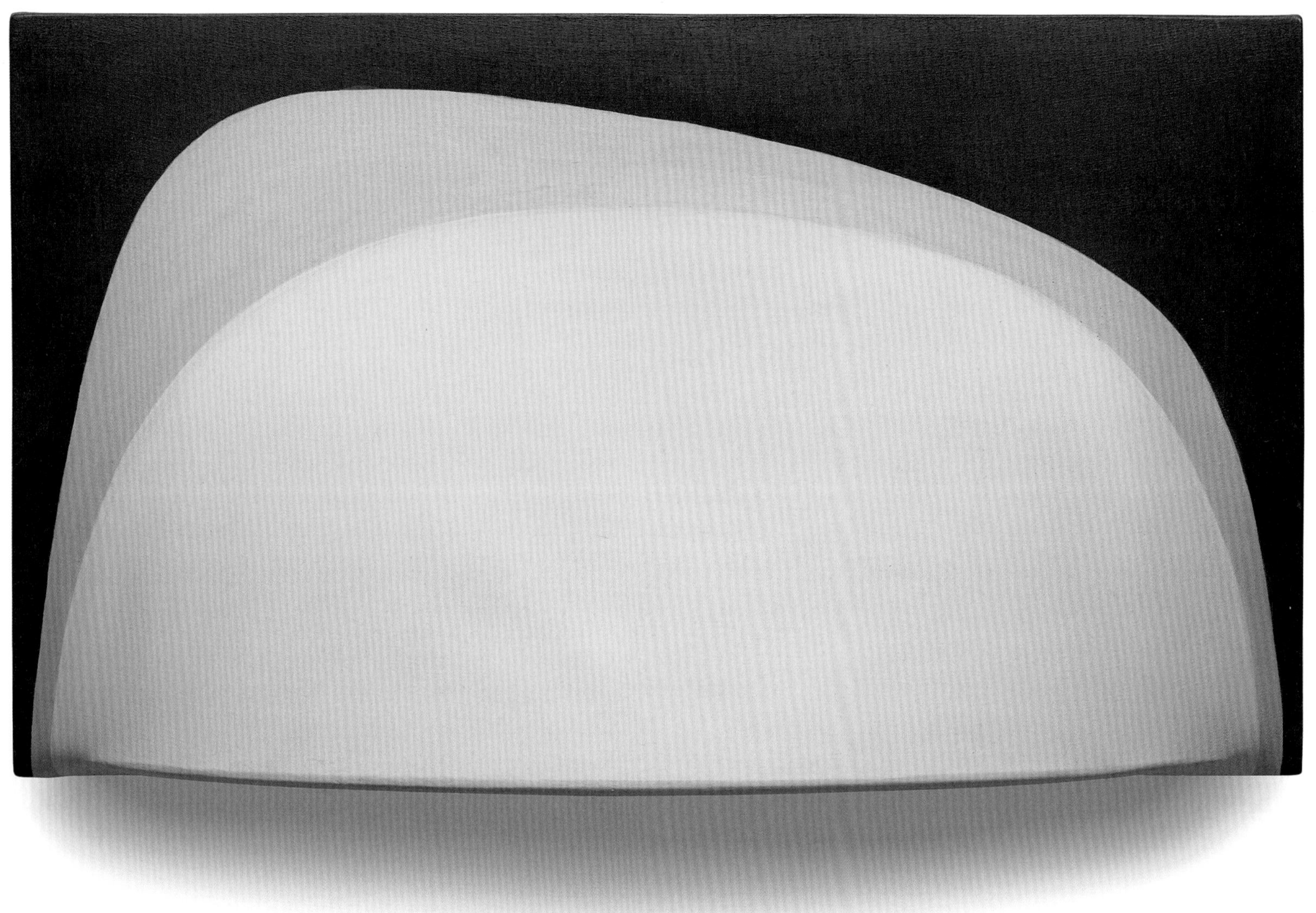

cat. 18   *Untitled*, 1962/90. Acrylic on stretched canvas, 15 × 25 × 8 in. (38.1 × 63.5 × 20.3 cm).
Collection of the artist, Courtesy Galerie Lelong & Co., New York.

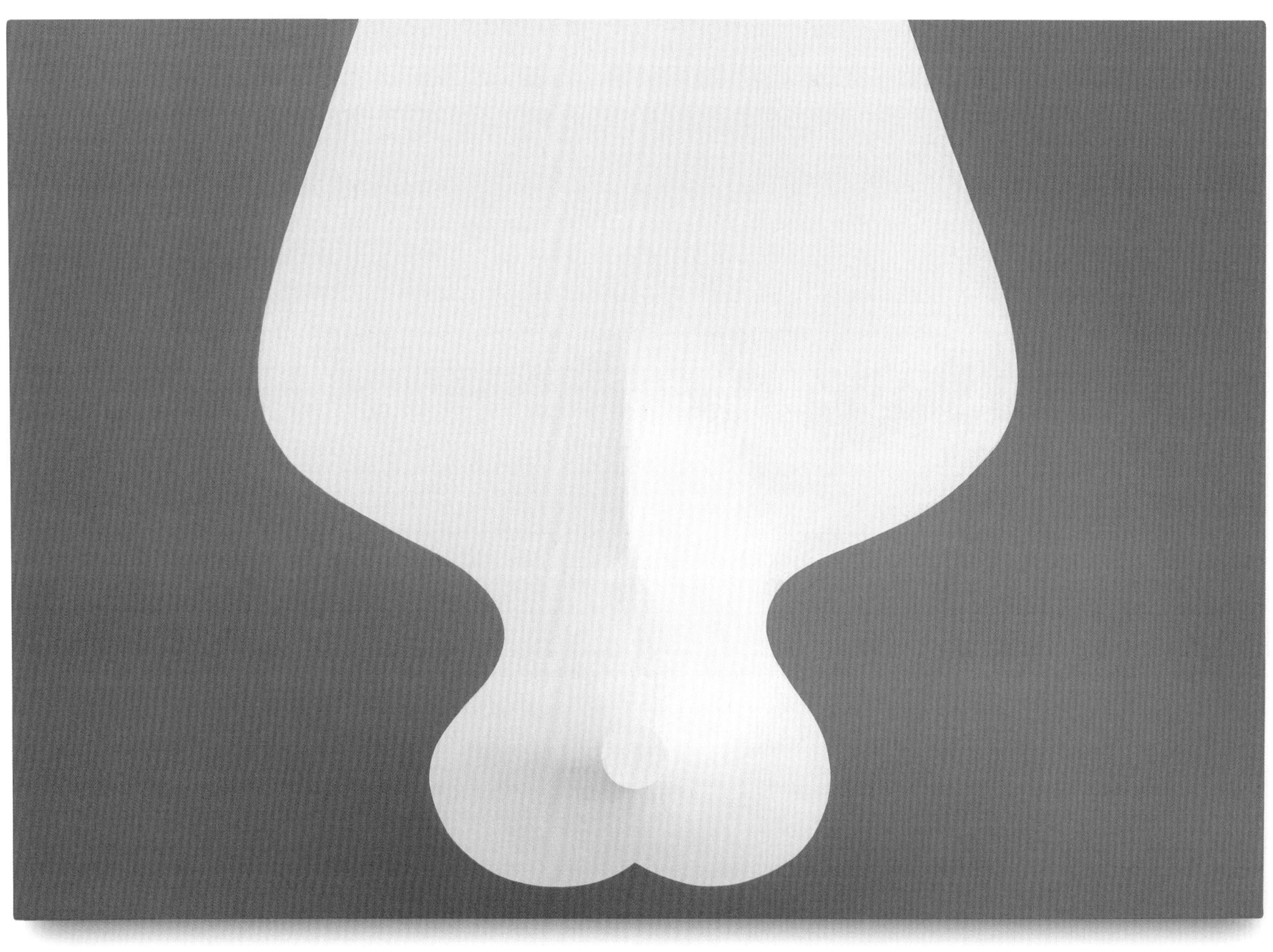

cat. 19   *Topología erótica* (Erotic Topology), 1960–71. Acrylic on stretched canvas, 41 × 56 × 13 in. (104.1 × 142.2 × 33 cm). Collection of Jose R. Landron, San Juan.

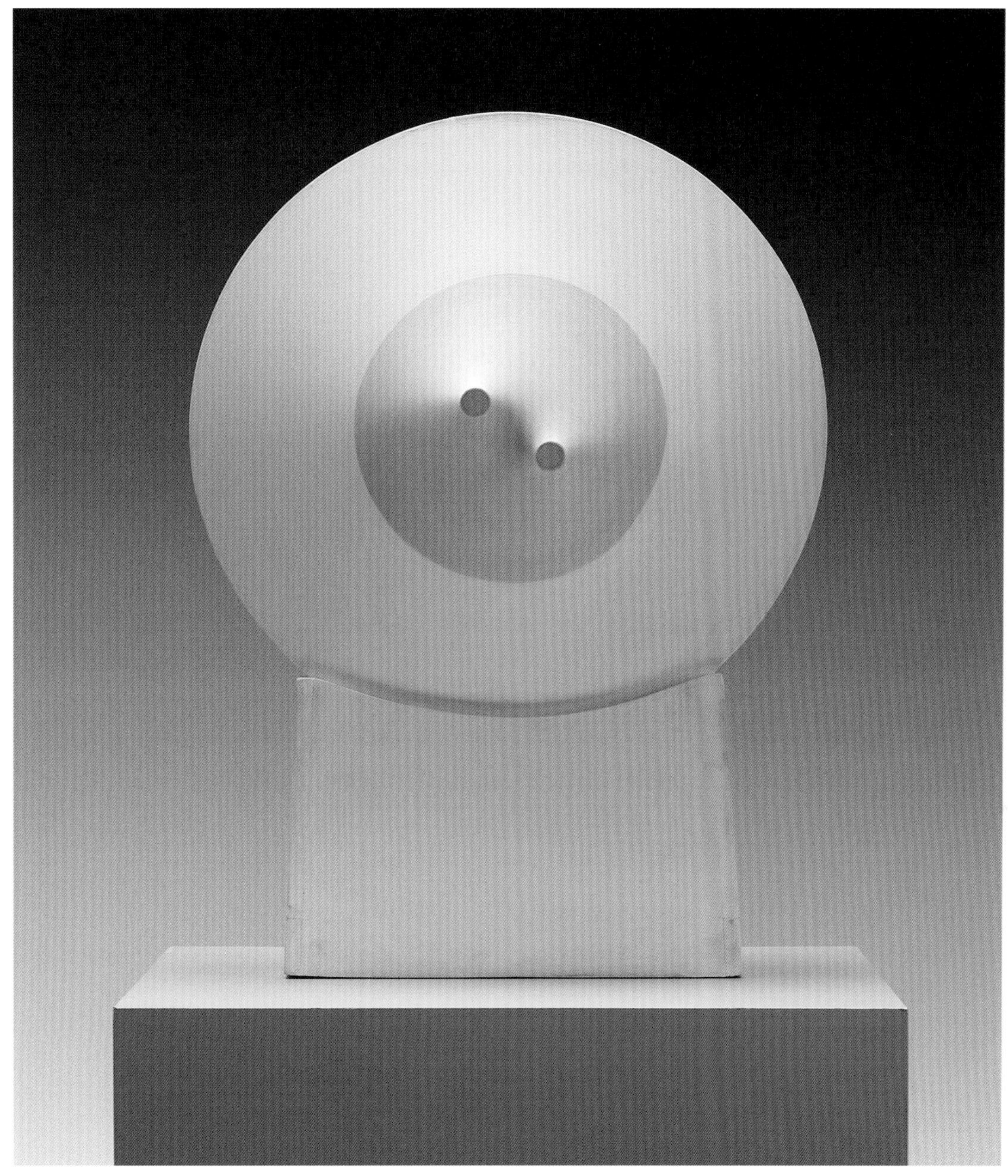

cat. 20 *Lunar blanco* (White Moon), 1964. Acrylic on stretched canvas, 33 ½ × 24 ½ × 5 ½ in. (85.1 × 62.2 × 14 cm).
Collection of Beth Rudin DeWoody, New York.

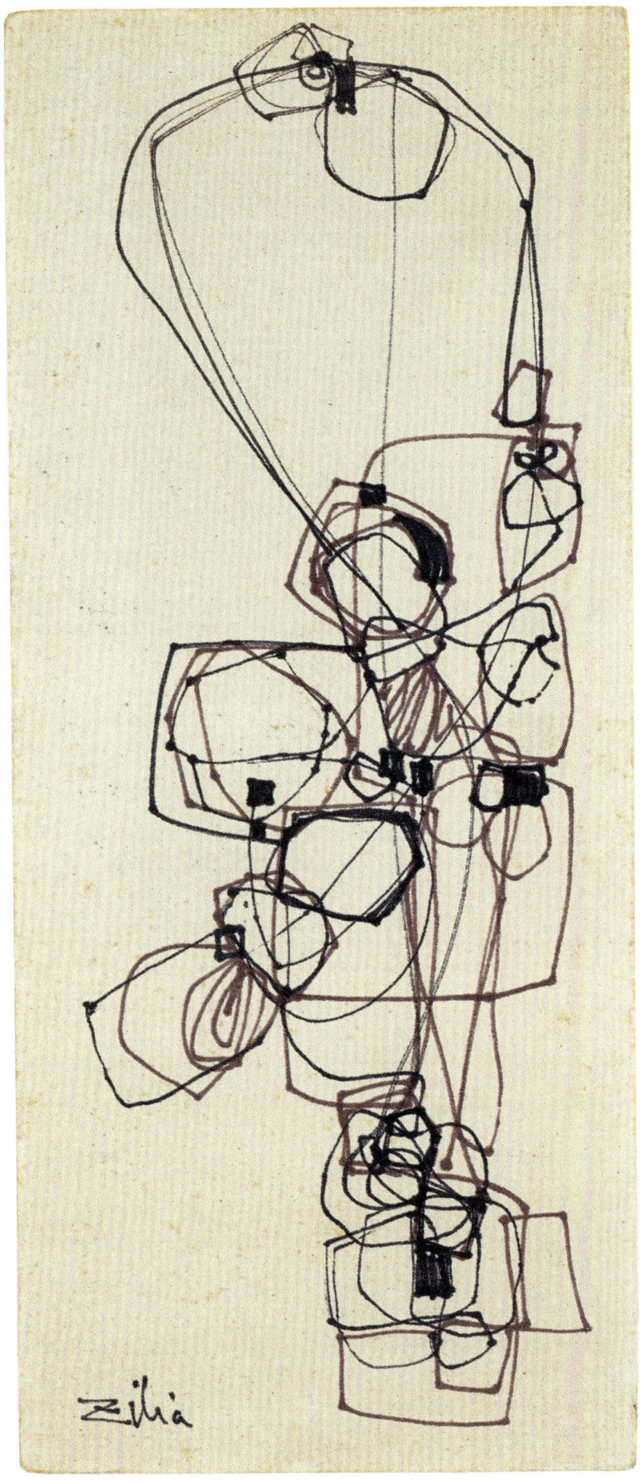
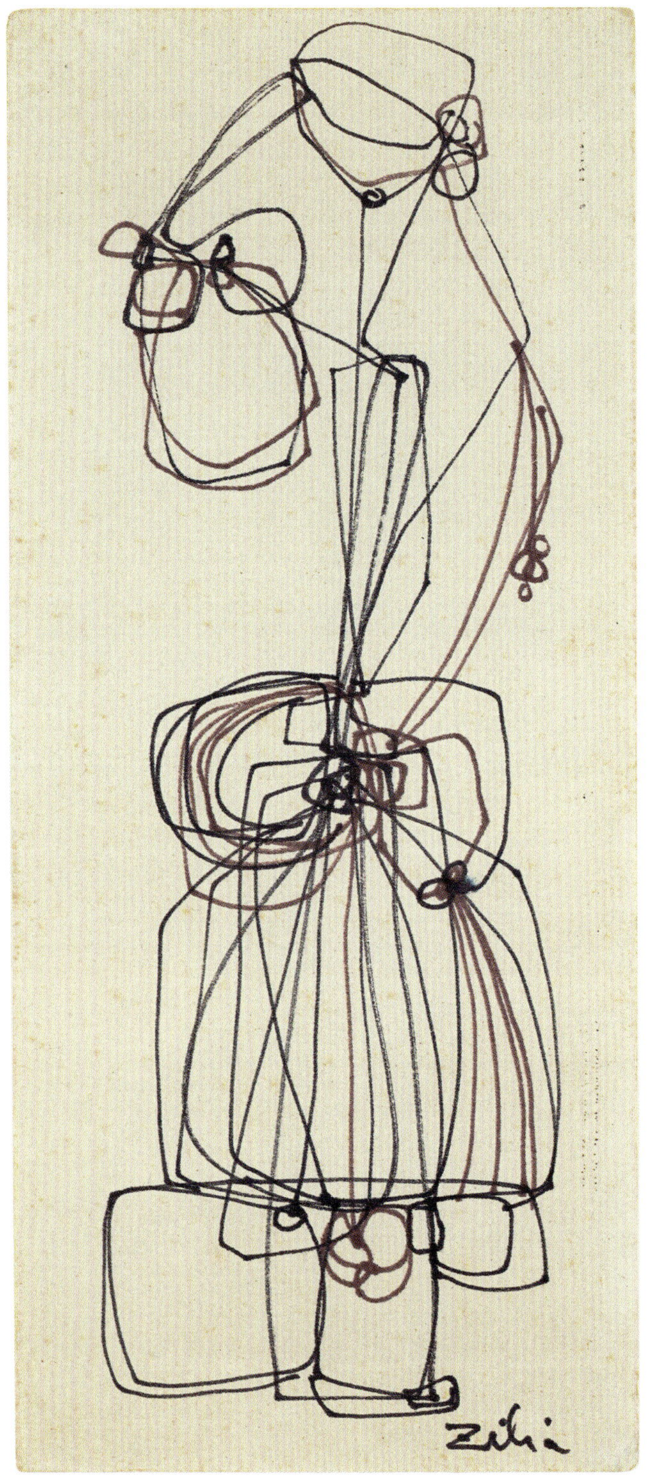

cat. 21 *Untitled*, c. 1965. Ink on paper, 9 ½ × 4 in. (24.1 × 10.2 cm). Collection of the artist, Courtesy Galerie Lelong & Co., New York.

cat. 22 *Untitled*, c. 1965. Ink on paper, 9 ½ × 4 in. (24.1 × 10.2 cm). Collection of Diane and Bruce Halle, Phoenix.

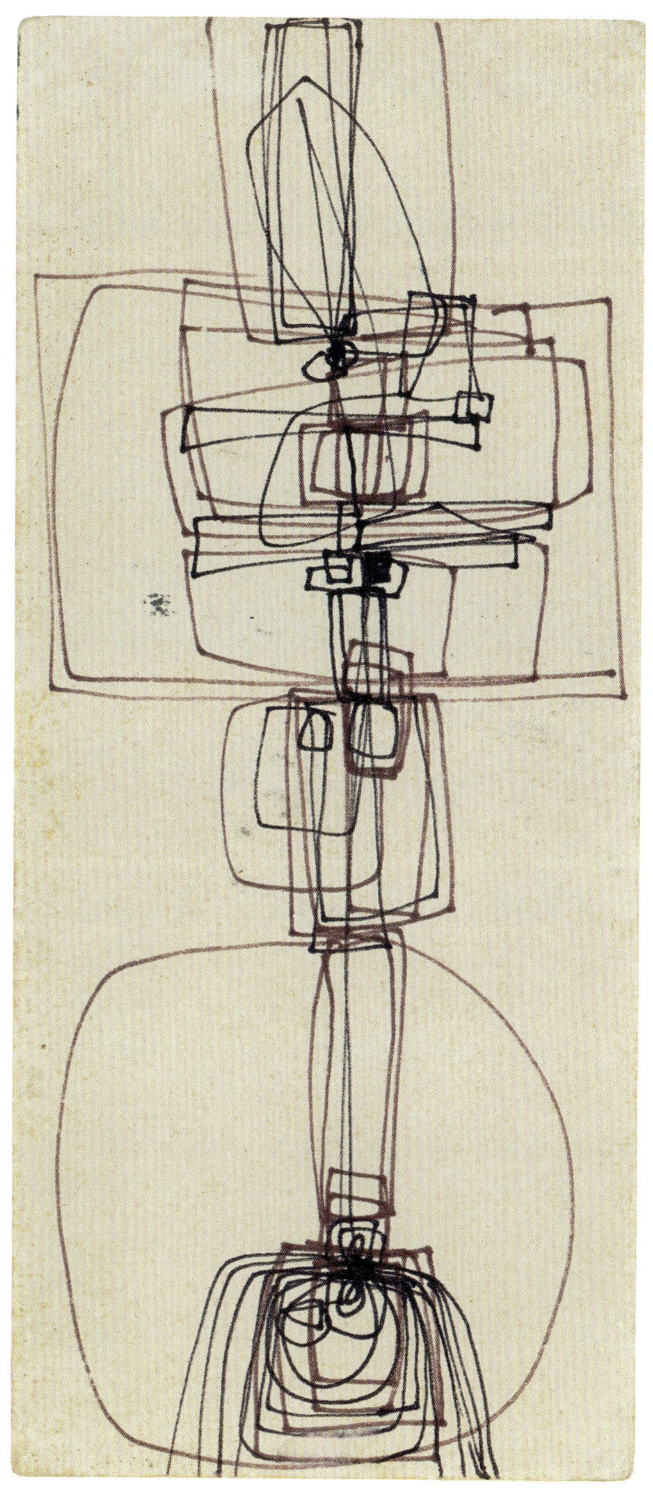

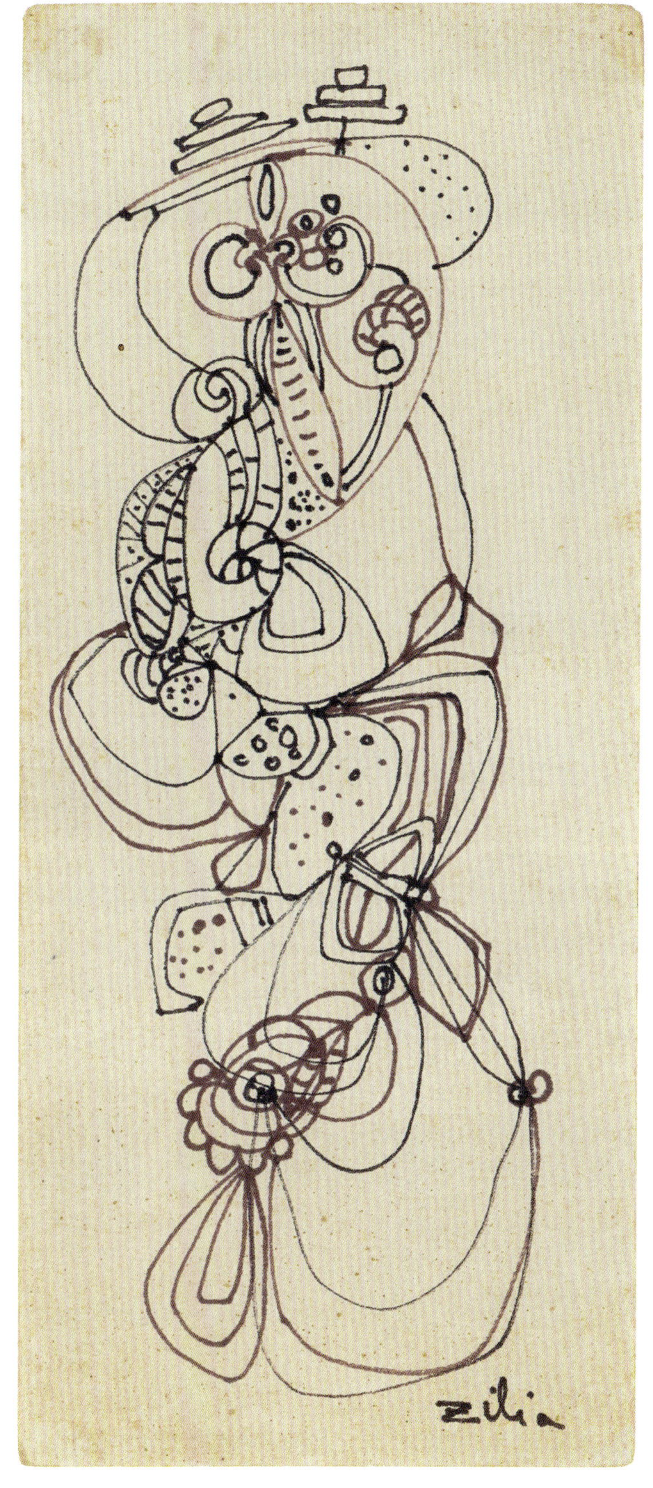

cat. 23 *Untitled*, c. 1965. Ink on paper, 9 ½ × 4 in. (24.1 × 10.2 cm). Collection of Diane and Bruce Halle, Phoenix.

cat. 24 *Untitled*, c. 1965. Ink on paper, 9 ½ × 4 in. (24.1 × 10.2 cm). Collection of Diane and Bruce Halle, Phoenix.

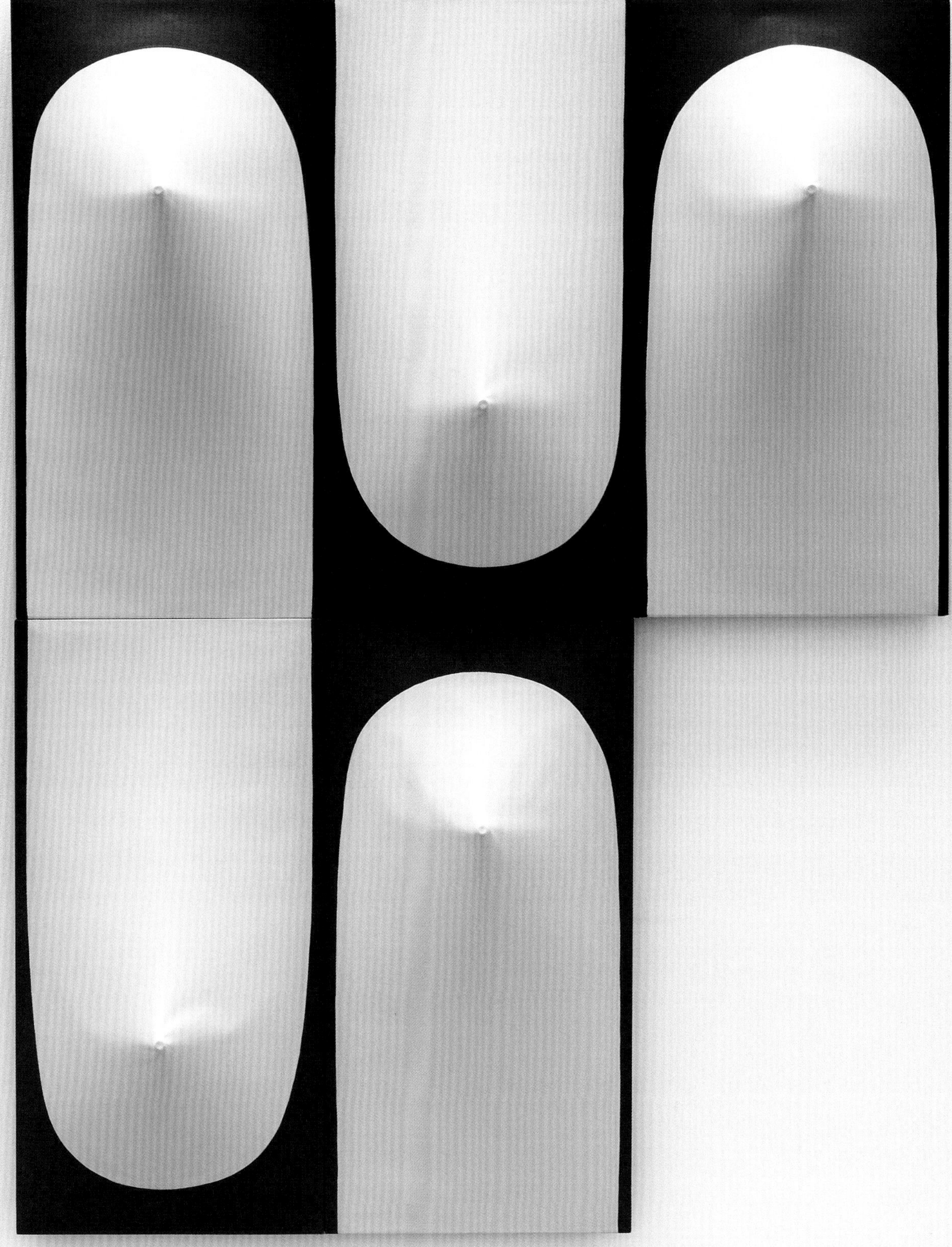

cat. 25 *Troyanas* (Trojan Women), polyptych, from the series *Módulos infinitos* (Infinite Modules), 1967. Acrylic on stretched canvas, 71 ¾ × 54 × 9 ½ in. (182.2 × 137.2 × 24.1 cm). Collection of Laura Delaney Taft and John Taft, promised gift to Walker Art Center, Minneapolis.

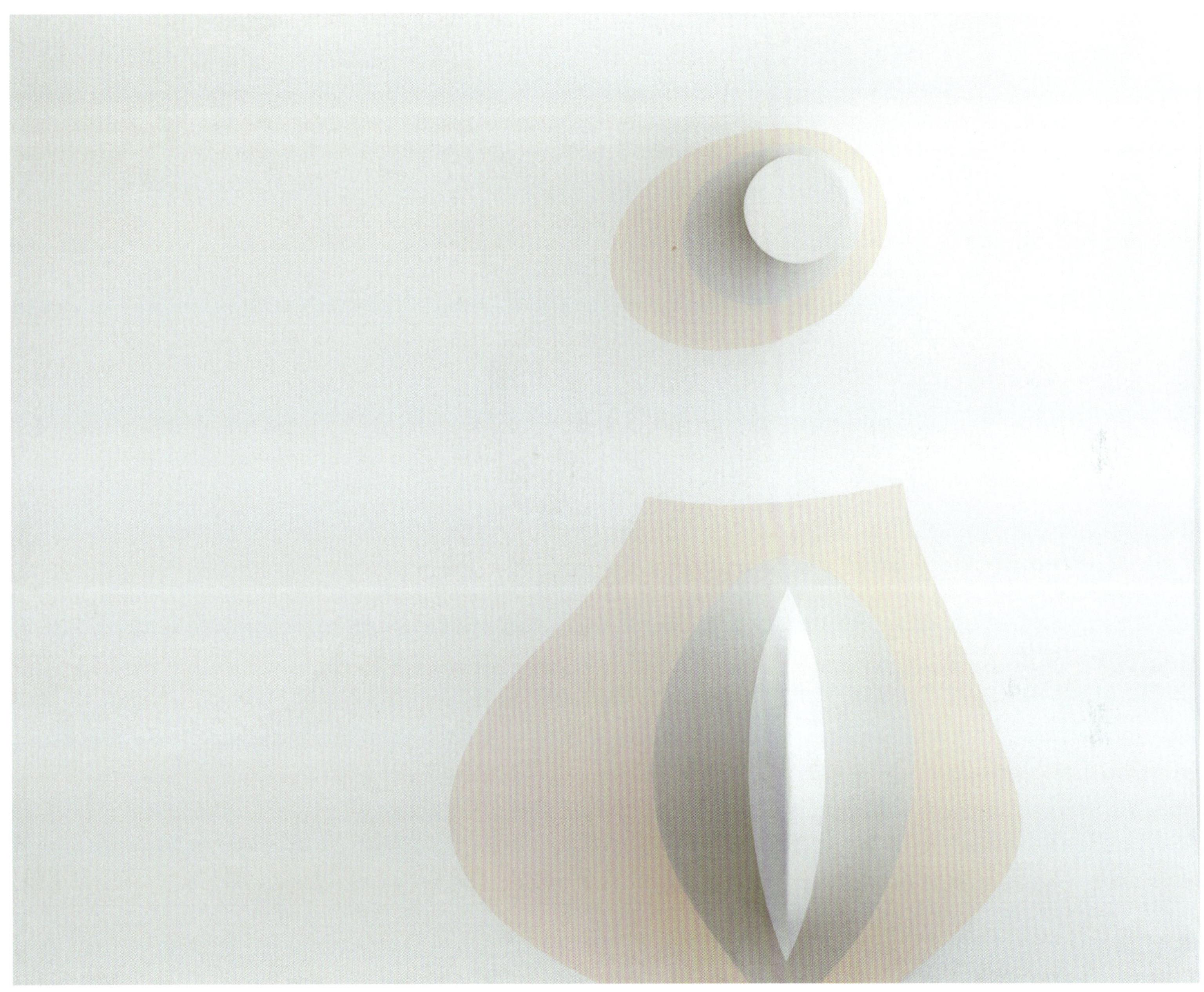

cat. 26 *Topología erótica* (Erotic Topology), 1968. Acrylic on stretched canvas, 36 × 43 × 12 in. (91.4 × 108 × 30.5 cm).
Collection of Cecilia and Ernesto Poma, Miami.

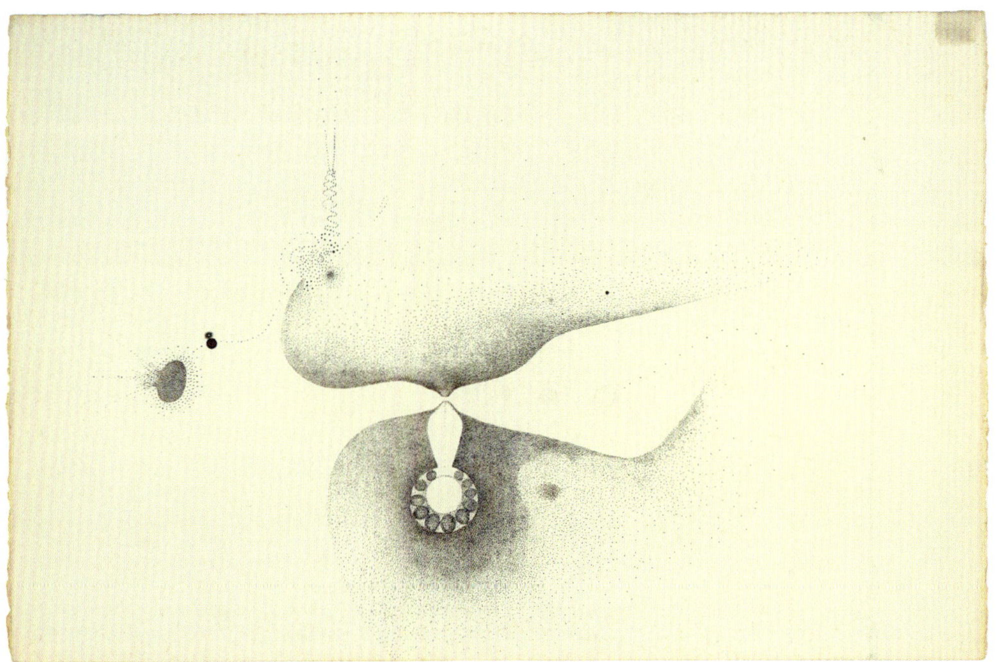

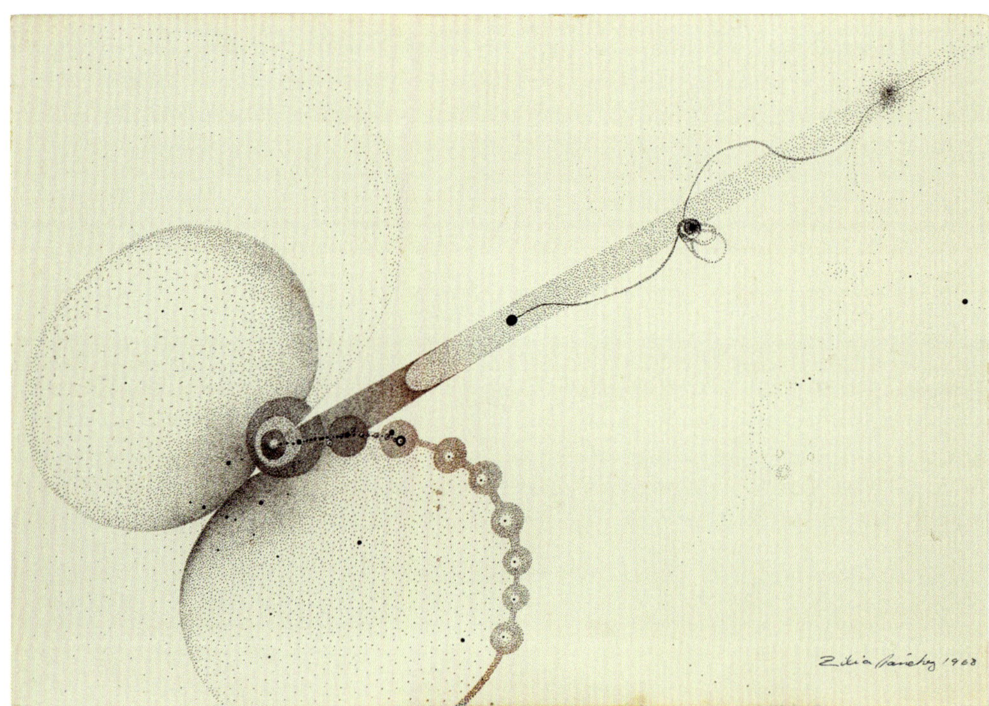

cat. 27   *El significado del significante* (The Signified of the Signifier), c. 1968. India ink on paper, 15 × 22 in. (38.1 × 55.9 cm).
Collection of the artist, Courtesy Galerie Lelong & Co., New York.

cat. 28   *El significado del significante* (The Signified of the Signifier), c. 1968. India ink on paper, 14 × 19 ¾ in. (35.6 × 50.2 cm).
Collection of the artist, Courtesy Galerie Lelong & Co., New York.

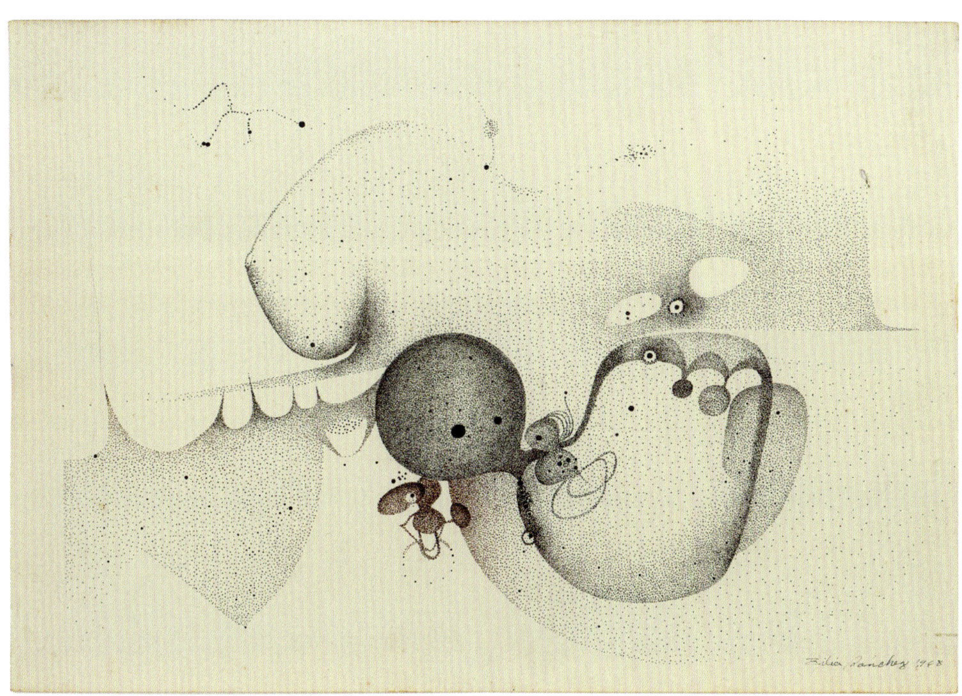

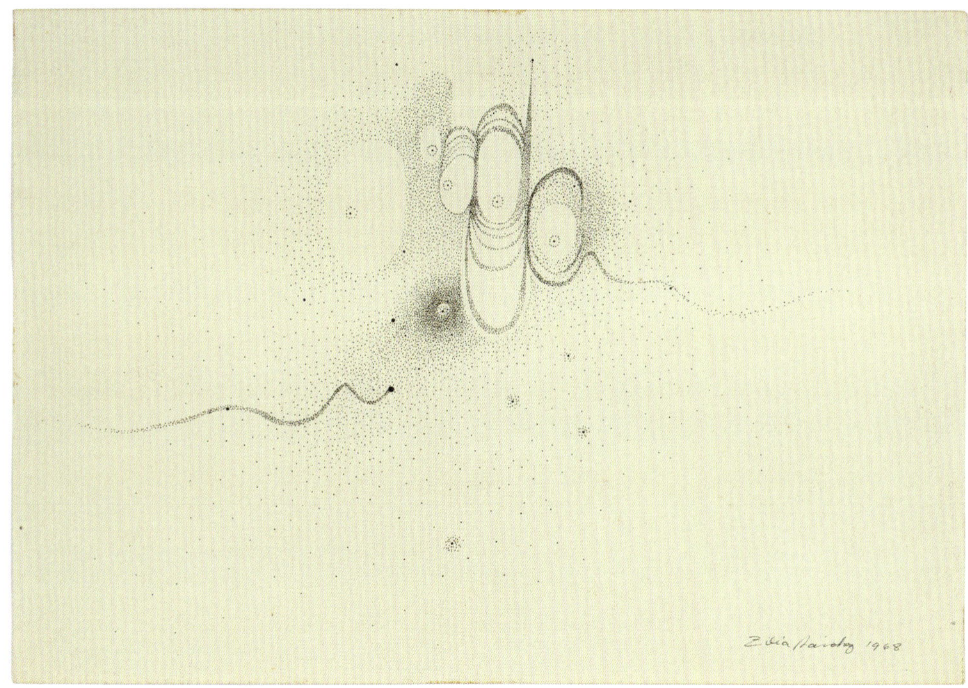

cat. 29 *El significado del significante* (The Signified of the Signifier), c. 1968. India ink on paper, 14 × 19 ¾ in. (35.6 × 50.2 cm). Collection of the artist, Courtesy Galerie Lelong & Co., New York.

cat. 30 *El significado del significante* (The Signified of the Signifier), c. 1968. India ink on paper, 14 × 19 ¾ in. (35.6 × 50.2 cm). Collection of the artist, Courtesy Galerie Lelong & Co., New York.

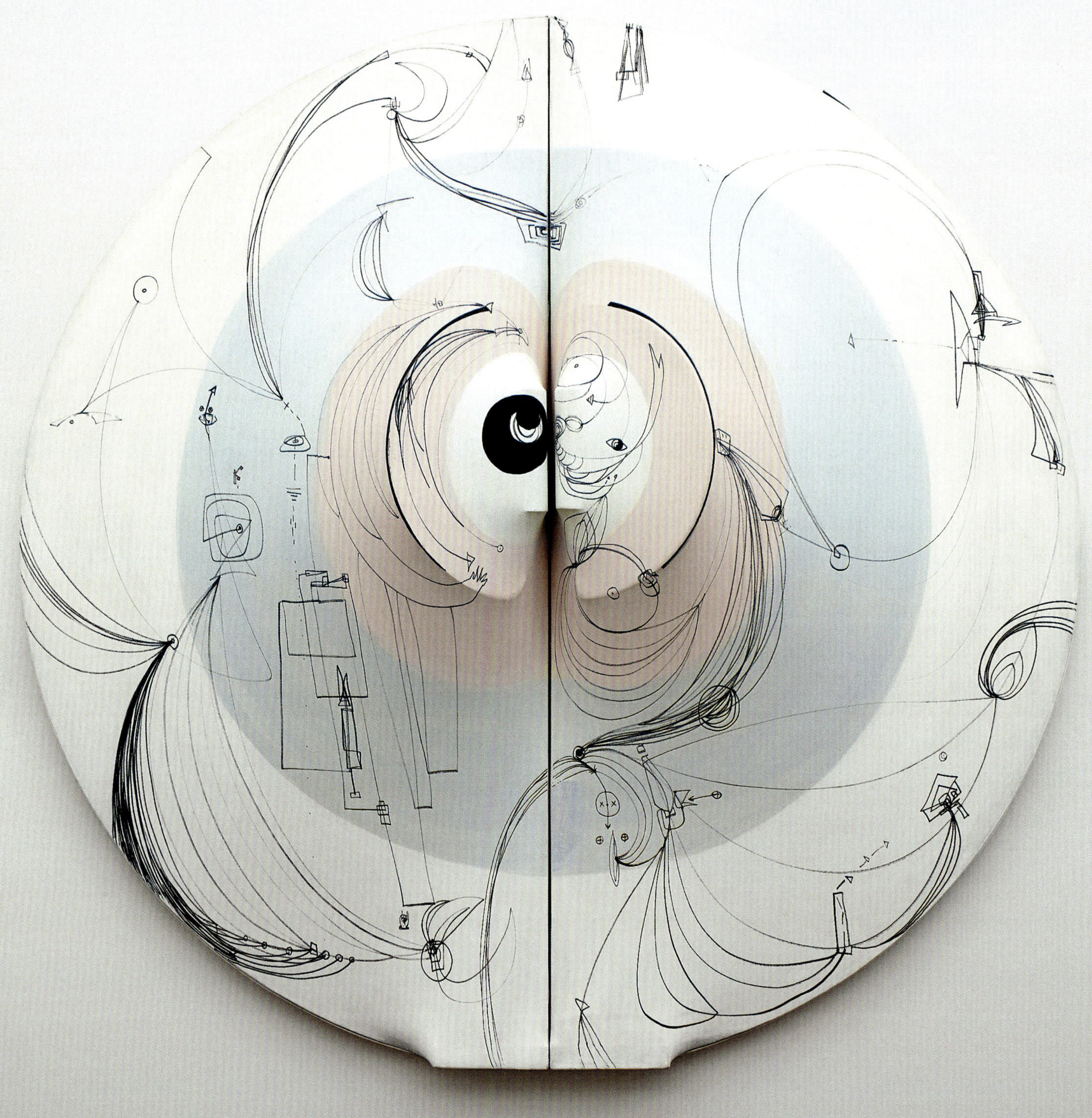

cat. 31 *Lunar con tatuaje* (Moon with Tattoo), c. 1968/96. Acrylic on stretched canvas, 71 × 72 × 12 in. (180.3 × 182.9 × 30.5 cm). Collection of the artist, Courtesy Galerie Lelong & Co., New York.

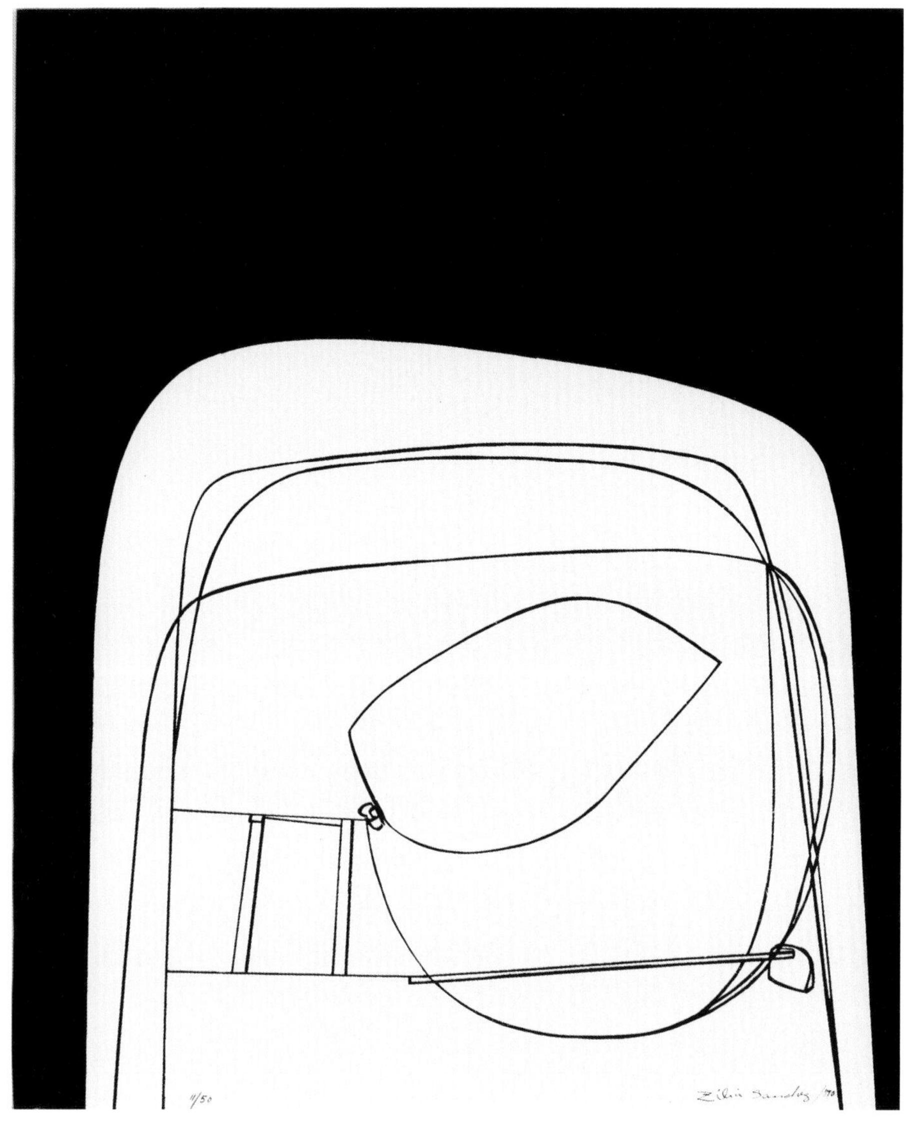

cat. 32　*Untitled*, 1970. Serigraph, ed. 11/30, 20 × 16 in. (50.8 × 40.6 cm). El Museo del Barrio, New York, Gift of Servando Sacaluga, 1985.

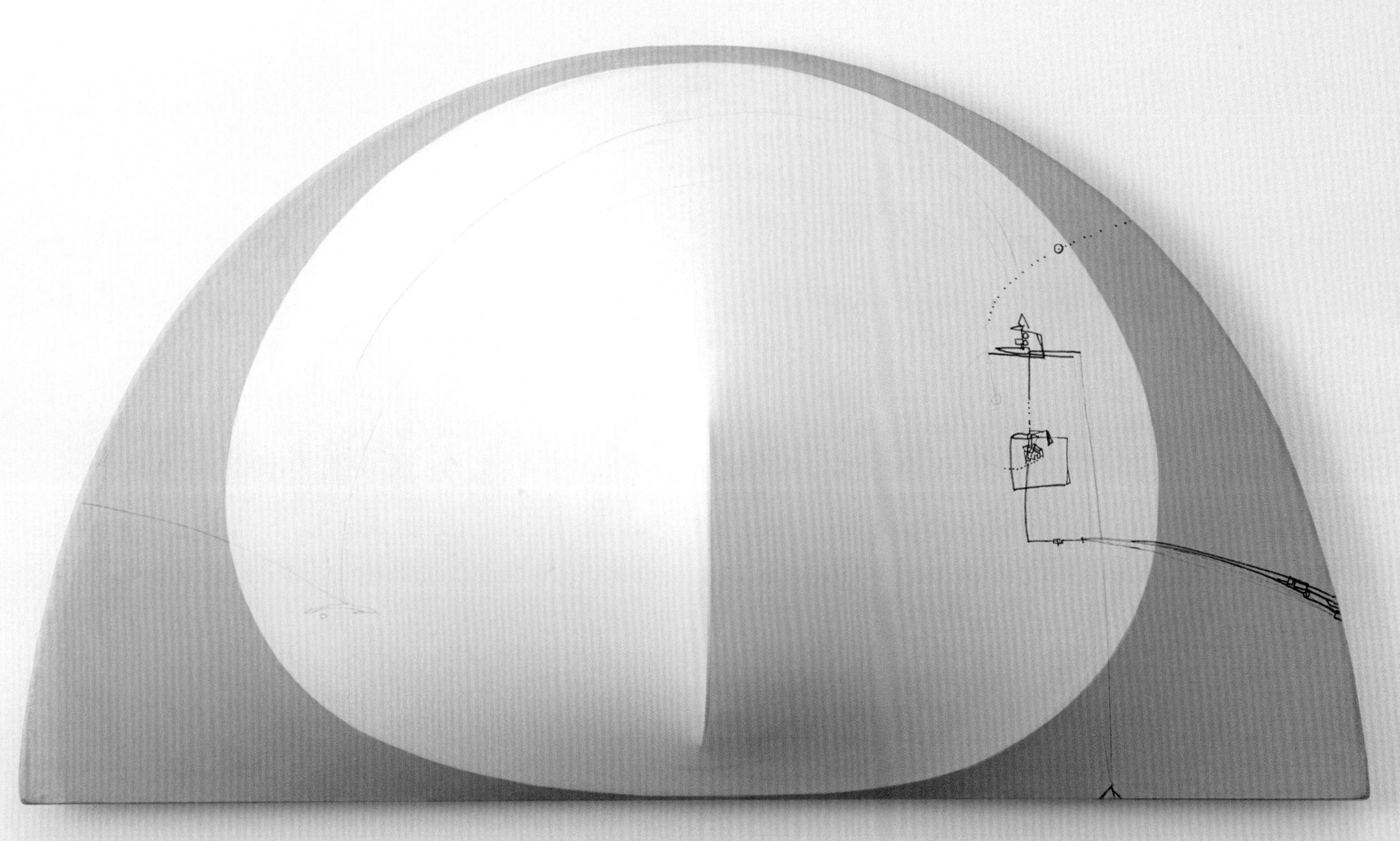

cat. 33 *Soy Isla* (I Am an Island), c. 1970. Acrylic and ink on stretched canvas, 19 ¾ × 35 × 14 in. (50.2 × 88.9 × 35.6 cm).
Collection of the artist, Courtesy Galerie Lelong & Co., New York.

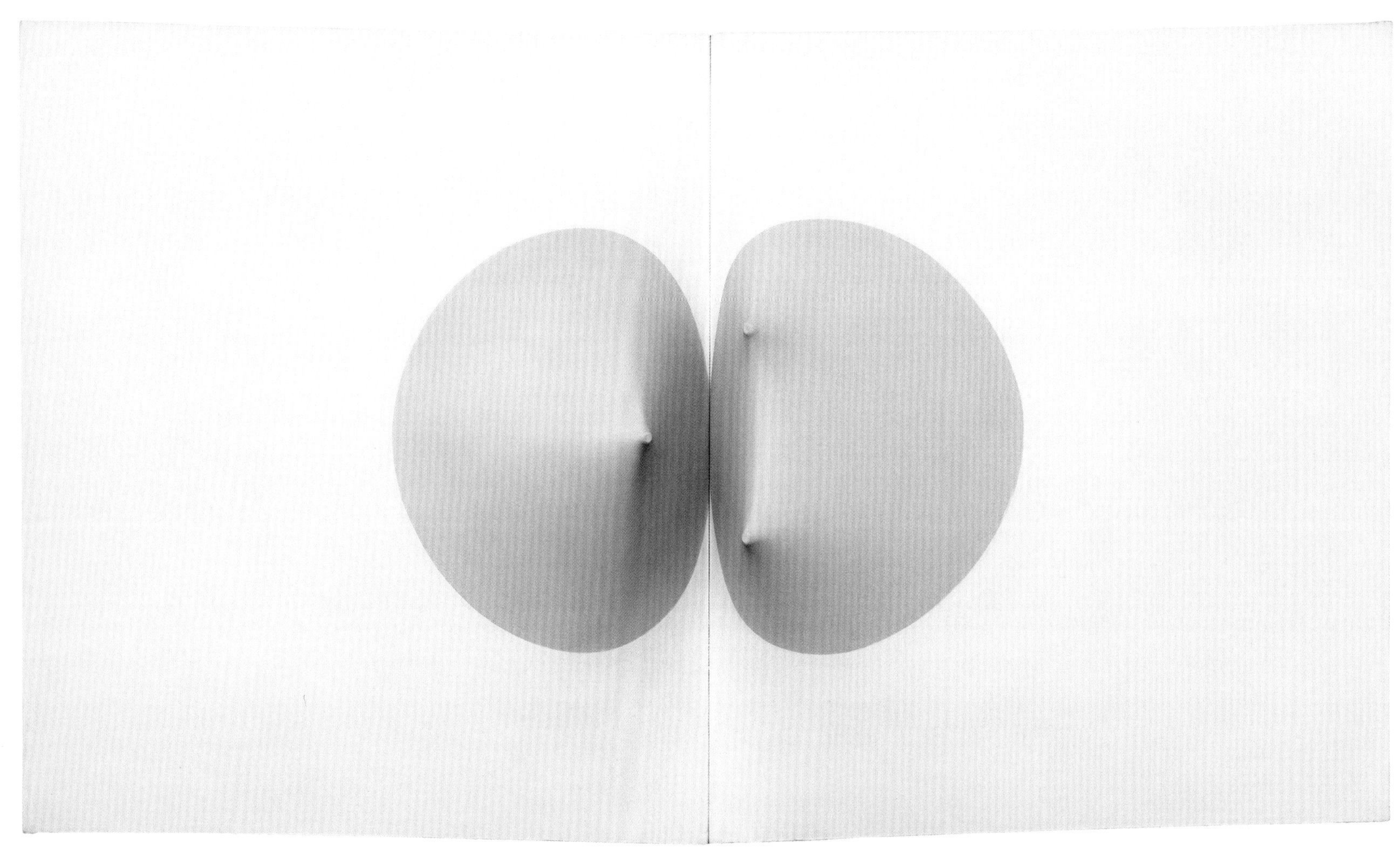

cat. 34　*Untitled*, 1971. Acrylic on stretched canvas, 43 × 73 × approx. 12 in. (109.2 × 185.4 × approx. 30.5 cm).
Pérez Art Museum Miami, Gift of Jorge M. Pérez.

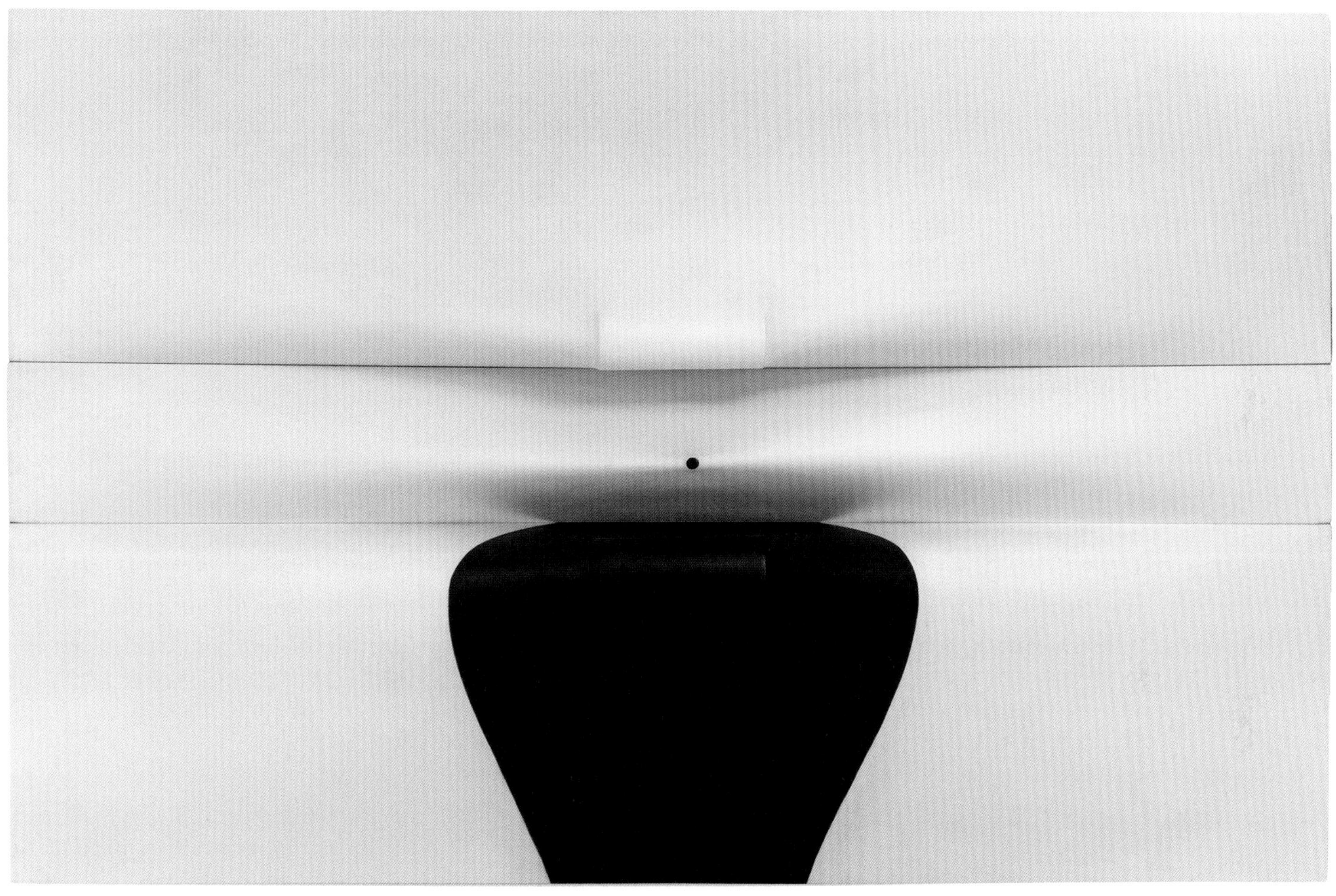

cat. 35 *Subliminal*, from the series *Amazonas* (Amazons), 1972. Acrylic on stretched canvas, 39 ½ × 40 ½ × 10 in. (100.3 × 102.9 × 25.4 cm). Private collection, San Juan.

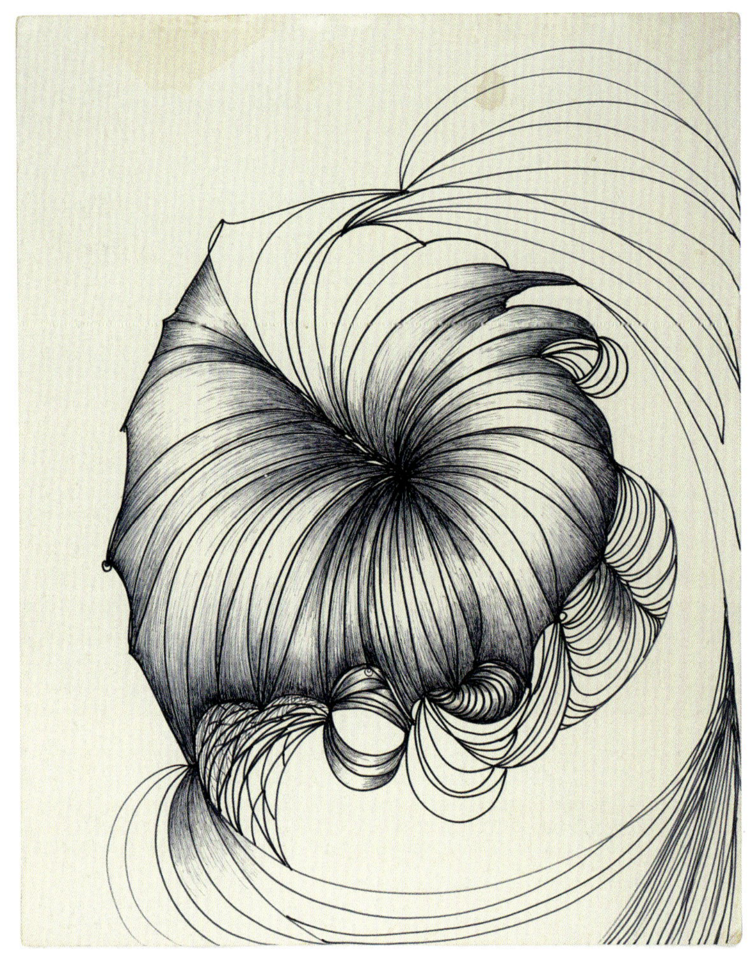

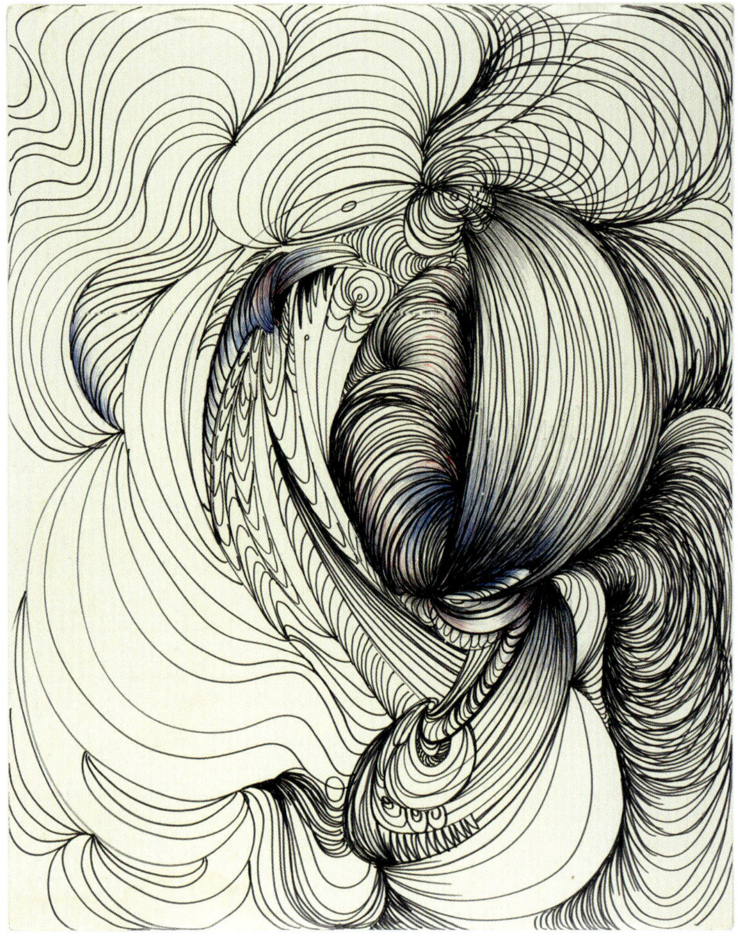

cat. 36 *Furia I* (Fury I), 1972. Ink on paper, 25 ½ × 20 in. (64.8 × 50.8 cm). Collection of the artist, Courtesy Galerie Lelong & Co., New York.

cat. 37 *Furia II* (Fury II), 1972. Ink on paper, 25 ½ × 20 in. (64.8 × 50.8 cm). Collection of the artist, Courtesy Galerie Lelong & Co., New York.

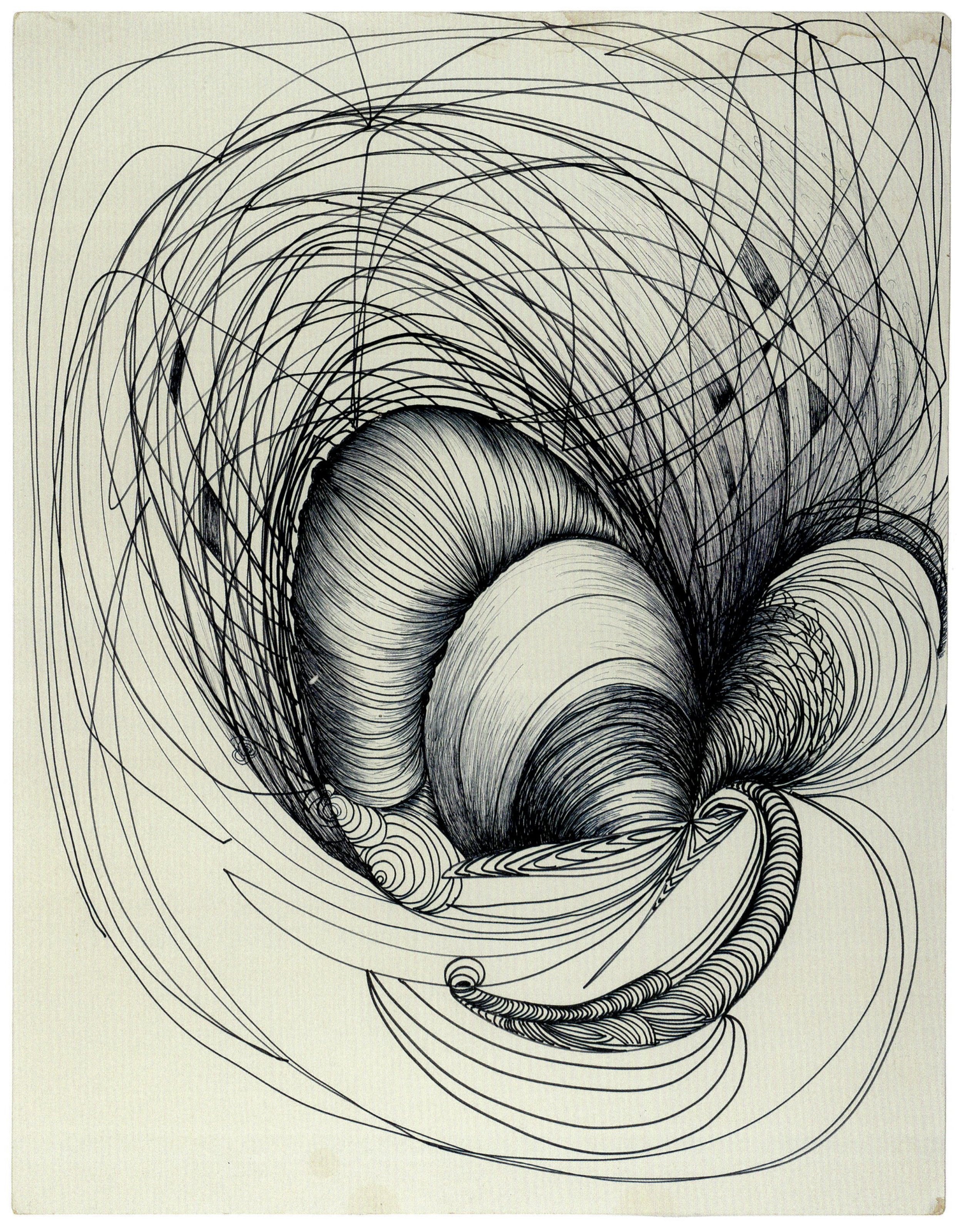

cat. 38   *Furia III* (Fury III), 1972. Ink on paper, 25 ½ × 20 in. (64.8 × 50.8 cm). Collection of the artist, Courtesy Galerie Lelong & Co., New York.

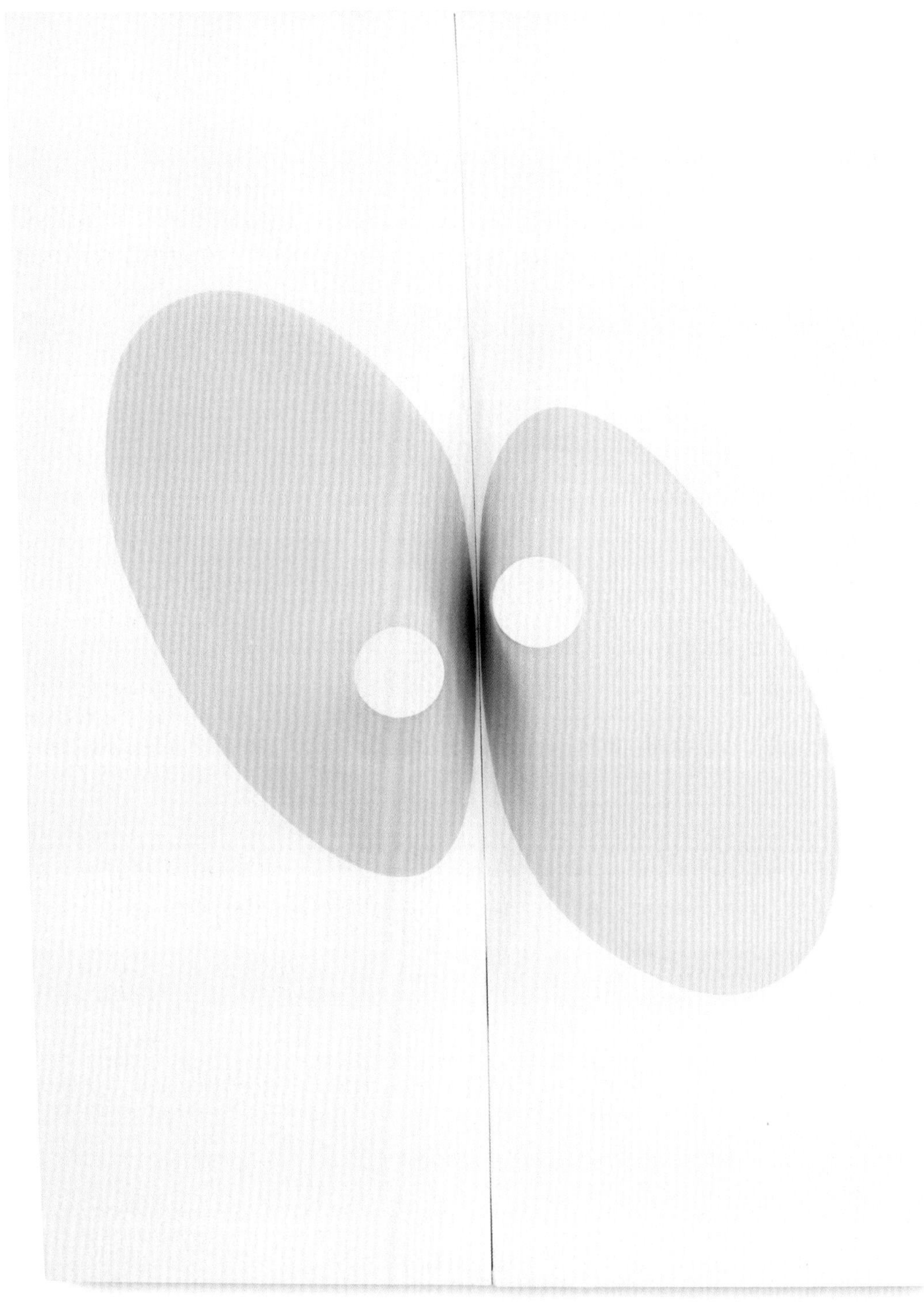

cat. 39 *Maqueta Soy Isla*, 1972/92. Acrylic on stretched canvas, 55 ½ × 39 ¾ × 9 ½ in. (141 × 101 × 24.1 cm).
Collection of Marie Lynn Arrieta-Tartak, San Juan.

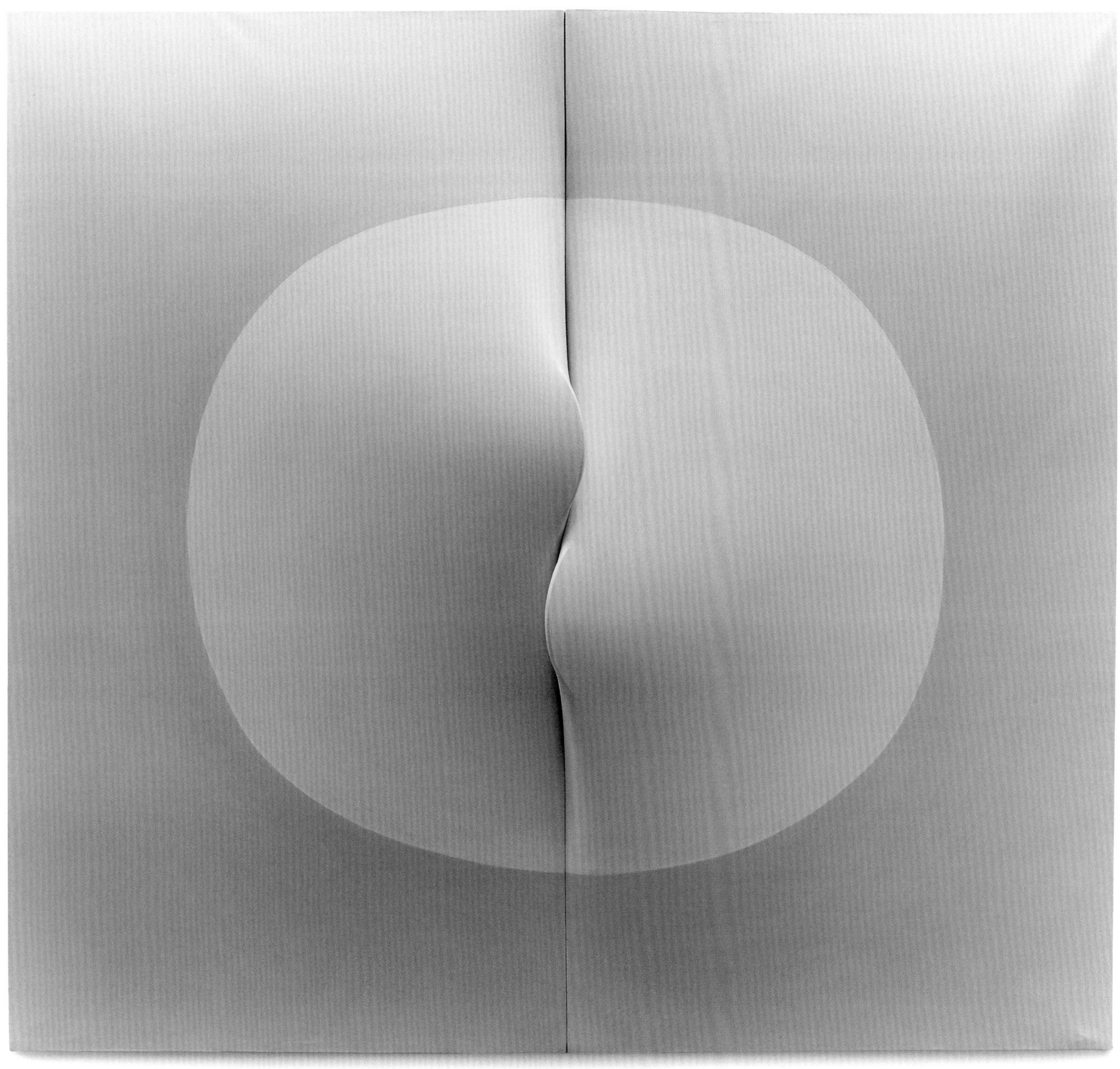

cat. 40   *Lunar V (Moon V)*, c. 1973. Acrylic on stretched canvas, 74 ¾ × 79 ½ × 10 in. (189.9 × 201.9 × 25.4 cm). Private collection, Seattle.

cat. 41   *Construcción: Topología erótica* (Construction: Erotic Topology), 1973. Acrylic on stretched canvas, 73 ¹³⁄₁₆ × 30 ⅞ × 5 ¼ in. (187.5 × 78.5 × 13 cm). Museo de Arte de Ponce, The Luis A. Ferré Foundation, Inc., PR.

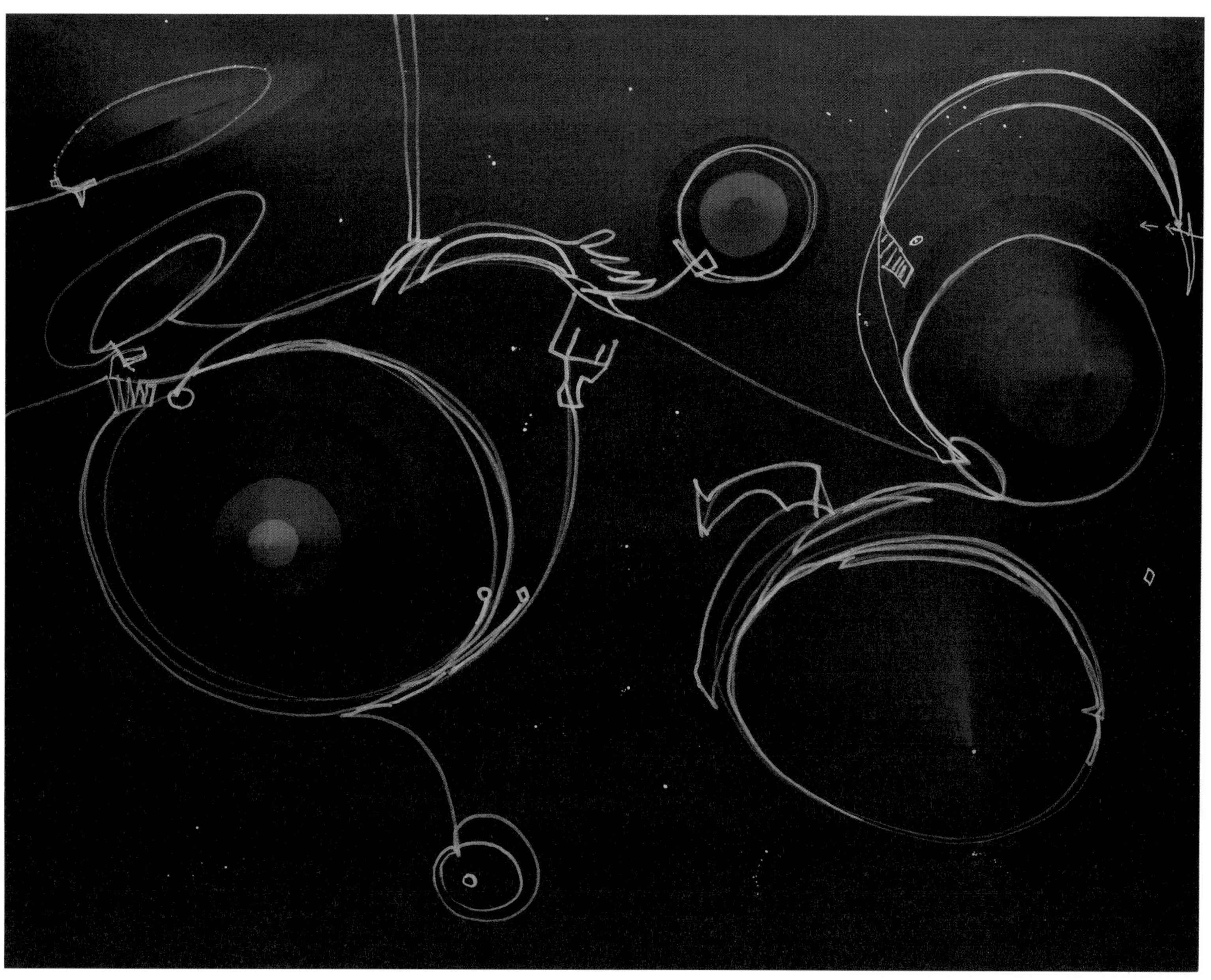

cat. 42 *Lunar negro con tatuaje* (Black Moon with Tattoo), 1975. Acrylic on stretched canvas, 33 × 43 ¾ × 8 ½ in. (83.8 × 111.1 × 21.6 cm). Colby College Museum of Art, Waterville, ME, Museum purchase from the Jere Abbott Acquisitions Fund, 2016.228.

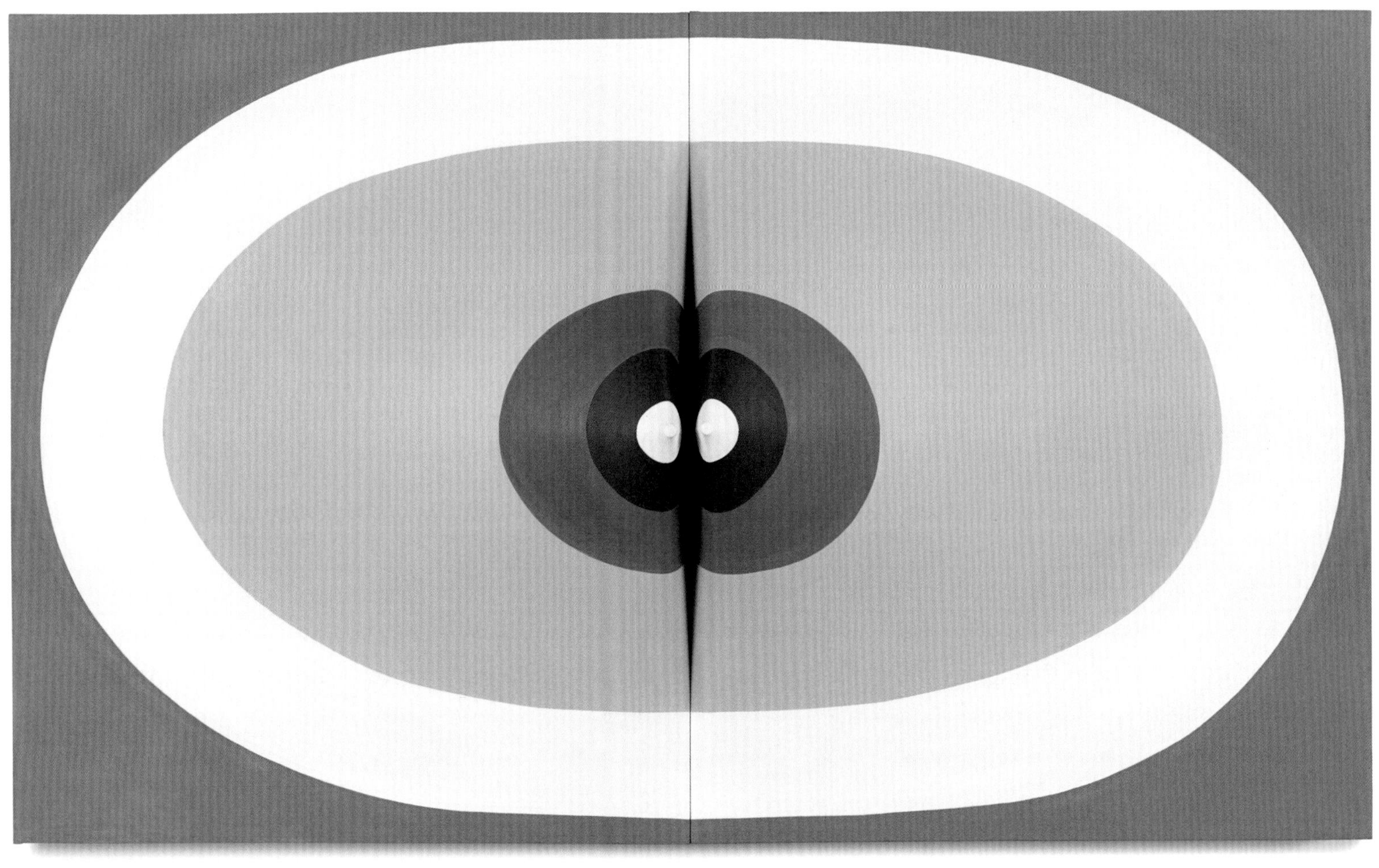

cat. 43   *Untitled*, 1978. Acrylic on stretched canvas, 72 × 117 ½ × 10 ½ in. (182.9 × 298.5 × 26.7 cm).
Collection of the artist, Courtesy Galerie Lelong & Co., New York.

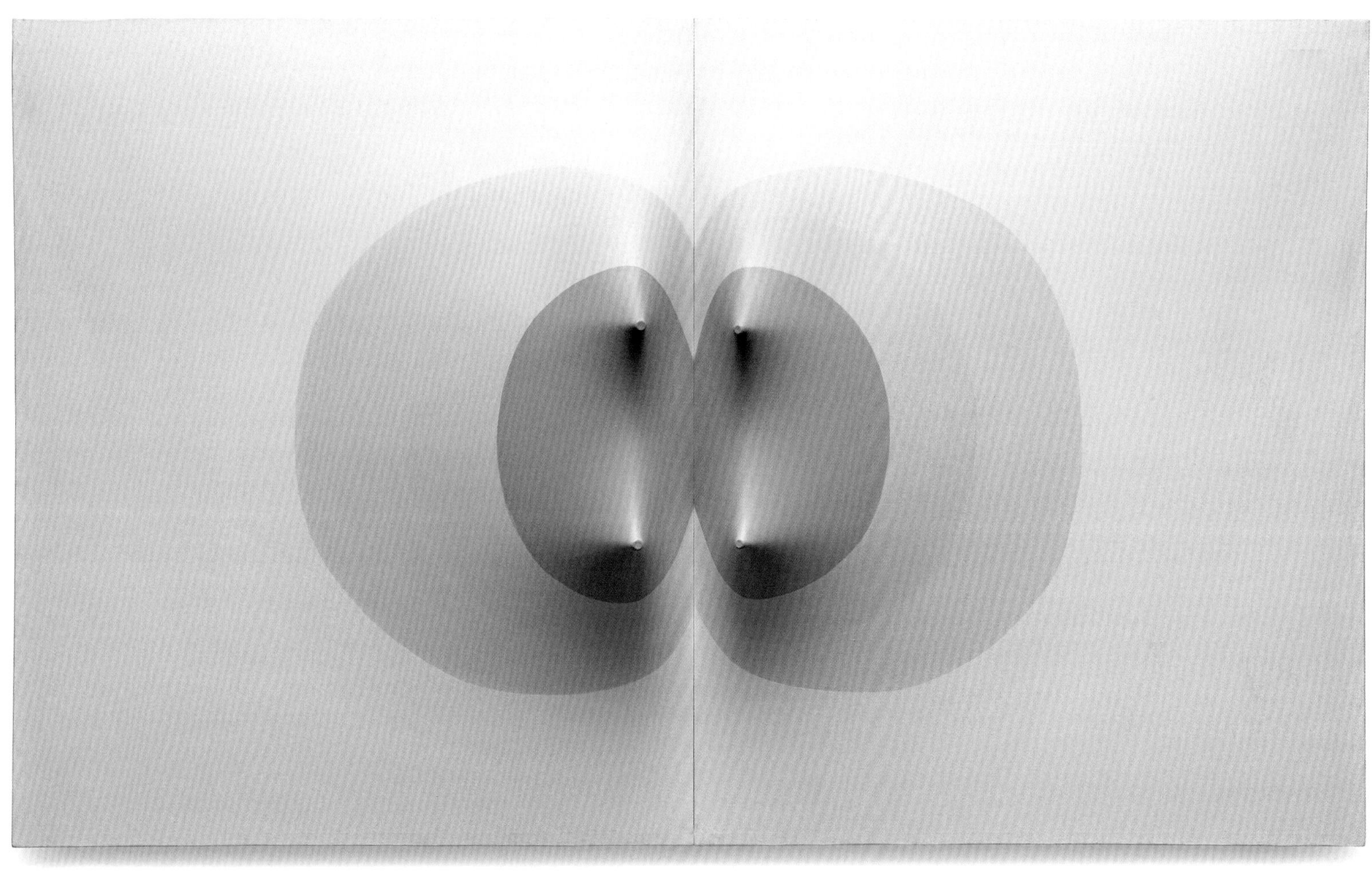

cat. 44   *Amazonas* (Amazons), from the series *Topologías eróticas* (Erotic Topologies), 1978. Acrylic on stretched canvas, 43 × 70 × 11 in. (109.2 × 177.8 × 27.9 cm). Princeton University Art Museum, NJ, Museum purchase, Fowler McCormick, Class of 1921, Fund, 2014-53.

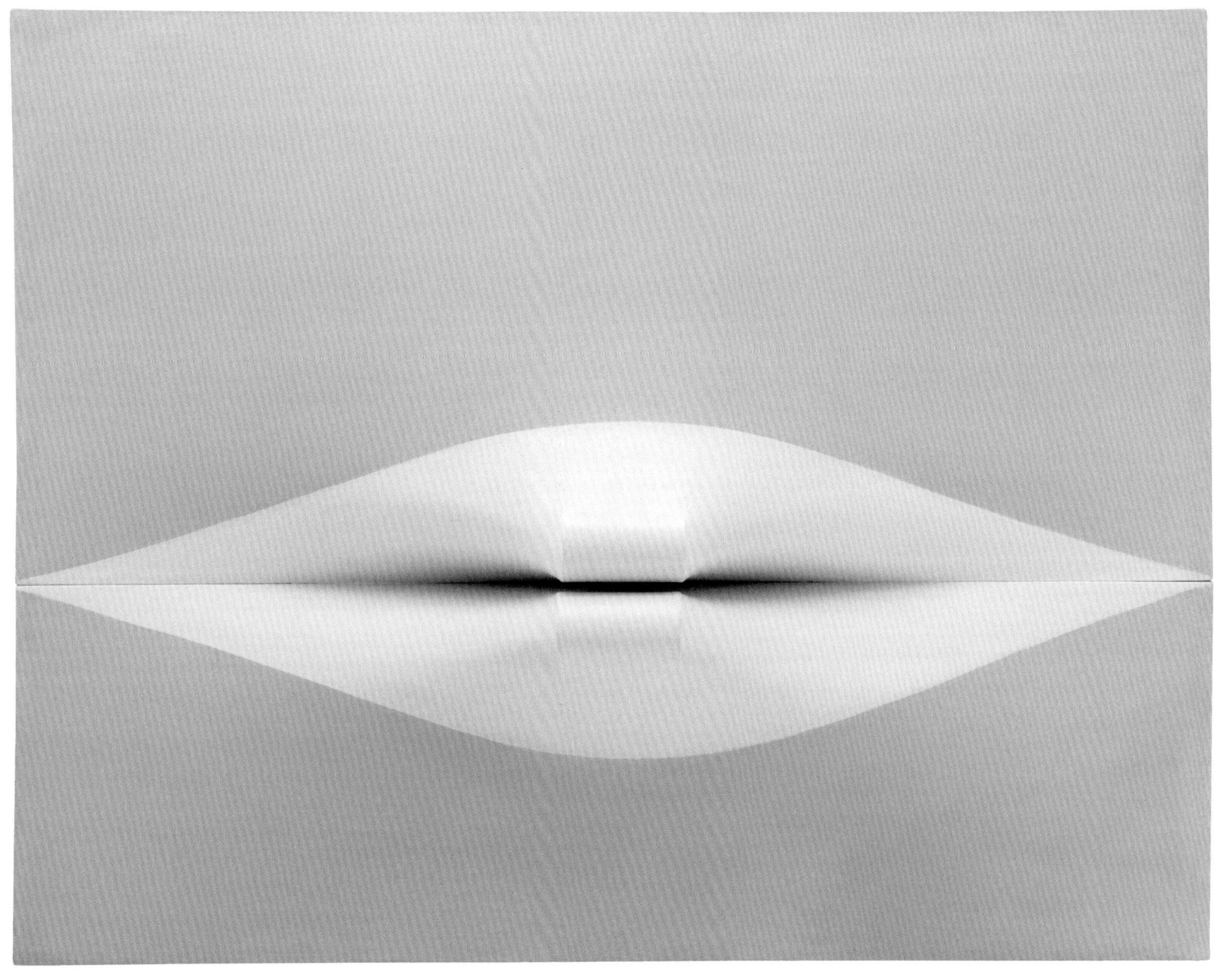

cat. 45　*El silencio de Eros* (The Silence of Eros), c. 1980. Acrylic on stretched canvas, 50 × 62 × 15 in. (127 × 157.5 × 38.1 cm). Collection of Diane and Bruce Halle, Phoenix.

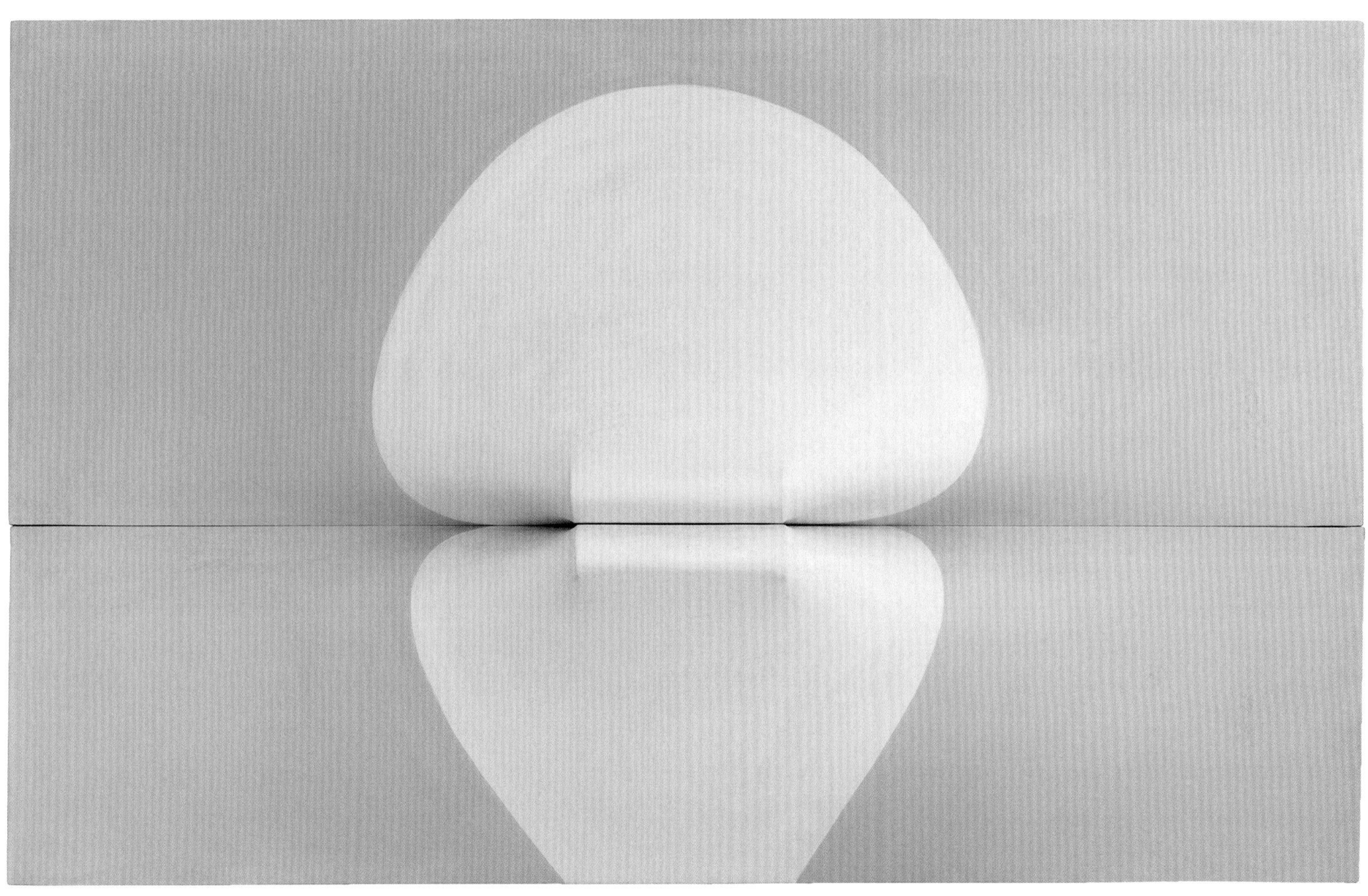

cat. 46 *El silencio de Eros* (The Silence of Eros), 1983. Acrylic on stretched canvas, 34 × 53 × 9 ½ in. (86.4 × 134.6 × 24.1 cm).
Collection of Marie Lynn Arrieta-Tartak, San Juan.

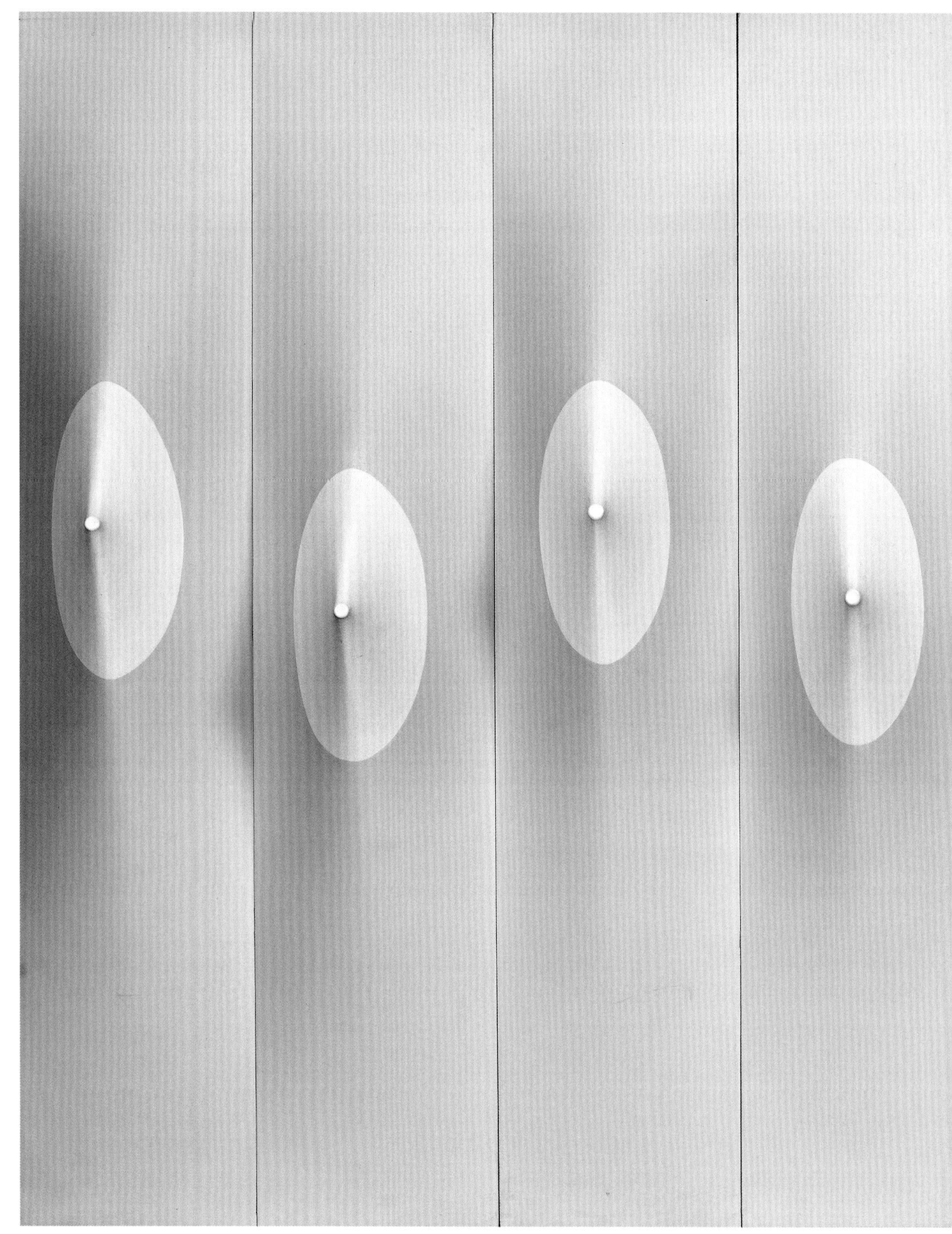

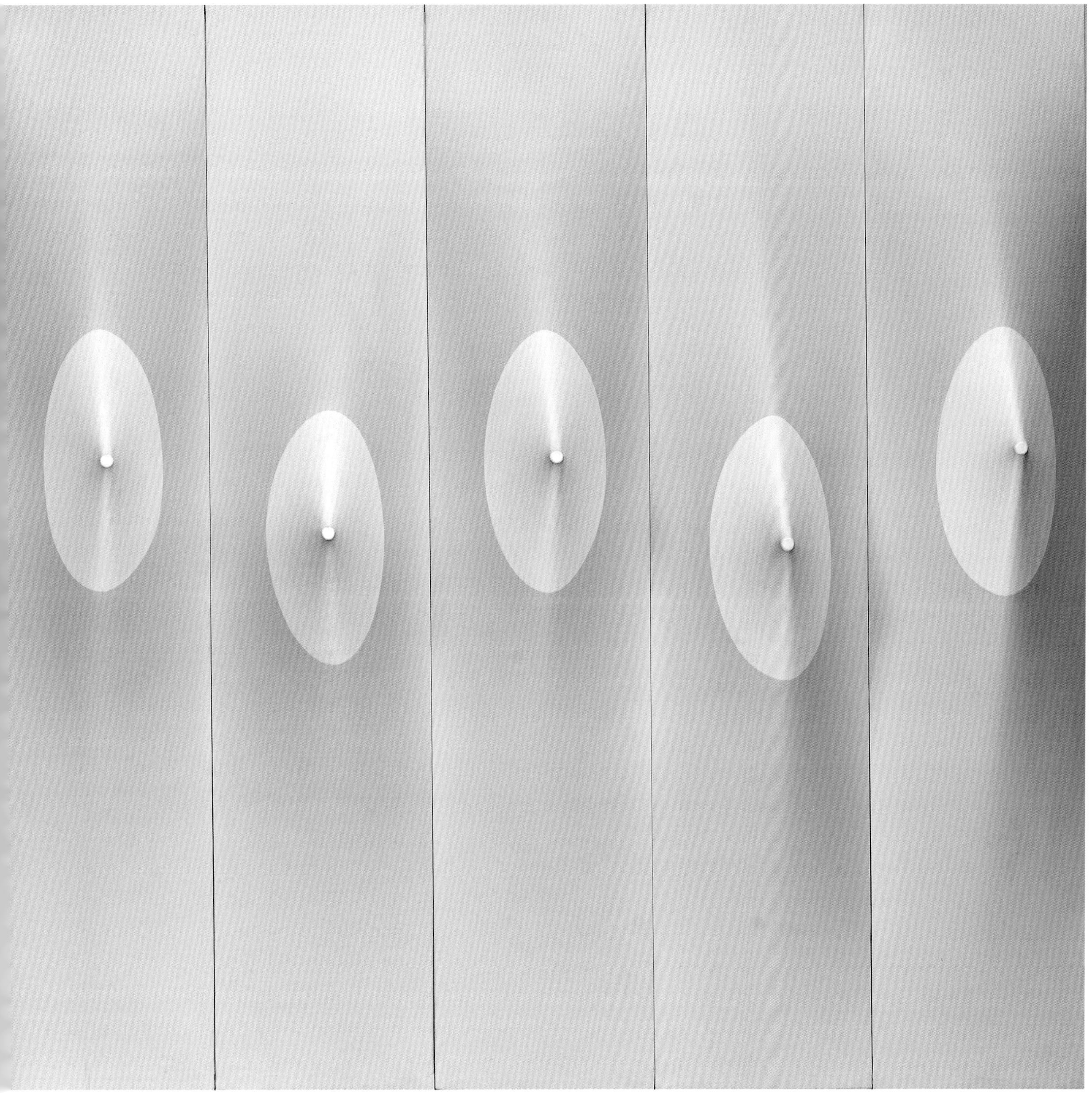

cat. 47 *Troyanas* (Trojan Women), 1984. Acrylic on stretched canvas, 54 × 95 ⅜ × 11 ¼ in. (137.2 × 242.3 × 28.6 cm).
Compañía de Turismo de Puerto Rico, San Juan.

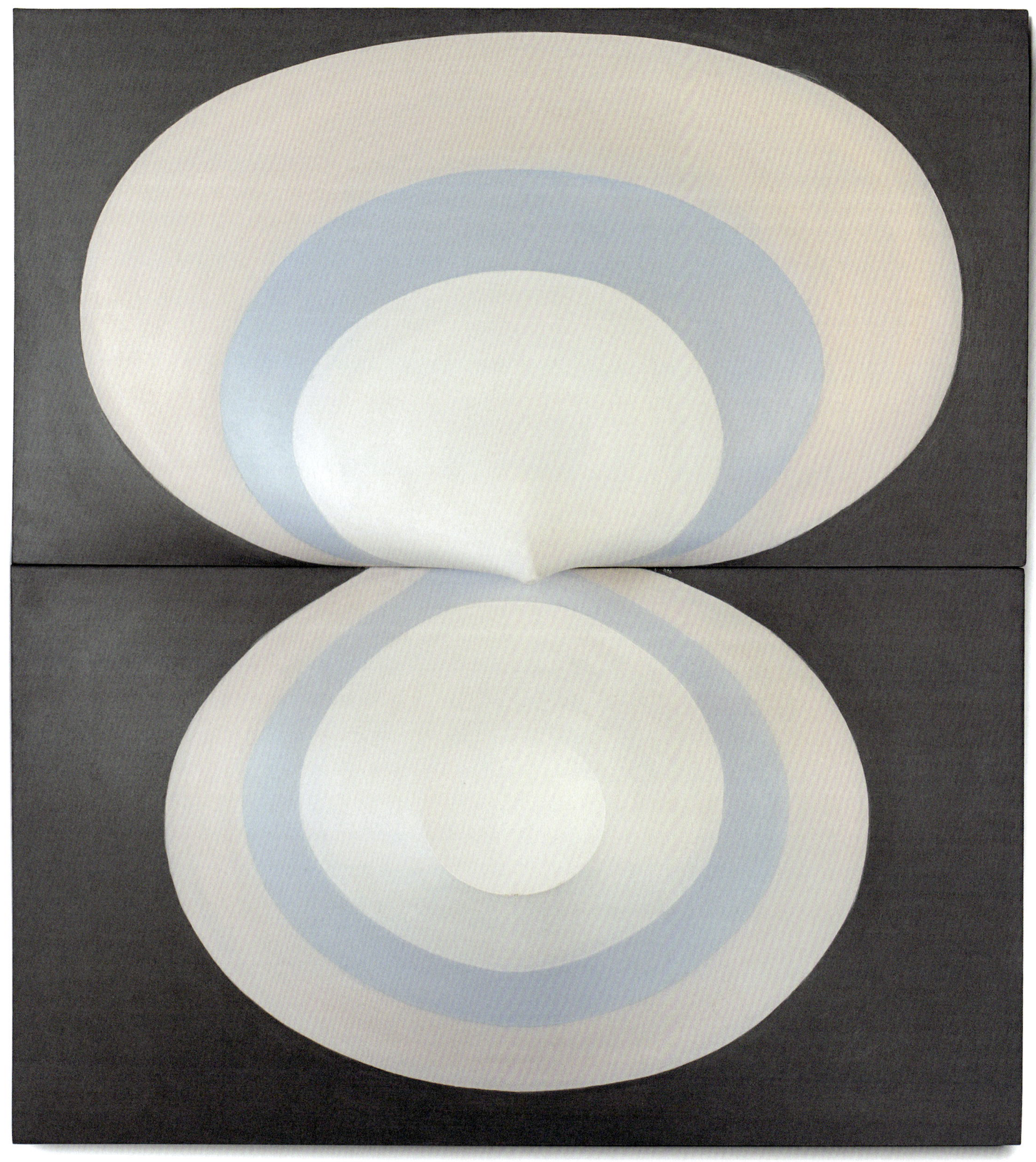

cat. 48 *El silencio de Eros III* (The Silence of Eros III), 1984. Acrylic on stretched canvas, 48 ¼ × 43 × 11 ¼ in.
(122.7 × 109.2 × 28.6 cm). Collection of Mima and César Reyes, San Juan.

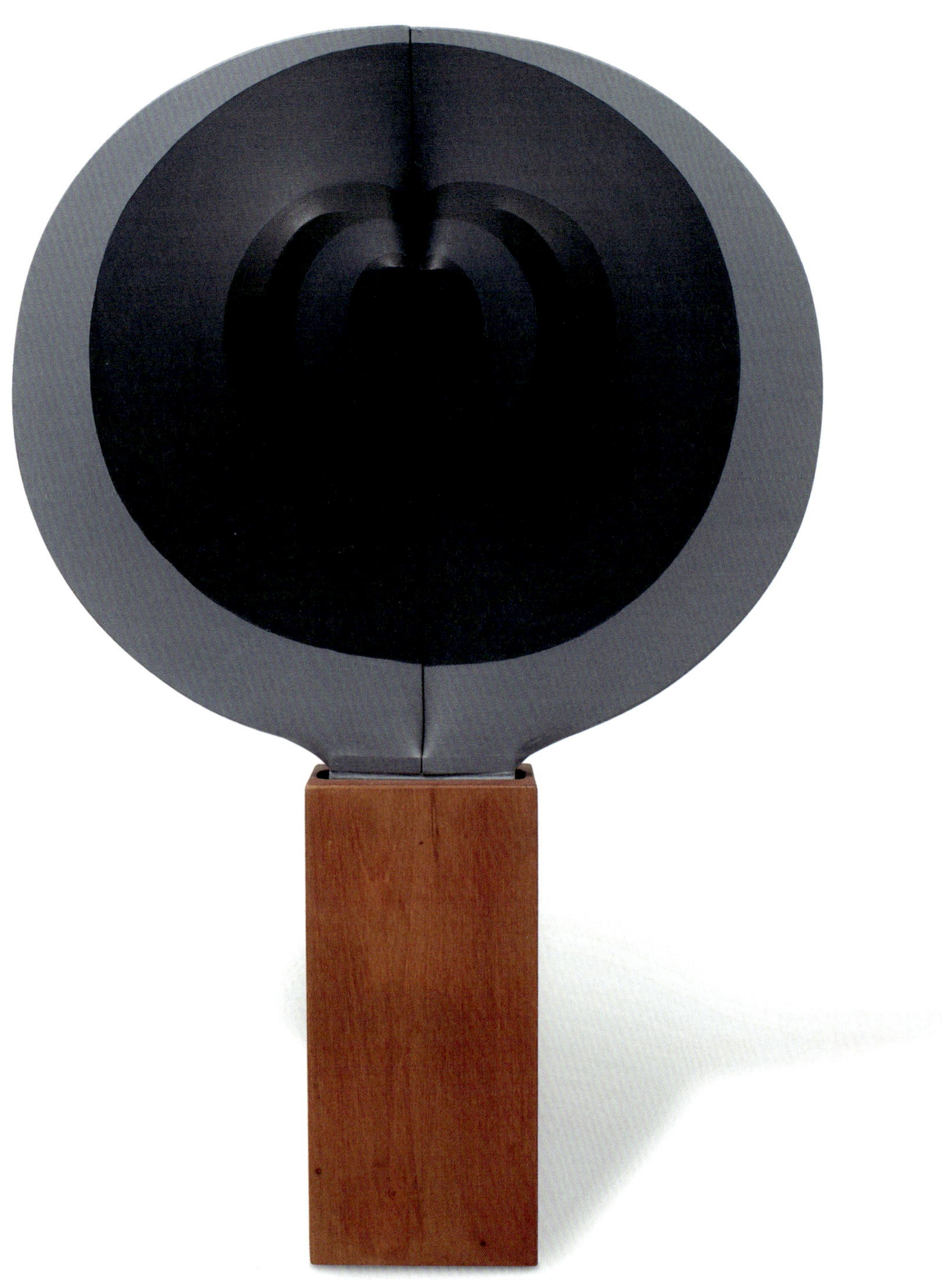

cat. 49   *Lunar* (Moon), c. 1980. Acrylic on stretched canvas with custom wooden base, 23 × 21 ¾ × 5 in.
(58.4 × 55.2 × 12.7 cm). Collection of Mima and César Reyes, San Juan.

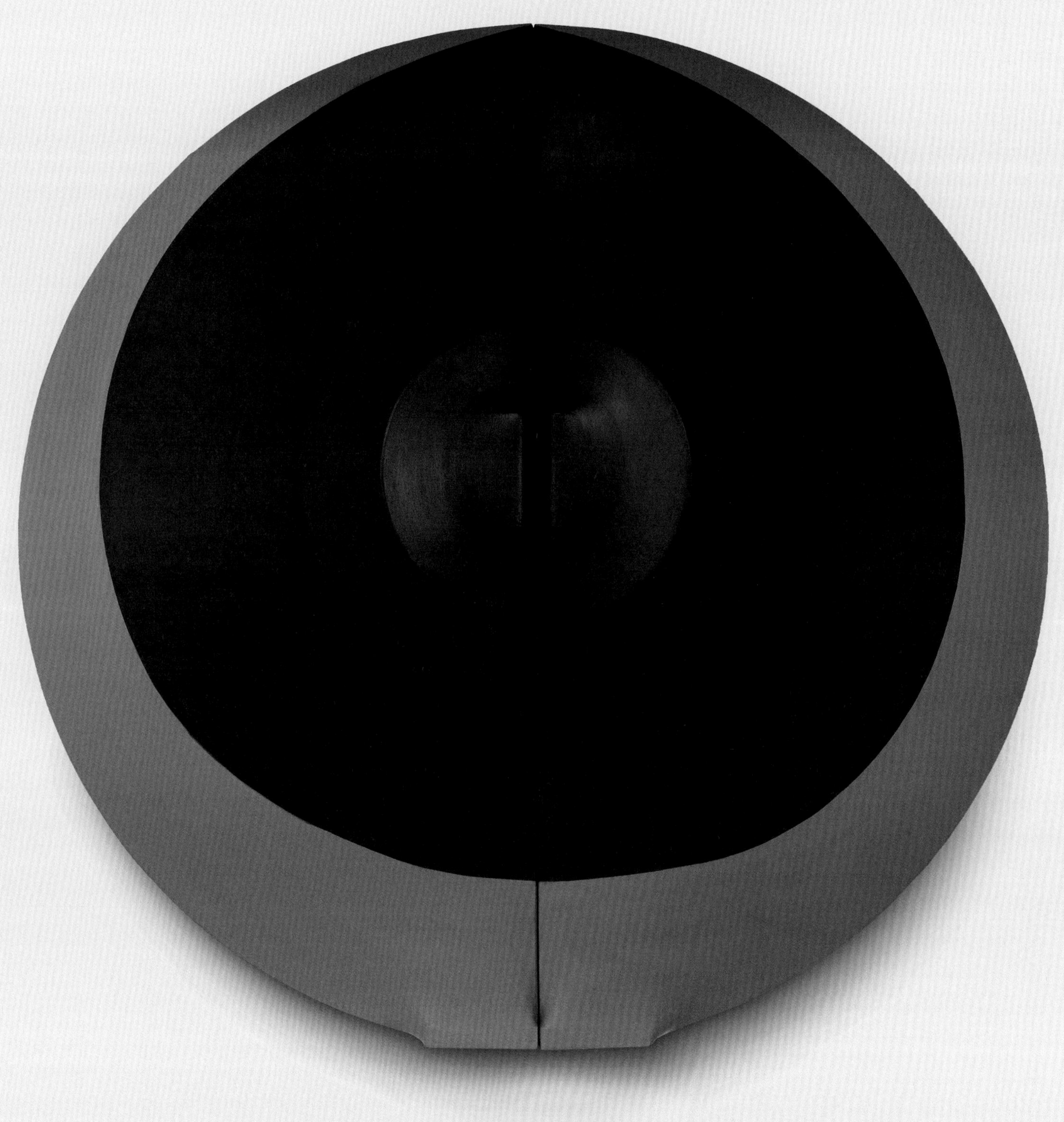

cat. 50 *Lunar* (Moon), 1985. Acrylic on stretched canvas, 71 ½ × 73 ½ × 14 in. (181.6 × 186.7 × 35.6 cm).
Collection of Ignacio J. López Beguiristain and Laura M. Guerra, San Juan.

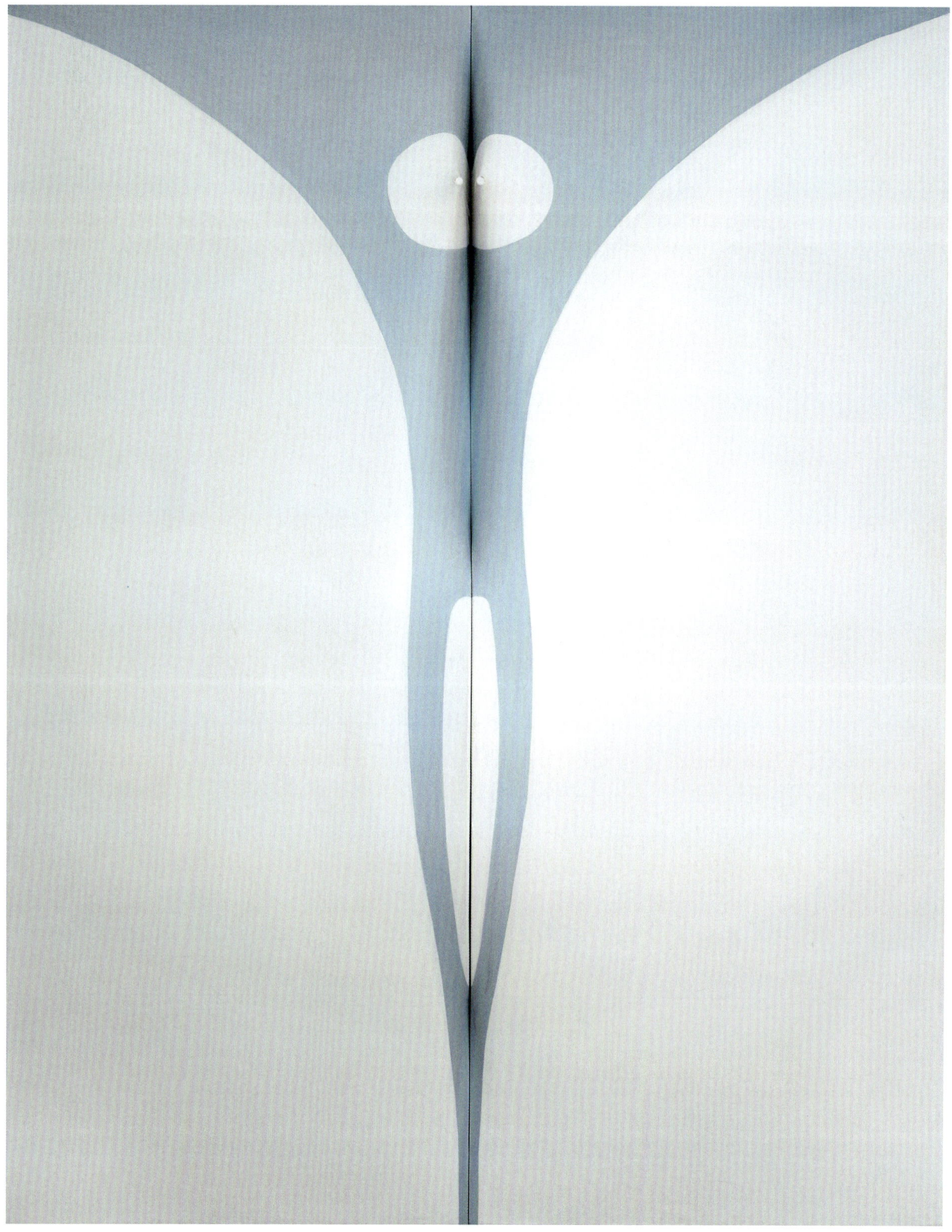

cat. 51   *Juana de Arco* (Joan of Arc), 1987. Acrylic on stretched canvas, 97 ¼ × 73 ¾ × 13 in. (247 × 187.3 × 33 cm).
Collection of Mima and César Reyes, San Juan.

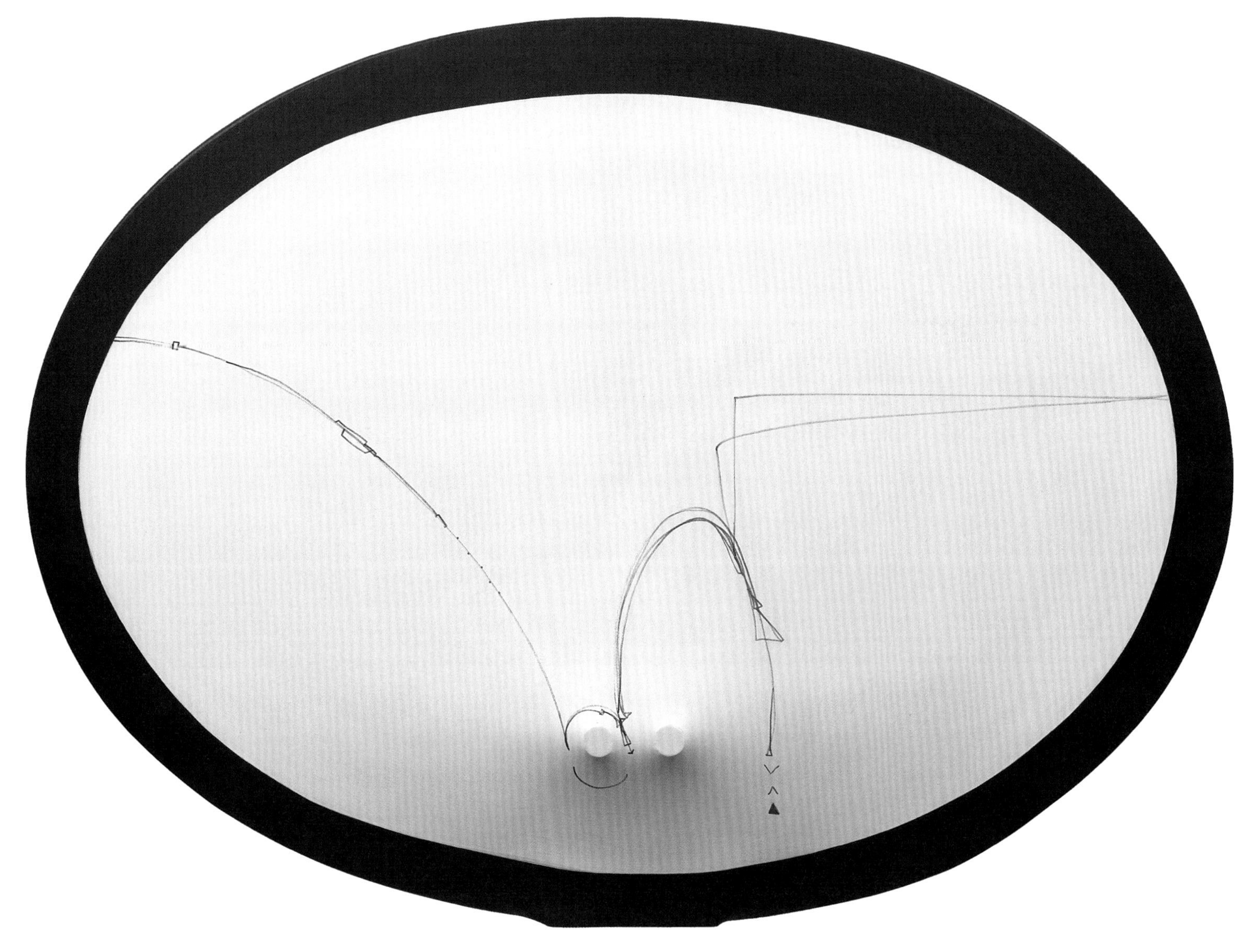

cat. 52   *Lunar con tatuaje* (Moon with Tattoo), 1989. Acrylic and ink on stretched canvas, 35 × 47 × 4 in. (88.9 × 119.4 × 10.2 cm).
Collection of the artist, Courtesy Galerie Lelong & Co., New York.

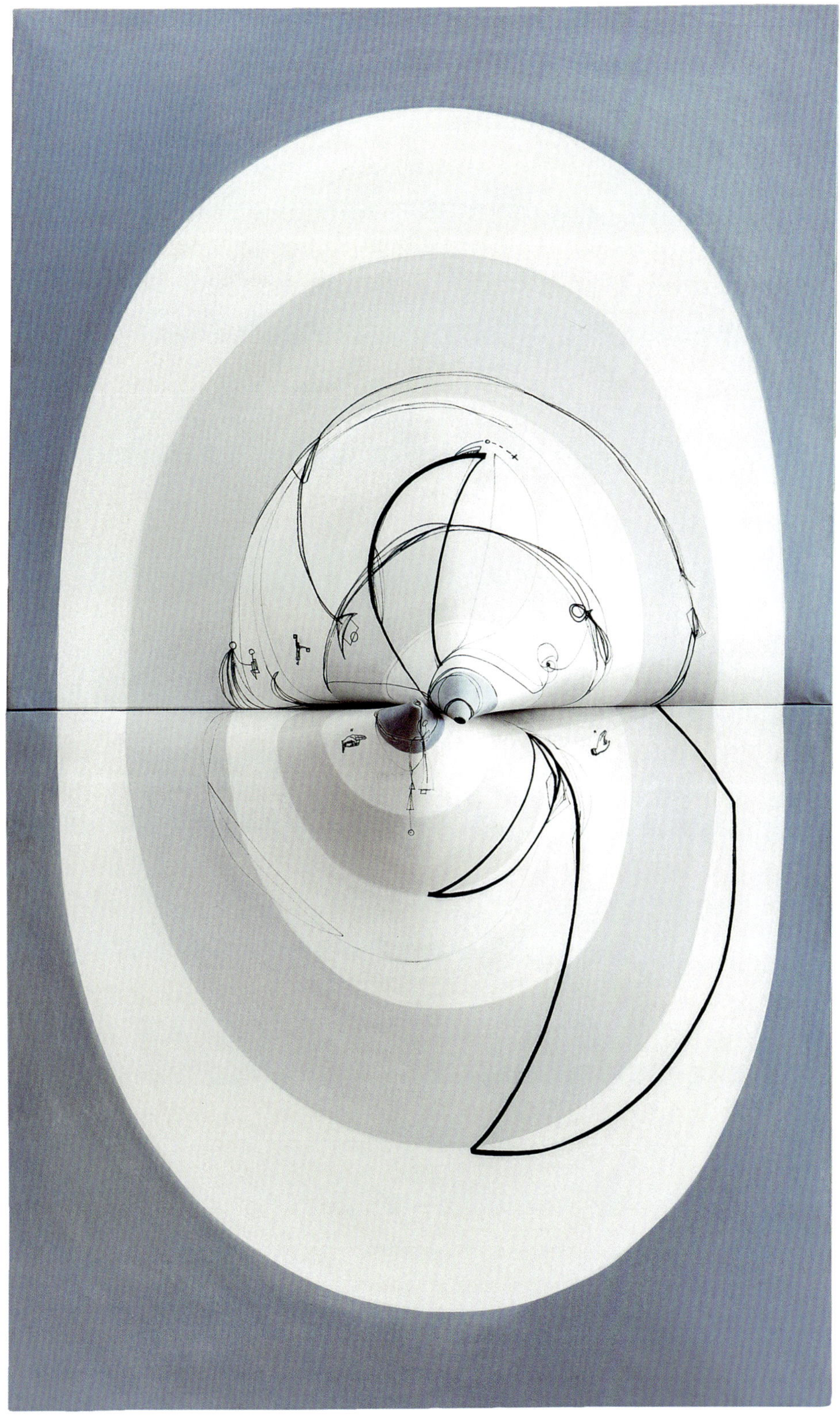

cat. 53 *Soy Isla: Compréndelo y retírate* (I Am an Island: Understand and Retreat), 1990. Acrylic and ink on stretched canvas,
72 ⅜ × 42 ⅛ × 10 in. (183.8 × 107 × 25.4 cm). Collection of the Andreu-Pietri Family, San Juan.

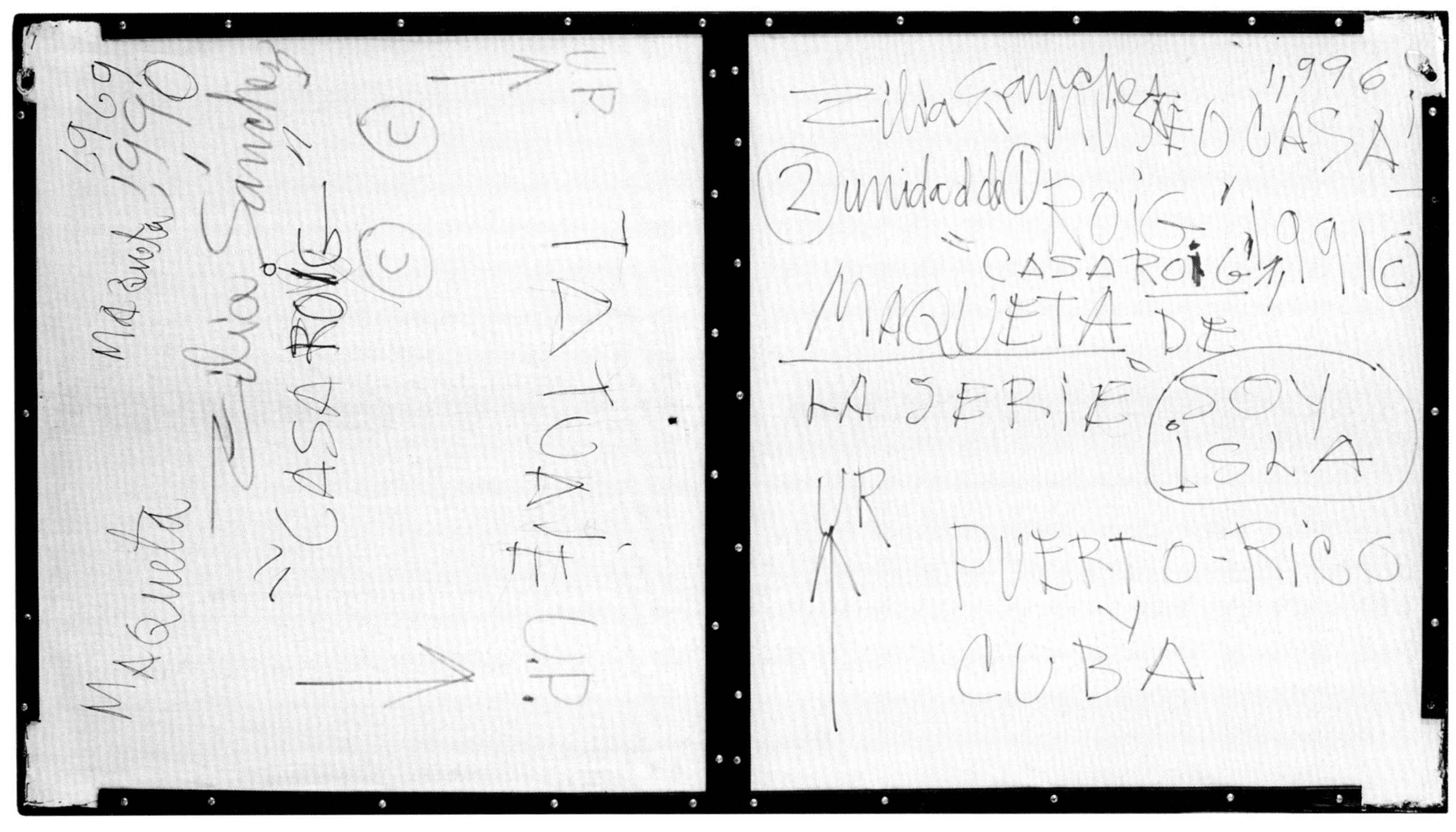
1969
Maqueta 1990
Zilia Sanchez
"CASA ROIG"
©
©
UP
TATUAJE UP.
Zilia Sanchez 1996
MUSEO CASA
2 unidades ROIG
"CASA ROIG" 1991 ©
MAQUETA DE
LA SERIE SOY ISLA
UP
PUERTO-RICO
Y
CUBA

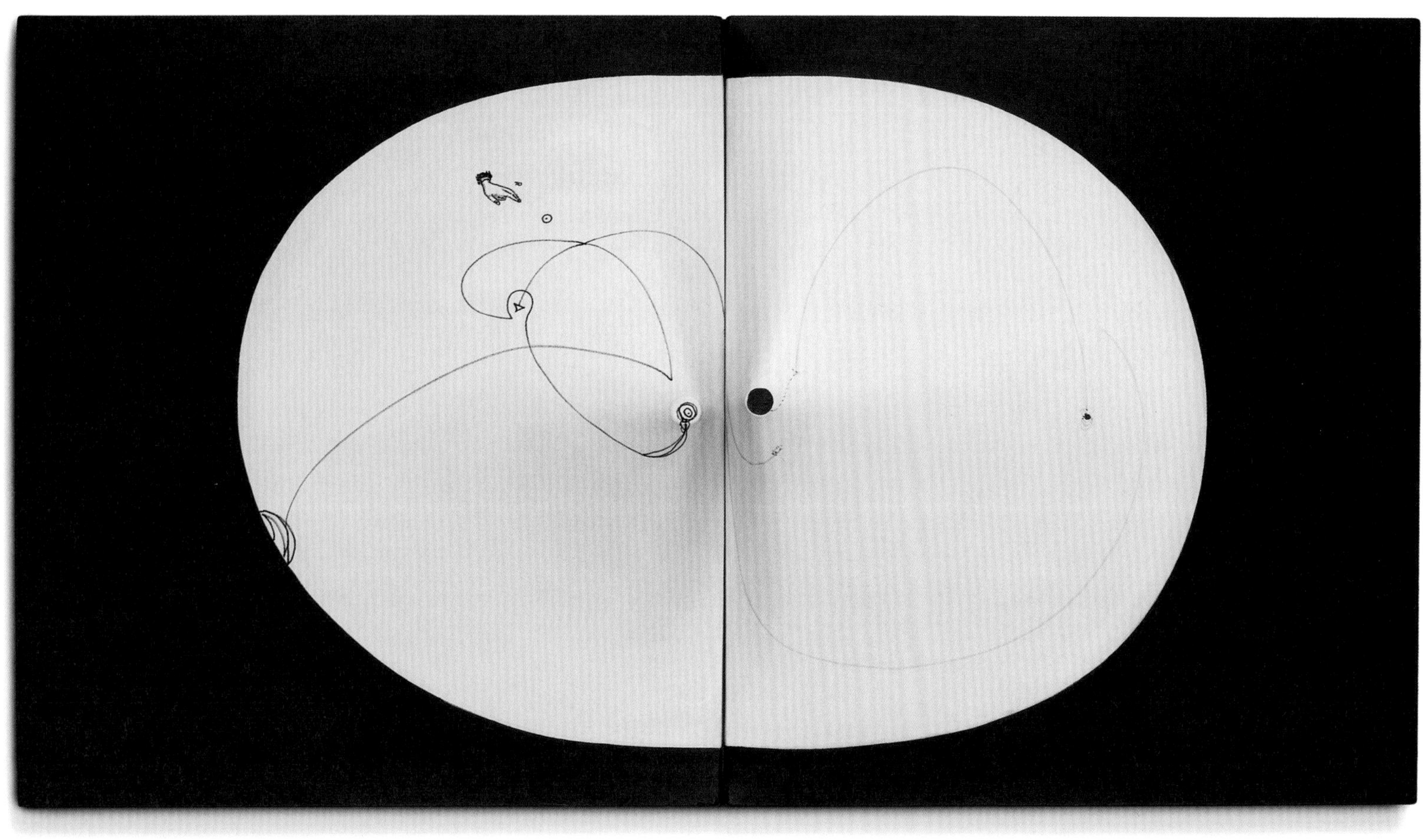

cat. 54 *Soy Isla: Compréndelo y retírate* (I Am an Island: Understand and Retreat), 1969–96. Acrylic and ink on stretched canvas, 24 ⅞ × 43 ¾ × 9 in. (63.2 × 111.1 × 22.9 cm). Collection of Luis R. de Corral, MD, San Juan. (Back view indicates object can be displayed vertically or horizontally.)

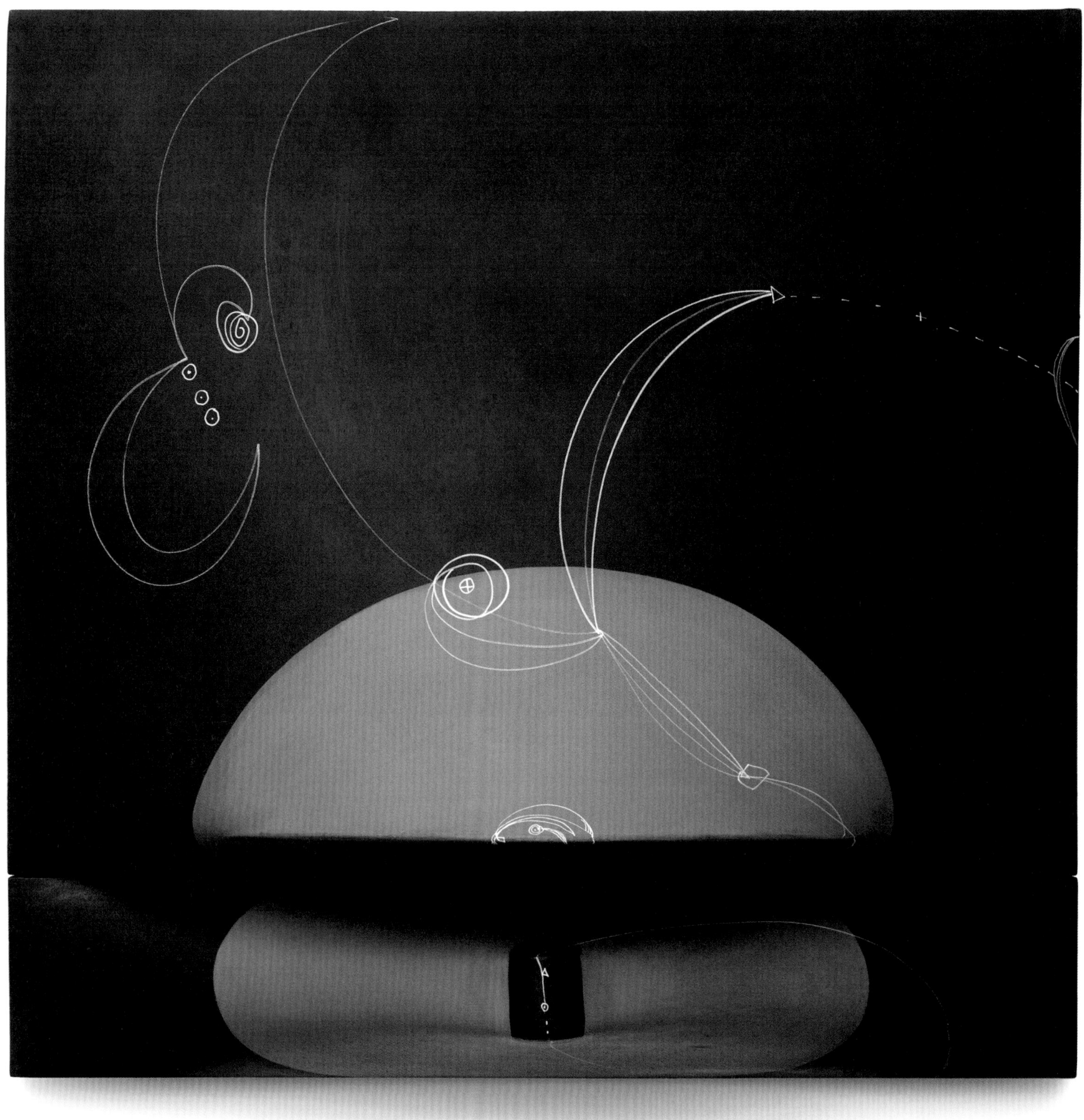

cat. 55 *Topología* (Topology), from the series *Tatuajes* (Tattoos), 1993. Acrylic on stretched canvas, 47 × 46 ¾ × 14 ½ in. (119.4 × 118.7 × 36.8 cm). Collection of the artist, Courtesy Galerie Lelong & Co., New York.

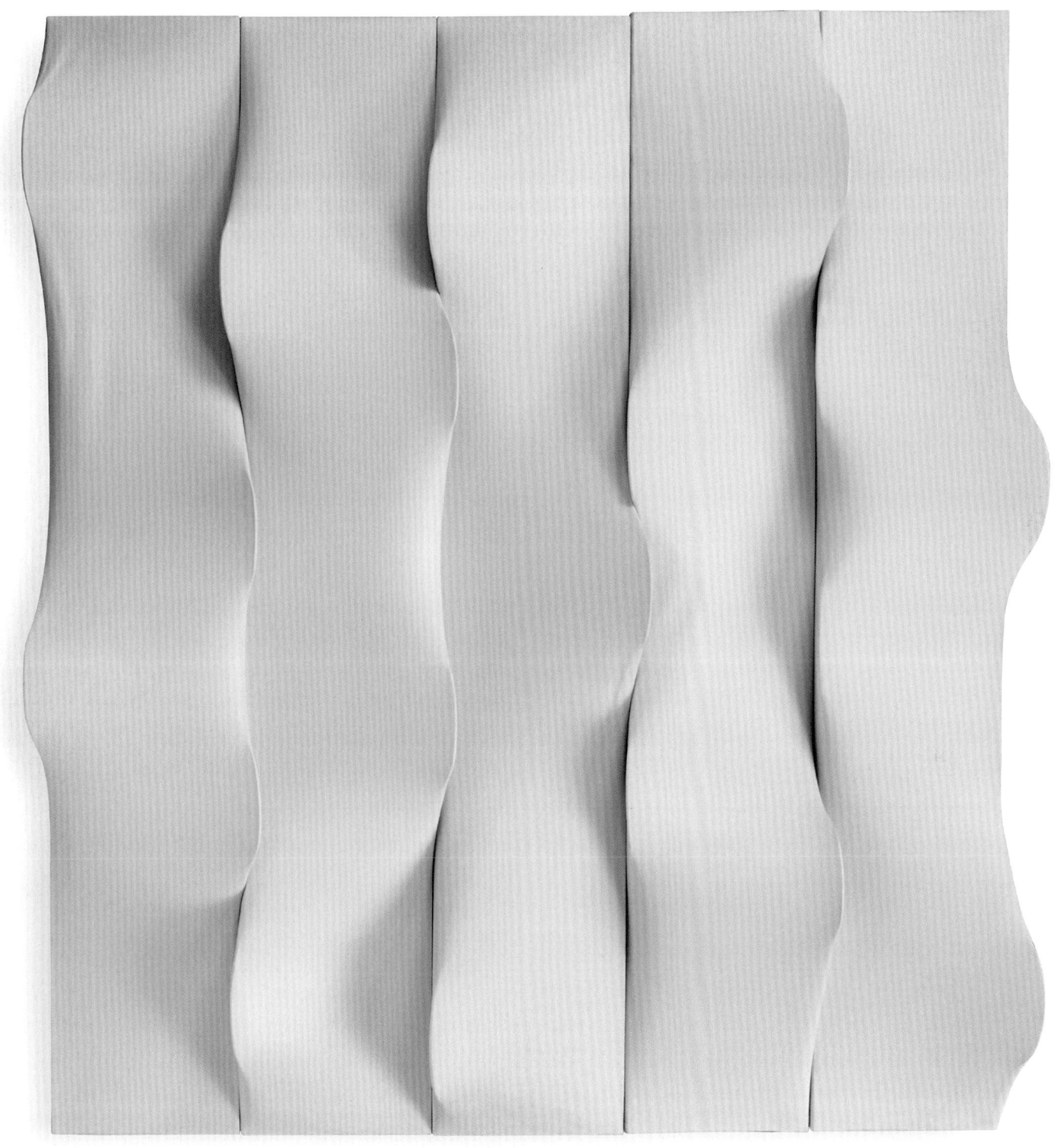

cat. 56 *Troyanas* (Trojan Women), from the series *Topologías eróticas* (Erotic Topologies), 1993. Acrylic on stretched canvas, 47 × 41 × 6 in. (119.4 × 104.1 × 15.2 cm). Collection of Mima and César Reyes, San Juan.

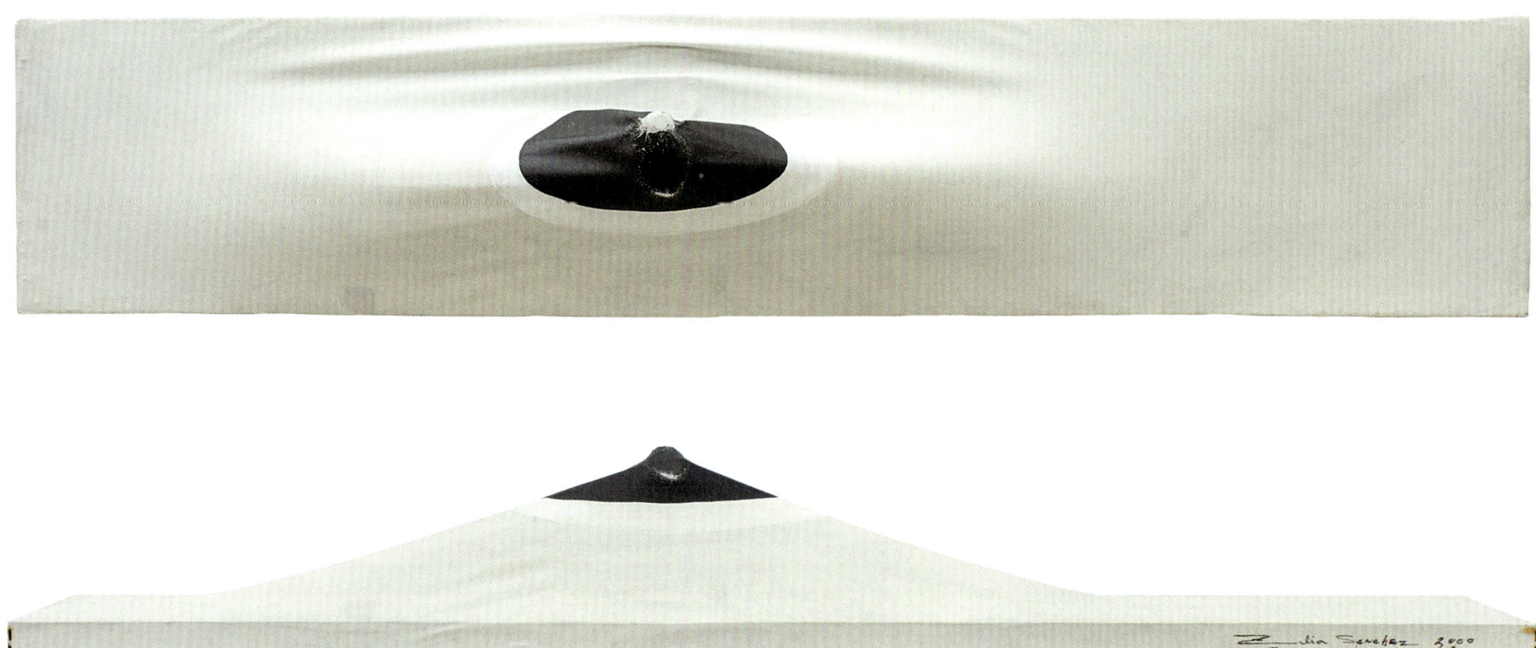

cat. 57b   *Soy Isla (I Am an Island)*, 2000. Acrylic on stretched canvas, 10 ¾ × 53 ¾ × 9 ¾ in. (27.3 × 136.5 × 22.9 cm).
From the performance *encuentrismo—ofrenda o retorno* (The Encounter—Offering or Return), from the series *Soy Isla: Compréndelo y retírate*
(I Am an Island: Understand and Retreat), 2000. Berezdivin Collection, San Juan.

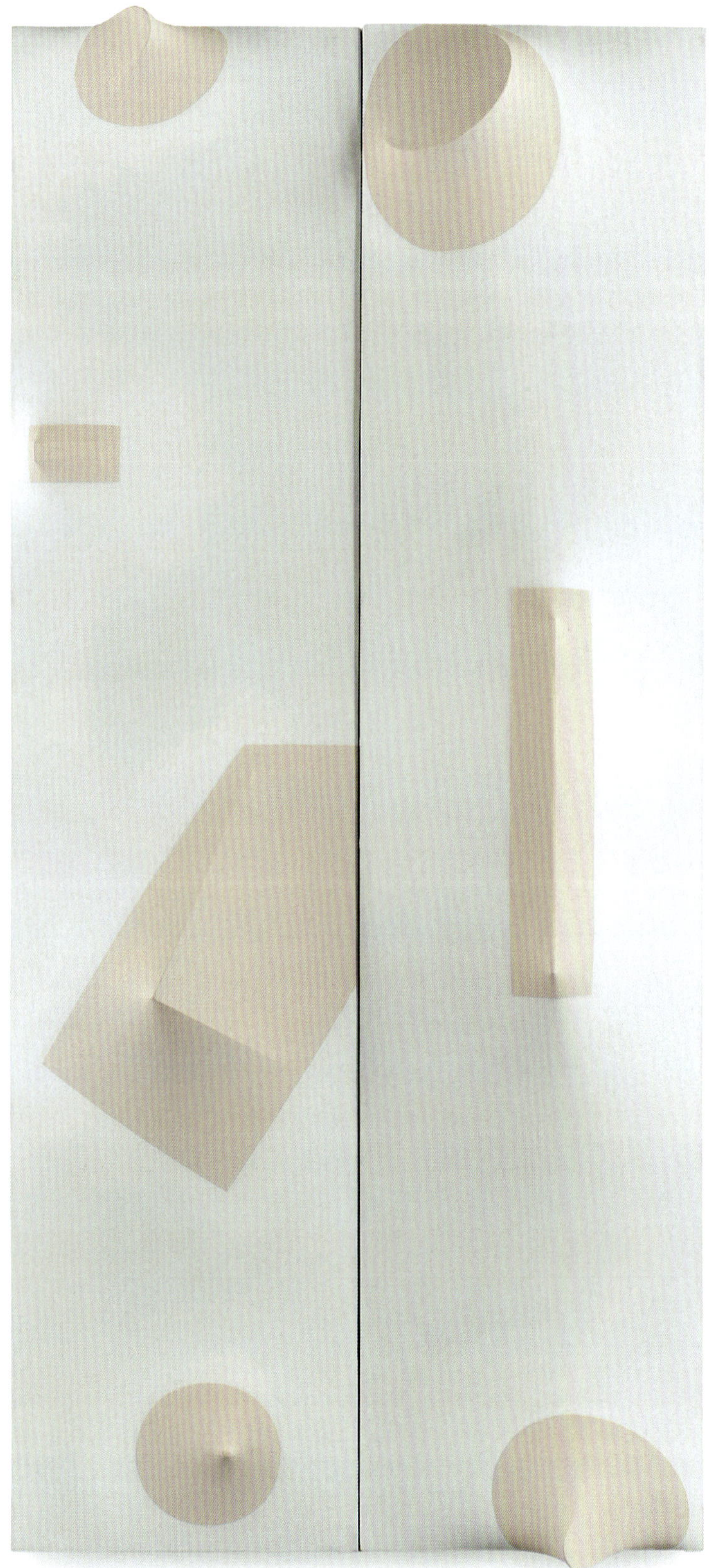

cat. 58   *Maquinista* (Machinist), diptych, 2008. Acrylic on stretched canvas, 61 × 27 ½ × 6 in. (154.9 × 69.8 × 15.2 cm).
The Phillips Collection, Washington, DC, Director's Discretionary Fund, 2016.

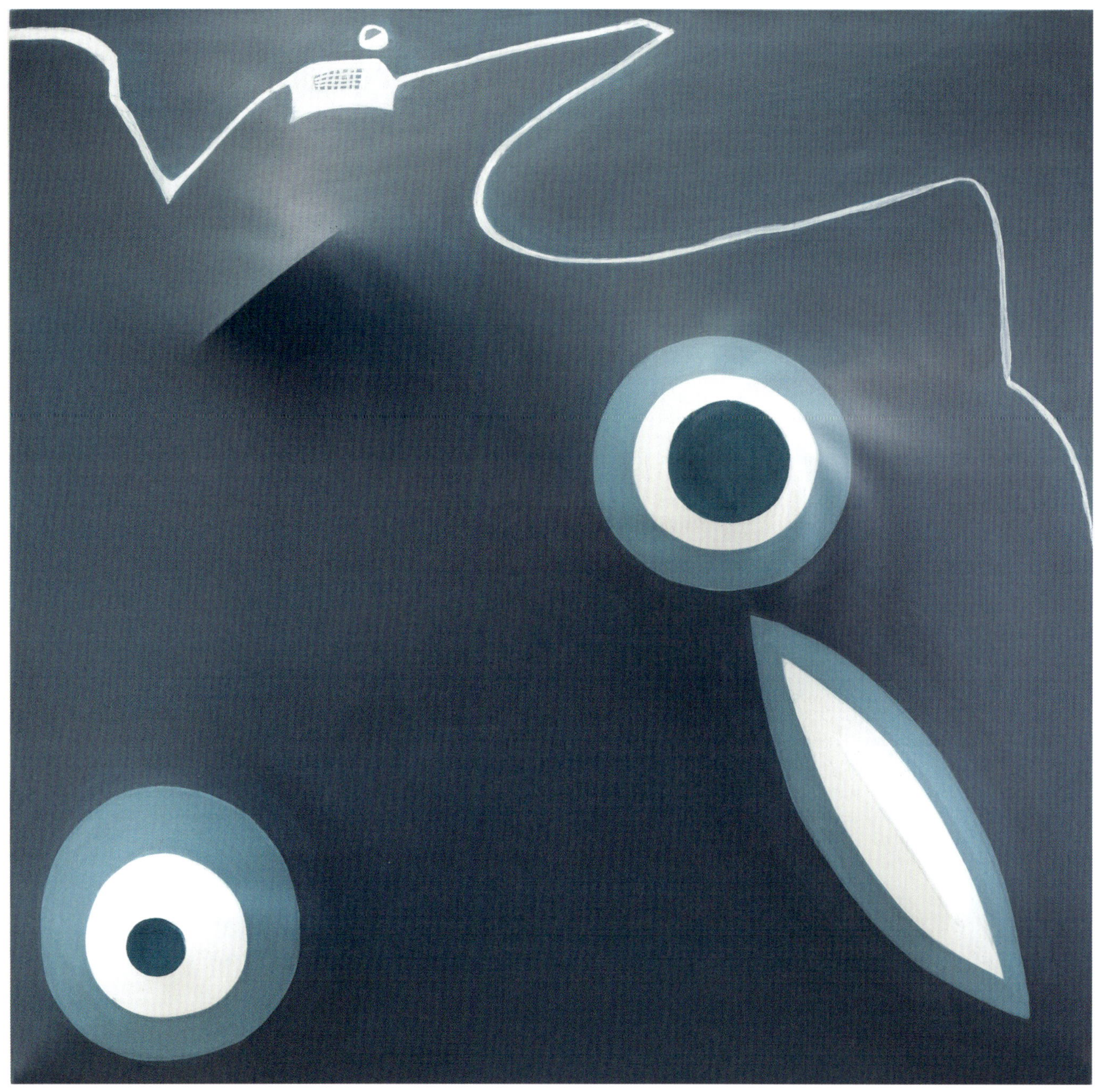

cat. 59 *Topología* (Topology), from the series *Azul azul* (Blue Blue), 2016. Acrylic on stretched canvas, 34 × 34 × 7 in. (86.4 × 86.4 × 17.8 cm). Collection of the artist, Courtesy Galerie Lelong & Co., New York.

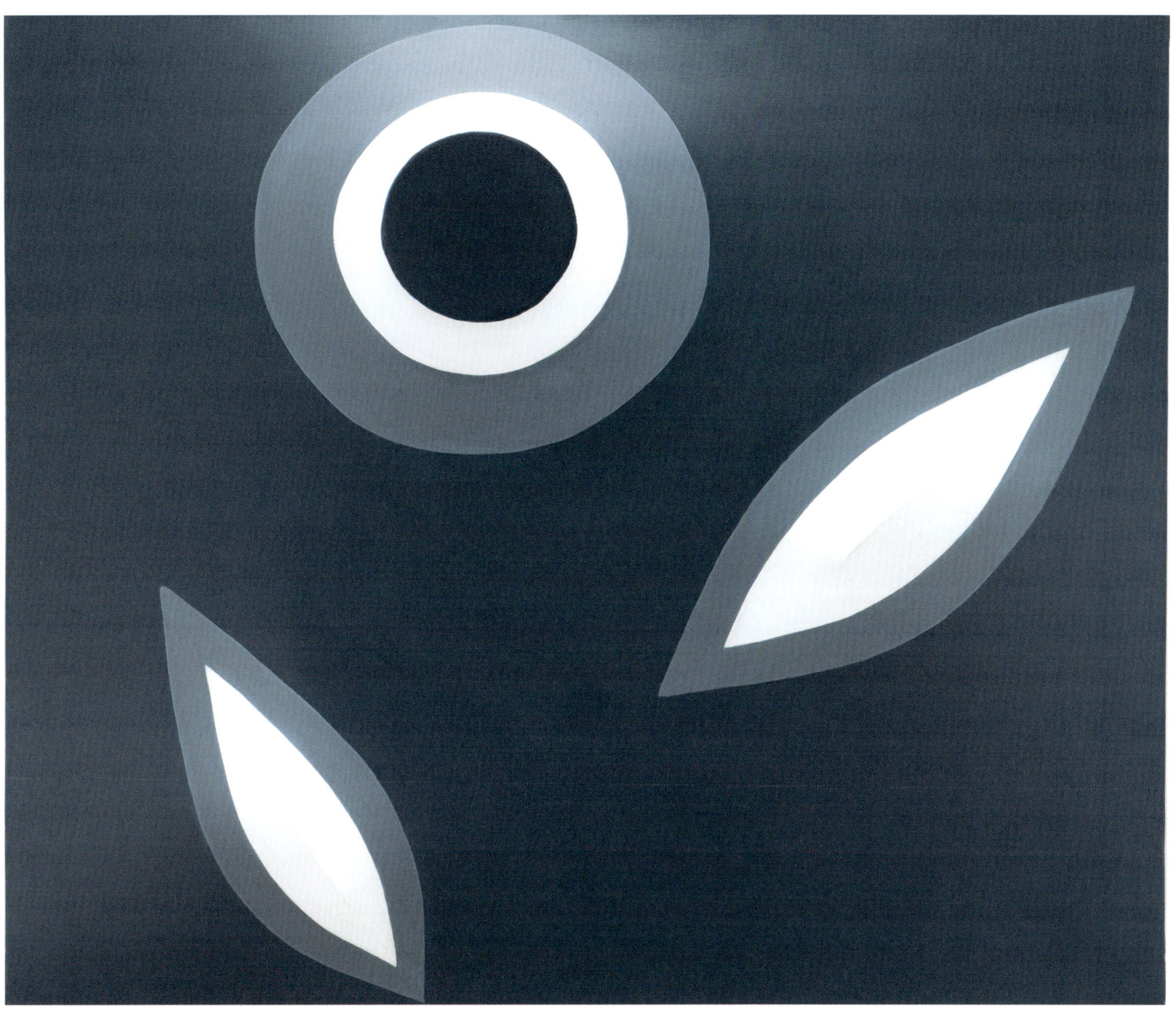

cat. 60   *Topología* (Topology), from the series *Azul azul* (Blue Blue), 2016. Acrylic on stretched canvas, 30 × 34 ¾ × 4 in. (76.2 × 88.3 × 10.2 cm).
Collection of the artist, Courtesy Galerie Lelong & Co., New York.

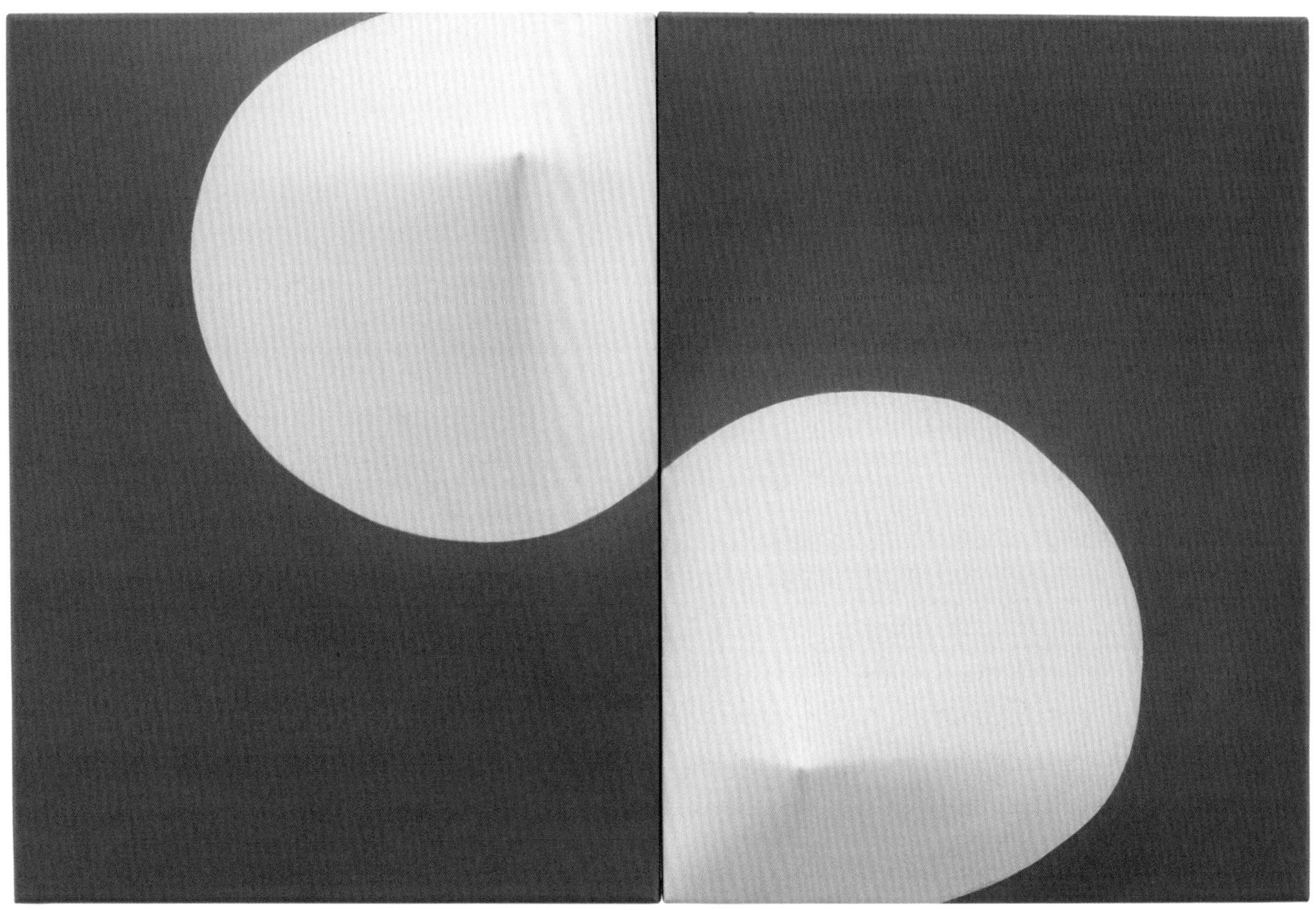

cat. 61   *Topología erótica* (Erotic Topology), from the series *Azul azul* (Blue Blue), 2016. Acrylic on stretched canvas, 17 ⅞ × 25 ⅞ × 4 ½ in. (45.4 × 65.7 × 11.4 cm). Collection of Ms. Cleusa Garfinkel, Miami.

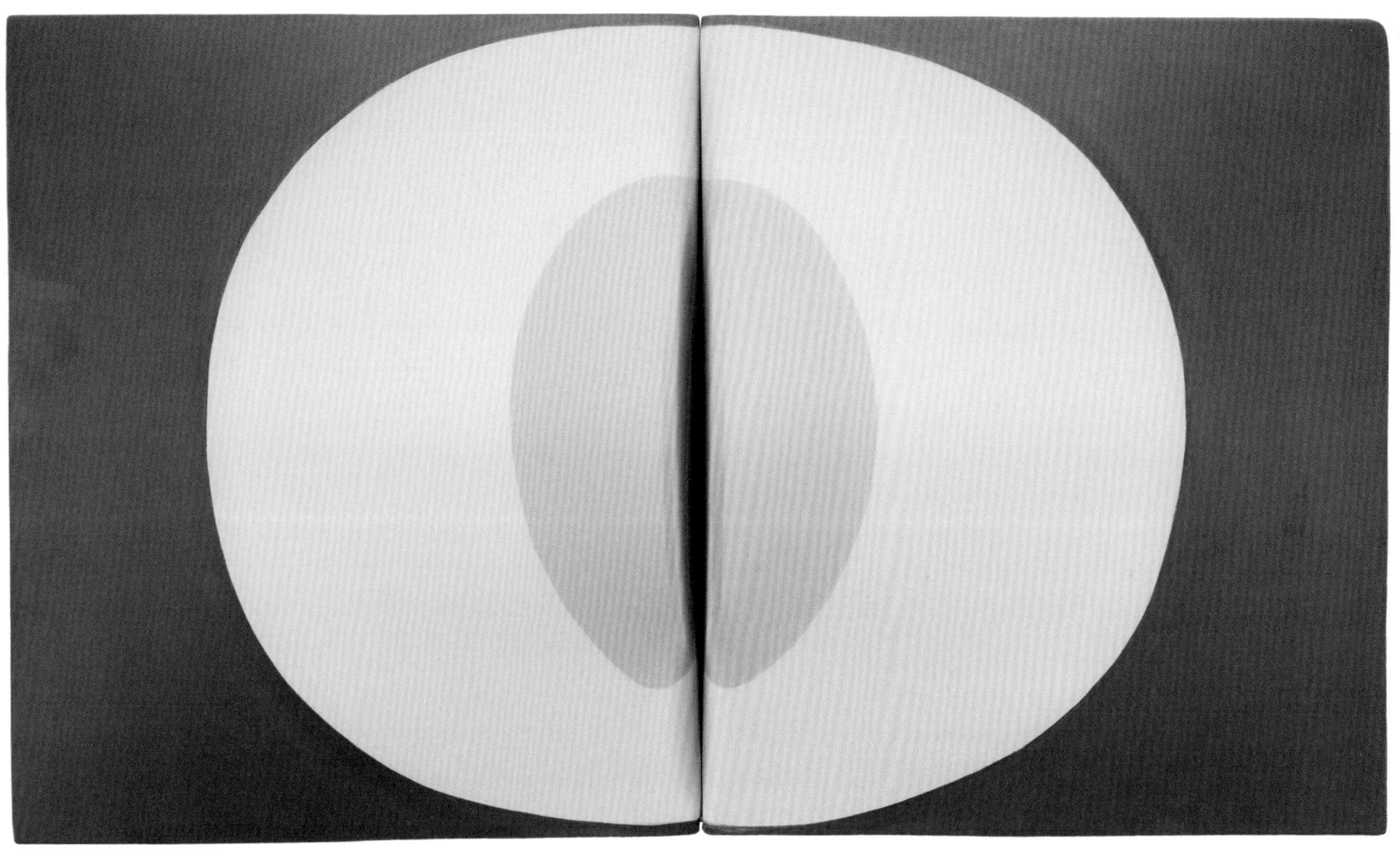

cat. 62 *Topología* (Topology), from the series *Azul azul* (Blue Blue), 2016. Acrylic on stretched canvas, 17 × 28 × 6 ½ in. (43.1 × 71.1 × 16.5 cm). Collection of Laura Delaney Taft and John Taft, promised gift to Walker Art Center, Minneapolis.

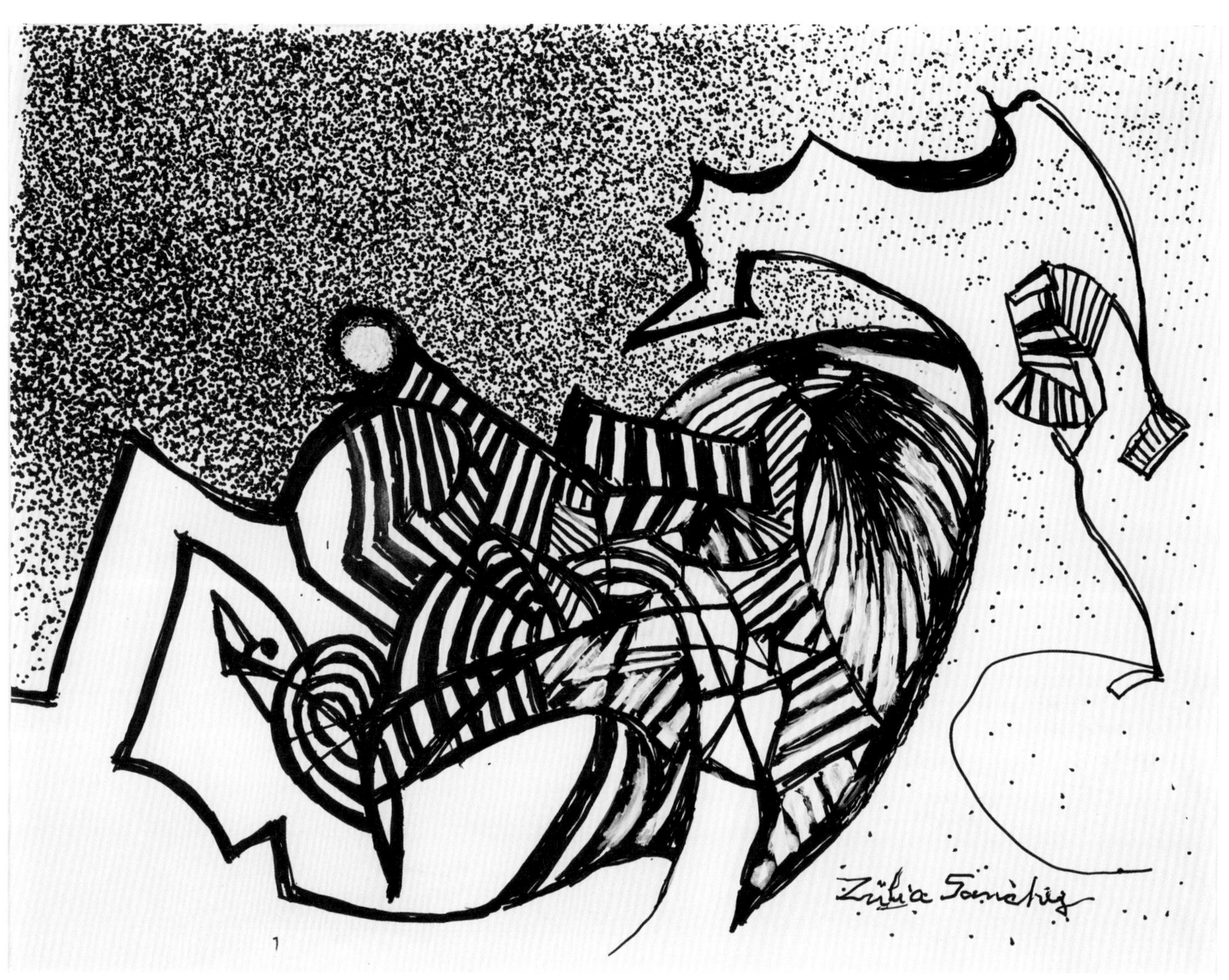

cat. 63   *Untitled*, 2018. Ink and correction fluid on paper, 13 ½ × 17 in. (34.3 × 43.2 cm). Collection of the artist,
Courtesy Galerie Lelong & Co., New York.

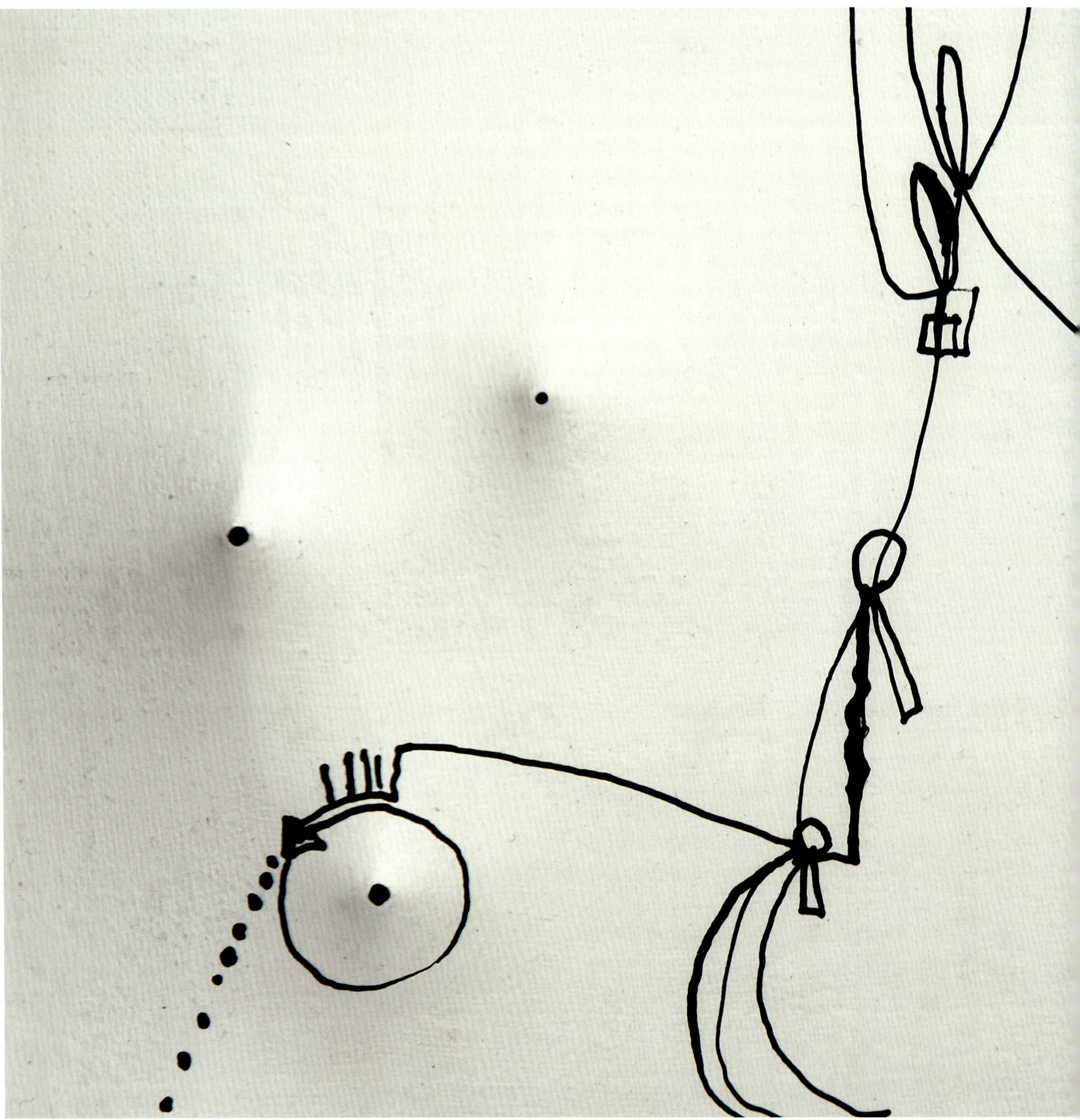

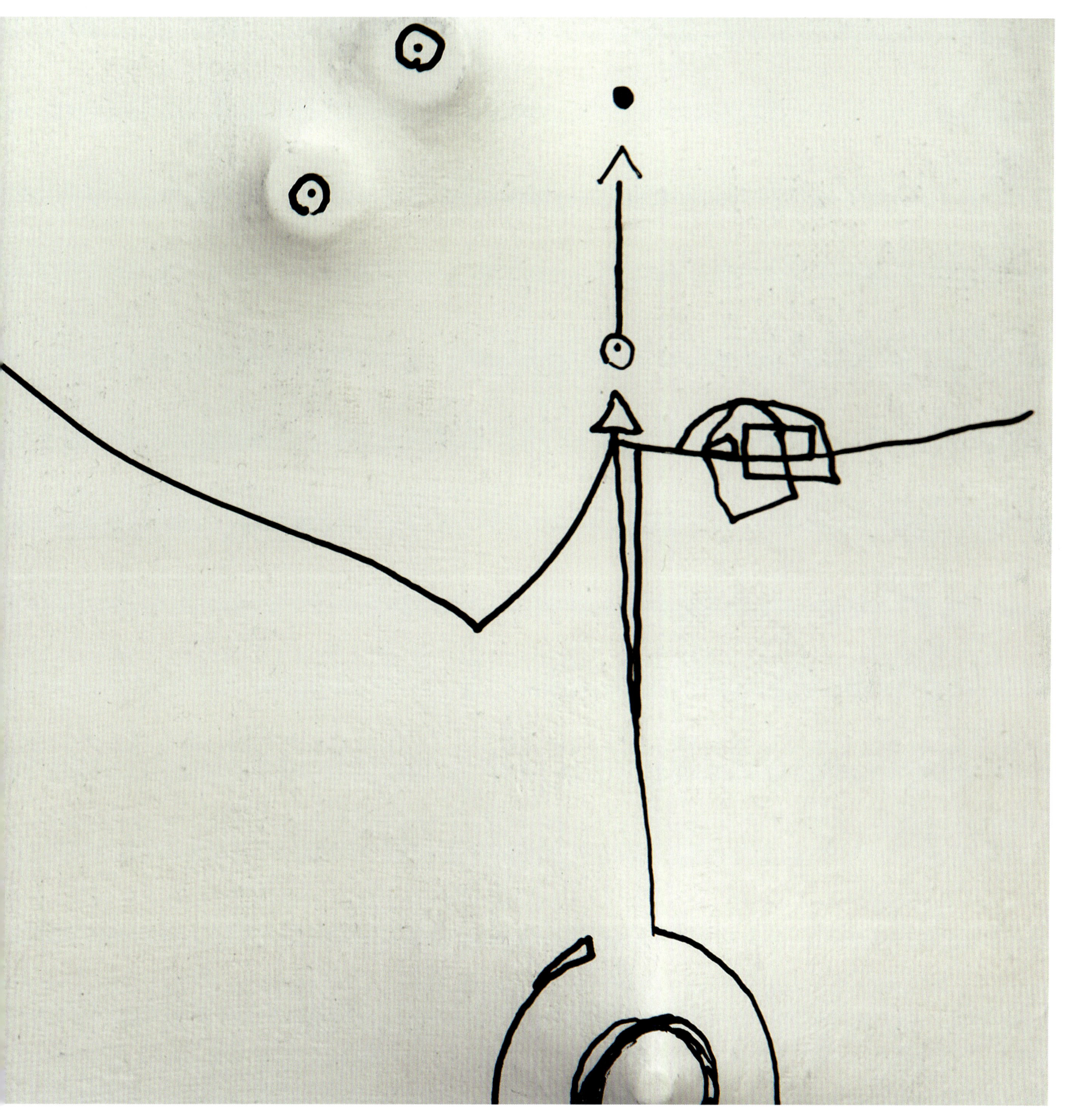

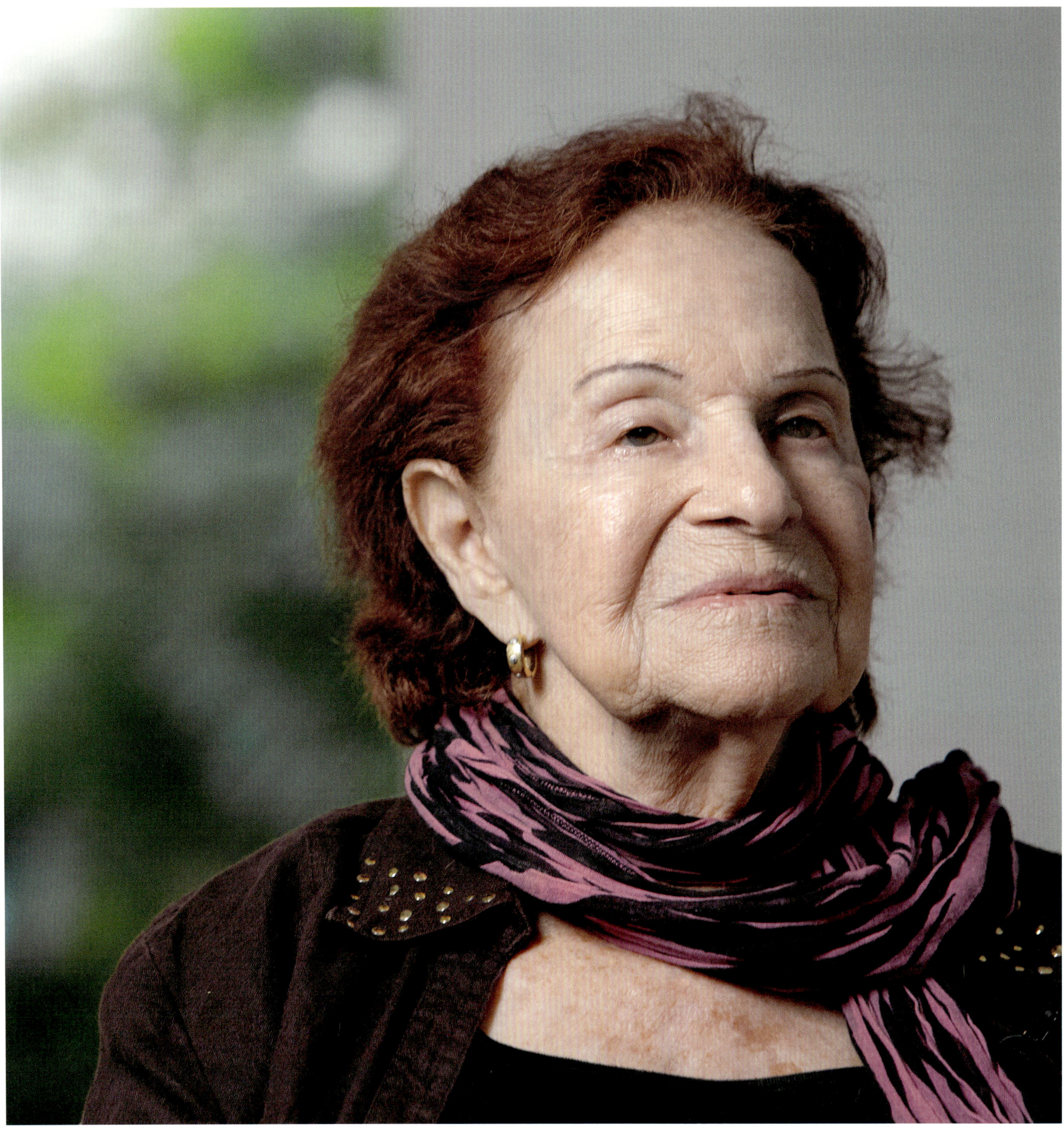

This chronology highlights the major events of Zilia Sánchez's career. It draws on a wide range of sources, including the artist's archives at Galerie Lelong, exhibition catalogues, journals, newspaper clippings, scholarly texts, correspondence with the artist's contemporaries and friends, and documentation provided by museums, galleries, libraries, universities, and foundations. While the chronology provides the best possible information drawn from these primary and secondary sources, there may be occasional inaccuracies due to missing records and some factual inconsistencies among sources.

Chronology

ALYSON CLUCK

1926

Zilia Sánchez Domínguez is born on July 12 in Havana, Cuba. Her father is an immigrant from Spain and works in business administration. Sánchez describes him as a "Sunday painter." Her mother is Cuban.

1930s

Growing up, Sánchez is deeply influenced by her neighbor and mentor Víctor Manuel (1897–1969), a leader of Cuba's first generation of vanguard painters.

1941–43

Sánchez completes two years of study at the Escuela Elemental de Artes Plásticas Aplicadas, a school in Havana that provides introductory training in the visual arts.

1943–48

In 1943 Sánchez enrolls in Cuba's national art school, the Escuela Nacional de Bellas Artes "San Alejandro," located in Havana. She receives outstanding marks in landscape and coloring and participates in the *II salón de otoño* at the Liceo Artístico y Literario de Regla in 1947. She graduates as a professor of drawing and painting in 1948.

1950

In July, Sánchez's painting *El guajiro* (The Peasant) appears in the *IV exposición nacional de pintura, escultura y grabado* at the Centro Asturiano in Havana. Returning after a four-year hiatus, the national salon offers an important platform for young artists like Sánchez to exhibit alongside the first and second generations of the Cuban vanguard.

1951

In March, Sánchez's work is included in the inaugural exhibition of the Sociedad Cultural Nuestro Tiempo, a new cultural center in Havana. Independently operated, Nuestro Tiempo becomes the main gathering point for left-wing artists, writers, and thinkers, helping to foster the formation of a revolutionary new generation of artists.

1952

On March 10, Fulgencio Batista — president of Cuba from 1940 to 1944 — seizes power by military coup and ends the country's constitutional democracy. He rules as a dictator for the next seven years.

1953

Sánchez participates in three group shows in Havana: the *VI salón nacional de pintura y escultura* at the Salones del Capitolio Nacional in January, *15 pintores y escultores jóvenes* at the Sociedad Cultural Nuestro Tiempo in February, and *Pintura, escultura, cerámica* at the Retiro Odontológico in July. Prominently featured in these exhibitions are the "under-thirties," including Sánchez, who reject forms of naturalistic representation and declare a rupture with the earlier Cuban vanguard.

In April, Cuba's first group of abstract artists, known as Los Once (The Eleven), has its inaugural exhibition. Named after its eleven initial participants, the group fluctuates in membership and size until its dissolution in June 1955. Although Sánchez retains her independence, she frequently exhibits alongside her peers in Los Once — all under-thirties who share an interest in gestural abstraction and a commitment to generational solidarity.

In November, Sánchez has her first solo exhibition of paintings, held at the Lyceum and Lawn Tennis Club in Havana, one of Cuba's most prestigious venues for modern art. The show features fifteen abstract compositions characterized by rich coloring and fluid lines and shapes.

1954

Sánchez joins a landmark exhibition, *Homenaje a José Martí: Exposición de plástica cubana contemporánea*, opening in January at Havana's Lyceum. An ideological and anti-Batista show of force, the exhibition — better known as the Anti-Bienal — commemorates the recent centennial of Cuba's independence hero, José Martí (1853–1895). It forms part of a wider, months-long protest led by dozens of Cuban artists and activists against the forthcoming *II bienal hispanoamericana* in Havana, an event purportedly set to honor Martí by the dictatorships of Batista in Cuba and Francisco Franco in Spain. After opening at the Lyceum, the Anti-Bienal travels to additional venues in Santiago de Cuba and Camagüey.

In May, coinciding with the arrival of the *II bienal hispanoamericana*, Sánchez again participates in a protest exhibition, the *Primer festival universitario de arte*, held at the Universidad de la Habana.

Throughout the year, Sánchez works as a scenographer for Las Máscaras (The Masks), an experimental theater company in Havana. Sánchez designs the sets for the entire sixth season: *Cándida*, *A puertas cerradas*, *Los padres terribles*, *Yerma*, *El cocktail party*, and *Picnic*. She has a small solo exhibition of her paintings in February in the vestibule of the group's performance space, the Palacio de los Yesistas, which doubles as a meeting place for anti-Batista youth.

In December, the Sociedad Cultural Nuestro Tiempo opens the Galería Nuestro Tiempo, a permanent installation of contemporary Cuban art. Sánchez is among three dozen painters and sculptors represented.

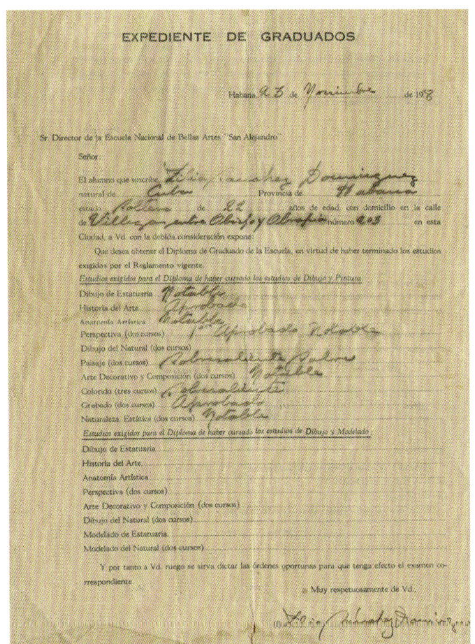

Sánchez's graduation record, Escuela Nacional de Bellas Artes "San Alejandro," 1948.

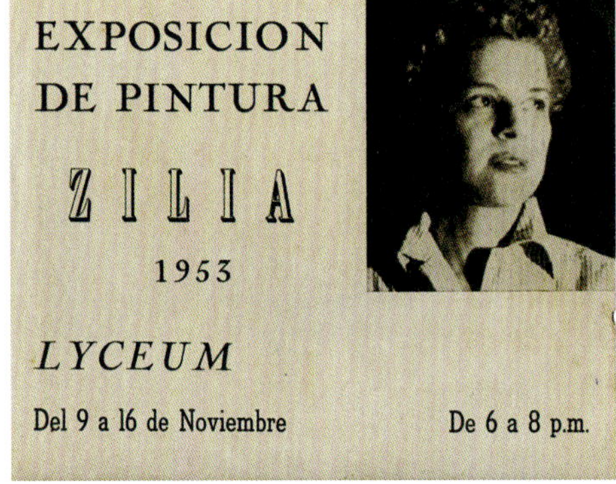

Announcement for Sánchez's exhibition at the Lyceum, 1953.

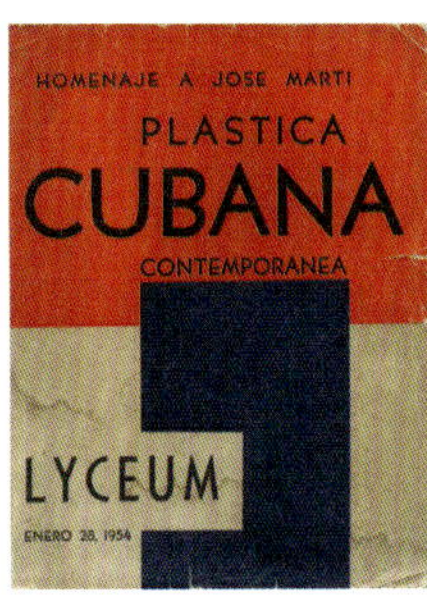

Catalogue for *Homenaje a José Martí*, 1954.

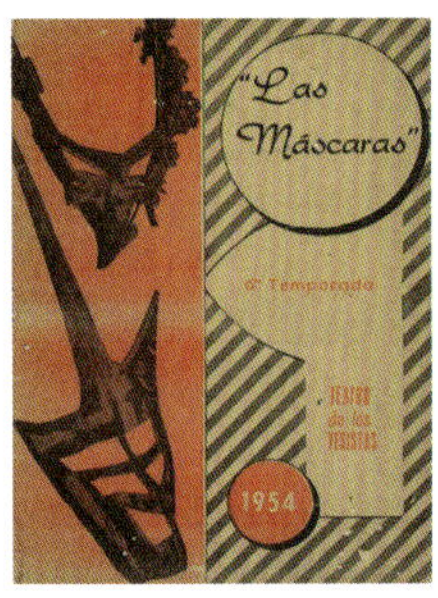

Brochure for Las Máscaras' sixth season, 1954.

1955

Two new journals, *Nuestro tiempo* (Our Time; 1954–59), founded the previous year by the cultural society, and *Ciclón* (Cyclone; 1955–59), offer an expanded platform for Cuba's literary youth to explore radical politics and aesthetics. Sánchez's close friend Severo Sarduy (1937–1993) and Antón Arrufat (b. 1935) both publish early poems in *Ciclón*. Arrufat's poem *Antígona*—the theme of which Sánchez will take up in her shaped canvases around 1970—appears in the November 1955 issue. It prefigures Arrufat's strategy of using Greek mythology to comment on contemporary politics, which gathers force in his later work, and in Caribbean literature and theater more generally, around 1968.

In March the Cuban journalist Ángel Huete organizes a group show at the Instituto de Cultura Hispánica in Madrid, featuring drawings and watercolors by Sánchez and three artists from Los Once. A protest ensues when the latter contingent—Hugo Consuegra, Guido Llinás, and Raúl Martínez—releases a statement claiming that they never approved the display of their art in a Francoist institution.

In May, works by Sánchez, members of Los Once, and the earlier vanguard artists appear in an exhibition at the Sociedad Cultural Nuestro Tiempo in honor of the Cuban art historian and professor Luis de Soto (1893–1955).

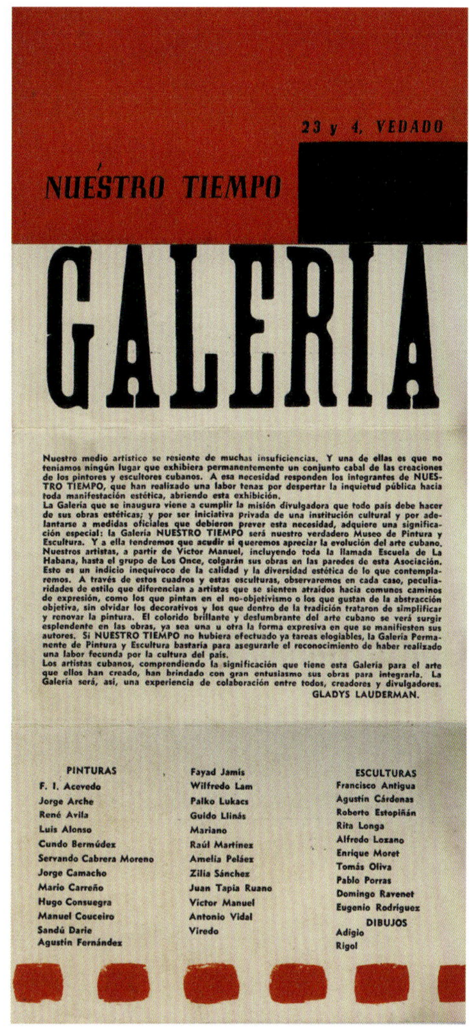

Nuestro medio artístico se resiente de muchas insuficiencias. Y una de ellas es que no teníamos ningún lugar que exhibiera permanentemente un conjunto cabal de las creaciones de los pintores y escultores cubanos. A esa necesidad responden los integrantes de NUESTRO TIEMPO, que han realizado una labor tenaz por despertar la inquietud pública hacia toda manifestación estética, abriendo esta exhibición.

La Galería que se inaugura viene a cumplir la misión divulgadora que todo país debe hacer de sus obras estéticas; y por ser iniciativa privada de una institución cultural y por adelantarse a medidas oficiales que debieron prever esta necesidad, adquiere una significación especial: la Galería NUESTRO TIEMPO será nuestro verdadero Museo de Pintura y Escultura. Y a ella tendremos que acudir si queremos apreciar la evolución del arte cubano. Nuestros artistas, a partir de Víctor Manuel, incluyendo toda la llamada Escuela de La Habana, hasta el grupo de Los Once, colgarán sus obras en las paredes de esta Asociación. Esto es un indicio inequívoco de la calidad y la diversidad estética de lo que contemplaremos. A través de estos cuadros y estas esculturas, observaremos en cada caso, peculiaridades de estilo que diferencian a artistas que se sienten atraídos hacia comunes caminos de expresión, como los que pintan en el no-objetivismo o los que gustan de la abstracción objetiva, sin olvidar los decorativos y los que dentro de la tradición trataron de simplificar y renovar la pintura. El colorido brillante y deslumbrante del arte cubano se verá surgir esplendente en las obras, ya sea una u otra la forma expresiva en que se manifiesten sus autores. Si NUESTRO TIEMPO no hubiera efectuado ya tareas elogiables, la Galería Permanente de Pintura y Escultura bastaría para asegurarle el reconocimiento de haber realizado una labor fecunda por la cultura del país.

Los artistas cubanos, comprendiendo la significación que tiene esta Galería para el arte que ellos han creado, han brindado con gran entusiasmo sus obras para integrarla. La Galería será, así, una experiencia de colaboración entre todos, creadores y divulgadores.

GLADYS LAUDERMAN.

PINTURAS		ESCULTURAS
F. I. Acevedo	Fayad Jamis	Francisco Antigua
Jorge Arche	Wilfredo Lam	Agustín Cárdenas
René Avila	Palko Lukacs	Roberto Estopiñán
Luis Alonso	Guido Llinás	Rita Longa
Cundo Bermúdez	Mariano	Alfredo Lozano
Servando Cabrera Moreno	Raúl Martínez	Enrique Moret
Jorge Camacho	Amelia Peláez	Tomás Oliva
Mario Carreño	Zilia Sánchez	Pablo Porras
Hugo Consuegra	Juan Tapia Ruano	Domingo Ravenet
Manuel Couceiro	Víctor Manuel	Eugenio Rodríguez
Sandú Darie	Antonio Vidal	DIBUJOS
Agustín Fernández	Viredo	Adigio
		Rigol

Brochure for the Galería Nuestro Tiempo, 1954.

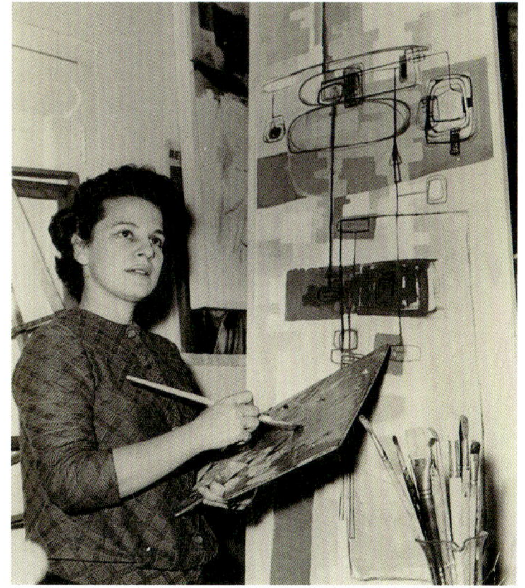

Sánchez painting in her studio, Havana, 1950s.

In June, Sánchez participates in Los Once's group exhibition at the Galería Habana.

In July, works by Cuban artists, including Sánchez, are featured in *Cuba en Tampa: La feria del progreso*, held in Tampa, Florida, in celebration of the city's centennial.

1956

A memorial exhibition for the art critic Guy Pérez Cisneros (1915–1953) is staged at the Lyceum in January. A strong showing of Cuban abstraction, it includes Sánchez and dozens of other artists supported in recent years by the Lyceum.

In March a museum exhibition of European postwar abstraction, *Pintura de hoy: Vanguardia de la escuela de París*, opens at Havana's Palacio de Bellas Artes. Organized by the artist Loló Soldevilla (1901–1971) on her return from Paris to Havana, it provides Sánchez and other Cuban artists with an opportunity to view recent forms of abstraction by forty-six leading practitioners. Over the next few years, Soldevilla will cofound the Galería Color-Luz in Havana and promote a group of geometric abstract artists known as Los Diez Pintores Concretos (The Ten Concrete Painters).

In late March, Sánchez is included in the exhibition *El tema religioso en la pintura cubana* at the Galería Cubana, a private venue in Havana founded in 1954 by the Venezuelan art dealer and critic Florencio García Cisneros.

In May, Sánchez has a solo show, *Zilia Sánchez: Óleos*, at the Galería Cubana. Severo Sarduy writes a short text for the exhibition.

Opening in late November at the Palacio de Bellas Artes, the *VIII salón nacional de pintura y escultura* features three paintings by Sánchez. A number of Sánchez's peers refuse to participate in the event and stage a counter-exhibition in a venue across the street.

1957

Sánchez receives a fellowship from the Instituto de Cultura Hispánica in Madrid and spends part of the year in Spain. During the 1950s, she travels to France and Italy as well.

In September, a solo exhibition of Sánchez's paintings is held at the Sala Clan, a combined bookstore and art gallery in Madrid. The accompanying brochure includes a paragraph by Spanish art critic José María Moreno Galván.

1958

Between 1956 and 1958, Florencio García Cisneros (owner of the Galería Cubana) helps to facilitate the display of Sánchez's art in Venezuela. Among Sánchez's exhibitions in the country are a group show at the Club del Comercio in Barquisimeto and a March 1958 group exhibition organized by García Cisneros at the Asociación Venezolana de Periodistas (AVP) in Caracas.

1959

On January 1, Fidel Castro's rebel army ousts Batista from power, signaling the triumph of the Cuban Revolution.

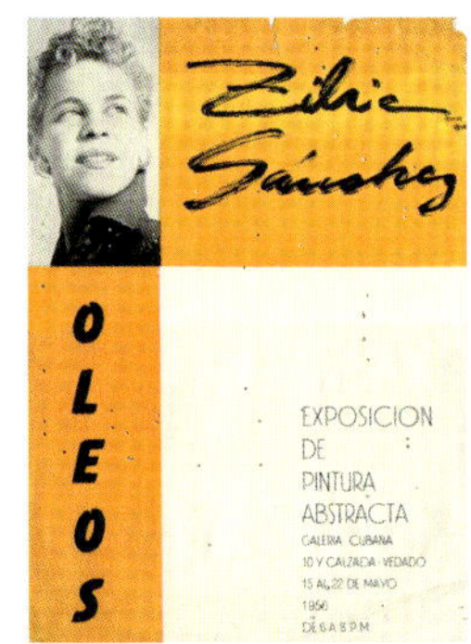

Poster for Sánchez's exhibition at the Galería Cubana, 1956.

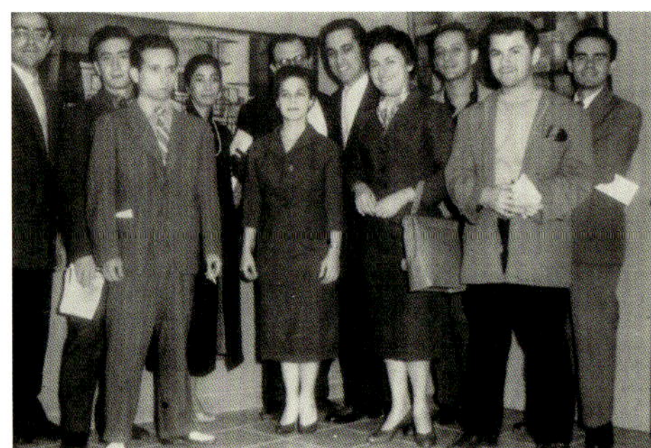

Sánchez (center) at the opening of her Sala Clan exhibition, 1957.

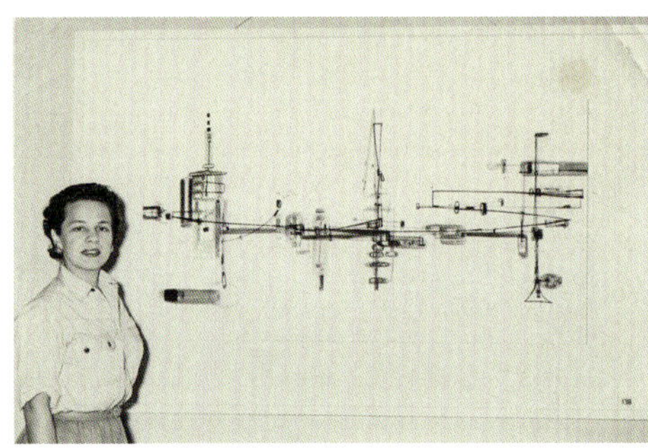

Sánchez with *Composición en blanco*, featured in the *V bienal de São Paulo*, 1959.

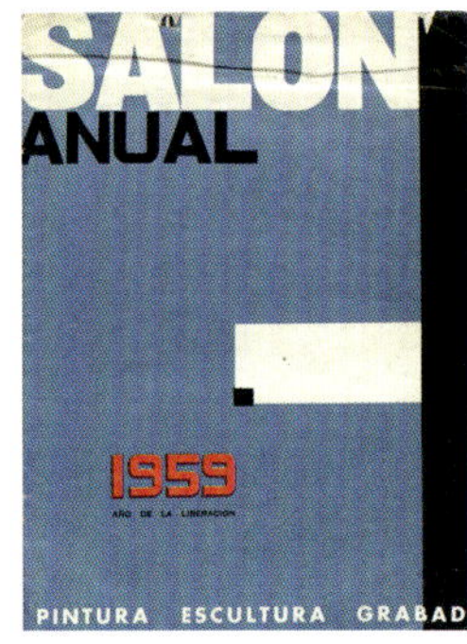

Catalogue for the *Salón anual*, 1959.

Sánchez participates in an exhibition of contemporary Cuban painters sponsored by the Woman's Club of Havana in February and in the exhibition *Operación cultura* at the Universidad de la Habana in April.

In the fall, Sánchez's painting *Composición en blanco* (Composition in White) appears in the *V bienal de São Paulo* in Brazil, one of the largest and most prestigious showings of international contemporary art. Sánchez is among seventeen Cuban painters selected for the event, and her work resonates with the year's dominant trend of gestural abstraction.

In October, Sánchez participates in Cuba's first national salon of the post-Batista era, the *Salón anual 1959: Pintura, escultura y grabado*, at the Palacio de Bellas Artes. The predominance of abstraction alarms some critics and party officials who believe that nonfigurative art is incapable of serving a new revolutionary society.

1960

Sánchez exhibits alongside sixty artists from Cuba and hundreds more from across the Americas in Mexico City's *II bienal interamericana de pintura, escultura y grabado*, which opens in September at the Museo Nacional de Arte Moderno in the Palacio de Bellas Artes.

In late 1960 Sánchez departs Havana and moves to New York. There she joins a growing émigré community of artists, poets, writers, and performers who have fled Cuba under Castro's regime. She will eventually settle in an apartment on East Eighty-First Street on the Upper East Side of Manhattan.

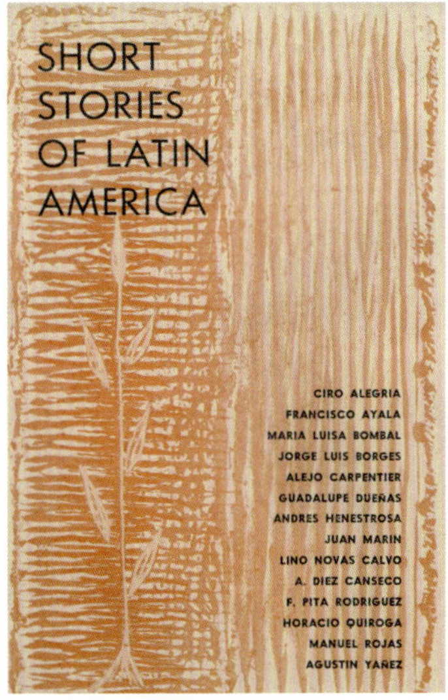

Book jacket design by Sánchez, 1963.

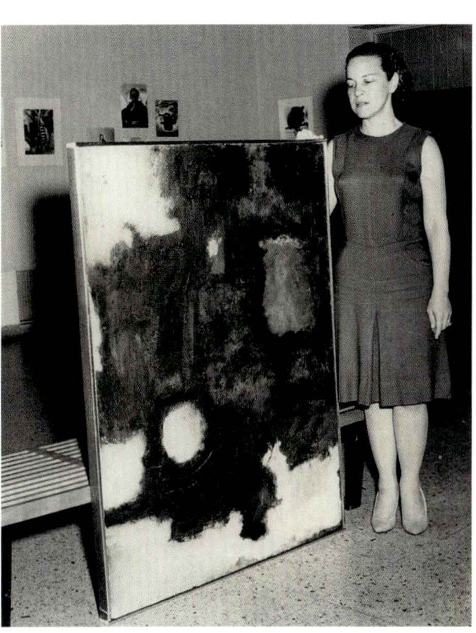

Sánchez with her painting, New York, 1966.

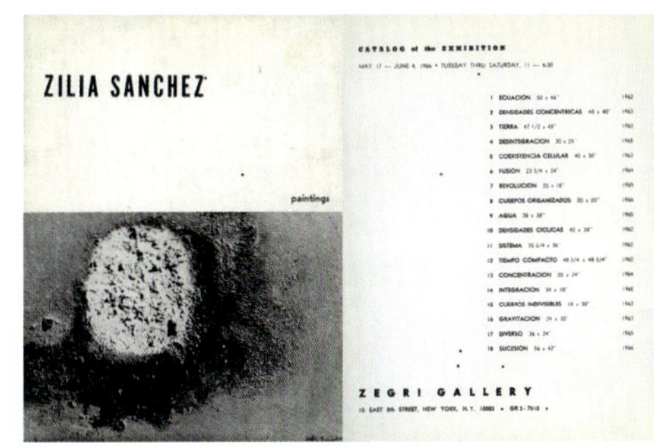

Catalogue for Sánchez's exhibition at
the Zegrí Gallery, 1966.

1962

Sánchez contributes drawings to two single-issue poetry magazines in New York: *Pa'Lante*, published by the League of Militant Poets, and *Protesta*, considered the first literary magazine by Cuban writers in exile. The latter project is spearheaded by Mercedes Cortázar (b. 1940), a founding member of the postrevolutionary movement of writers and poets in Havana known as El Puente (The Bridge). Cortázar departed Cuba for New York in January 1961. Another founding member of El Puente, Isel Rivero (b. 1941), who moved to New York alongside Sánchez, also collaborates on *Protesta*.

Sánchez takes printmaking classes at the Pratt Graphic Art Center in Manhattan in 1962 and 1963. An extension of Pratt Institute, the center offers innovative instruction, equipment, and studio space to professional artists experimenting in print media. The center attracts a wide range of local and international artists in the early to mid-1960s, including Luis Camnitzer, Jim Dine, Gego (Gertrud Goldschmidt), Barnett Newman, Claes Oldenburg, and Liliana Porter.

1963

In the early 1960s, Sánchez works in an antiques and art restoration shop and also as an illustrator and designer for Las Américas Publishing Company, a New York publishing house that specializes in classic and contemporary literature by Spanish and Latin American authors. In 1963 she designs the book jackets for *The Affable Hangman* by Ramón Sender, *Short Stories of Latin America*, and *Poems* by Giacomo Leopardi.

Sánchez creates several abstract prints for the cover and interior of Isel Rivero's book *Tundra: Poema a dos voces*, published by Las Américas.

1965

Sánchez designs the cover and interior of *2 poèmes de Mercedes Cortázar*, a bilingual French and Spanish edition of Cortázar's poetry published in February. Servando Sacaluga, a professor at Columbia University, writes the introduction and French translation. He later acquires and donates two prints made by Sánchez to El Museo del Barrio in New York.

In July, Sánchez has a solo exhibition of twenty-five paintings at the Museo de la Universidad de Puerto Rico in San Juan. Made in the Informel style, these works represent the culmination of her seven years of experimentation with diverse materials and mixtures such as resins, wax, and sawdust, which result in a rough, matte surface. Sánchez identifies herself with the Spanish Informel artists, whose work she would have seen in Spain in 1957 and who achieved international success at the 1958 Venice Biennale.

1966

In May, the Zegrí Gallery in New York hosts a solo exhibition of eighteen paintings in the Informel style by Sánchez. Isel Rivero and Eleanor Hakim contribute essays to the catalogue. The Zegrí Gallery, formerly called the Galería Sudamericana, was one of the city's earliest and most prominent venues for contemporary Latin American art. Its founder and director, Armando Zegrí, gave hundreds of artists from the region — including dozens from Cuba — the opportunity to present their work in New York.

In the summer, Sánchez is one of six recipients of a 1966–67 CINTAS Fellowship, a $3,000 award given to arts professionals of Cuban citizenship or "lineage" who are residing outside Cuba. Sánchez uses her stipend to further her studies in Spain.

In the fall, Sánchez moves to Madrid and enrolls in a year of coursework at the Instituto Central de Conservación y Restauración (ICCR), where she specializes in techniques to restore artworks on canvas and panel. In 1966 the ICCR — located in the Casón del Buen Retiro, a building that is now part of the Museo Nacional del Prado — allows students to work directly with artworks and objects in the country's national museums.

1967

In March, the Galería El Bosco in Madrid opens a solo exhibition of fourteen paintings by Sánchez. Local critics praise her clean, graphic style and striking black-and-white palette. Fernando Chueca Goitia, director of the Museo Nacional de Arte Contemporáneo in Madrid, writes a short essay for the exhibition brochure.

In Barcelona, the Instituto Catalán de Cultura Hispánica presents a solo show of Sánchez's paintings in July. A statement by Spanish art critic Adolfo Castaño appears in the accompanying brochure.

In September seven artists, including Sánchez, are featured in *Contemporary American Paintings and Watercolors*, a show at the Herbert E. Feist Gallery in New York, where Sánchez works in art restoration.

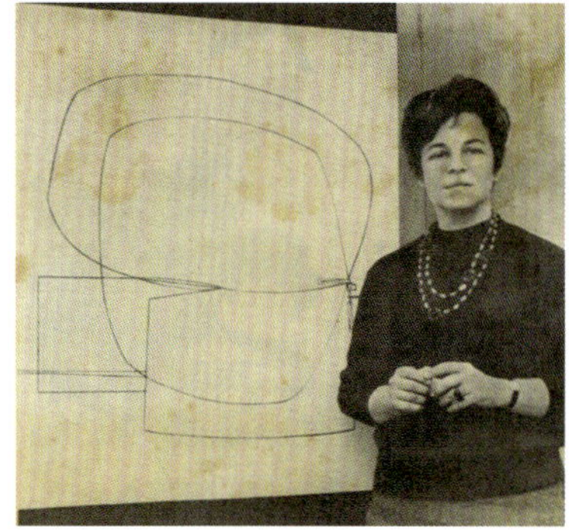

Newspaper photo of Sánchez with her painting, Galería El Bosco, 1967.

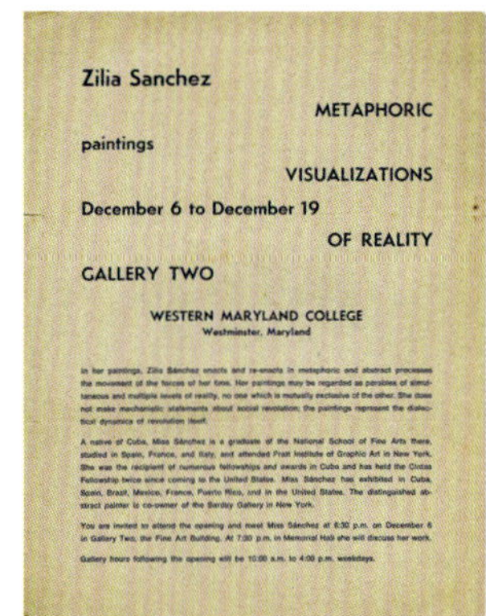

Flyer for Sánchez's exhibition at Western Maryland College, 1969.

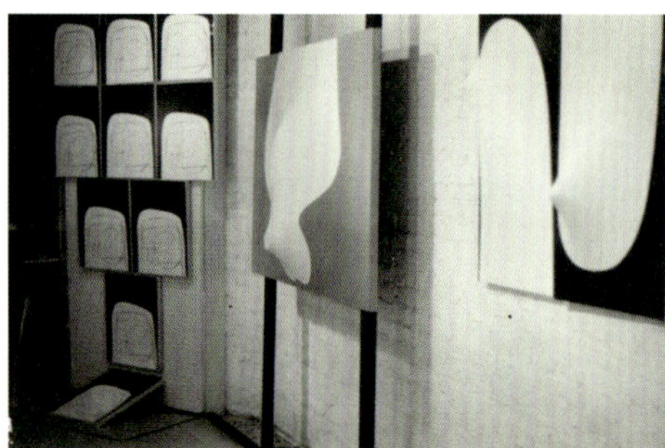

Installation view of Sánchez's works, c. 1970.

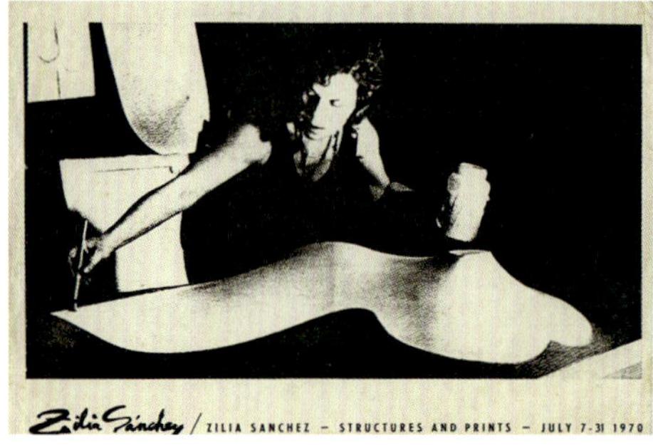

Poster for Sánchez's exhibition at the Sarduy Gallery, 1970.

1968

Sánchez receives a second CINTAS Fellowship for the year 1968–69. The artists Waldo Díaz-Balart (b. 1931) and Carmen Herrera (b. 1915), both abstract painters from Cuba living in New York, also receive fellowships this year.

1969

In a preopening event, the Sarduy Gallery in New York features Sánchez in a show of five contemporary Cuban painters. Founded by RosaMaría García Sarduy, a cousin of the poet Severo Sarduy, the gallery presents exhibitions and literary events at its East Eighty-Fifth Street location, a gathering point for Cuban artists and writers.

Sánchez illustrates the March/April issue of *La nueva sangre* (The New Blood; 1968–72), a literary and cultural magazine formed by several Cuban and Puerto Rican poets in New York, including Mercedes Cortázar, Rolando Campins (b. 1940), Víctor Fernández-Fragoso (1944–1982), and Dolores Prida (1943–2013). Favoring aesthetics over political ideology, the magazine provides an outlet for a new generation of writers and critics to publish their work in Spanish and also to stay connected with the Cuban and Latin American diaspora. Sánchez appears multiple times in the magazine's pages as both an illustrator and subject.

In the spring and summer, Sánchez is the scenographer for two theater productions by Cuban directors: *Antígona* (dir. René Buch), copresented by the Greenwich Players and Las Artes, Inc., and *Dos viejos pánicos* (dir. Mario Peña), written by Cuban playwright Virgilio

Piñera (1912–1979) and staged by the Duo Theater. The productions take place within New York's flourishing Hispanic theater movement of the late 1960s and 1970s.

Sánchez codesigns the autumn issue of *La nueva sangre*, devoted in part to Vietnamese poetry and the antiwar movement.

In December, Western Maryland College in Westminster, Maryland, presents a solo exhibition of Sánchez's paintings and hosts a lecture by the artist. The title of the show, *Zilia Sánchez: Metaphoric Visualizations of Reality*, is adopted from Eleanor Hakim's 1966 essay in the Zegrí Gallery catalogue.

1970

Three of Sánchez's lithographs are included in the *Primera bienal de San Juan del grabado latinoamericano*, which is organized by the Instituto de Cultura Puertorriqueña (ICP) in San Juan and features nearly 180 artists from Puerto Rico and across Latin America. As the Caribbean's first art biennial, the event seeks to position Puerto Rico, already home to a robust printmaking culture, at the center of Latin America's graphic arts revival.

Sánchez unsuccessfully applies for a Guggenheim Fellowship in the spring, proposing to "combine pictorial elements with sounds and movements."

In July, she has a solo exhibition of recent work at the Sarduy Gallery. Titled *Structures and Prints*, the show includes a number of three-dimensional shaped-canvas paintings and black-and-white silkscreens. Many of the works are serial or modular in form, composed of

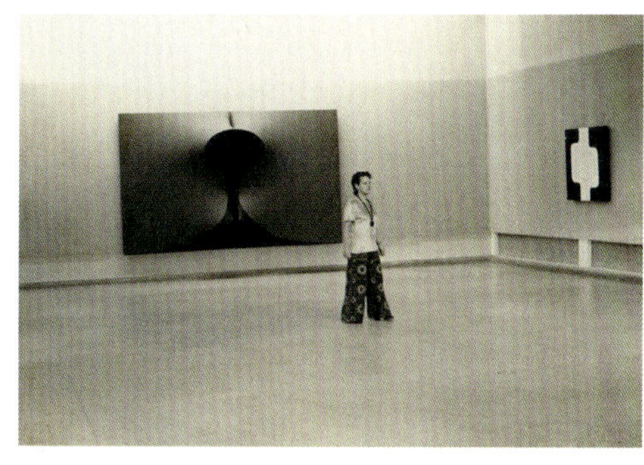

Installation view of *Estructuras en secuencia* with Sánchez, 1970.

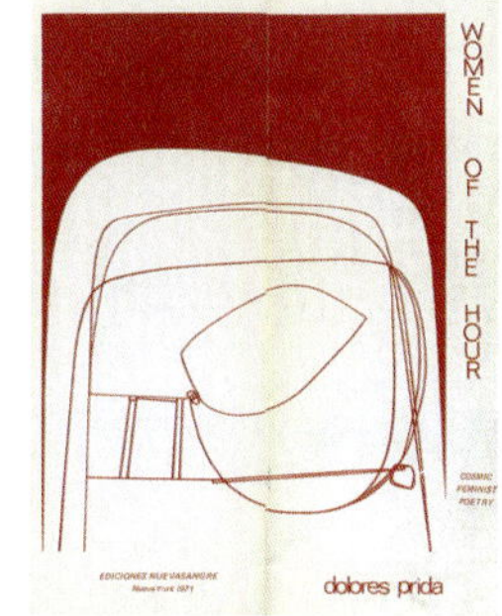

Cover illustration by Sánchez, 1971.

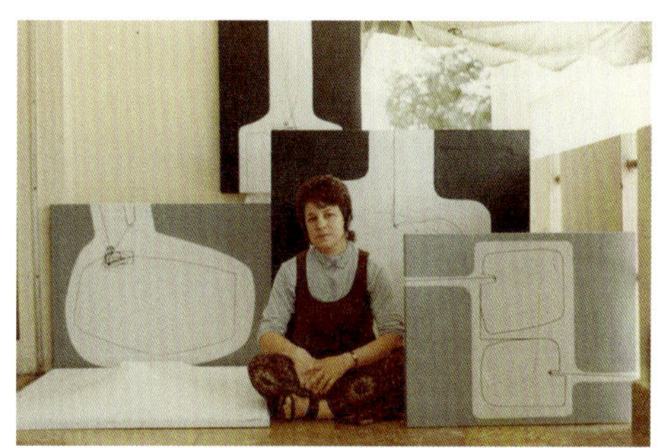

Sánchez with her works in San Juan, c. 1971.

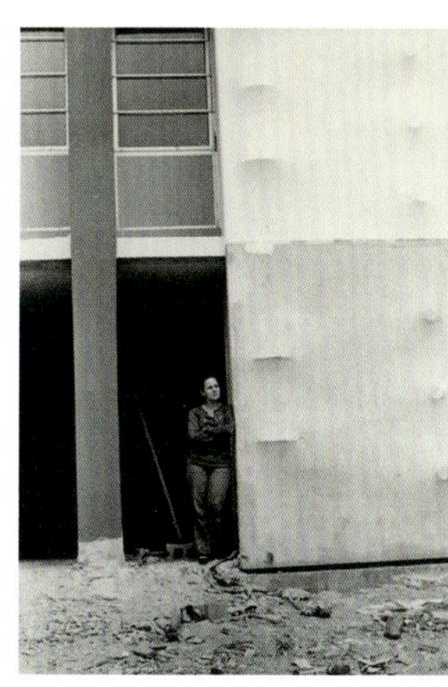

Sánchez next to her mural in Laguna Gardens, 1971.

individual, repeated units that can be arranged in various configurations. Sánchez began exploring this concept, which she calls *módulos infinitos* (infinite modules), around 1967.

In September, the Museo de la Universidad de Puerto Rico presents *Estructuras en secuencia*, a solo exhibition of Sánchez's shaped-canvas paintings and silkscreens. The accompanying catalogue contains an essay by Severo Sarduy that examines Sánchez's shaped canvases—known as *topologías eróticas* (erotic topologies)—in relation to minimalism and to earlier phases of the artist's career, as well as a statement by Gordon Brown, senior editor of *Arts Magazine*.

In October, Sánchez is included in the exhibition *Fourteen Latin American Painters*, organized by the Inter-American Development Bank Staff Association in Washington, DC.

1971

A print by Sánchez is featured on the covers of the February issue of *La nueva sangre* and Dolores Prida's poetry collection *Women of the Hour: Cosmic Feminist Poetry*, published in March.

During the year, Sánchez settles permanently in San Juan and opens a studio in the neighborhood of Santurce.

Sánchez creates a monumental mural in concrete that adorns the facades of two high-rise apartment buildings in the new Laguna Gardens housing complex in Isla Verde, a district east of San Juan. The site's developer, Henry Gutiérrez, is an exiled Cuban architect.

1972

In January, Sánchez contributes three serigraphs to the *Segunda bienal de San Juan del grabado latinoamericano*.

The Liga de Estudiantes de Arte de San Juan, a local art association, hires Sánchez to teach a studio art course that examines the properties and technical possibilities of materials such as paper, wood, and canvas. This marks the beginning of Sánchez's successful, decades-long teaching career in San Juan at the Liga de Arte and as a professor at the Escuela de Artes Plásticas. Her courses include subjects that range from color theory and practice to the principles of basic design.

Sánchez collaborates with Puerto Rican writers Rosario Ferré (1938–2016) and Olga Nolla (1938–2001) on the creation of their literary magazine, *Zona. Carga y descarga* (Zone. Charge and Discharge [or Load and Unload]; 1972–75), which seeks to revolutionize traditional moral and aesthetic values on the island. Using photo-collage and experimental typography, Sánchez establishes the magazine's distinct layout and design. She contributes to the first four issues of *Zona*, which begins publication in September, then departs from the group after the editors define *Zona* in support of Puerto Rican independence and socialist revolution.

The Argentine art critic Marta Traba (1930–1983), who teaches at the Universidad de Puerto Rico for one year, writes "El erotismo y la comunicación," an essay on the eroticism of Sánchez's shaped canvases that is published in the November/December issue of *Zona*.

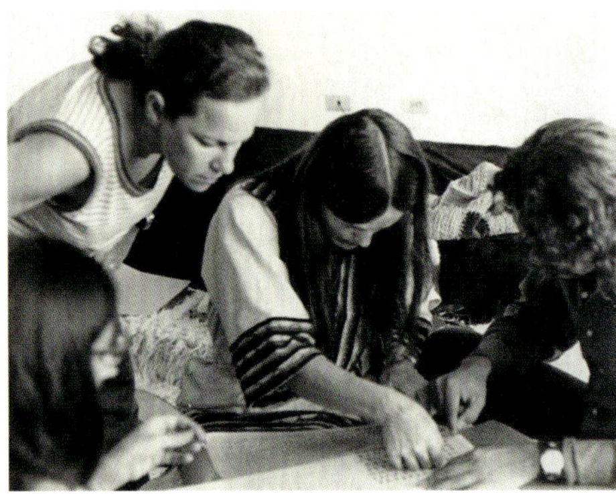

Sánchez working with students in San Juan, early 1970s.

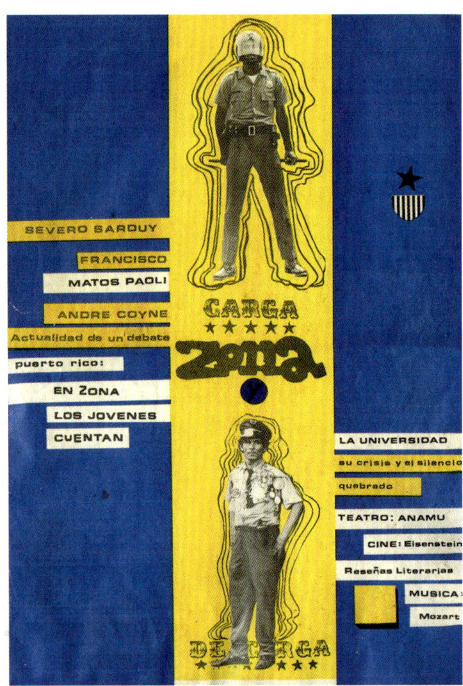

Cover design by Sánchez for *Zona. Carga y descarga* 1, no. 3 (January–February 1973).

1974

Three of Sánchez's recent prints are included in the *Tercera bienal de San Juan del grabado latinoamericano*.

1975

Sánchez participates in *Cuatro pintoras y una escultora* at the Galería María Rechany in San Juan. The exhibition celebrates the work of five women artists in Puerto Rico: Elvira Goya, Doris Rodríguez, Noemí Ruiz, Sánchez, and Esther Shelley.

In May, the Museo de la Universidad de Puerto Rico hosts a solo exhibition of Sánchez's shaped canvases. Antonio J. Molina, a Cuban exile and art critic living in San Juan who writes about Sánchez on several occasions, reviews her work in the newspaper *El mundo*.

1977

Sánchez designs the cover and interior of *Vertizonte* (1977, 1980), a book by the Cuban émigré poet and professor Rita Geada (b. 1934). In New York, Geada participated in the same 1960s literary and artistic circles as Sánchez. Geada also helps to facilitate the donation of one of Sánchez's shaped canvases to the school where Geada teaches, Southern Connecticut State University.

1978

In January, Sánchez takes part in the *IV salón de pintura de la UNESCO* at the Museo de la Universidad de Puerto Rico, where she receives first prize ($1,000) for her *Topología erótica*.

1979

In October, the Liga de Estudiantes de Arte de San Juan presents a solo exhibition of Sánchez's shaped canvases. In the coming years, Sánchez frequently participates in the Liga de Arte's group exhibitions as a member of its teaching faculty.

1981

Two of Sánchez's *Topologías eróticas* (1980) are selected for the *IV bienal de arte de Medellín* held at the Palacio de Exposiciones in Medellín, Colombia, from May to July. The exhibition features more than two hundred artists from Colombia and abroad. It constitutes a major triumph for Sánchez, who in addition to having one of her paintings purchased by the biennial's organizers, is awarded one of six first prizes by the Museo de Arte Moderno de Cali.

Sánchez submits two shaped canvases and a freestanding sculpture to the *Quinta muestra de pintura y escultura puertorriqueña*, hosted by the ICP.

1982

The Unión de Cubanos en el Exilio (Union of Cuban Exiles), known as the UCE, organizes *Obra puertorriqueña de artistas cubanos* at the Museo Casa Blanca in San Juan. Sánchez is one of twelve Cuban émigrés featured in the exhibit, which commemorates the twentieth anniversary of the UCE's activities in Puerto Rico.

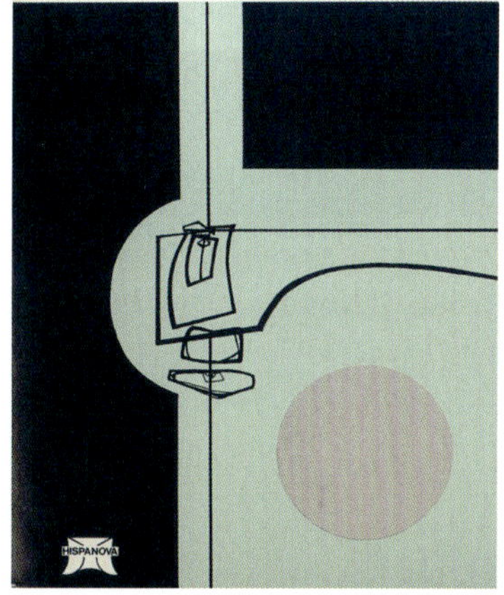

Cover illustration by Sánchez, 1977.

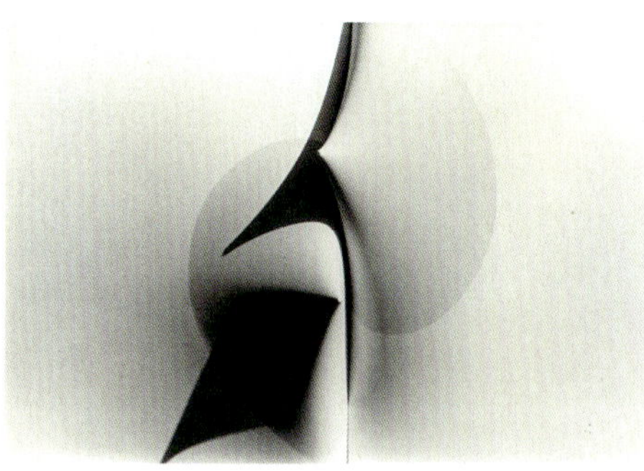

Sánchez's *Topología erótica* (1980), acquired by the organizers of the *IV bienal de arte de Medellín*, 1981.

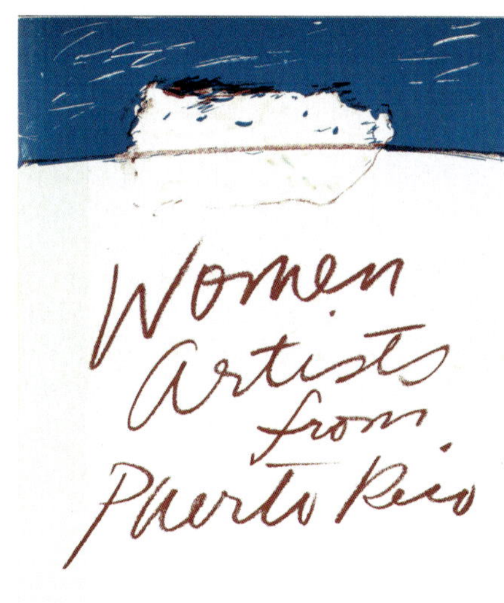

Catalogue for the exhibition at the Cayman Gallery, 1983.

1983

Sánchez participates in *Arte actual: Puerto Rico 1983*, which surveys recent work by artists on the island and marks the fifteenth anniversary of the Liga de Arte in San Juan.

Sánchez is a founding member of the Asociación de Mujeres Artistas de Puerto Rico, a collective of women artists that first meets in March. In November, the group has its inaugural exhibition, which includes three shaped canvases by Sánchez, at the Cayman Gallery in New York. Following its debut, *Women Artists from Puerto Rico* travels to several venues, including Lehigh University (Bethlehem, PA) and the Pontiac Creative Arts Center (Pontiac, MI). Over the next decade, the group's members participate in museum exhibitions and organize a show every March in celebration of the Semana de la Mujer (Women's Week). The annual event takes place at Plaza Las Américas, a shopping center in San Juan, where artists like Sánchez can present their work to a wider audience.

1984

In May, Sánchez participates in the *Primer congreso de artistas abstractos de Puerto Rico*, an exhibition and forum sponsored by the ICP. Chaired by artist and professor Luis Hernández Cruz (b. 1936), the event calls together the island's abstract artists and surveys their diverse practices.

In November, the INTAR Latin American Gallery in New York opens *Zilia Sánchez: Erótica*, an exhibition that showcases the artist's shaped canvases. INTAR — short for International Art Relations — emerged as a theater company in the late 1960s, founded by a group of Cuban and Puerto Rican writers and artists. In the late 1970s, Cuban-born painter Inverna Lockpez (b. 1941) became the director of INTAR's new art gallery, foregrounding the work of emerging and established Latin American and Latino artists.

1985

In 1984 and 1985, Sánchez unsuccessfully applies for a Guggenheim Fellowship, her second and third attempts. In 1985 she proposes to conduct "in-depth study and work with marble and brass relating to structuralism and its application to the concept of my *Erotic Topologies*."

During the fall, the Galería Espiral in San Juan presents *Arte erótico*, a group exhibition featuring Sánchez's shaped canvases.

1986

In February, Sánchez's work is included in *Artistas abstractos de Puerto Rico* at the Galería de Arte Moderno in Santo Domingo, Dominican Republic. Sponsored by the ICP, the exhibition is affiliated with the 1984 *Primer congreso de artistas abstractos* in San Juan.

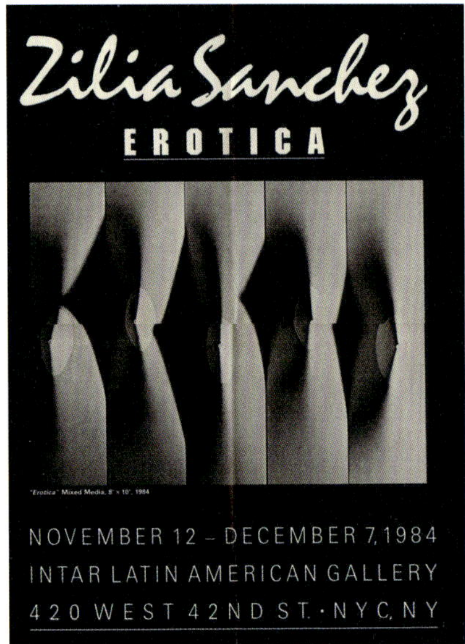

Flyer for Sánchez's exhibition at INTAR Latin American Gallery, 1984.

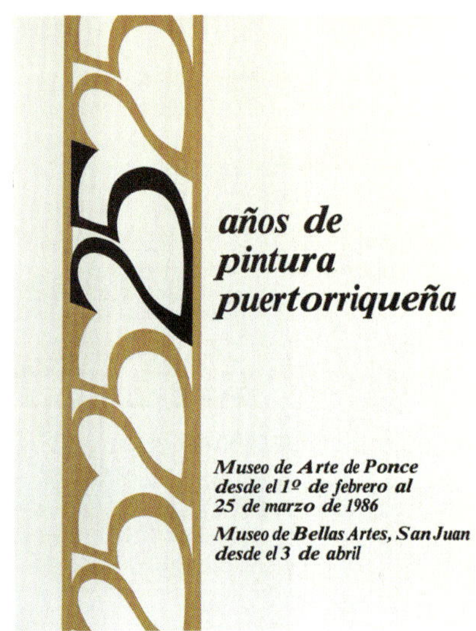

Catalogue for *25 años de pintura puertorriqueña*, 1986.

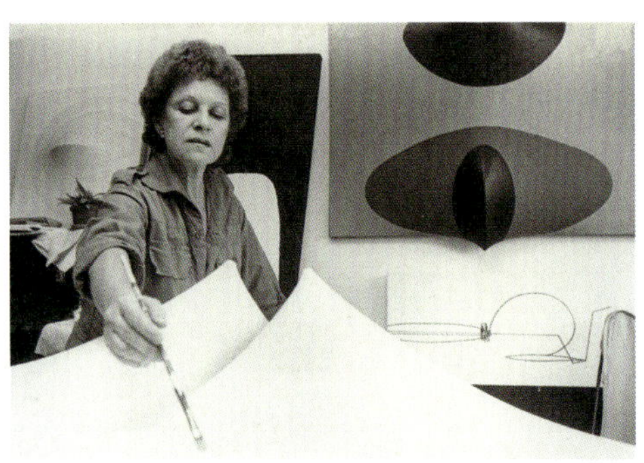

Sánchez working in her studio in San Juan, 1980s.

Sánchez's shaped canvas *Lunar 10* (Moon 10) represents the year 1973 in the exhibition *25 años de pintura puertorriqueña*, a retrospective survey of Puerto Rican art. The show opens in February at the Museo de Arte de Ponce before traveling north to the Museo de Bellas Artes in San Juan.

The Asociación de Mujeres Artistas de Puerto Rico organizes *Mujeres artistas de Puerto Rico*, its second major exhibition and the first to take place on the island. The show opens in February at the Museo de Bellas Artes and spotlights three dozen artists, including Sánchez, working in a variety of mediums and styles.

1987

Sánchez is featured in *Outside Cuba/Fuera de Cuba*, a landmark exhibition in the United States that highlights six generations of contemporary Cuban artists living permanently outside Cuba. The show identifies Sánchez as part of the island's third generation — the last to come of age in Havana before the start of the 1960s exodus. The show opens in March at the Jane Voorhees Zimmerli Art Museum, Rutgers University, New Jersey, before traveling to venues in New York, Ohio, Puerto Rico, Florida, and Georgia over the next two years.

1989

A *Topología erótica* (1978) by Sánchez appears in *Pintura y escultura de los años setenta en Puerto Rico*. Organized by the Museo de Arte Contemporáneo de Puerto Rico, the exhibition takes place from June to August at the Universidad del Sagrado Corazón in San Juan.

1990

Sánchez participates in *Mujeres artistas: Protag-onistas de los ochenta*, organized by the Asocia-ción de Mujeres Artistas de Puerto Rico. After its debut in March at the Museo de las Casas Reales in Santo Domingo, Dominican Republic, the show travels to the Museo de Arte Con-temporáneo de Puerto Rico in San Juan.

In December, Sánchez contributes two small paintings and a sculpture to *Pequeño formato 90*, an annual exhibition of artworks, each no larger than one square foot in size, made by artists in Puerto Rico during the previous year. Hosted by the Galería Luigi Marrozzini in San Juan for several consecutive years, the event regularly features new work by Sánchez.

1991

In August the Museo Casa Roig in Humacao, Puerto Rico, opens *Zilia Sánchez: Tres décadas*, a major survey of Sánchez's career through the 1960s, 1970s, and 1980s. The catalogue contains an essay by Margarita Fernández Zavala, along with a reprint of Marta Traba's 1972 essay and a selection of critical commentary.

1997

Sánchez is included in *Breaking Barriers: Selec-tions from the Museum of Art's Permanent Contemporary Cuban Collection* at the Museum of Art in Fort Lauderdale, Florida. The exhibition contains a modular work by Sánchez, *Eros y la comunicación sublimada no. 1* (Eros and Sub-limated Communication no. 1; 1970/85), composed of six shaped canvases donated by RosaMaría García Sarduy in 1996.

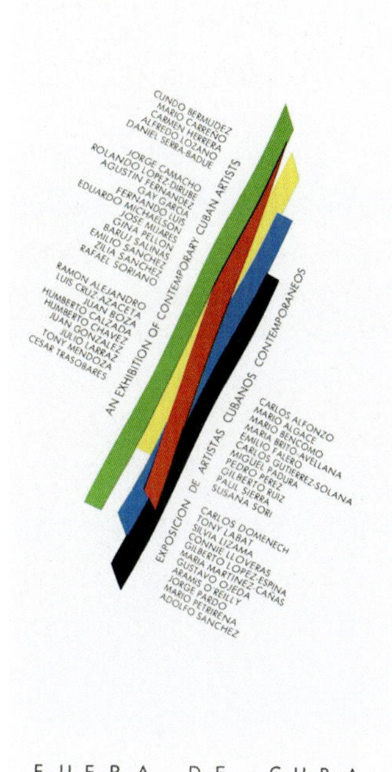

Brochure for the exhibition at the Zimmerli Art Museum, 1987.

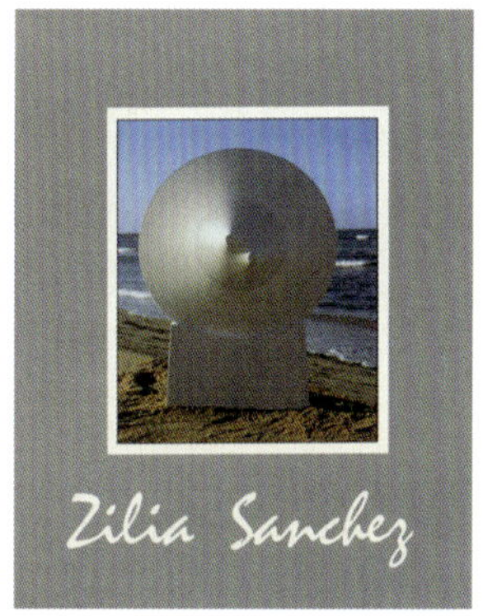

Postcard for *Zilia Sánchez: Tres décadas*, 1991.

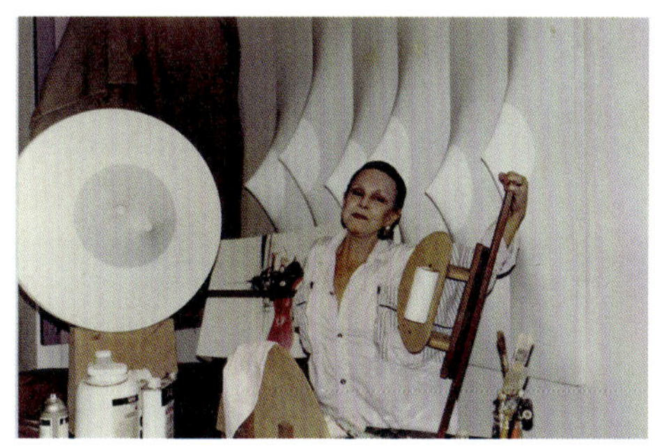

Sánchez in her studio with the structural support for a work, c. late 1980s–early 1990s.

1998

Sánchez participates in *100 años después… 100 artistas contemporáneos: Reflexiones en torno a la presencia norteamericana*, an exhibi-tion in San Juan.

1999

Opening in October at the Fundació Joan Miró in Barcelona, the installation *Tu-Tran* by Charles Juhasz Alvarado (b. 1965) contains artwork by Sánchez. The project is part of the museum's yearlong exhibition cycle "An Oasis in the Blue Desert," which invites the participation of six young artists from Puerto Rico.

2000

In April, Sánchez presents her work in a solo exhibition, *Heróicas eróticas*, at the Museo de las Américas in San Juan. The catalogue includes texts by Servando Sacaluga and Manuel Álvarez Lezama, as well as a reprint of Severo Sarduy's 1970 essay.

In October, Sánchez participates in *U/topistas: Estudios para proyectos contemporáneos*, an exhibition of utopian proposals by contempo-rary artists in Puerto Rico. The event forms part of a weeklong series of collective inter-ventions across San Juan under the title *Puerto Rico '00 (Paréntesis en la "ciudad")*.

2001

In May the show *Metáforas* at the Galería Petrus in San Juan brings together three women art-ists, including Sánchez, who explore the female figure in their work.

2004

Sánchez takes part in *Plan D: Acercamientos al dibujo* at the Galería Raíces in San Juan. The show is devoted to contemporary drawing practices and highlights Sánchez's shaped canvases containing *tatuajes* (tattoos).

2006

At CIRCA Puerto Rico '06, an international art fair in San Juan, Sánchez participates in *SOLO*, an exhibition that promotes the work of five independent, contemporary artists without gallery representation.

2007

The Museo de Arte de Puerto Rico organizes a long-term exhibition of its permanent collection, titled *Contexto puertorriqueño: Del rococó colonial al arte global*. It features one of Sánchez's largest shaped canvases, *Nacimiento de Eros* (Birth of Eros; 1971), measuring approximately 7 ½ feet by 9 ½ feet.

2009

In April the Casa Sofía de Puerto Rico in San Juan hosts *Construcciones en secuencia*, a solo exhibition of Sánchez's work that includes shaped canvases from the 1960s to the present. Manuel Álvarez Lezama contributes to the catalogue.

In New York, an untitled serigraph (c. 1970) by Sánchez appears in El Museo del Barrio's exhibition *Voces y visiones: Four Decades through El Museo del Barrio's Permanent Collection*.

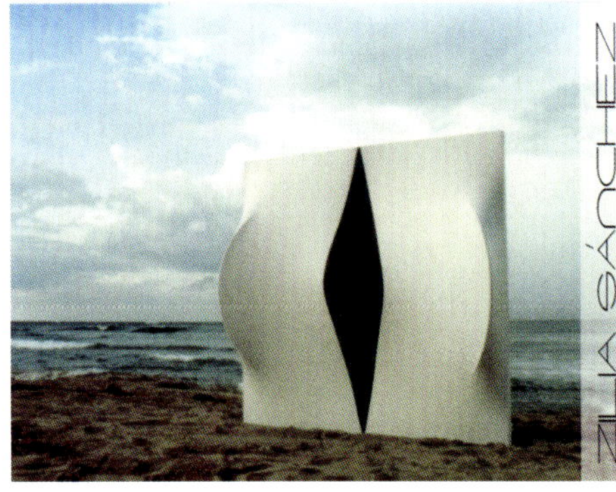

Postcard for CIRCA Puerto Rico '06, 2006.

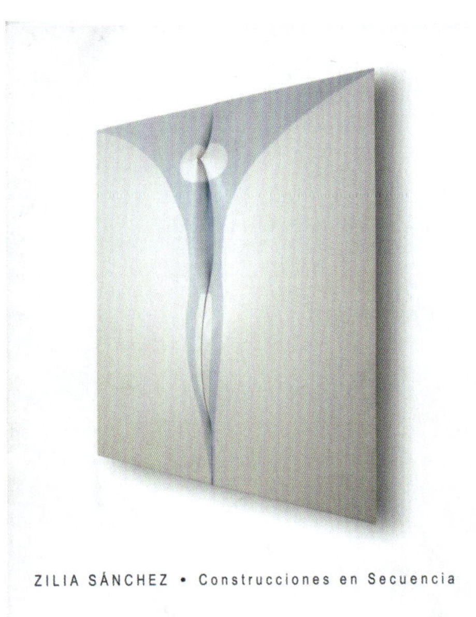

Catalogue for Sánchez's exhibition at the Casa Sofía de Puerto Rico, 2009.

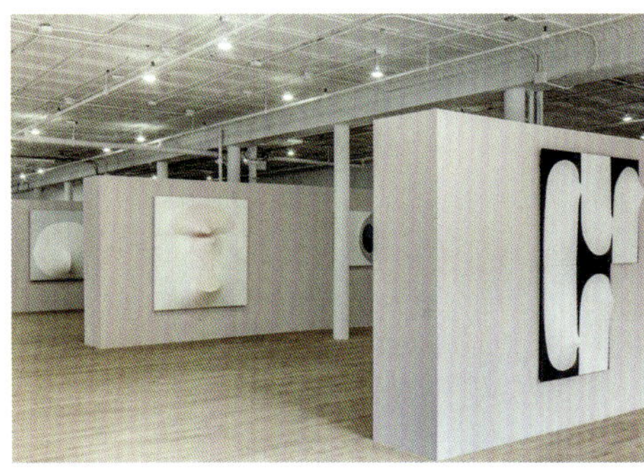

Installation view of *Zilia Sánchez* at Artists Space, 2013.

2013

From April to June, Artists Space presents *Zilia Sánchez*, a survey of the artist's career and her first solo exhibition in New York since 1984. Sánchez receives an award for Best Exhibition by a Puerto Rican Artist Abroad, given by the International Art Critics Association (AICA), Puerto Rico Chapter.

2014

Zilia Sánchez: Heróicas eróticas en Nueva York, a solo exhibition of shaped canvases, sculptures, and works on paper, opens in May at Galerie Lelong in New York. The catalogue includes contributions by Irene V. Small and Marimar Benítez.

Sánchez's work appears in *Museum Starter Kit: Open with Care* at El Museo del Barrio and *Looking Back: The 8th White Columns Annual*, both in New York.

2015

Organized by the ICP, the *16a edición de la muestra nacional de artes* pays tribute to the careers of Sánchez and Olga Albizu (1924–2005), both pioneering women artists who have lived in Puerto Rico and New York.

2016

Galerie Lelong presents *Diálogos constructivistas en la vanguardia cubana*, an exhibition highlighting the geometric and constructivist tendencies of three Cuban painters: Amelia Peláez (1896–1968), Loló Soldevilla, and Sánchez. The catalogue contains an essay by guest curator Ingrid W. Elliott.

Sánchez's art appears in *The Illusive Eye* at El Museo del Barrio, the *Segunda gran bienal tropical* in Puerto Rico, and *Verboamérica* at the Museo de Arte Latinoamericano de Buenos Aires (MALBA) in Argentina.

2017

Sánchez participates in *Viva arte viva*, the main section of the fifty-seventh Venice Biennale in Italy, held from May to November.

The Hammer Museum in Los Angeles includes Sánchez in *Radical Women: Latin American Art, 1960–1985*, an exhibition that encompasses more than one hundred women artists from fifteen countries. After opening at the Hammer Museum, the show is intended to travel to the Brooklyn Museum in New York and the Pinacoteca do Estado de São Paulo in Brazil.

Additional group shows featuring Sánchez's art take place at the Approach Gallery and the Stephen Friedman Gallery, both in London; El Museo del Barrio; the Newcomb Art Museum in New Orleans; the Coral Gables Museum in Florida; and the Pérez Art Museum Miami.

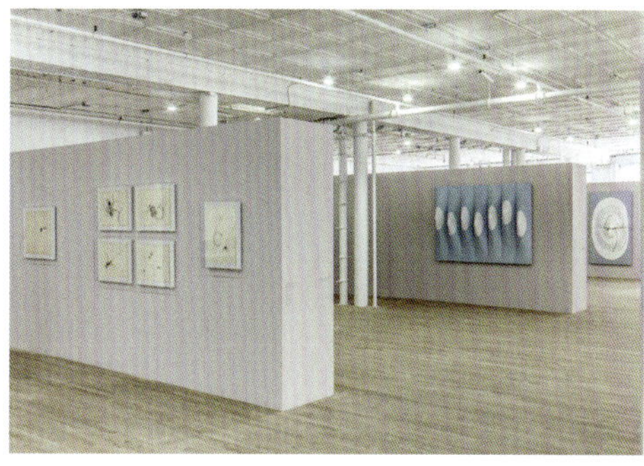

Installation view of *Zilia Sánchez* at Artists Space, 2013.

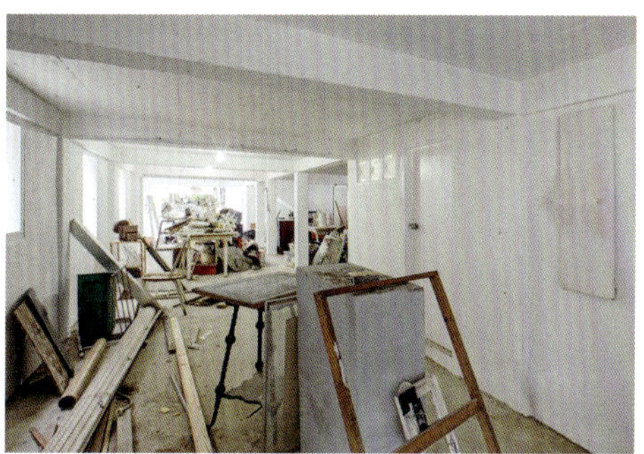

Sánchez's studio in San Juan, 2018.

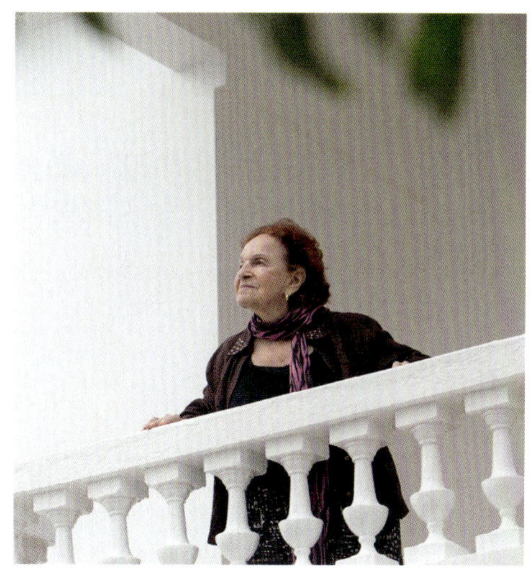

Sánchez on the balcony of her studio, February 2018.

In September, Hurricane Maria wreaks havoc on the island of Puerto Rico and damages Sánchez's studio. Sánchez herself is temporarily displaced from her apartment.

2018

After a complete renovation, Sánchez's studio reopens in the spring. Sánchez continues to live and work in San Juan.

Alyson Cluck is a PhD candidate, Modern and Contemporary Art, at the University of Maryland.

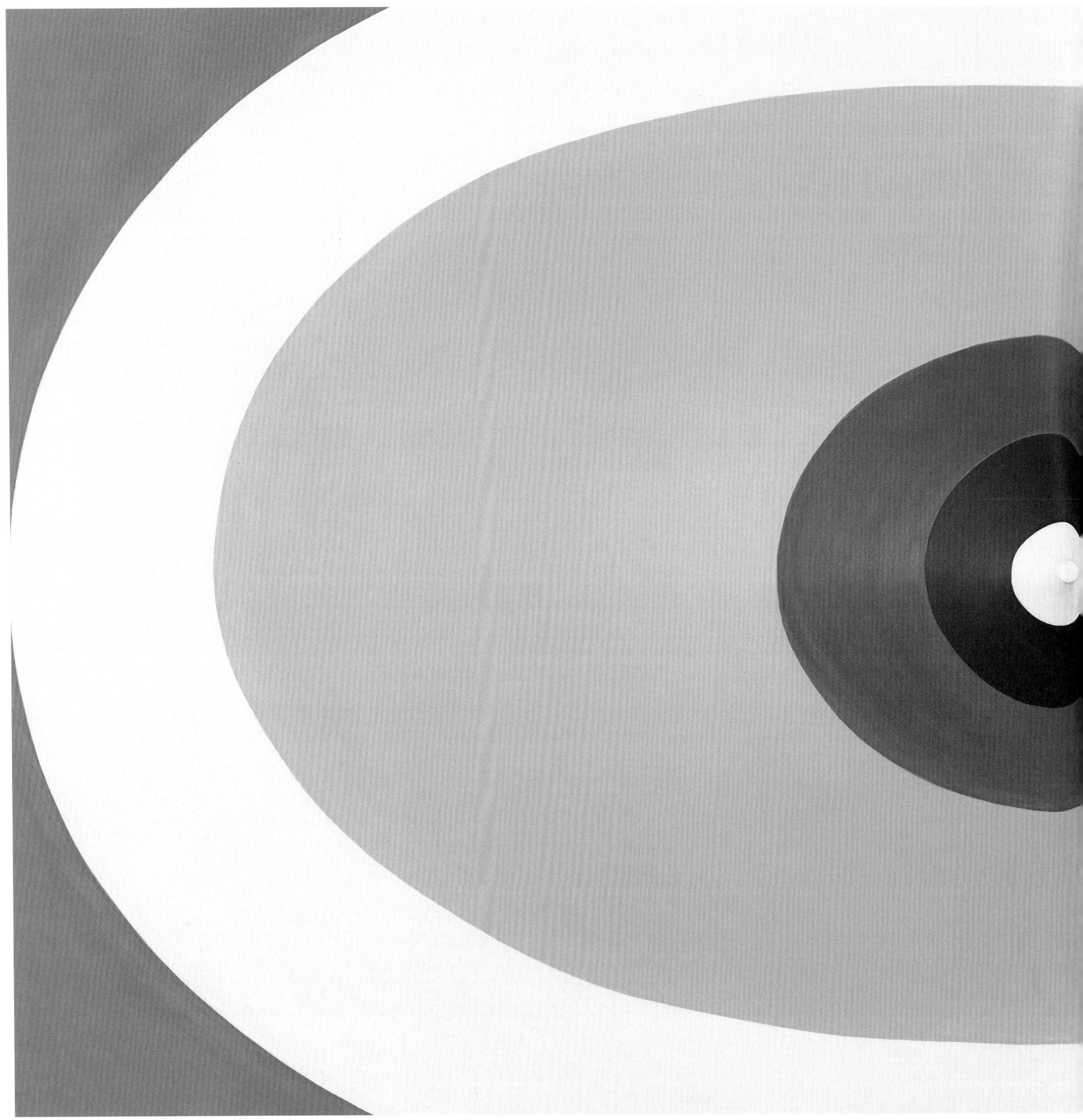

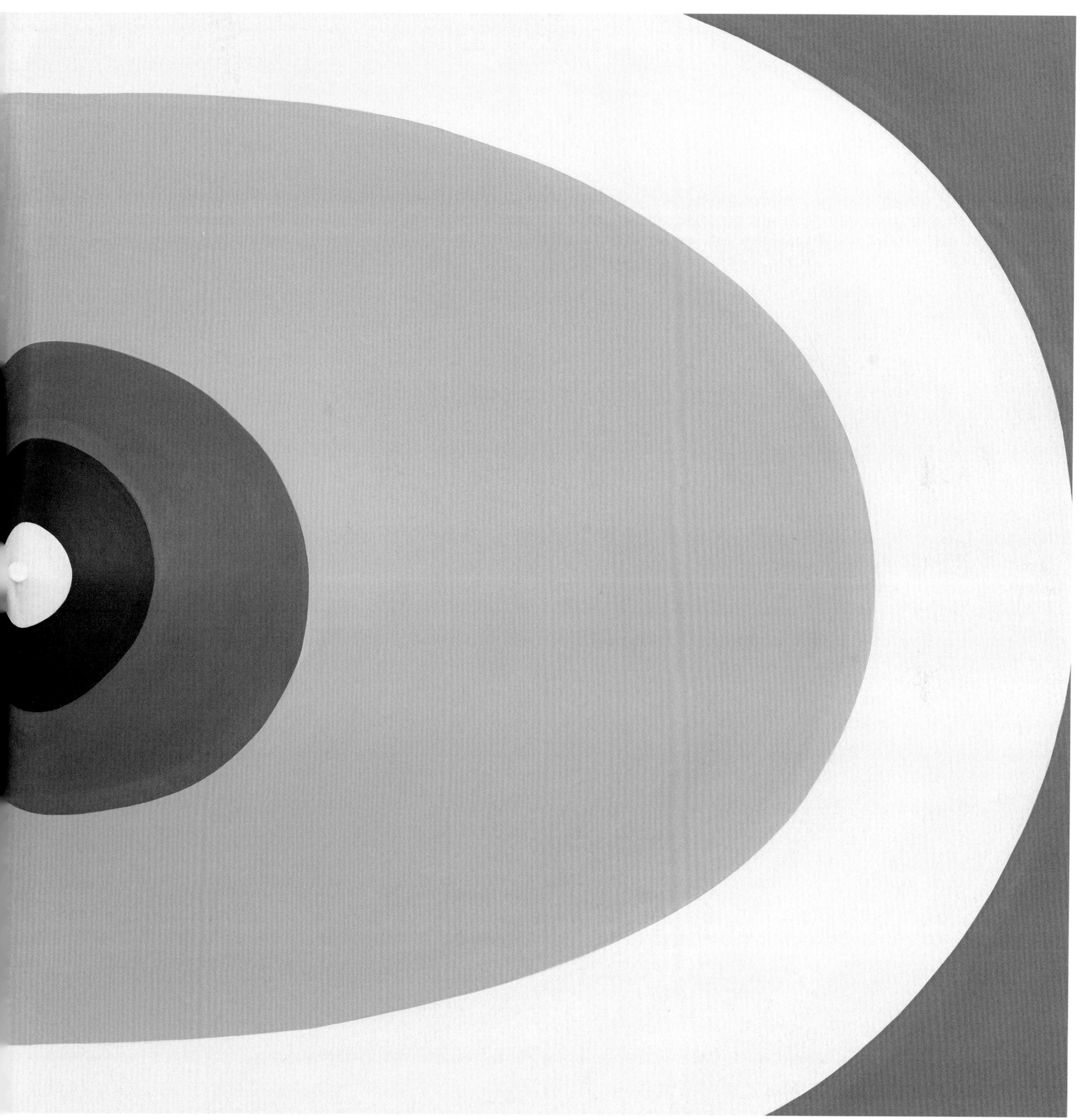

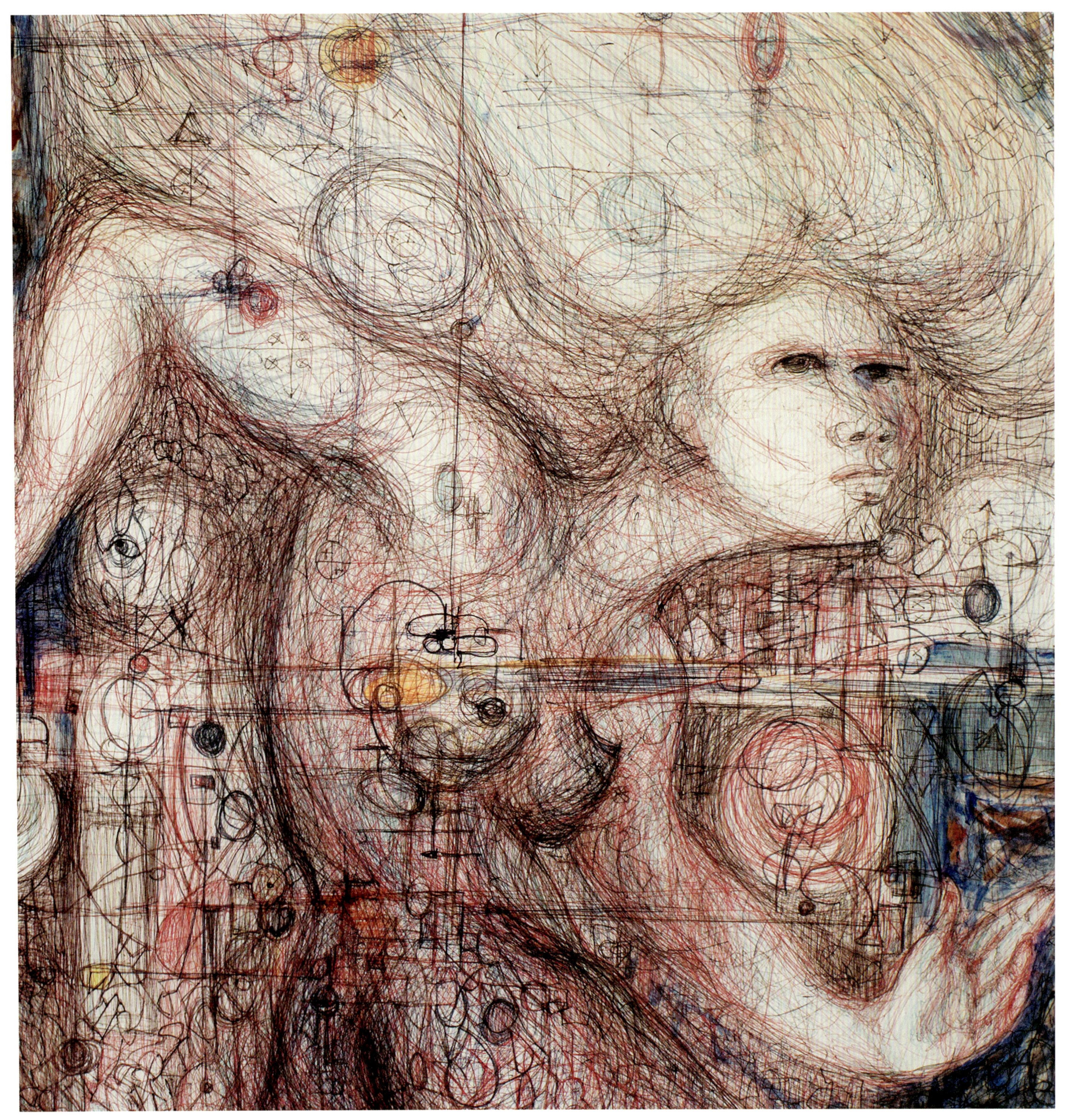

Works within each section are arranged chronologically.

Interviews

Júpiter. "Una pintora abstracta, Zilia Sánchez, muy joven, dice sus propósitos y sus convicciones estéticas." *Diario de la marina* (Havana), May 20, 1956.

Blanc, Giulio V. "Conversación con Zilia Sánchez." *Mariel* (New York) 2, no. 7 (Fall 1984): 37.

Kalmár, Stefan, and Richard Birkett. "Zilia Sánchez Interview." San Juan, March 2013. Translated by Carla Acevedo-Yates. Artists Space video. http://artistsspace.org/materials /zilia-sanchez-interview.

Fuchs, Eva. "Zilia Sánchez at Galerie Lelong, New York." *Ocula Insight*, June 10, 2016. https:// ocula.com/magazine/insights/zilia-sanchez -at-galerie-lelong-new-york.

Barral, Alberto. "Zilia Sánchez." *Art Nexus*, no. 104 (March–May 2017): 48–51.

See also Vesela Sretenović, "In Retrospect: Talking with Zilia Sánchez," in this catalogue.

Catalogues and Brochures: Solo Exhibitions

Zilia Sánchez: Óleos. Statement by Severo Sarduy. Havana: Galería Cubana, 1956.

Zilia Sánchez: Exposición pintura. Statement by J. M. Moreno Galván. Madrid: Sala Clan, 1957.

Zilia Sánchez. San Juan: Museo de la Universidad de Puerto Rico, 1965.

Zilia Sánchez: Paintings. Essays by Eleanor Hakim, "Zilia Sánchez: Metaphoric Visualizations of Reality," and Isel Rivero, "Historical Situation and Retrospective." New York: Zegrí Gallery, 1966.

Zilia Sánchez. Essay by Fernando Chueca Goitia. Madrid: Galería El Bosco, 1967.

Zilia Sánchez. Statement by Adolfo Castaño. Barcelona: Instituto Catalán de Cultura Hispánica, 1967.

Estructuras en secuencia. Essay by Severo Sarduy, "Las *topologías eróticas* de Zilia Sánchez," and statement by Gordon Brown. San Juan: Museo de la Universidad de Puerto Rico, 1970.

Zilia Sánchez: Erótica. New York: INTAR Latin American Gallery, 1984.

Zilia Sánchez: Tres décadas. Essays by Margarita Fernández Zavala, "Zilia Sánchez: El desarrollo de un lenguaje plástico," and Marta Traba, "El erotismo y la comunicación," 1972 (reprint), and a selection of critical commentary. Humacao, PR: Museo Casa Roig, 1991.

Zilia Sánchez: Heróicas eróticas. Essays by Servando Sacaluga, "Las topologías heróicas eróticas de Zilia Sánchez"; Manuel Álvarez Lezama, "Heróicas/eróticas: Zilia Sánchez y sus necesarias seducciones"; and Severo Sarduy, "Las *topologías eróticas* de Zilia Sánchez," 1970 (reprint). San Juan: Museo de las Américas, 2000.

Zilia Sánchez: Construcciones en secuencia. Essay by Manuel Álvarez Lezama, "Zilia Sánchez: Poeta de la sensualidad." San Juan: Casa Sofía de Puerto Rico, 2009.

Selected Bibliography

COMPILED BY
ALYSON CLUCK

Zilia Sánchez: Heróicas eróticas en Nueva York. Essay by Irene V. Small, "On Zilia Sánchez's Surface," and artist's chronology by Marimar Benítez. New York: Actar / Galerie Lelong, 2014.

Catalogues: Group Exhibitions

II salón de otoño. Havana: Liceo Artístico y Literario de Regla, 1947.

IV exposición nacional de pintura, escultura y grabado. Havana: Centro Asturiano, 1950.

VI salón nacional de pintura y escultura. Havana: Salones del Capitolio Nacional, 1953.

Pintura, escultura, cerámica. Havana: Retiro Odontológico, 1953.

Homenaje a José Martí: Exposición de plástica cubana contemporánea. Havana: Lyceum, 1954.

Exposición en homenaje a Luis de Soto. Havana: Sociedad Cultural Nuestro Tiempo, 1955.

Cuba en Tampa: La feria del progreso. N.p., 1955.

El tema religioso en la pintura cubana. Havana: Galería Cubana, 1956.

VIII salón nacional de pintura y escultura. Havana: Palacio de Bellas Artes, 1956.

V bienal de S. Paulo. São Paulo: Museu de Arte Moderna, 1959.

Salón anual 1959: Pintura, escultura y grabado. Havana: Palacio de Bellas Artes, 1959.

II bienal interamericana de pintura, escultura y grabado (1960). Mexico City: Artes de México, 1961.

Contemporary American Paintings and Watercolors. New York: Herbert E. Feist Gallery, 1967.

Primera bienal de San Juan del grabado latinoamericano. San Juan: Instituto de Cultura Puertorriqueña, 1970.

Fourteen Latin American Painters. Washington, DC: Inter-American Development Bank Staff Association, 1970.

Segunda bienal de San Juan del grabado latinoamericano. San Juan: Instituto de Cultura Puertorriqueña, 1972.

Tercera bienal de San Juan del grabado latinoamericano. San Juan: Instituto de Cultura Puertorriqueña, 1974.

Cuatro pintoras y una escultora. San Juan: Galería María Rechany, 1975.

IV bienal de arte de Medellín. Medellín: Corporación Bienal de Arte, 1981.

Quinta muestra de pintura y escultura puertorriqueña. San Juan: Instituto de Cultura Puertorriqueña, 1981.

Obra puertorriqueña de artistas cubanos: Homenaje de la Unión de Cubanos en el Exilio (UCE) al pueblo de Puerto Rico. San Juan: Unión de Cubanos en el Exilio, 1982.

Arte actual: Puerto Rico 1983. San Juan: Liga de Estudiantes de Arte de San Juan, 1983.

Women Artists from Puerto Rico. New York: Cayman Gallery, 1983.

Primer congreso de artistas abstractos de Puerto Rico. San Juan: Instituto de Cultura Puertorriqueña, 1984.

Artistas abstractos de Puerto Rico. San Juan: Instituto de Cultura Puertorriqueña, 1986.

25 años de pintura puertorriqueña. Ponce, PR: Museo de Arte de Ponce, 1986.

Mujeres artistas de Puerto Rico. San Juan: Museo de Bellas Artes/Instituto de Cultura Puertorriqueña, 1986.

Outside Cuba/Fuera de Cuba: Contemporary Cuban Visual Artists (1987–89). New Brunswick, NJ: Office of Hispanic Arts, Rutgers; Coral Gables, FL: Research Institute for Cuban Studies, University of Miami, 1989.

Pintura y escultura de los años setenta en Puerto Rico. San Juan: Museo de Arte Contemporáneo de Puerto Rico, 1989.

Mujeres artistas: Protagonistas de los ochenta. San Juan: Museo de Arte Contemporáneo de Puerto Rico, 1990.

Pequeño formato 90. San Juan: Galería Luigi Marrozzini, 1990.

Breaking Barriers: Selections from the Museum of Art's Permanent Contemporary Cuban Collection. Fort Lauderdale, FL: Museum of Art, 1997.

100 años después… 100 artistas contemporáneos: Reflexiones en torno a la presencia norteamericana. San Juan: Comité de los Cien, 1998.

Puerto Rico '00 (Paréntesis en la "ciudad") (2000). San Juan: M&M Proyectos, 2001.

Contexto puertorriqueño: Del rococó colonial al arte global. San Juan: Museo de Arte de Puerto Rico, 2007.

16a edición de la muestra nacional de artes: Dedicada a la obra de Olga Albizu y Zilia Sánchez. San Juan: Instituto de Cultura Puertorriqueña, 2015.

Diálogos constructivistas en la vanguardia cubana: Amelia Peláez, Loló Soldevilla, y Zilia Sánchez. Essay by Ingrid W. Elliott, "Between the Real and the Invisible." New York: Galerie Lelong, 2016.

Verboamérica. Buenos Aires: Fundación Eduardo F. Costantini—MALBA, 2016.

Viva arte viva: 57th International Art Exhibition. Venice: La Biennale di Venezia, 2017.

Painting on the Edge: A Historical Survey. London: Stephen Friedman Gallery, 2017.

On the Horizon: Contemporary Cuban Art from the Jorge M. Pérez Collection. Miami: Pérez Art Museum Miami, 2017.

Radical Women: Latin American Art, 1960–1985. Los Angeles: Hammer Museum and DelMonico Books/Prestel, 2017.

Books

Traba, Marta. "A la búsqueda del signo perdido." In *Dos décadas vulnerables en las artes plásticas latinoamericanas, 1950–1970*, 154–79. Mexico City: Siglo Veintiuno Editores, 1973.

Routté Gómez, Eneid. "Zilia Sánchez y sus múltiples memorias." In *Conversando con nuestros artistas*, 86–89. San Juan: Museo de Arte Contemporáneo de Puerto Rico, 1999.

Bleys, Rudi C. *Images of Ambiente: Homotextuality and Latin American Art, 1810–Today*. New York: Continuum, 2000.

Veigas, José, et al. *Memoria: Cuban Art of the 20th Century*. Los Angeles: California/International Arts Foundation, 2002.

McEwen, Abigail. *Revolutionary Horizons: Art and Polemics in 1950s Cuba*. New Haven, CT: Yale University Press, 2016.

Suárez, Osbel. "Los Once." In *La isla concreta: Abstração geométrica em Cuba*, 17–19. São Paulo: Dan Galeria, 2016.

Trigo, Benigno. *Malady and Genius: Self-Sacrifice in Puerto Rican Literature*. Albany: State University of New York Press, 2016.

Articles

Huete, Ángel. "Encuentro con Zilia Sánchez." *Artes* (Havana) 1, no. 3 (May 1959): 10–11.

"Dibujos de Zilia Sánchez." *Lunes de Revolución* (Havana), December 14, 1959.

Skerrett, Lillian. "Expone en la UPR: Pintora es exponente de los 'informalistas.'" *El mundo* (San Juan), July 22, 1965.

Alonso, Alberto. "Alucinante exactitud del mundo de hoy en obras de Z. Sánchez." *El diario–La prensa* (New York), May 20, 1966.

"Galería de arte: Zilia Sánchez." *Dígame* (Madrid), April 4, 1967.

Castaño, Adolfo. "Itinerario de exposiciones: Zilia Sánchez." *La estafeta literaria* (Madrid), April 8, 1967.

Castro Arines, José de. "Zilia Sánchez." *Diario de Barcelona*, April 8, 1967.

Prados de la Plaza, Francisco. "Galería de arte: Zilia Sánchez." *Arriba* (Madrid), April 9, 1967.

"Cuban Talent." *Spanish Daily News* (Madrid), April 26, 1967.

Fuentes, Juan E. "Two Young Painters." *Guidepost Magazine* (Madrid), May 12, 1967.

"Abstract Artist Displays Paintings in Gallery Two." *Gold Bug* (Western Maryland College), December 12, 1969.

Spector, Stephen. "Cecilia [*sic*] Sánchez at Sarduy." *Arts Magazine* 44 (Summer 1970): 60.

"La exposición de Zilia Sánchez." *El tiempo* (New York), July 9, 1970.

Soretsky, Leo. "Gallery Scene." *City East* (New York) 3, no. 11 (August 1970): 9.

Ruiz de la Mata, Ernesto J. "Zilia Sánchez." *San Juan Star Magazine*, September 20, 1970.

Prida, Dolores. "El erotismo espacial en la pintura de Zilia Sánchez." *La nueva sangre* 3, no. 9 (October 1970): 9–10.

Peña, Mario. "El minimalismo con poesía de Zilia." *El tiempo* (New York), January 4, 1971.

Molina, Antonio J. "Arte en Puerto Rico: Liga Estudiantes de Arte contrata servicios pintora." *El mundo* (San Juan), January 23, 1972.

Borrás, Gloria. "La liberación de Rosario Ferré." *El mundo* (San Juan), *Puerto Rico ilustrado*, October 1, 1972.

Traba, Marta. "El erotismo y la comunicación." *Zona. Carga y descarga* (San Juan) 1, no. 2 (November–December 1972): 11.

Sarduy, Severo. "Las *topologías eróticas* de Zilia Sánchez" (1970). *La provincia* (Las Palmas, Spain), April 8, 1973.

Molina, Antonio J. "Zilia Sánchez y su obra." *El mundo* (San Juan), *Puerto Rico ilustrado*, May 5, 1975.

"Premio de la UNESCO a Zilia." *El nuevo día* (San Juan), January 20, 1978.

Bourbakis, Jorge C. "Zilia Sánchez." *Vanidades continental*, October 1979, 42–45.

Ruiz de la Mata, Ernesto J. "Purely Decorative? Why Not?" *San Juan Star Magazine*, November 4, 1979.

"Usted escoge! [en la Bienal]." *El colombiano* (Medellín), May 27, 1981.

"La escultura de Zilia Sánchez: La forma y el color hacen su erotismo." *El mundo* (Medellín), June 2, 1981.

Gómez Gómez, Sonia. "La figura humana se insinúa en las *Topologías eróticas* de Zilia Sánchez." *El colombiano* (Medellín), June 3, 1981.

"Colombia: Zilia Sánchez en la Bienal de Arte de Medellín." *Plástica* (San Juan), no. 7 (July 1981): 42–43.

"Obra realizada en Puerto Rico: Primer premio en el Museo Moderno de Cali." *El vocero* (San Juan), July 6, 1981.

Molina, Antonio J. "Zilia Sánchez triunfa en Colombia." *El mundo* (San Juan), July 28, 1981.

Niurka, Norma. "Zilia sublimiza el cuerpo femenino." *El Miami Herald*, January 24, 1982.

Cherson, Samuel B. "El arte cubano en Puerto Rico y en el mundo." *Plástica* (San Juan), no. 9 (August 1982): 32–36.

Miller, Jeannette. "Afinidades e influencias en el arte: Zilia Sánchez y Bismark Yermenos." *El caribe* (Santo Domingo, Dominican Republic), April 21, 1984.

Pérez Ruiz, José Antonio. "Zilia Sánchez." *El reportero* (San Juan), sec. Viva, August 6, 1984.

Buján, Juan. "Erotismo y comunicación: Zilia Sánchez en Intar Gallery." *La voz hispana* (New York), December 6–12, 1984.

"Juego erótico en la Espiral." *El mundo* (San Juan), sec. Diario Vivir, November 14, 1985.

Zimmer, William. "6 Generations of Cuban Artists at Rutgers's Zimmerli Museum." *New York Times*, April 19, 1987.

Alegre Barrios, Mario. "Zilia Sánchez: Una 'cangrejera' de La Habana." *El nuevo día* (San Juan), sec. Por Dentro, March 5, 1991.

Rodríguez, Myrna. "Sánchez's Works on Exhibit at Casa Roig in Humacao." *San Juan Star*, September 5, 1991.

García Gutiérrez, Enrique. "Eros y Zilia Sánchez." *El nuevo día* (San Juan), October 6, 1991.

Alegre Barrios, Mario. "Catarsis y pequeño formato con Luigi Marrozzini." *El nuevo día* (San Juan), sec. Por Dentro, December 5, 1991.

Álvarez Lezama, Manuel. "Zilia Sánchez Reveals Mysteries of the Human Body." *San Juan Star*, February 20, 1994.

———. "La metáfora como reto." *El nuevo día* (San Juan), sec. Por Dentro, April 9, 2000.

Pérez Ruiz, José Antonio. "Zilia Sánchez: Heróicas eróticas." *El vocero* (San Juan), sec. Escenario, July 11, 2000.

"Tres mujeres, tres vertientes." *El nuevo día* (San Juan), sec. Por Dentro, April 29, 2001.

Jiménez, Ivelisse. "Zilia Sánchez." *BOMB* (New York), no. 86 (Winter 2003/2004): 36–37.

Rodríguez, Jorge. "Artistas y galeristas al acecho." *El vocero* (San Juan), sec. Escenario, June 15, 2004.

Delgado Castro, Ileana. "Encuentro con Zilia Sánchez." *El nuevo día* (San Juan), sec. Revista Domingo, March 20, 2005.

Pérez Rivera, Tatiana. "Solos y diversos en CIRCA." *El nuevo día* (San Juan), May 24, 2006.

Trigo, Benigno. "*Zona. Carga y descarga*: Minor Literature in a Penal Colony." *MLN* 124, no. 2 (March 2009): 481–508.

González, Leyra E. "Aferrada a su obra." *El nuevo día* (San Juan), April 15, 2009.

Álvarez Lezama, Manuel. "Zilia Sánchez: Casa Sofía." *Art Nexus* 8, no. 74 (September–November 2009): 129–31.

Mulero, Lillian, and Jan Galligan. "Zilia Sánchez: Lunare, la marca de la belleza." *Claridad/En rojo* (San Juan), September 5, 2011.

Cotter, Holland. "Zilia Sánchez." *New York Times*, June 14, 2013.

Noriega Costas, Rebeca. "Lienzos elásticos, lienzos de piel." *El nuevo día* (San Juan), August 2, 2013.

Young, Gillian. "Zilia Sánchez: Artists Space." *Art in America* 101, no. 8 (September 2013): 142–43.

Barral, Alberto. "Zilia Sánchez: Artists Space." *Art Nexus* 12, no. 90 (September–November 2013): 121–22.

Zaya, Octavio. "Zilia Sánchez: An Approach to the Topographies of Desire." *Arte al día international* 144 (November 2013–January 2014): 24–31.

DíazCasas, Rafael. "Zilia Sánchez: A Minimalist *Mulata*—A Caribbean Island." *Art OnCuba*, no. 1 (December 2013–February 2014): 40–43.

Schwabsky, Barry. "Zilia Sánchez." *Artforum International* 53, no. 1 (September 2014): 373–74.

Roulet, Laura. "Zilia Sánchez: Minimalist Mulata." *Sculpture* 34, no. 1 (January/February 2015): 44–49.

Benítez, Marimar. "Zilia Sánchez." *Revista del ICP* (San Juan) 3, no. 3 (December 2015): 172–77.

Beckenstein, Joyce. "Zilia Sánchez, María Magdalena Campos-Pons, and Glenda León: Three Cuban Artists, Three Generations, Three Perspectives." *Woman's Art Journal* 37, no. 2 (Fall/Winter 2016): 20–28.

Noguera Osuna, Male. "Zilia llega a Venecia." *Àrea* (Guaynabo, PR) 7, no. 3 (Spring 2017): 56–58.

Biesenbach, Klaus, Christopher Gregory, and Ariana McLaughlin. "In Puerto Rico, Artists Rebuild and Reach Out." *New York Times*, January 28, 2018.

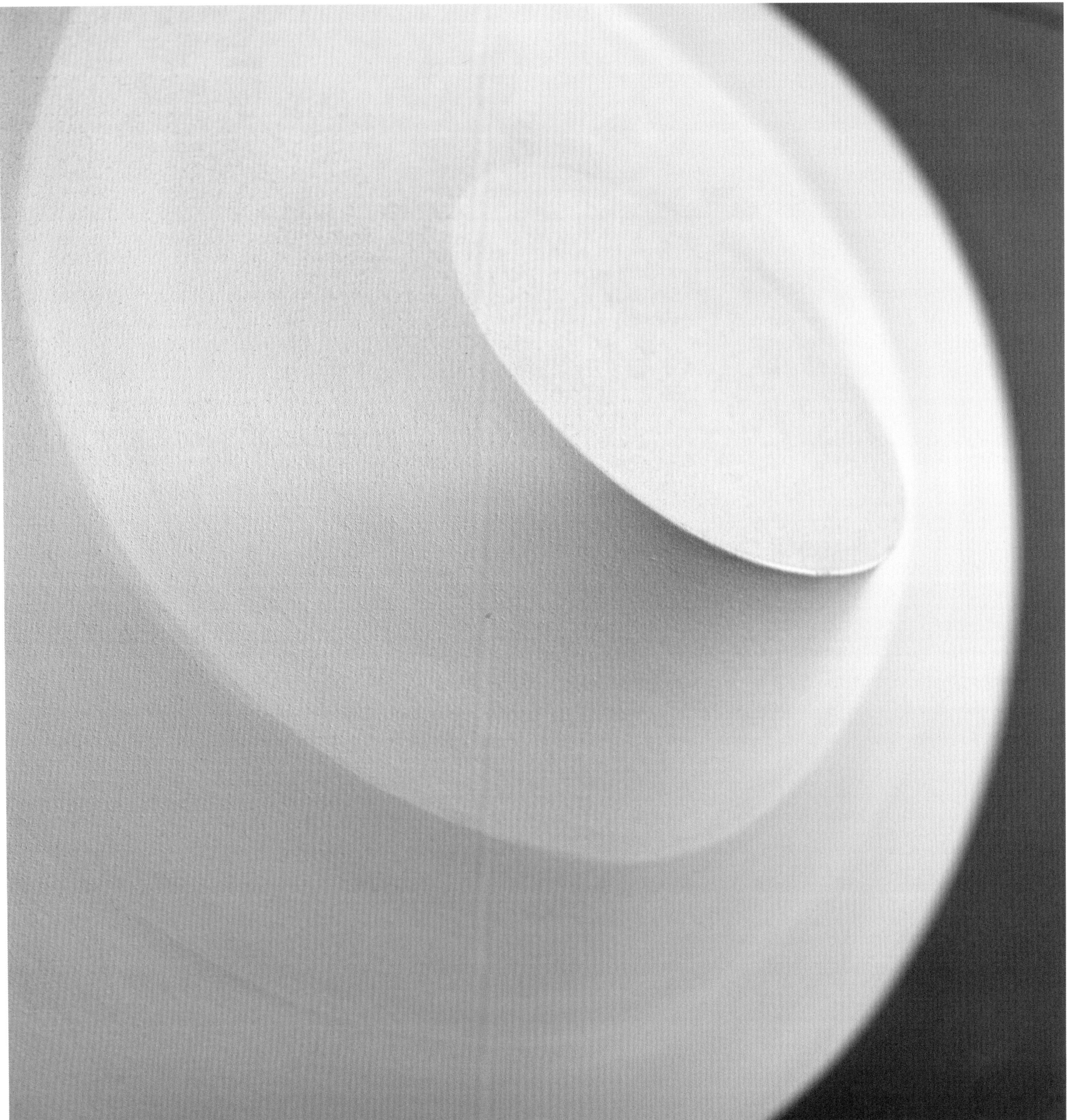

Works in
the Exhibition

Self Portrait, 1954
Pen and ink on paper
26 × 20 ⅛ in. (66.2 × 51.1 cm)
Collection of the artist, San Juan
Cat. 1

Untitled, c. mid-1950s
Acrylic on canvas
22 ¼ × 11 ¼ in. (56.5 × 28.6 cm)
Collection of RosaMaría García Sarduy, Miami
Cat. 2

Untitled, mid-1950s–1962
Acrylic on canvas
16 × 18 in. (40.6 × 45.7 cm)
Collection of Cecilia and Ernesto Poma, Miami
Cat. 9

Azul azul (Blue Blue), 1956
Acrylic on canvas
21 × 23 in. (53.3 × 58.4 cm)
Collection of the artist, Courtesy Galerie
Lelong & Co., New York
Cat. 3

Untitled, 1956–99
Ink on stretched canvas
7 × 9 ¼ × 2 ¾ in. (17.8 × 23.5 × 7 cm)
Collection of Ignacio J. López Beguiristain
and Laura M. Guerra, San Juan
Cat. 4

Afrocubano, 1957
Oil on canvas
27 ½ × 21 ½ in. (70 × 54.5 cm)
Private collection, Madrid
Page 44

Untitled, from the series *Afrocubanos,* 1957
Acrylic and ink on canvas laid on board
36 × 28 in. (91.4 × 71.1 cm)
Collection of the artist, Courtesy Galerie
Lelong & Co., New York
Cat. 6

Lo que es de isla y piel (Belonging to Island
and Skin), from the series *Afrocubanos,* 1958
Acrylic and ink on canvas
39 ½ × 40 ½ in. (100.3 × 102.9 cm)
Collection of Mima and César Reyes, San Juan
Cat. 5

Untitled, 1958
Ink and watercolor on coated paper
20 × 14 ⅝ in. (50.8 × 37.1 cm)
Collection of the artist, Courtesy Galerie
Lelong & Co., New York
Cat. 7

Untitled, 1958
Acrylic and ink on canvas
34 × 49 ⅞ in. (86.4 × 126.7 cm)
Collection of Mima and César Reyes, San Juan
Cat. 8

Untitled, 1959
Ink and gouache on paper
14 × 20 in. (35.6 × 50.8 cm)
Collection of RosaMaría García Sarduy, Miami
Cat. 10

Tierra (The Earth), 1959
Mixed media on canvas
48 ½ × 48 ¼ in. (123.2 × 122.6 cm)
CINTAS Foundation Fellows Collection, Miami
Cat. 11

Untitled, c. 1960s
Mixed media on canvas
38 × 42 in. (96.5 × 106.7 cm)
Private collection, Miami
Cat. 14

Untitled, c. 1960s
Mixed media on stretched canvas
31 × 23 × approx. 2 in. (78.7 × 58.4 × approx. 5 cm)
CINTAS Foundation Fellows Collection, Miami
Cat. 16

Topologia eròtica (Erotic Topology), 1960–71
Acrylic on stretched canvas
41 × 56 × 13 in. (104.1 × 142.2 × 33 cm)
Collection of Jose R. Landron, San Juan
Cat. 19

Untitled (Agua), 1961
Mixed media on canvas
38 ¼ × 37 ⅞ in. (97.2 × 96.2 cm)
Collection of RosaMaría García Sarduy, Miami
Cat. 12

Untitled, 1962/90
Acrylic on stretched canvas
15 × 25 × 8 in. (38.1 × 63.5 × 20.3 cm)
Collection of the artist, Courtesy Galerie
Lelong & Co., New York
Cat. 18

Concepto Z, 1964
Acrylic on canvas
23 ⅛ × 28 ⅛ in. (58.7 × 71.4 cm)
Instituto de Cultura Puertorriqueña, San Juan
Cat. 15

Lunar blanco (White Moon), 1964
Acrylic on stretched canvas
33 ½ × 24 ½ × 5 ½ in. (85.1 × 62.2 × 14 cm)
Collection of Beth Rudin DeWoody, New York
Cat. 20

Untitled, c. 1965
Ink on paper
9 ½ × 4 in. (24.1 × 10.2 cm)
Collection of the artist, Courtesy Galerie
Lelong & Co., New York
Cat. 21

Untitled, c. 1965
Ink on paper
9 ½ × 4 in. (24.1 × 10.2 cm)
Collection of Diane and Bruce Halle, Phoenix
Cat. 22

Untitled, c. 1965
Ink on paper
9 ½ × 4 in. (24.1 × 10.2 cm)
Collection of Diane and Bruce Halle, Phoenix
Cat. 23

Untitled, c. 1965
Ink on paper
9 ½ × 4 in. (24.1 × 10.2 cm)
Collection of Diane and Bruce Halle, Phoenix
Cat. 24

Untitled, 1965
Mixed media on canvas
33 ½ × 36 in. (85.1 × 91.4 cm)
Collection of RosaMaría García Sarduy, Miami
Cat. 13

Topología (Topology), 1965/93
Acrylic and ink on canvas
15 × 20 in. (38.1 × 50.8 cm)
Collection of the artist, Courtesy Galerie
Lelong & Co., New York
Cat. 17

Troyanas (Trojan Women), polyptych,
from the series *Módulos infinitos* (Infinite
Modules), 1967
Acrylic on stretched canvas
71 ¾ × 54 × 9 ½ in. (182.2 × 137.2 × 24.1 cm)
Collection of Laura Delaney Taft and John Taft,
promised gift to Walker Art Center, Minneapolis
Cat. 25

Lunar con tatuaje (Moon with Tattoo),
c. 1968/96
Acrylic on stretched canvas
71 × 72 × 12 in. (180.3 × 182.9 × 30.5 cm)
Collection of the artist, Courtesy Galerie
Lelong & Co., New York
Cat. 31

El significado del significante
(The Signified of the Signifier), c. 1968
India ink on paper
15 × 22 in. (38.1 × 55.9 cm)
Collection of the artist, Courtesy Galerie
Lelong & Co., New York
Cat. 27

El significado del significante
(The Signified of the Signifier), c. 1968
India ink on paper
14 × 19 ¾ in. (35.6 × 50.2 cm)
Collection of the artist, Courtesy Galerie
Lelong & Co., New York
Cat. 28

El significado del significante
(The Signified of the Signifier), c. 1968
India ink on paper
14 × 19 ¾ in. (35.6 × 50.2 cm)
Collection of the artist, Courtesy Galerie
Lelong & Co., New York
Cat. 29

El significado del significante
(The Signified of the Signifier), c. 1968
India ink on paper
14 × 19 ¾ in. (35.6 × 50.2 cm)
Collection of the artist, Courtesy Galerie
Lelong & Co., New York
Cat. 30

Topología erótica (Erotic Topology), 1968
Acrylic on stretched canvas
36 × 43 × 12 in. (91.4 × 108 × 30.5 cm)
Collection of Cecilia and Ernesto Poma, Miami
Cat. 26

Soy Isla: Compréndelo y retírate (I Am an Island:
Understand and Retreat), 1969–96
Acrylic and ink on stretched canvas
24 ⅞ × 43 ¾ × 9 in. (63.2 × 111.1 × 22.9 cm)
Collection of Luis R. de Corral, MD, San Juan
Cat. 54

Soy Isla (I Am an Island), c. 1970
Acrylic and ink on stretched canvas
19 ¾ × 35 × 14 in. (50.2 × 88.9 × 35.6 cm)
Collection of the artist, Courtesy Galerie
Lelong & Co., New York
Cat. 33

Antígona (Antigone), 1970
Acrylic on stretched canvas
30 × 36 × 10 in. (76.2 × 91.4 × 25.4 cm)
Museum of Modern Art, New York, Acquired
through the generosity of Agnes Gund,
María Luisa Ferré Rangel, Bertita and Guillermo
L. Martínez, Luisa Rangel de Ferré, an
anonymous donor, and the Latin American
and Caribbean Fund
Page 64

Untitled, 1970
Serigraph, ed. 11/30
20 × 16 in. (50.8 × 40.6 cm)
El Museo del Barrio, New York, Gift of
Servando Sacaluga, 1985
Cat. 32

Untitled, 1971
Acrylic on stretched canvas
43 × 73 × approx. 12 in.
(109.2 × 185.4 × approx. 30.5 cm)
Pérez Art Museum Miami, Gift of Jorge M. Pérez
Cat. 34

Furia I (Fury I), 1972
Ink on paper
25 ½ × 20 in. (64.8 × 50.8 cm)
Collection of the artist, Courtesy Galerie
Lelong & Co., New York
Cat. 36

Furia II (Fury II), 1972
Ink on paper
25 ½ × 20 in. (64.8 × 50.8 cm)
Collection of the artist, Courtesy Galerie
Lelong & Co., New York
Cat. 37

Furia III (Fury III), 1972
Ink on paper
25 ½ × 20 in. (64.8 × 50.8 cm)
Collection of the artist, Courtesy Galerie
Lelong & Co., New York
Cat. 38

Subliminal, from the series *Amazonas*
(Amazons), 1972
Acrylic on stretched canvas
39 ½ × 40 ½ × 10 in. (100.3 × 102.9 × 25.4 cm)
Private collection, San Juan
Cat. 35

Maqueta Soy Isla, 1972/92
Acrylic on stretched canvas
55 ½ × 39 ¾ × 9 ½ in. (141 × 101 × 24.1 cm)
Collection of Marie Lynn Arrieta-Tartak,
San Juan
Cat. 39

Lunar V (Moon V), c. 1973
Acrylic on stretched canvas
74 ¾ × 79 ½ × 10 in. (189.9 × 201.9 × 25.4 cm)
Private collection, Seattle
Cat. 40

Construcción: Topología erótica
(Construction: Erotic Topology), 1973
Acrylic on stretched canvas
73 ¹³⁄₁₆ × 30 ⅞ × 5 ¼ in. (187.5 × 78.5 × 13 cm)
Museo de Arte de Ponce, The Luis A. Ferre
Foundation, Inc., PR
Cat. 41

Lunar negro con tatuaje
(Black Moon with Tattoo), 1975
Acrylic on stretched canvas
33 × 43 ¾ × 8 ½ in. (83.8 × 111.1 × 21.6 cm)
Colby College Museum of Art, Waterville, ME,
Museum purchase from the Jere Abbott
Acquisitions Fund, 2016.228
Cat. 42

Amazonas (Amazons), from the series
Topologías eróticas (Erotic Topologies), 1978
Acrylic on stretched canvas
43 × 70 × 11 in. (109.2 × 177.8 × 27.9 cm)
Princeton University Art Museum, NJ, Museum
purchase, Fowler McCormick, Class of 1921,
Fund, 2014-53
Cat. 44

Untitled, 1978
Acrylic on stretched canvas
72 × 117 ½ × 10 ½ in. (182.9 × 298.5 × 26.7 cm)
Collection of the artist, Courtesy Galerie
Lelong & Co., New York
Cat. 43

El silencio de Eros (The Silence of Eros), c. 1980
Acrylic on stretched canvas
50 × 62 × 15 in. (127 × 157.5 × 38.1 cm)
Collection of Diane and Bruce Halle, Phoenix
Cat. 45

Lunar (Moon), c. 1980
Acrylic on stretched canvas with custom
wooden base
23 × 21 ¾ × 5 in. (58.4 × 55.2 × 12.7 cm)
Collection of Mima and César Reyes, San Juan
Cat. 49

El silencio de Eros (The Silence of Eros), 1983
Acrylic on stretched canvas
34 × 53 × 9 ½ in. (86.4 × 134.6 × 24.1 cm)
Collection of Marie Lynn Arrieta-Tartak,
San Juan
Cat. 46

Troyanas (Trojan Women), 1984
Acrylic on stretched canvas
54 × 95 ⅜ × 11 ¼ in. (137.2 × 242.3 × 28.6 cm)
Compañía de Turismo de Puerto Rico, San Juan
Cat. 47

El silencio de Eros III (The Silence of Eros III), 1984
Acrylic on stretched canvas
48 ¼ × 43 × 11 ¼ in. (122.7 × 109.2 × 28.6 cm)
Collection of Mima and César Reyes, San Juan
Cat. 48

Lunar (Moon), 1985
Acrylic on stretched canvas
71 ½ × 73 ½ × 14 in. (181.6 × 186.7 × 35.6 cm)
Collection of Ignacio J. López Beguiristain
and Laura M. Guerra, San Juan
Cat. 50

Juana de Arco (Joan of Arc), 1987
Acrylic on stretched canvas
97 ¼ × 73 ¾ × 13 in. (247 × 187.3 × 33 cm)
Collection of Mima and César Reyes, San Juan
Cat. 51

Lunar con tatuaje (Moon with Tattoo), 1989
Acrylic and ink on stretched canvas
35 × 47 × 4 in. (88.9 × 119.4 × 10.2 cm)
Collection of the artist, Courtesy Galerie
Lelong & Co., New York
Cat. 52

Soy Isla: Compréndelo y retírate
(I Am an Island: Understand and Retreat), 1990
Acrylic and ink on stretched canvas
72 ⅜ × 42 ⅛ × 10 in. (183.8 × 107 × 25.4 cm)
Collection of the Andreu-Pietri Family, San Juan
Cat. 53

Topología (Topology), from the series
Tatuajes (Tattoos), 1993
Acrylic on stretched canvas
47 × 46 ¾ × 14 ½ in. (119.4 × 118.7 × 36.8 cm)
Collection of the artist, Courtesy Galerie
Lelong & Co., New York
Cat. 55

Troyanas (Trojan Women), from the series
Topologías eróticas (Erotic Topologies), 1993
Acrylic on stretched canvas
47 × 41 × 6 in. (119.4 × 104.1 × 15.2 cm)
Collection of Mima and César Reyes, San Juan
Cat. 56

Represión (Repression), 1998
White cement with iron bars
24 × 24 × 2 in. (61 × 61 × 5.1 cm)
Collection of the artist, Courtesy Galerie
Lelong & Co., New York
Page 10

encuentrismo — ofrenda o retorno (The
Encounter — Offering or Return), from the
series *Soy Isla: Compréndelo y retírate* (I Am
an Island: Understand and Retreat), 2000
Video of performance
Berezdivin Collection, San Juan
Cat. 57a

Soy Isla (I Am an Island), 2000
Acrylic on stretched canvas, painting
from performance
10 ¾ × 53 ¾ × 9 ¾ in. (27.3 × 136.5 × 22.9 cm)
Berezdivin Collection, San Juan
Cat. 57b

Maquinista (Machinist), diptych, 2008
Acrylic on stretched canvas
61 × 27 ½ × 6 in. (154.9 × 69.8 × 15.2 cm)
The Phillips Collection, Washington, DC,
Director's Discretionary Fund, 2016
Cat. 58

Topología (Topology), from the series
Azul azul (Blue Blue), 2016
Acrylic on stretched canvas
34 × 34 × 7 in. (86.4 × 86.4 × 17.8 cm)
Collection of the artist, Courtesy Galerie
Lelong & Co., New York
Cat. 59

Topología (Topology), from the series
Azul azul (Blue Blue), 2016
Acrylic on stretched canvas
30 × 34 ¾ × 4 in. (76.2 × 88.3 × 10.2 cm)
Collection of the artist, Courtesy Galerie
Lelong & Co., New York
Cat. 60

Topología (Topology), from the series
Azul azul (Blue Blue), 2016
Acrylic on stretched canvas
17 × 28 × 6 ½ in. (43.1 × 71.1 × 16.5 cm)
Collection of Laura Delaney Taft and
John Taft, promised gift to Walker Art Center,
Minneapolis
Cat. 62

Topología erótica (Erotic Topology),
from the series *Azul azul* (Blue Blue), 2016
Acrylic on stretched canvas
17 ⅞ × 25 ⅞ × 4 ½ in. (45.4 × 65.7 × 11.4 cm)
Collection of Ms. Cleusa Garfinkel, Miami
Cat. 61

Untitled, 2018
Ink and correction fluid on paper
13 ½ × 17 in. (34.3 × 43.2 cm)
Collection of the artist, Courtesy Galerie
Lelong & Co., New York
Cat. 63

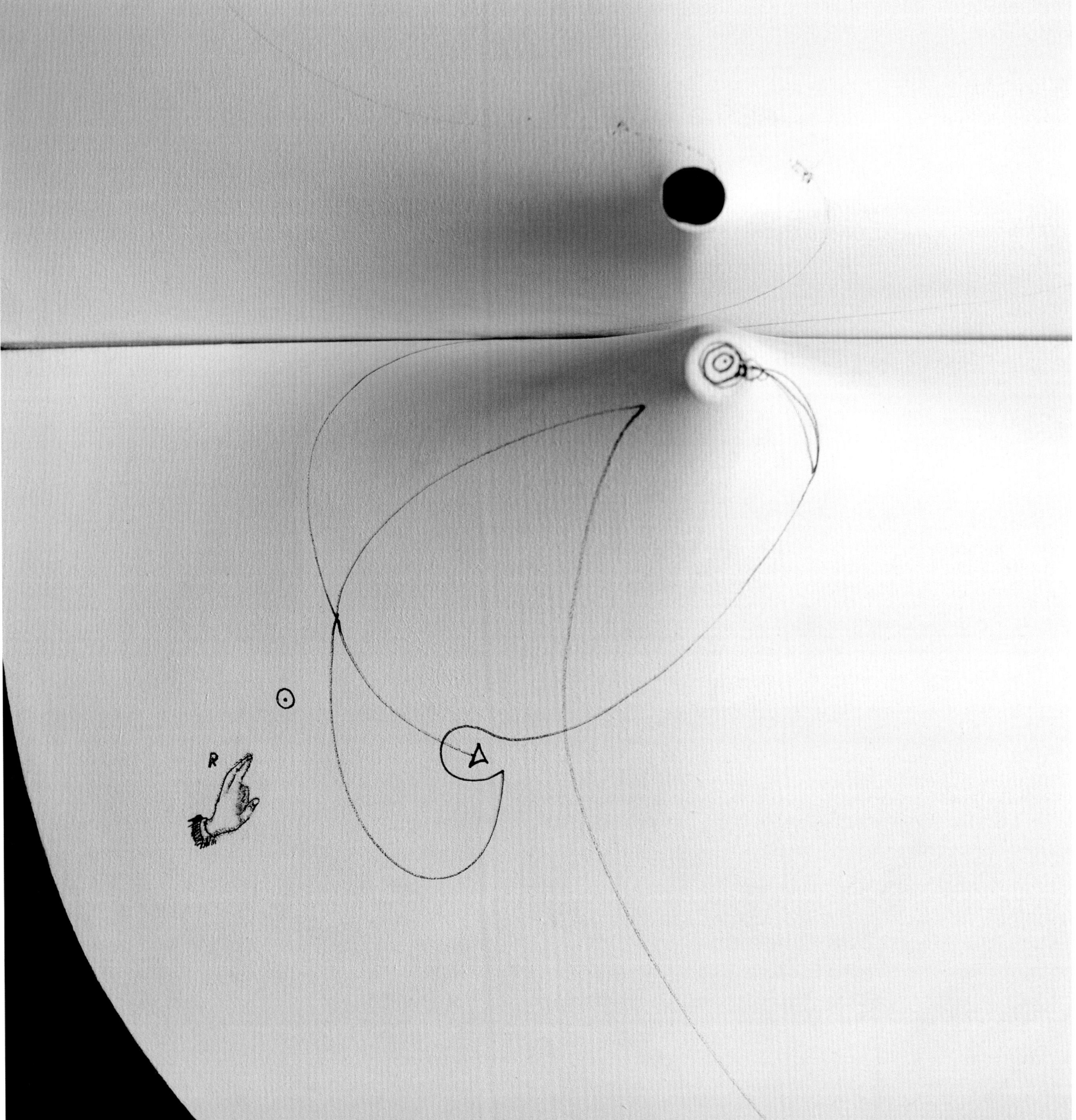

R

Lenders to the Exhibition

The Andreu-Pietri Family, San Juan

Marie Lynn Arrieta-Tartak, San Juan

Ignacio J. López Beguiristain and Laura M. Guerra, San Juan

Berezdivin Collection, San Juan

CINTAS Foundation Fellows Collection, Miami

Colby College Museum of Art, Waterville

Compañía de Turismo de Puerto Rico, San Juan

Luis R. de Corral, MD, San Juan

Cuban Heritage Collection, University of Miami Libraries, Coral Gables, FL

Beth Rudin DeWoody, New York

Galerie Lelong & Co., New York

Cleusa Garfinkel, Miami

Diane and Bruce Halle Foundation, Scottsdale

Instituto de Cultura Puertorriqueña, San Juan

Jose R. Landron, San Juan

Museo de Arte de Ponce, PR

El Museo del Barrio, New York

Museum of Modern Art, New York

Pérez Art Museum Miami

Cecilia and Ernesto Poma, Miami

Princeton University Art Museum, NJ

Private collection, Madrid

Private collection, Miami

Private collection, San Juan

Private collection, Seattle

César and Mima Reyes, San Juan

Zilia Sánchez, San Juan

RosaMaría García Sarduy, Miami

Laura Delaney Taft and John Taft, Minneapolis

Index

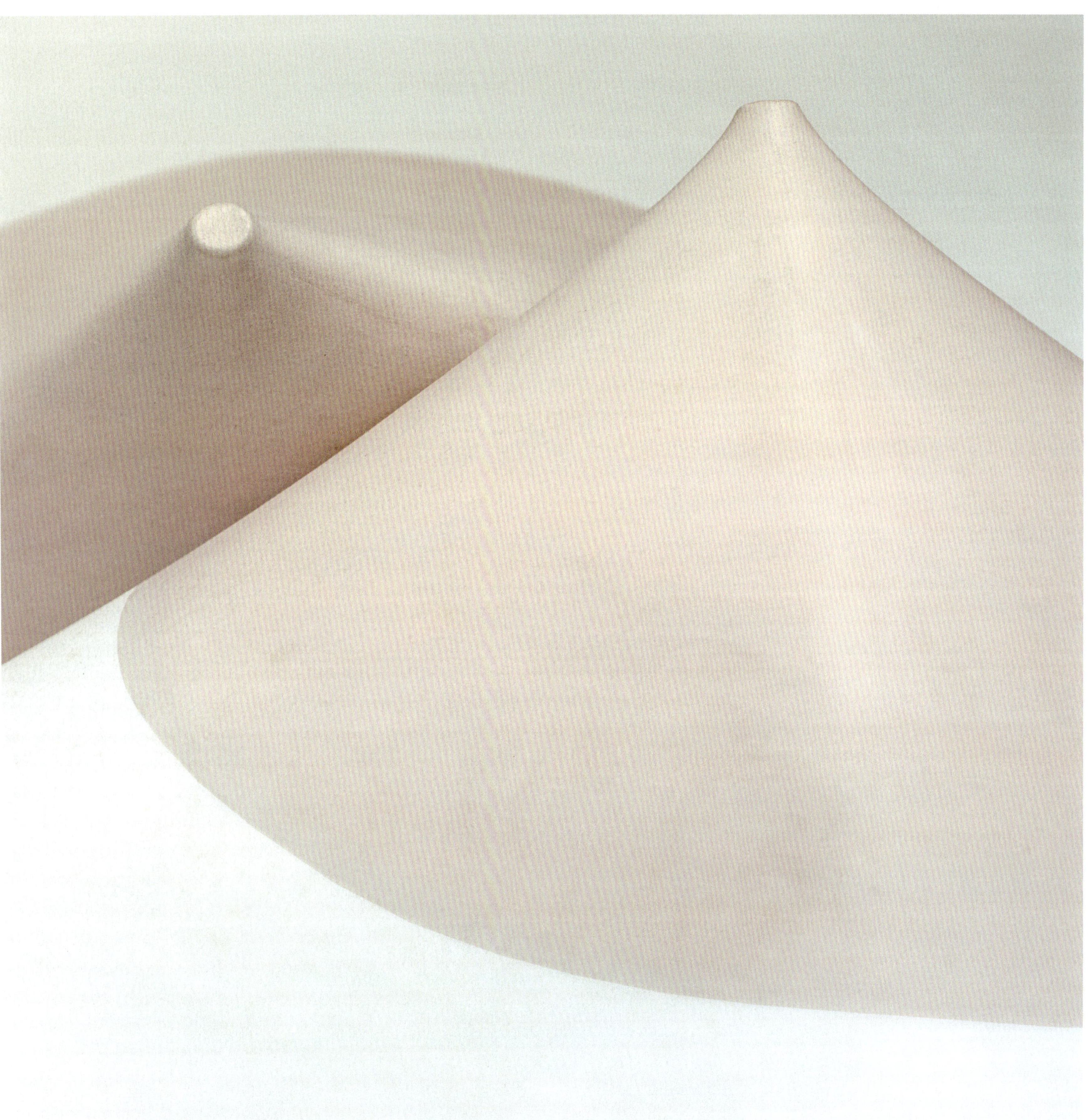

Photo Credits

© Albright-Knox Art Gallery / Art Resource, NY: Sretenović 6

© Archivio Agostino Bonalumi, Milano: Sretenović 8

© CHC Miami: McEwen 7; Cortázar 4

© CINTAS Foundation Fellows Collection / Photo by Mariano Costa Peuser: Cats. 11, 16

© Colby College Museum of Art: Cat. 42

© 2018 Comissió Tàpies / Artists Rights Society (ARS), New York / VEGAP, Madrid: Sretenović 4

© DeA Picture Library / Art Resource, NY: Sretenović 5

© Instituto de Cultura Puertorriqueña, San Juan, PR: Sretenović 13; Cat. 15

© Pablo Linés: page 44

© MNBA, Havana: Sretenović 1; Elliott 5, 9, 12

© Museo de Arte de Puerto Rico: Cat. 47

© El Museo del Barrio, New York: Cat. 32

Image © Museum of Modern Art, New York / Licensed by SCALA / Art Resource, NY: Elliott 1, 7

© Pérez Art Museum Miami, Photo by Oriol Tarridas: Cat. 34

Photography © Raquel Pérez-Puig: Sretenović 9–11, 15–17; Cats. 1, 4, 5, 8, 19, 35, 39, 46, 48–51, 54, 56, 57b

Photography © Mariano Costa Peuser: Cats. 2, 9–10, 12–13, 26

© The Phillips Collection, Washington, DC: Cat. 58

© Bertrand Prévost, CNAC / MNAM / Dist. RMN-Grand Palais / Art Resource, NY: Sretenović 3

Image © Smithsonian American Art Museum, Washington, DC / Art Resource, NY: Sretenović 7

© Zilia Sánchez, courtesy Galerie Lelong & Co., New York: Sretenović 12–14; Elliott 3–4, 11; Acevedo-Yates 1–6; Cortázar 3, 5–6; Cats. 3, 6–7, 17–18, 20–25, 27–31, 33, 36–38, 40–41, 43–45, 52–53, 55, 59–63

© The Solomon R. Guggenheim Foundation / Art Resource, NY: Sretenović 4

© Tate, London / Art Resource, NY: Sretenović 2

All images of the artist from February 2018 featured in the interview and the chronology are © Raquel Pérez-Puig.

All ephemera illustrated in the chronology are from the artist's archives, courtesy Galerie Lelong & Co., New York, except the 2013 installation photography on pages 162–63, which is © Artists Space, New York.

All works by Zilia Sánchez are © the artist.

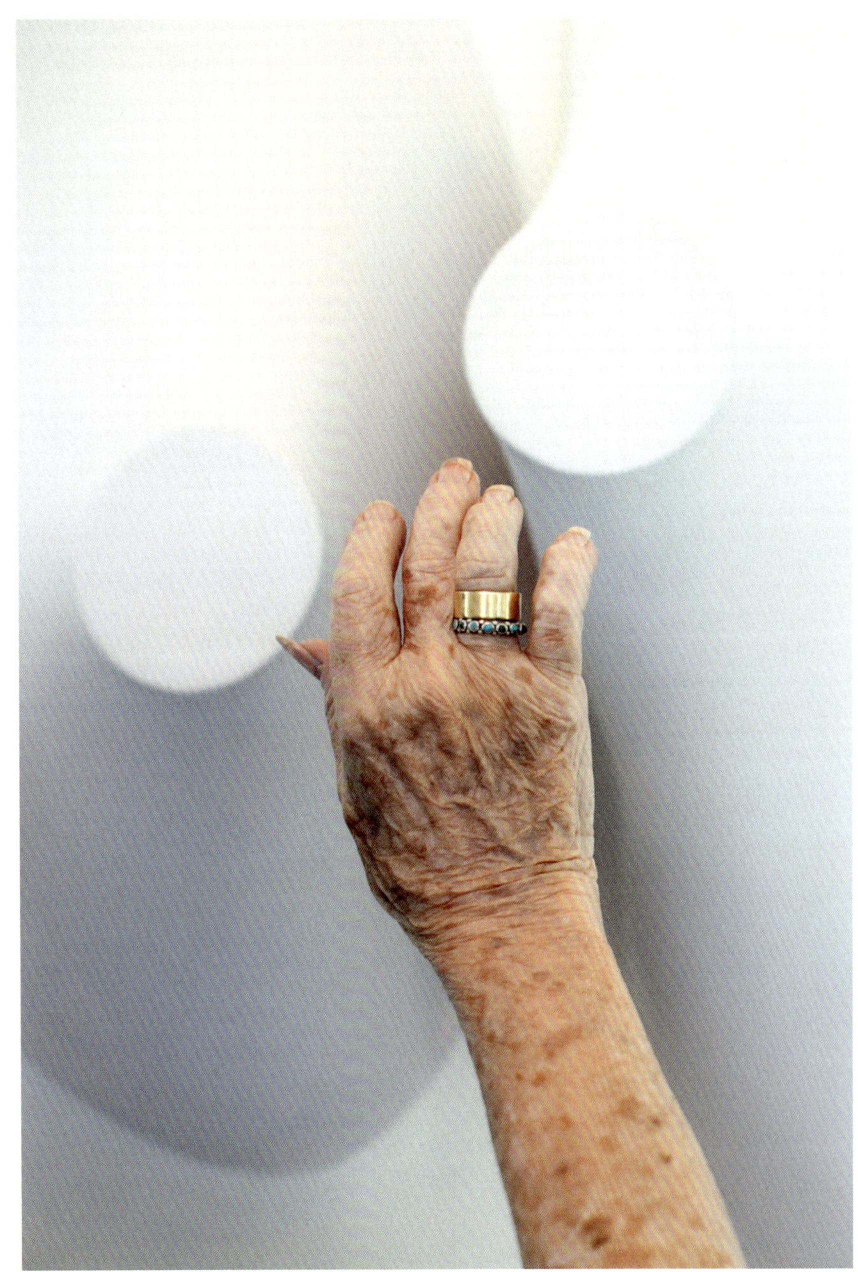

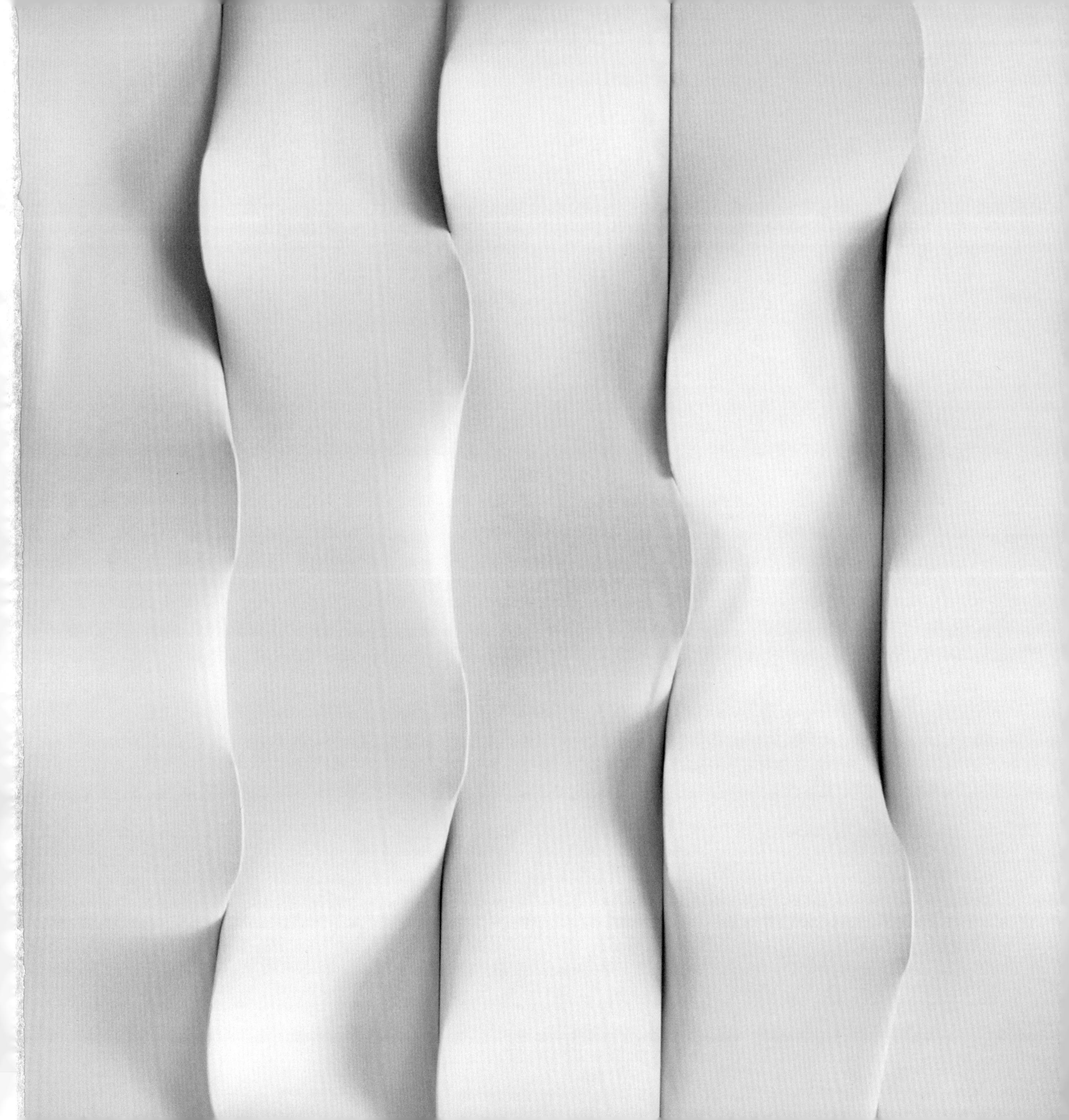